OXFORD THEOLOGICAL MONOGRAPHS

OXFORD THEOLOGICAL MONOGRAPHS

Theodore the Stoudite

The Ordering of Holiness

ROMAN CHOLIJ

OXFORD
UNIVERSITY PRESS

OXFORD
UNIVERSITY PRESS

Great Clarendon Street, Oxford OX2 6DP

Oxford University Press is a department of the University of Oxford.
It furthers the University's objective of excellence in research, scholarship,
and education by publishing worldwide in

Oxford New York

Athens Auckland Bangkok Bogotá Buenos Aires Cape Town
Chennai Dar es Salaam Delhi Florence Hong Kong Istanbul Karachi
Kolkata Kuala Lumpur Madrid Melbourne Mexico City Mumbai Nairobi
Paris São Paulo Shanghai Singapore Taipei Tokyo Toronto Warsaw

with associated companies in Berlin Ibadan

Oxford is a registered trade mark of Oxford University Press
in the UK and in certain other countries

Published in the United States
by Oxford University Press Inc., New York

© Roman Cholij 2002

The moral rights of the author have been asserted
Database right Oxford University Press (maker)

First published 2002

British Library Cataloguing in Publication Data
Data available

Library of Congress Cataloging in Publication Data
Cholij, Roman, 1956–
Theodore the Stoudite: the ordering of holiness/by Roman Cholij.
p. cm.—(Oxford theological monographs)
Includes bibliographical references and index.

1. Theodore, Studites, Saint, 759–862. I. Title. II. Series.
BR1720.T38 C46 2002   270.3′092—dc21   [B]   2001046488

ISBN 0–19–924846–X

1 3 5 7 9 10 8 6 4 2

Typeset in Baskerville
by Hope Services (Abingdon) Ltd
Printed in Great Britain
on acid-free paper by
Biddles Ltd, Guildford and King's Lynn

CONTENTS

ACKNOWLEDGEMENTS

It gives me great pleasure to thank those who have been instrumental in seeing this book to print. This work started life as a doctoral dissertation at Oxford University where I spent a number of rewarding years as a member of Christ Church. My gratitude is thus first expressed to all those who tutored me during my student years as a postgraduate, but most particularly Dr Kallistos Ware who, with much patience, good humour, and great learning, guided me through the uneven terrain of eastern Christian studies and to the award of the M.Phil. and D.Phil. degrees.

Secondly, sincere thanks are due to those scholars from whose insightful and expert advice I profited much in the preparation of this book, especially my examiners Professor Averil Cameron, Warden of Keble College, Oxford, and Professor Andrew Louth of Durham University, Dr. Ken Parry, external reader, Dr Joseph Munititz SJ of Campion Hall, Oxford, Professor John Behr, and Professor John Erickson, both of St. Vladimir's Orthodox Theological Seminary, New York. Any defects in this book are due entirely to the author and not to his guides and mentors!

My gratitude is directed next to those who sponsored my studies at Oxford University: Aid to the Church in Need and the London Oratory (in particular to the late Very Revd Michael Napier), Bishop Basil Losten of the Ukrainian Catholic Diocese of Stamford, Connecticut, USA, and to my mother Wiktoria. I am also indebted to Campion Hall, Oxford, the Pontifical Oriental Institute, Rome, and Bishop Michael Kuchmiak of the Ukrainian Catholic Exarchate of Great Britain for the critical support I received in the final stages of my doctoral studies. Although my personal circumstances have changed since these years of study, I hope and trust that this book will be some reward to my sponsors for their investment in me.

The writing of this study was the easy part! The real work lay in seeing it through to publication, which fell on an outstanding editorial team at Oxford University Press. This team includes Hilary O'Shea, Jenny Wagstaffe, Enid Barker, and Lucy Qureshi, whom I thank for their highly professional work.

Finally, I wish to thank one special individual who has been a major inspiration and source of encouragement and without whose patient insistence this book would not have seen the light of day—Louise de Muscote, fellow member of Christ Church, linguist, and my wife. It is to her I dedicate this book.

Roman Cholij

Michaelmas 2001

ABBREVIATIONS

AA.SS	*Acta Sanctorum*
AnBoll.	*Analecta Bollandiana*
BF	*Byzantinische Forschungen*
BHG	Bibliotheca hagiographica graeca
BMGS	*Byzantine and Modern Greek Studies*
BZ	*Byzantinische Zeitschrift*
CCL	Corpus Christianorum. Series Latina
CSCO	Corpus scriptorum christianorum orientalium
CSEL	Corpus scriptorum ecclesiasticorum latinorum
CSHB	Corpus Scriptorum Historiae Byzantinae
DOP	*Dumbarton Oaks Papers*
DS	*Dictionnaire de spiritualité*
DTC	*Dictionnaire de théologie catholique*
EEC	*Encyclopaedia of the Early Church*, 2 vols. (Cambridge, 1992)
EH	Dionysios the Pseudo-Areopagite, *Ecclesiastical Hierarchy*, ed. G. Heil and A. M. Ritter, *Corpus Dionysiacum*, Patristiche Texte und Studien, 36 (Berlin, 1991)
EL	*Ephemerides Liturgicae*
EO	*Échos d'Orient*
Ep.	Epistula
Ep.	*Epitimia*
GCS	Griechischen christlichen Schriftsteller
GOAR	J. Goar (ed.), Εὐχολόγιον sive Rituale Graecorum . . . , 2nd edn. (Venice, 1730)
JEH	*Journal of Ecclesiastical History*
Joannou	P.-P. Joannou, *Fonti*, 9, *Discipline Générale Antique*, (Grottaferrata/Rome, 1962–3)
JÖB	*Jahrbuch der Österreichischen Byzantinistik* (before 1969, *Jahrbuch der Österreichischen byzantinischen Gesellschaft*)
JTS	*Journal of Theological Studies*
MC	Theodore the Stoudite, *Magna Catechesis*. Cited according to *Sancti Theodori Studitae Sermones Magnae Catecheseos*, ed. J. Cozza-Luzi, in A. Mai, *Nova Patrum Bibliotheca* (Rome, 1888, 1905)
MGH	*Monumenta Germaniae historica*

NPB	Nova Patrum Bibliotheca
OCA	Orientalia Christiana Analecta
OCP	*Orientalia Christiana Periodica*
ODB	*Oxford Dictionary of Byzantium*
PC	Theodore the Stoudite, *Parva Catechesis*. Cited according to: Μικρὰ Καιήχηοις. Τοῦ ὁσίου πατρὸς ἡμῶν καὶ ὁμολογητοῦ Θεοδώρου ἡγουμένου τῶν Στουδίου μικρὰ κατήχησις, ed. N. Skretta, 'Ορθόδοξος Κυψέλη (Thessalonica, 1984), ii
PG	*Patrologiae cursus completus. Series graeca*, ed. J. P. Migne
PK	Papadopoulos-Kerameus ed. of Τοῦ ὁσίου Θεοδώρου τοῦ Στουδίτου Μεγάλη Κατήχησις. Βιβλίον δεύτερον, ἐκδοθὲν ὑπο τῆς Αὐτοκρατορικῆς Ἀρχαιογραφικῆς 'Επιτροπῆς (St Petersburg, 1904).
PL	*Patrologiae cursus completus. Series latina*, ed. J. P. Migne
RB	*Regulae Brevius Tractatae (RB)*
REB	*Revue des études byzantines*
RF	*Regulae Fusius Tractatae*
SC	Sources chrétiennes
SVThQ	*Saint Vladimir's Theological Quarterly*
TC	*Tvorenija Catechesis*, unedited Catechesis in Russian translation, in *Tvorenija prepodobnago otsa nashego i ispovidnyka Feodorja Studitja v russkom perevod*, 2 vols. (St Petersburg, 1907). *TC* I: Book I of the Great Catecheses; *TC* III: Book III of the Catecheses (in vol. ii)
TDNT	*Theological Dictionary of the New Testament*
TM	*Travaux et mémoires*
TU	Texte und Untersuchungen zur Geschichte der altchristlichen Literatur
TWNT	*Theologishen Wörterbuch zum Neuen Testament*
Viz. Vrem.	*Vizantijskij vremennik*

INTRODUCTION

This book started life as a doctoral dissertation from the University of Oxford, Faculty of Theology, defended in late 1996. Significant scholarship since that time has been incorporated into the text of this present work and noted in the bibliography.

Theodore the Stoudite has in recent times become increasingly popular as a subject for study. This is partly due to advances in ninth-century Byzantine historical scholarship in general, and partly to progress made in critical editions of texts ascribed to Theodore.

Up until the latter part of the nineteenth century, and the beginning of the twentieth, comparatively little was known about Theodore or his writings outside restricted monastic circles. This changed when a handful of patristic scholars (especially French, German, and Russian) decided to take an interest. Biographies appeared (one in English by Alice Gardner) together with some monographs on Theodore's monastic activities, and critical editions of some parts of his catechetical writings were produced.

Many studies have since appeared on various aspects of Theodore's life. Advances with critical editions of minor literary works were made in the 1960s but the bulk of the writings most consulted by scholars still remained unedited or in an unsatisfactory state. Only recently, in 1992, did a critical edition of his most important writings—his letters—appear. This work, by the German Byzantinist George Fatouros (*Theodori Studitae Epistulae, Corpus Fontium Historiae Byzantinae*, 31 (Berlin, 1992)), which also includes painstaking annotations and indices, has since stimulated even more quality writing on the Stoudite and has borne its first major fruit in a biographical study by Thomas Pratsch: *Theodoros Studites (759–826)—zwishen Dogma und Pragma* (Frankfurt, 1998).

Theodore the Stoudite has always been important to historians who have interested themselves in ninth-century Byzantium because of the great deal of first-hand accounts of events that he provides. This is particularly true of the period of the second phase of iconoclasm in which Theodore lived. No history book on Byzantium, as a consequence, neglects mention of the Stoudite.

Nor has there been a lack of important studies, especially within the last forty years, on second iconoclasm and image theory, and the Byzantine ecclesiastical issues of Theodore's time.

Important, too, have been the studies on the monastic writings and monastic life of Theodore (to which Julien Leroy OSB contributed so much).

Despite all of this, as the Byzantinist Rosemary Morris commented in 1995, 'it is surprising that there is no full-length modern study of Theodore the Stoudite' (*Monks and Laymen in Byzantium 843–1118* (Cambridge, 1995), 14 n. 13). Thomas Pratsch has now filled part of the gap, but his study, although meticulously documented, has an intentionally narrow focus. It is based almost entirely on the letters, and although it admirably unravels and expertly expounds on the major political events of Theodore's life, it does not interest itself in the religious or intellectual part of Theodore's life and activities. A full-length biographical study requires both an accurate account of the political and ecclesiastical issues of the time (the domain of historians such as Pratsch) and an understanding of the theological and spiritual traditions within which Theodore worked (the domain of the theologian). In other words, an inclusive full-length biography of Theodore the Stoudite is an interdisciplinary task.

Another difficulty in producing a comprehensive full-length biography on Theodore revolves around the source material. Part of the edited source material, the Catecheses, is difficult to access. Also, a new critical edition of the entire corpus of Catecheses is much needed. Furthermore, in the past (with the exception, perhaps, of the pioneering Russian scholars) the source material has rarely been studied in its entirety. Historians have tended to neglect the Catecheses, which due to their preaching tone have been of less immediate interest to them, whereas theological specialists such as Leroy and Hausherr have devoted themselves almost exclusively to the study of the Catecheses, being more interested in the religious mind of Theodore and less in his political activities, which are reflected in the letters. A full study of the life and thought of Theodore requires familiarity with and an understanding of both these major sources. Besides, much theology is contained in the letters and interesting insights into daily Byzantine life and its concerns, and Theodore's own life and concerns, is found in the Catecheses.

There were two reasons for the choice of subject of this work. The first, as Rosemary Morris had correctly noted, was that there was no modern full-length study of Theodore, and therefore biography, that accurately set the context for the study of particular issues, or for his theological thought. Many fine specialized studies had been produced since the writing of the early biographies (which are still useful today), and there had been many advances in Byzantine historical sciences, but these had not been pulled together to update the story of Theodore. The work by Pratsch leaves many important areas untouched.

The intention of the first part of this book is to offer an updated and comprehensive account of the life and work of Theodore to those who might have little familiarity with this intriguing figure and who would prefer to become more familiar through reading about it in English. Whilst it uses a wide base of secondary sources, this account also draws directly on the primary sources. As a result, certain details are given which are not found in any of the published literature. Also, sections 1.10.1 and 1.10.2, which give an explanation and analysis of the Small and Great Catecheses, will hopefully prove to be helpful to the more specialized reader struggling to make sense of these particular sources.

The second reason for this study was the keen awareness that explanations of Theodore's involvement in the ecclesiastical issues of the day found in the literature often fail to give adequate weight to the Stoudite's theological outlook, and the place this had within wider Byzantine church society. In other words, historians have not maximized the resources of theology in their effort adequately to portray this churchman.

To understand Theodore's involvement in the controversies of his time requires some understanding of what it meant for him to be a Christian, a member of the church, and a member of the Byzantine Christian society. Theodore was, after all, first and foremost a monastic reformer. This point is often forgotten by historians, and its implications ignored. A monk was, to Theodore, simply a 'true Christian'. The theological principles behind his monastic reform, therefore, were the same principles which should direct the whole of Christian society. Thus, as a help to other Byzantinists, and as a theological research project, I had wanted to analyse carefully Theodore's theology of the Christian life.

Theodore's theology is underpinned by the truism that the end or purpose of this life is the attainment of holiness and salvation. At the same time there is a way or manner by which this end should be attained, a manner which is not haphazard or spontaneous, but ordered. Hence the subtitle: *The Ordering of Holiness*. The order follows on the principles of the Gospel and its interpretation by the Fathers of the church, by their sole authority or in synodal pronouncements. And the church has its spiritual traditions and internal life. It exercises its ministry through preaching the Word and through its rites of sanctification. Hence the division of this book into Part 2, Principles of Order, and Part 3, Principles of Holiness.

It was Patrick Henry's excellent doctoral dissertation, *Theodore of Studios: Byzantine Churchman* (Yale University, 1969), which unfortunately was never published as a whole work, and which analysed the question of church and authority, that inspired the content and structure of Part II. The account given of the *theological* grounds for obedience and Theodore's theological understanding of authority are a necessary complement, and at times corrective, to Henry's work. Chapter 2 is entitled Obedience and Authority. The main issues studied and discussed by Henry are re-evaluated in the light of this theological analysis. To complete Part II, and for the sake of comprehensiveness, a fresh look is taken at the much-worked subject of church and state (Ch. 3, Church and Emperor). This argues that Theodore cannot be taken as a representative of a non-Byzantine ideal of church autonomy.

Part III, Principles of Holiness, consists of three chapters. Chapter 4, Rites of Sanctification, is an essay in historical theology which offers some new insights to theologians and students of theology on matters of eastern liturgy and sacraments during a period of history that has kept many of its secrets. What scant and scattered information Theodore gives in his writings concerning ritual practices, and their probable meaning, is described. A fuller context for these rites is also given for the sake of those not specialized in these fields.

The two principal rites of sanctification, baptism and eucharist, are treated separately, together with the subject of heresy, in Ch. 5. This is done out of convenience since the issue of the validity of heretical sacraments, also examined, and which receives some discussion in Theodore's writings, primarily affects these two rites.

Chapter 6, Sanctification of Lay Person and Monk, is the culmination of all the previous chapters that analyse the requirements
for holiness. Although given some examination in Part II, greater
attention is paid in this chapter to the differences in the lay and
monastic vocations. It is argued that both share the same fundamental Christian vocation based on baptism and that there are no
grades of perfection in this identical calling, only levels of difficulty
in living it out. According to Theodore, the monk is privileged—
by the protected society in which he lives and the absence of family and worldly cares—in having a more secure path to God than
the lay person. Seeing the monk as essentially a lay person living
within monastery walls does have implications for the Byzantinist.
For monastic theology becomes, with appropriate nuances, the
theology of the laity.

If Theodore's theology, or approach to Christianity, was shared
by Christians at large in Byzantine society—and it is argued that
such seems to have been the case in the period dealt with—then a
study of this theology helps the Byzantinist to understand better
the world-view of the Byzantine citizen. This being the case,
Theodore's Catecheses become just as important as his letters to
the historian seeking to understand (as far as this is possible to a
twentieth-century researcher) ninth-century Byzantine society.

In this work the whole corpus of Theodore's writings was studied, with the exception of the hymns that are attributed to him only
by tradition. The corpus includes over 550 letters and 390
Catecheses, some twenty other works, and a few by later authors
but attributed to Theodore. The Catecheses are cited by a system
explained in Part I.

A TEXTUAL NOTE

With regard to translations, where these already existed they were
used, often with some changes being made. Patrick Henry, in particular, is the source for several citations from the letters, which
have been excellently translated, taken from his thesis or articles.
They are found mostly in Part II. I have not noted this in the text,
but these occur when his work or his material are being discussed.
The great majority of translations, however, which includes all the
Catecheses, are my own. I have been selective in citing the Greek

original, especially with long translations, so as not to overload the footnotes which are already very substantial. Transliterating Greek names seems always to be a problem in English. By and large I have tried to give them in their Greek, rather than Latin, forms. Examples would be 'Nikephoros' in place of 'Nicephorus', or 'Athanasios' in place of 'Athanasius' (unless this occurs in a title or citation from another author). Although this manner of spelling is less familiar to English readers, it corresponds more to what is accepted by Byzantinists. The *Oxford Dictionary of Byzantium* has been my main guide. Occasionally, when the name thus transliterated would appear very odd, I have left it in a more familiar form. References to works by, or attributed to, Theodore published in volume 99 of Migne, *Series Graeca*, are usually cited with a Latin title. This has been the convention in most of the secondary literature and a convention I have chosen to maintain. The only exceptions I have made (in keeping with a newer convention) are the *Hypotyposis* and *Epitimia* (spelt with Latin characters) in place of *Constitutiones Studitanae* and *Poenae Monasteriales* respectively. Biblical quotations are usually taken from the Revised Standard Version (unless from an author's citation).

PART I

Biography

1
Life and Times of Theodore the Stoudite

1.1 INTRODUCTION

Theodore the Stoudite (759–826) led anything but an uneventful, uninteresting, and unproductive life. As abbot of the monastery of Stoudios[1] he became a major personality in church and court circles in early ninth-century Byzantium and is today commemorated in both East and West as a saintly member of the heavenly court.[2] Yet in his time he defended and propagated views that were decidedly at odds with those of other revered men, such as his contemporaries Patriarchs Tarasios (784–806) and Nikephoros (806–15).

He was exiled three times by the emperor for his refusal to compromise on what for him were major matters of church doctrine— issues relating to Emperor Constantine VI's 'adulterous' marriage and to Leo V's revival of iconoclasm—but equally he could influence, in better times, decisions of imperial state policy. His exceptional monastic leadership resulted in his being recognized by subsequent generations as one of the greatest organizers of coenobitic monasticism in the East. He was compared by his supporters to Saint Basil the Great.[3]

---

[1] The name of the monastery with which Theodore's name is inextricably associated is given in the sources as ἡ τοῦ Στουδίου μονή or ἡ μονὴ τῶν Στουδίου. It was founded by an eastern consul by name of Studius (see also Ch. 1.6) in the quarter of the city of Constantinople that became known as τὰ Στουδίου. Hence the monks of this monastery— Stoudites—were the monks of the monastery of Studius or the city quarter of Studius. See H. Delehaye, 'Stoudion—Stoudios', *AnBoll.* 52 (1934), 64–5. It is therefore inexact to refer to the monastery as 'the Stoudion' or 'Studium'. In the secondary literature Theodore himself is variously referred to as Theodore of Stoudios, Theodore Stoudite or Stoudites, and— as used in this study—Theodore the Stoudite. The Latin convention of spelling (Studite), invariably used by Western scholars until recent years, is not followed here.

[2] *Synaxarium Ecclesiae Constantinopolitanae*, ed. H. Delehaye, Propylaeum ad AA.SS Novembris (Brussels, 1902), 214–16 (November 11); *Martyrologium Romanum ad formam editionis typicae scholiis historicis instructum*, Propylaeum ad AA.SS Decembris (Brussels, 1940), 513 (November 12).

[3] *Vita B*, ch. 1. *PG* 99. 236A.

A by-product of his reform was that his Stoudite monastic confederation played a role in the cultural and humanistic revival of
the ninth century, this being associated especially with the use of
minuscule or cursive script in the copying of texts in the monastic
scriptoria.[4]

Theodore's leadership, expressed in protest action and extensive
writings, over those who like him were willing to suffer persecution
and exile avowedly for the sake of the integrity of Orthodox faith
and morals, also earned him various other eulogistic epithets. His
biographer, Michael the Monk, describes Theodore as a 'Moses',[5]
and Theodore's successor and closest disciple, Naukratios, writes
that he was the 'mouth-piece of the Church', 'glory of priests', 'col-
umn of faith', 'sun of the Orthodox Faith', 'oecumenical teacher',
'fountain of dogmas', 'tuneful lyre of the Spirit'.[6] Anastasius
Bibliothecarius (d. 878), a near contemporary in the Western
church and an early translator of one of Theodore's sermons into
Latin, described him as a 'vir valde mirabilis'.[7] Subsequent trans-
lators and commentators have likewise been unsparing in their
praise. Theodore had on at least one occasion compared his own
epistolary activity in exile to that of St Cyprian of Carthage,[8] little
knowing that one day he would be compared to this great Western
saint in other ways too.[9] To those who appreciated the Roman

---

[4] P. Lemerle, *Le Premier Humanisme byzantin: Notes et remarques sur enseignement et culture à Byzance des origines au Xe siècle* (Paris, 1971), 109–28. The idea that the minuscule script itself was invented in the Stoudios monastery, held by an earlier generation of scholars, is far from certain. What is certain, however, is that it was soon used in the monastery. The Uspensky Gospel, for example, the earliest surviving example of a book written in minus-cule, may have been copied by Nikolaos the Stoudite in 834/5: B. Flusin, 'Les Débuts de l'humanisme byzantin', in *Le Livre au Moyen Âge* (Paris, 1988), 122 ff.

[5] *Vita B*, ch. 1. *PG* 99. 236A.

[6] *Naucratii confessoris encyclica de obitu sancti Theodori Studitae* (BHG 1756), ed. F. Combefis, *PG* 99. 1825–49, at 1828A.

[7] *Anastasius Bibliothecarius in Praefatione ad S. Theodori Studitae sermonem de S. Bartholomaeo apos-tolo. PG* 99. 99C; U. Westerbergh, *Anastasius Bibliothecarius Sermo Theodori Studitae de Sancto Bartholomeo Apostolo: A Study*, Studia Latina Stockholmiensia, 9 (Stockholm, 1963), 19–20.

[8] Ep. 120. 19–20. This analogy may well have been inspired by a passage from Gregory of Nazianzus, *Oratio XXIV, In Laudem S. Cypriani, PG* 35. 1188A.

[9] *Praefatio posthumae Sirmondianae editioni praemissa, PG* 99. 57–92, esp. 57–9 (taken from the posthumous publication, prepared by J. de la Beaune, of J. Sirmond, *Opera varia, v. Sancti Theodori Studitae epistolae* (Paris, 1696)). Thus, for example, the author writes of Cyprian: 'qui doceret poenitentiam lapsos, veritatem haereticos, schismaticos unitatem, filios Dei pacem et evangelicam legem', adding thereafter: 'Quae quidem omnia magni Cypriani propria sic fuerunt, ut prorsus eadem in Theodorum Studitam mirifice conveniant.' *PG* 99. 58A.

Catholic significance of his life, Theodore was 'fidei et morum christianorum defensor intrepidus'.[10]

Listing Theodore's admirers and cataloguing the virtues attributed to him, however, should not leave the impression that Theodore has been spared criticism or negative appraisal. Authors have not been lacking who interpret his religious zeal in upholding and propagating positions that even his co-religionists disagreed with as fanatical, arrogant, and intolerant. Confessional allegiance has in the past coloured judgement on Theodore, rendering the chasm between saint or sectarian unbridgeable by scholarship alone.[11] Some modern scholars, such as Karlin-Hayter, try to cut through religious sympathies and focus on Theodore's interventions seen in sociopolitical context and from a personal motive perspective. She concludes, not without providing her reasons, that Theodore is little more than a 'byzantine politician in a monk's gown'.[12] Peter Hatlie and Thomas Pratsch are more cautious in their judgements and acknowledge the complexities of both Theodore as a man and the controversies of his day:[13] 'Whatever the exact characterization, an all too common picture of Theodore has been that of a watchful and slightly prying guardian who, inspired by a strong sense of righteousness, was quick to call his monks into action whenever he was convinced that gross abuses in the church—and to some extent state-affairs—had occurred.'[14]

My hope in this work is to provide an insight into Theodore's faith, and in particular, into his monastic beliefs, such that

---

[10] E. Herman, in *Textus selecti ex operibus commentatorum byzantinorum iuris ecclesiastici*, ed. I. Croce, Fonti, S. Congregazione per la chiesa orientale, Codificazione canonica orientale, 2/5 (Vatican City, 1939), 10.

[11] Carl Thomas (*Theodor von Studion und sein Zeitalter* (Osnabrück, 1892), 3) expresses the position evident last century. Scholars, he says, have made of Theodore: 'entweder zu einem Heiligen und Martyrer oder aber zu einem Schwärmer und Fanatiker. Vom ersteren Gesichtspunkte aus betrachten ihn fast alle Historiker der römischen Kirche, vom letzteren die meisten Protestanten.'

[12] P. Karlin-Hayter, 'A Byzantine Politician Monk: Saint Theodore Stoudite', *JÖB* 44 (1994), 217–32, p. 217.

[13] P. Hatlie, 'Abbot Theodore and the Stoudites: A Case Study in Monastic Social Groupings and Religious Conflict in Constantinople (787–826)', Ph.D. dissertation (unpublished), Fordham University, 1993; 'The Politics of Salvation: Theodore of Stoudios on Martyrdom (Martyrion) and Speaking Out (Parrhesia)', *DOP* 50 (1996), 263–87. T. Pratsch, *Theodoros Studites (759–826)—zwischen Dogma und Pragma: Der Abt des Studosklosters in Konstantinopel im Spannungsfeld von Patriarch, Kaiser und eigenem Anspruch* (Frankfurt, 1998).

[14] Hatlie, 'Abbot Theodore', 39.

Theodore's public actions can be placed in a much broader perspective and evaluated more contextually.

1.1.1 *Note on Prior Scholarship and Historical Sources*

The bibliography on Theodore the Stoudite and the Stoudios monastery is very extensive, especially if other more general works covering the same historical period are to be included.[15] The classic and most comprehensive monograph on Theodore and his monks, published in 1913–14, is that by the Russian church historian Alexander Pavlovich Dobroklonskij. This is still a useful source, albeit dated and difficult to use (even apart from the Russian language).[16] Around the turn of the century considerable interest in Theodore had been taken by German and French as well as other Russian scholars[17] and a valuable, if somewhat popular, study also appeared in English.[18] Since the early years of this century numerous more specialized studies have appeared on

---

[15] See the Bibliography at the end of this book, for example.

[16] A. P. Dobroklonskij, *Prepodobnij Feodor, ispovednik i igumen Studijskij*, i. *Ego epoha, dzizn i deyatelnost*. ii. *Ego tvoreniya* (Odessa, 1913–14). Dobroklonskij taught church history at the Moscow Theological Academy, Moscow University, Odessa University, and finally, from 1920, at the Belgrade Orthodox Theological Faculty. Biographical details are to be found in the Obituary Notice of *Bogoslovlje, Journal of the Orthodox Theological Faculty of Belgrade*, 13 (1938), 80–7.

[17] German scholarship is represented particularly by Carl. Thomas and by G. A. Schneider (see Bibliography). The French produced the first critical edition of the most popular of Theodore's works, the *Parva Catechesis*: E. Auvray, Τοῦ ὁσίου πατρὸς ἡμῶν καὶ ὁμολογητοῦ Θεοδώρου ἡγουμένου τῶν Στουδίου μικρὰ κατήχησις (Paris, 1891) (= *Sancti patris nostri confessoris Theodori Studitis praepositi parva catechesis*), with an introduction by A. Tougard. The work by E. Marin, *De Studio coenobio Constantinopolitano* (Paris, 1893) is still the standard work on Theodore's monastery, although his *Saint Théodore (759–826)* (Paris, 1906) is a popular work and has prompted Patrick Henry ('Theodore of Studios: Byzantine Churchman', Ph.D. dissertation, Yale University, 1969, p. 8) to remark that it 'adds little to our knowledge, but elicits our amazement at the capacity of the French language for panegyrical fulsomeness'.

The Russians before Dobroklonskij also produced notable scholarship. For example, the first critical edition of the *Magna Catechesis* (Book II) was produced under the auspices of the Imperial Commission for the Study of Ancient Texts, St Petersburg, 1904: Τοῦ ὁσίου Θεοδώρου τοῦ Στουδίτου Μεγάλη Κατήχησις. Βιβλίον δεύτερον ἐκδοθὲν ὑπὸ τῆς Αὐτοκρατορικῆς Ἀρχαιογραφικῆς Ἐπιτροπῆς. The principal collaborator of those who worked on the edition was the Greek A. Papadopoulos-Kerameus, and it is usually cited under his name despite the fact that his name does not appear on the cover. A complete translation of Theodore's works was produced in Russian. Details in Dobroklonskij, *Prepodobnij Feodor*, ii. 27–8, 33–5, and G. Fatouros (ed.), *Theodori Studitae Epistulae* (Berlin, 1992), Prolegomena, 124*–5*.

[18] Alice Gardner, *Theodore of Studium, his Life and Times* (London, 1905). Reviewed in *AB* 26, p. 348.

many aspects of Theodore's career and interests. These will be referred to, when occasion arises, in the pages that are to follow and in the bibliography.

As for the primary sources of the life and career of Theodore, we are fortunate in having much first-hand material from the pen of Theodore himself, especially his letters.[19] Particularly valuable for Theodore's early life are the funeral encomia to his mother Theoktista[20] and to his uncle Plato.[21] An ancient biography, written by the Stoudite monk Michael, and known as *Vita B*,[22] was written some forty-two years or more after Theodore's death.[23] It was written according to the norms of ninth-century hagiography (already a sophisticated literary genre), meaning that historical details have to be treated with caution until substantiated by more reliable sources. It was also based on the funeral encomia, especially on the one to Plato.[24]

Four main variants of the *Vita* of Theodore are in fact known to scholars, but *Vita B* is recognized as being the most ancient, and of the four is the most reliable.[25] The others are designated in modern literature as *Vita A*,[26] *C*,[27] and *D*.[28] A more reliable source than

---

[19] On these, and Theodore's other writings, see below.

[20] *Laudatio Funebris in Matrem Suam* (BHG 2422), *PG* 99. 884–901, repr. from A. Mai, NPB 6/2 (Rome, 1853), 364–78.

[21] *Laudatio Sancti Platonis Hegumeni* (BHG 1553), *PG* 99. 804–49, repr. from *Acta Sanctorum* (1st edn.) collegit I. Bollandus etc. (Antwerp, 1643, Brussels, 1925), April. I (1675), pp. xlvi–liv; G. da Costa-Louillet, 'Saints de Constantinople au VIIIᵉ, IXᵉ et Xᵉ siècles', *Byzantion*, 24 (1954), 230 ff.

[22] *PG* 99. 233–328 (BHG 1754), repr. from Mai, NPB 6/2 (1853), 293–363.

[23] The *terminus post quem* is AD 868 as *Vita B*, 42 suggests that the Stoudite monk Nikolaos is already deceased at the time of writing the biography. The latter died in 868 (*Vita S. Nicolai Studitae*, *PG* 105. 905B).

[24] T. Pratsch, *Theodorus Studites (759–826)*, Berliner Byzantinistische Studien, 4 (Frankfurt am Main), 8.

[25] J. Leroy, 'La Réforme studite', *Il monachesimo orientale: Atti del convegno di studi orientali che sul predetto tema si tenne a Roma, sotto la direzione del pontificio istituto orientale, nei giorni 9,10,11 e 12 Aprile 1958*, OCA 153 (Rome, 1958), 181–214, p. 187 n. 45; Fatouros, *Theodori Studitae Epistulae*, Prolegomena, 4*.

[26] *PG* 99. 113–232, repr. from J. Sirmond, *Opera Varia*, 5 (Paris, 1696), 1–79; (Venice, 1728), 1–62. BHG 1755. This is the first of the *Vitae* to have been edited and is attributed in several MSS to Theodoros Daphnopates, a contemporary of Constantine VII Porphyrogennetos (945–59). See B. Latyšev, *VizVrem.* 21 (1914), 222, 256; L. G. Westerink, in *Théodore Daphnopatès. Correspondance*, ed. J. Darrouzès (Paris, 1978), Introduction.

[27] BHG 1755d; B. Latyšev, *VizVrem* 21 (1914), 258–304. The same text had just been edited by Dobroklonskij, *Prepodobnij Feodor*, i. pp. xxxiv–xc (*in fine voluminis*), but with several errors. Cf. Latyšev, 'Vita S. Theodori Studitae in codice Mosquensi musei Rumianzoviani nº 520. Praemonenda', *VizVrem.* 21 (1914), 255–7.

[28] The text remains unedited and is found in *Codex Monacensis gr. 467*. It was analysed

the *Vita* for details of the place of death of Theodore is a panegyric
by an unknown Stoudite monk commemorating an anniversary of
the recent transfer (*translatio*) of the mortal remains of Theodore,
and his brother Archbishop Joseph, from the island of Prinkipo to
the Stoudios monastery in Constantinople on 26 January 844.[29] It
was thus composed somewhat earlier than the *Vita*.[30] A letter cir-
culated to the monks by Naukratios, Theodore's successor, soon
after the latter's death, also corrects details given in the *Vita*.[31]

Other *Vitae* of saints may also provide valuable information.
Hagiography in general is designed for edification, not information, with the miraculous usually having a prominent place.
Chronology is also often handled artificially in order to give
greater scope for the activities of the hero with bias and misinfor-
mation not infrequently colouring the account. None the less, a
discerning reading can reveal details of events, attitudes, and
underlying moods that are of great value to the historian.[32]
Helpful in reconstructing the history of Theodore's time are the
Vitae of Patriarch Tarasios, Patriarch Nikephoros, Nikolaos
Stoudite, Niketas, Leo, and several others.[33]

Of prime importance for the historical context of Theodore's
life and activity are the accounts of the Byzantine chroniclers.
Theophanes the Confessor (who ends his account in 813)[34] and the

---

briefly by Latyšev, *VizVrem.* 21 (1914), 222–54, esp. 222–5, who concluded that it was the
same text of *Vita A* (BHG 1755) by Theodoros Daphnopates, the latter differing from the
11th-cent. MS only because of copying error. The text is not in fact listed in Halkin, BHG.
A different opinion was expressed by Julien Leroy, who was not convinced of the strict relationship between *A* and *D*, and who believed the latter was sufficiently different to warrant
a separate BHG listing: 'Les Petites Catéchèses', 333; 'La Réforme studite', 187.

[29] εἰς τὴν ἀνακομιδὴν καὶ κατάθεσιν τῶν λειψάνων τοῦ ὁσίου πατρὸς ἡμῶν καὶ
ὁμολογητοῦ Θεοδώρου, ed. Ch. van de Vorst, 'La Translation de S. Théodore Studite
et de S. Joseph de Thessalonique', *AnBoll.* 32 (1913), 27–61 (text: 50–61); Dobroklonskij,
Prepodobnij Feodor, i. pp. i–xv (*in fine voluminis*). BHG 1756t.

[30] Van de Vorst, 'La Translation de S. Théodore et S. Joseph', 27–35. *Vita B* i, *PG* 99.
233B, makes an allusion to the prior existence of both poetic compositions by disciples of
Theodore extolling his virtues and more developed encomia in prose style composed by
other ecclesiastics. It is possible that this panegyric is being included in the latter category.

[31] *Naucratii confessoris encyclica de obitu sancti Theodori Studitae, PG* 99. 1828A.

[32] C. Mango, *Byzantium:The Empire of the New Rome* (London, 1980), 246–51; R. Morris,
Monks and Laymen in Byzantium 843–1118 (Cambridge, 1995), 4–5, 11; T. Pratsch, *Theodorus
Studites,* 8–9.

[33] See the list of hagiographical sources in the bibliography of W. Treadgold, *The
Byzantine Revival,* 465–75, esp. pp. 365, 470. Also see Pratsch, *Theodorus Studites,* 13–14.

[34] Theophanes, *Chronographia,* ed. C. de Boor, 2 vols. (Leipzig, 1883). H. Turtledove, *The
Chronicle of Theophanes: An English Translation of Anni Mundi 6095–6305 (A.D. 602–813),* with

Scriptor Incertus (who covers the years 812–16)[35] provide us with information contemporary to the occurrence of these events. The main narrative sources for the next years come from the tenth century, with the exception of the world chronicle of George the Monk (Hamartolos), written either at the end of the reign of Michael III (842–67) or soon after, and ending in the year 842. This particular chronicle is regarded as being of little historical value.[36] The tenth-century chronicles use sources for the period after Theophanes ends his account, which are now lost. The anonymous author of the first part of the chronicle commissioned by Constantine VII, *Theophanes Continuatus* or *Scriptores post Theophanem*, covered the period 813–67.[37] The chronicle of Genesios also covers these same years and is closely related to the account of the continuator of Theophanes.[38] Both accounts, which are iconophile biased and seemingly dependent on the Life of Patriach Nikephoros, need to be read with discernment.[39] Symeon the Logothete and the so-called Pseudo-Symeon are the other two main tenth-century sources that provide information for our period.[40] All these sources, together with some other even later chronicles,[41] provide us with sufficient secure information to place Theodore the Stoudite within a proper historical context.[42]

Introduction and Notes (Philadelphia, 1982); C. Mango and R. Scott, *The Chronicle of Theophanes Confessor*, trans. with Introduction and Commentary (Oxford, 1997).

[35] Scriptor Incertus [Sergius Confessor?], *Historia de Leonae Bardae Armenii Filio*, in Leo Grammaticus, *Chronographia*, ed. I. Bekker, CSHB (Bonn, 1842), 335–62.

[36] G. Ostrogorsky, *History of the Byzantine State*, 2nd edn. (Oxford, 1968), 147, calls it 'a typical product of monastic circles' while Warren Treadgold, *The Byzantine Revival*, 388, describes it as a 'rather stupid chronicle'.

[37] *Theophanes Continuatus*, ed. I. Bekker (Bonn, 1838). This work is in fact a collection of four independent chronicles found in a single preserved MS. For details and bibliography, see A. Kazhdan, 'Theophanes Continuatus', *ODB* iii. 2061–2.

[38] *Regum libri Quattuor*, ed. A. Lesmüller-Werner and H. Thurn (Berlin, 1978). On the complicated relationship between these two chronicles, see A. Kahzdan, 'Genesios', *ODB*, ii. 828–9.

[39] Treadgold, *The Byzantine Revival*, 389; Pratsch, *Theodorus Studites*, 11.

[40] Pseudo-Symeon Magistros provides a better transmitted text of the Scriptor Incertus; Symeon Logothete (Magistros) is more important for the period 842–948. The account coinciding with Theodore's life often resembles the text of George the Monk. Treadgold, *The Byzantine Revival*, 389–90; A. Kahzdan, 'Symeon Logothete', 'Symeon Magistros. Pseudo-', *ODB* iii. 1982–3.

[41] e.g. the 11th-cent. John Skylitzes for the years 811 onwards.

[42] Mention should also be made of the *Historia Syntomos (Breviarium)* of Patriarch Nikephoros (602–769) and the Acts of the Synod of Nicaea (787) for the period of Theodore's early life. Some additional information for this historical period can also be

1.2 THE HISTORICAL CONTEXT OF
THEODORE'S FIRST YEARS

Theodore was born in Constantinople in 759 during the reign of
the iconoclast Emperor Constantine V (741–75). The city of
Constantinople had barely recovered from the great plague of 747
resulting in a serious underpopulation that was partially offset by
the resettlement of groups from Greece and the Aegean islands.
This left a population of perhaps 50,000 people, although by 780 it
may have grown to about 100,000. With unrepaired damage from
a serious earthquake in 740, many buildings and monuments lay
abandoned or ruined. Municipal reconstruction was sure but
gradual.[43]

Constantinople was the capital of an insecure Empire, much
reduced in size from its heyday under Justinian or even Herakleios.
At the time of Constantine V, North Africa, much of Spain, Egypt,
Palestine, and Syria were in the hands of the Muslim Arabs who
constantly posed a serious threat to the existing southern and eastern borders of Byzantium. However, with the transfer of the
caliphate from Damascus to Baghdad in 750 (following on the
overthrow of the Umayyad dynasty by the Abassids) the danger to
the south was somewhat reduced, but bi-annual incursions from
the east were the least to be expected. The Christian communities
of the ancient patriarchates of Alexandria, Jerusalem, and Antioch
were under Islamic rule and their leaders, who resided outside
their traditional sees, were severely hampered in exercising their
traditional roles both within their own territories and within the
greater orbit of Christendom. They no longer commanded the traditional respect of bygone centuries. The Empire was also threatened from the north. Constantine's main preoccupation for the
security of the Empire was in fact the threat from the Bulgars in the
north Balkans, a warrior race originally of Turkish origin. To these
most of his military campaigns, in which he was generally successful, were directed. The wars would be continued by his successors.

gleaned from non-literary sources, especially from numismatics and sigillography.
Treadgold, *The Byzantine Revival*, 390.

   [43] Many ruins also dated to the time of the old city in parts that had long been abandoned.

Eight years before Theodore was born a major setback for Constantine occurred in the West which was to have dramatic consequences. The exarchate of Ravenna fell into the hands of the Lombards and was never to be returned to the Empire. Not only did this mean that Byzantine control over north and central Italy ceased to exist, but the integrity of the duchy of Rome was now threatened. As a result Pope Stephen II entered into negotiations with King Pepin of the Frankish kingdom, having been disappointed at the lack of effective response from Constantine. This alliance, which would be renewed by subsequent popes, eventually led to the creation of the Papal States and to secession from the Empire of the East. It also led to the creation of a Western Holy Roman Empire.[44] Tensions with Constantinople had been acute under Constantine's father, Emperor Leo III (717–41), who had tried to impose a more efficient tax system on lands under the direct control of the papacy, as yet part of the Empire, but who had been hindered by Pope Gregory II (715–30) because of the resulting loss of his patrimonies. East Illyricum, Sicily, and Calabria had also been wrested from the ecclesiastical jurisdiction of Rome and placed under that of Constantinople, a situation never accepted by the Roman pontiffs.[45] Rome had also protested at the iconoclasm of Leo III, the forced resignation of Patriarch Germanos (730), and the imperial order to remove icons from Roman churches. A Roman Synod of 731 officially condemned Byzantine iconoclasm thus bringing the Churches into schism. Despite this, the popes still continued to show political loyalty to the East, expecting Constantinople to fulfil its obligations towards the Old Rome. When this failed to materialize a new realignment of powers was formed, with the duchy of Rome becoming a protectorate of the Franks. The crowning of Charlemagne as emperor by Pope Leo III in 800 sealed the political break between Rome and Constantinople.

Despite Constantine's achievements in his military campaigns, structural works in the city of Constantinople,[46] efficient military

---

[44] On the fall of Ravenna and all the events that followed, see the excellent analysis by Judith Herrin, *The Formation of Christendom* (London, 1989), 370 ff. with notes and bibliography.

[45] Ibid. 349–52. But cf. Ostrogorsky, *History of the Byzantine State*, 170 and n.

[46] Especially the rebuilding of the principal aqueduct of the city, the aqueduct of Valens, destroyed by the Avars in 626 during the reign of Herakleios.

administration of the Empire and creation of the mobile *tagmata* forces,[47] iconophile historians record his memory in the blackest of terms. Neither he nor his father are given credit for having restored imperial authority nor for having put an end to the political crisis from previous ineffectual reigns that had nearly brought down the Byzantine empire.[48] Constantine, like Leo III, was an iconoclast. Therefore he was a bad emperor. Theophanes begins the account of his reign thus:

Constantine's actions were impiously carried out from the tenth indiction—the first year of his reign—to the fourteenth indiction—the year of his end. For he was a totally destructive bloodsucking wild beast who used his power tyrannically and illegally. First, he sided against our God and Saviour Jesus Christ, His altogether immaculate Mother, and all the Saints. He was deceived by wizardry, licentiousness, blood sacrifices of horses, dung and urine. Effeminacy and summoning demons pleased him, and ever since he was a boy he had partaken in absolutely every sort of soul-destroying practice.[49]

In this year [741] Constantine, the persecutor of the laws handed down from the fathers, became Emperor by divine judgment because of the multitude of our sins.[50]

Theophanes also calls him the Forerunner of the Antichrist.[51] Iconophile literature, furthermore, gave Constantine nicknames by which he would be derisively remembered: Kaballinos ('groom')[52] and especially Kopronymos ('dung-named') for supposedly having opened his bowels during his baptism.[53]

The literature on Byzantine iconoclasm (726–87; 815–43) is very extensive.[54] There is no one accepted explanation for its origins,

[47] Treadgold, *The Byzantine Revival*, 26–7; Herrin, *Formation of Christendom*, 360–3.

[48] Cf. J. Herrin, 'The Context of Iconoclast Reform', in *Iconoclasm*, ed. A. Bryer and J. Herrin (Birmingham, 1977), 15–20.

[49] Theophanes, *Chronographia*, AM 6232, pp. 412–13.

[50] Ibid. AM 6233, p. 414.   [51] Ibid. AM 6211, p. 400: Ἀντιχρίστου πρόδρομος.

[52] Cf. the anonymous iconophile tract, written between 765 and 787, *Adversus Constantinum Caballinum*, PG 95. 309–44 and Theodore Stoudite, ep. 421. 17 (cf. ep. 417. 13 where the name is also given to Leo V).

[53] Theophanes, *Chronographia*, AM 6211, p. 400: 'While Germanos the chief prelate was baptizing Leo's successor (in both his evil and his rule) Constantine, the boy, because he was so young, gave a terrible, foul-smelling harbinger: he defecated in the holy font, as say those who were accurate eyewitnesses.' Cf. Vita *B*, 236B; Vita *A*, 117B: Vita *C*, no. 5.

[54] For a good general introduction to the problem of iconoclasm, see R. Cormack, *Writing In Gold: Byzantine Society and its Icons* (London, 1985), esp. pp. 95 ff., and Kenneth Parry, *Depicting the Word: Byzantine Iconophile Thought of the Eighth and Ninth Centuries* (Leiden, 1996). More specialized studies include: G. Ostrogorsky, *Studien zur Geschichte des*

theories being almost as numerous as Byzantinists.[55] Constantine's iconoclasm, which he inherited from his father,[56] is particularly notorious because of its violence and divisive effects on society.[57] He himself seems to have been a talented, if misguided, theologian, systematizing and raising the theological discourse from the level of biblical injunction against idolatry to that of Christology.[58] But unlike his father, who seems to have acted with some caution and showed no particular theological pretensions, Constantine went much further in treating the matter as if icon veneration were an aberration from the true doctrine of the Apostolic Church. Those who venerated icons or defended them, or who even kept iconophile literature, would be treated not only as enemies of the state but also as heretics.[59] But for this he needed the endorsement of the ecclesiastical authorities. This he received from the carefully planned Synod of Hieria (754).[60] In its canons and anathemas the Council forbade the production of images, their veneration, erection in churches or private homes, or concealment. Bishops, presbyters, and deacons who disregarded this ordinance were to be

byzantinischen Bilderstreites (Breslau, 1929); idem, 'Les Débuts de la querelle des images', *Mélanges Charles Diehl* (Paris, 1930), i. 235–55; E. J. Martin, *A History of the Iconoclastic Controversy* (London, 1930); P. J. Alexander, *The Patriarch Nicephorus of Constantinople* (Oxford, 1958); A. Bryer and J. Herrin (eds.), *Iconoclasm*; S. Gero, *Byzantine Iconoclasm During the Reign of Leo III, with Particular Attention to the Oriental Sources*, CSCO 346 suppl. 41 (Louvain, 1973); idem, *Byzantine Iconoclasm During the Reign of Constantine V, with Particular Attention to the Oriental Sources*, CSCO 348 suppl. 52 (Louvain, 1977); A. Grabar, *L'Iconoclasme byzantin: Le Dossier archéologique*, 2nd edn. (Paris, 1984); D. Stein, *Der Beginn des byzantinischen Bilderstreites und seine Entwicklung* (Munich, 1980).

[55] Cf. P. A. Hollingsworth and A. Cutler, 'Iconoclasm', in *ODB* ii. 975–7.

[56] The documentation on the persecution of image-venerators under Leo III is quite scanty compared to that of his son.

[57] The standard works on Constantine V and his policies are A. Lombard, *Constantin V, empereur des Romains (740–775)* (Paris, 1902), and Gero, *Constantine V*.

[58] He composed at least two 'enquiries' (πεύσεις) which he himself read to assemblies of the clergy. He also arranged *silentia* in several places where he or one of his sympathizers explained his views.

[59] According to the evidence we have, punishments were meted out to iconophiles not because of their 'errancy' in doctrine, but because of opposition to imperial will and resistance to imperial law. See the stimulating article by P. J. Alexander, 'Religious Persecution and Resistance in the Byzantine Empire of the Eighth and Ninth centuries: Methods and Justifications', *Speculum*, 52/2 (1977), 238–64.

[60] The *Definition (Horos)*, but not the Acts, have been preserved as part of the Seventh Ecumenical Council, where it was read out to be refuted point by point in the sixth session: I. D. Mansi, *Sacrorum Conciliorum Nova et Amplissima Collectio etc.* (Florence, 1767), xiii. 205–364. English trans. D. J. Sahas, *Icon and Logos: Sources in Eighth-Century Iconoclasm* (Toronto, 1986). The *Horos* was based on an edited version of the writings of Constantine.

deposed and recalcitrant monks or laymen were to be anathematized and subjected to prosecution under the imperial laws as foes
of God's commandments and the teaching of the Fathers.[61]

The resolutions of the Council, which gave itself an ecumenical
title, were soon put into effect. Constantine required the army and
the populace of Constantinople to take an oath that they would not
venerate images. Monks and monasteries were also particularly targeted. *Hegoumenoi* received new novices under pain of death. There
was to be no communion with monks nor were they even to be
greeted.[62] They may have been the most resistant to the new doctrine and policies, but the emperor seems also to have had his own
motives for a personal crusade against them.[63] He referred to them
publicly as 'unmentionables' (ἀμνημόνευτοι) and to monasteries in
general as 'the order of darkness'.[64] A propaganda campaign,
attacking the very *raison d'être* of monasticism, was initiated.[65]

Despite the impression given by the sources, iconoclasm was
essentially a Constantinopolitan phenomenon, other parts of the
Empire being affected to the extent of their proximity to the capital
and to the extent of the efforts of individual agents to put into effect
the emperor's policies.[66] Furthermore, only from the 760s is iconoclastic violence towards monks first reliably recorded.[67] A
graphic account is given by Theophanes of the cruel determination of the *strategos* of the Thracesian theme, Michael
Lachanodrakon, to implement his master's will, resulting in the
extermination of the monastic order in the theme.[68] Of the named

---

[61] Mansi, *Sacrorum Conciliorum Nova et Amplissma Collectio etc.* xiii, 328BC.

[62] Cf. *Vita S. Stephani Iunioris*, BHG 1666, M.-F. Auzépy (ed), *La Vie d'Étienne le Jeune par Étienne le Diacre*, Birmingham Byzantine and Ottoman Monographs, 3, Aldershot, 1997, c.24, 119–20; c. 40, 131–40 (= *PG* 100, 1112A; 1137B).

[63] Stephen Gero has convincingly argued in 'Byzantine Iconoclasm and Mona-chomachy', *JEH* 28 (1977), 241–8, that throughout the iconoclastic crisis there was no necessary relationship between 'iconomachy' and 'monachomachy' and that Constantine's persecution of the monks was due to personal motives and antipathy. See also the discus-sion in Morris, *Monks and Laymen*, 12–13.

[64] Auzépy, *Vie d'Etienne le Jeune*, ch. 24. 119–20 (and *passim*).

[65] Nikephoros, *Antirrheticus iii*, *PG* 100. 517B. Cf. Theodore the Stoudite, ep. 489. 14–38, in defence of the (apostolic) institution of monasticism.

[66] H. Ahrweiler, 'The Geography of the Iconoclast World', in Bryer and Herrin (eds.), *Iconoclasm*, 21–7.

[67] The persecution was, of course, aimed at all troublesome iconophiles including high-ranking officials of the government and army. Cf. Theophanes, *Chronographia*, AM 6257, pp. 437–38.

[68] Ibid. 6263, p. 446.

iconophile martyrs (of which there are surprisingly few),[69] the most prominent was Stephen the Younger, monk of the monastery of St Auxentios in Bithynia and martyred, according to Theophanes, in 765.[70] The *Vita* of St Stephen was composed *c.*806 by Stephen the Deacon and influenced many authors who subsequently wrote on iconoclasm.[71]

1.3 THEODORE'S FAMILY BACKGROUND AND EDUCATION

Born in 759, Theodore the Stoudite was about 5 years of age when Stephen was martyred and when Constantine's iconoclasm and anti-monastic violence was at its height. His family was wealthy and socially well-connected: Theodote, a cousin on his mother's side, would be crowned Augusta in 795 and become the second wife to Emperor Constantine VI.[72] Although reputedly iconophile and from Constantinople, his immediate family does not seem to have been adversely affected by Constantine's policies, which seems to suggest that there were ways of conscientious coexistence with the emperor's religious regime.[73]

Theodore's father, Photeinos, was a highly placed official of the imperial treasury[74] and appears to have been learned, even beyond what would be expected of a civil servant.[75] Precious little is known of his blood relations.[76] The *Vita* informs us that he was

[69] The only ones recorded are St Andrew Kalybites, from a community at Blachernai, who was whipped to death in the hippodrome, Peter the Stylite, St Andreas the Cretan, and Stephen the Younger. Cf. S. Gero, *Constantine V*, 122–5.

[70] Theophanes, *Chronographia*, AM 6257, p. 437.

[71] *PG* 100. 1069–186. This document is full of precious details although styled on earlier hagiography. An account of its contents is found in Cormack, *Writing in Gold*, 118–21. Cf. Gero, 'Byzantine Iconoclasm and Monachomachy', 242–3.

[72] On Theodore's relations and family background, see Dobroklonskij, *Prepodobnij Feodor*, i. 285–90; J. Pargoire, 'Saint Théophane le chronographe et ses rapports avec Saint Théodore Studite', *VizVrem.* 9 (1902), 31–102; 35 ff.: Pratsch, *Theodoros Studites*, 17–67.

[73] Cf. *Vita A*, 116D, which simply alludes to the fact that Theodore's father refused to be moved by the iconomachs. See also, Pratsch, *Theodoros Studites*, 42–5: 'Die Familie des Theodoros und der erste Ikonoklasmus'.

[74] *Vita B*, 236D; *Vita A*, 116D: *Vita C*, no. 4. See also, Pratsch, *Theodoros Studites*, 18–21.

[75] This is suggested by a letter written in 815 to Naukratios, ep. 103. 19–20, in which Theodore asks his disciple to obtain a work for him of exegesis on St John belonging to (or possibly written by?) his 'father according to the flesh.'

[76] According to *Vita B*, 241A and *Laudatio Funebris in Matrem Suam* 889C, Photeinos had three brothers (who also embraced monastic life).

a pious man and had lived in religious continence with his wife for
some five years before their mutual decision, in 781, to embrace
union with God in the life of monasticism.[77] He may subsequently
have been ordained a deacon.[78] Photeinos is rarely mentioned in
Theodore's writings, and it has been suggested that he died sometime between 797 and 800.[79]

Photeinos was married to Theoktista. She figures prominently
as a major influence in Theodore's young life and as a comfort in
the first real trials of his monastic life.[80]

Theoktista was from a senatorial family but had endured a
difficult childhood as a result of having lost her parents, Sergios
and Euphemia, along with other relatives, in the great plague of
747.[81] She seems to have received minimal education as a child
and taught herself to read only after she had married. A woman of
genuine and strong piety, Theodore tells us she had quickly
learned to commit the whole Psalter to memory, which aided her
in the religious upbringing of her children.[82] Theoktista is said to
have had a forceful personality and, with it, a quick temper which
was a cause of mortification for her. She was remembered as being
a true mistress of the household, being strict but also considerate
with children and servants alike. Theodore was greatly devoted to
his mother, and was especially grateful for his religious upbringing
which made him think of her as a 'double' mother ($\delta\iota\mu\eta\tau\eta\rho$)—in
flesh and in spirit.[83] She became an exemplary religious, but was

[77] *Vita B*, 236D; 241A Cf. *Vita A*, 116D, 121A; *Vita C*, nos. 4, 8. In *Laudatio Funebris in Matrem Suam*, 885CD, Theodore is also clear that this was due to his mother's initiative and insistence. With the widespread conviction that asceticism was the culmination of the Christian life, marital continence was not in itself an unusual practice. It is commended by Theodore in his eulogy of his mother and in advice he gives to pious laywomen. An example is his letter to the Protospatharia Albeneka, ep. 395 (*ann.* 815–19), where he suggests that Albeneka, married to a very high state official, should try to persuade her husband to let her enter a nunnery. Failing this, Theodore states, she is permitted to follow God's calling even with a protesting husband!

[78] Cf. the reference in ep. 1. 88: ὁ κύριος διάκονος καὶ πατὴρ ἡμῶν, which also indicates that Photeinos would have accompanied Theodore into exile to Thessalonica. For a discussion on the evidence to suggest this interpretation, see Pratsch, *Theodoros Studites*, 23–4.

[79] Ibid. 23.

[80] The most recent discussion on Theoktista's life is ibid. 26–41. Earlier works include: C. Diehl, 'A Middle Class Woman of the Eighth Century', *Byzantine Portraits*, trans. Harold Bell (New York, 1927), 105–24; B. Hermann, *Theoktista aus Byzanz, die Mutter zweier Heiligen* (Freiberg, 1919); Dobroklonskij, *Prepodobnij Feodor* i. 294 ff.; A. Gardner, *Theodore of Studium*, 15 ff.

[81] *Laudatio S. Platonis Hegumeni* 805B–808B. *Laudatio Funebris in Matrem Suam* 885B.

[82] *Laudatio Funebris* 885B.   [83] Ibid. 901A.

still a mother to him in his suffering.[84] Theodore corresponded
with her and composed a eulogy after she died when in her 50s
(between the years 797 and 800).[85]

Theodore was the eldest of four children. His brother Joseph, born
around 762, was destined to become an outstanding hymnographer[86] and archbishop of Thessalonica (around the end of 806), and
to share in many of the trials of Theodore's later life. He died on 15
July 832, thereafter being numbered among the saints in glory by the
Eastern church.[87] Very little is known of the life of his sister, whose
name is not even recorded, except that she died young.[88] The
Benjamin of the family, Euthymios, also had a short life, being born
between 769 and 774 in Constantinople. Theodore records a
pathetic scene of how the young Euthymios despaired at being separated from his mother when the family split up to follow the monastic calling.[89] With time he seems to have settled into his new life, for
he was still with his brother seventeen years later. Theodore writes to
him in March or April 797 at the beginning of the moechian controversy, encouraging him to persevere and to be faithful whilst being
held as an imperial prisoner.[90] It is very probable that within the next
year Euthymios tragically drowned in the Marmara Sea, when he
would have been not far from 30 years of age. Together with nine
other monks from Sakkoudion he had set sail from Bithynia towards
the capital city (perhaps to set up a new foundation) but had been
caught in a violent storm. Theodore speaks of this in a catechetical
oration of the period. There was a happy ending to the story:
Euthymios had appeared in dreams to four monks of the community
to assure them that all the deceased had found salvation.[91]

---

[84] Cf.ibid. 893B–D; ep. 3. 75–80.

[85] The one letter to survive, ep. 6 (*ann.* 797–9), was written to console his mother who
had fallen gravely ill. On the date of Theoktista's death, see Pratsch, *Theodoros Studites*, 41.

[86] But not to be confused with Joseph the Hymnographer, a younger contemporary who
belonged to the poetic school of Stoudios.

[87] Cf. J. Pargoire, 'Saint Joseph de Thessalonique', *EO* 9 (1906), 278–82; 351–6; C. van
de Vorst, 'La Translation', 36 ff.

[88] She is mentioned in *Vita A*, 121A; *Vita B*, 241A; and *Vita C*, no. 8 in connection with
the whole family embracing monasticism, and in ep. 6. 9 to Theoktista where her death is
recorded. She therefore must have died between 797 and 799.

[89] *Laudatio Funebris* 892CD.

[90] Ep. 1 (March–April ann. 797) to Plato, 63–74. Euthymios was being held with Plato in
Constantinople.

[91] *Tvorenija prepodobnago otsa nashego i ispovidnyka Feodorja Studitja v russkom perevod* (2 vols.; St
Petersburg, 1907), i. 588 (= *TC* I. 54. 588). Although Theodore does not expressly identify

Apart from his mother, the major influence on Theodore's young life was his uncle Plato, Theoktista's brother, who was to become Theodore's spiritual father ('my father who gave spiritual birth to me')[92] and mentor for many a year.[93] Born in 735, Plato was raised by his uncle, a high-ranking financial official, who taught him the profession of notary and was instrumental in helping him become a *zygostates* of the treasury.[94] In 759, around the time when Theodore was born, he decided to abandon the world, giving away his accumulated wealth (to, among others, his two sisters, one of whom was Theoktista)[95] and took the monastic habit at the monastery of Symboloi (or Symbola) in the region of Mt. Olympos in Bithynia.[96] He returned to Constantinople at least briefly in the early reign of Leo IV (775–80), where his reputation as an exceptional spiritual teacher and guide was such that he was offered, alternatively, the abbacy of a monastery within the capital and the bishopric of Nikomedia, both of which he declined.[97] He was present at the Second Council of Nicaea (787) where he was part of the moderate party of invited *hegoumenoi*,[98] supporting Patriarch Tarasios in his attempt to create unity in a very divided church.[99] He experienced imprisonment and exile for his uncom-

---

Euthymios as his blood brother there are good reasons to think that this was the case. From the letter to his gravely ill mother, ep. 6. 10 (*ann.* 797–9), we know he was already deceased. Thus he would have died not too long after his release from captivity and return to Bithynia (August 797). Cf. J. Leroy, 'La Réforme Studite', 203 n. 180.

[92] PK 65. 456.

[93] Details on his birth and career are found in Theodore's eulogy *Laudatio S. Platonis Hegumeni* 803–49; G. da Costa-Louillet, 'Saints de Constantinople au VIIIᵉ, IXᵉ et Xᵉ siècles', *Byzantion*, 24 (1954), 230–40 (French summary with comments of eulogy). For his chronology, see J. Pargoire, 'A quelle date l'higoumène saint Platon est-il mort?' *EO* 4 (1900–1), 164–70. See also Pratsch, *Theodoros Studites*, 47–8.

[94] i.e. an official concerned with checking the quality of the gold solidus.

[95] *Laudatio Platonis* 805B, 809B; *Vita A*, 121A. The other sister remained 'in the world'.

[96] *Laudatio Platonis* 813A. On this monastery, see R. Janin, *Les Églises et les monastères des grands centres byzantins* (Paris, 1975), 181–3.

[97] *Laudatio Platonis* 808B, 810B, 820B–821D. Theodore places Plato in Constantinople after the persecution was over, but before the reign of Irene or the patriarchate of Tarasios.

[98] At this time he was the abbot and archimandrite of Sakkoudion (on which see below). On the Second Council of Nicaea, see G. Dumeige, *Nicée II: Histoire des conciles oecuméniques* (Paris, 1978). For an insight into its theological arguments, see M.-F. Auzépy, 'Manifestations de la propagande en faveur de l'orthodoxie', in *Byzantium in the Ninth Century: Dead or Alive? Papers from the Thirtieth Spring Symposium of Byzantine Studies, Birmingham, 1996*, ed. Leslie Brubaker (Aldershot, 1998), 85–99.

[99] On the divisions among the monks over the reconciliation of iconoclast and simoniac bishops, see M.-F. Auzépy, 'La Place des moines à Nicée II (787)', *Byzantion*, 58 (1988), 5–21, p. 19. No mention of Plato's participation in the Council is made by Theodore in his eulogy

promising stand towards the second marriage of Constantine VI
in 797, and again from 809–11. He died on 4 April 814, being
commemorated as a saint soon afterwards by the Stoudite community.[100]

As the son of a court official, Theodore would have been given the
education appropriate for his position in society and as one
expected to follow in his father's footsteps.[101] At the age of 7
Theodore began his elementary education, προπαιδεία, under
the supervision of an instructor or γραμματιστής.[102] This consisted of learning to read aloud, to count, and to acquire the rudi-
ments of grammar.[103] Following this came his secondary or
general education, ἐγκύκλιος παίδευσις, which when completed
would have consisted of a cycle of literary studies (equivalent to the
medieval *trivium*), namely grammar, dialectic, and rhetoric, and a
cycle of scientific studies (*quadrivium*), namely arithmetic, geometry,
music, and astronomy. On completion Theodore would have been
around 18 and ready for higher studies.[104] At this time in
Constantinople there is no known organized educational institution that Theodore could have been sent to for his education, and
it is to be presumed that all his learning was directed by private
tutors.

The *Vita* makes no mention of the *quadrivium*, presumably
because specific allusion to such 'profane' knowledge would have
been of little interest to monastic readers. In his writings, however,

to his uncle, written probably in 814. A probable reason for this is that Theodore was, at
this time, highly critical of the actions of Patriarch Tarasios over the moechian affair. On
Theodore's changing attitudes to the Council, see P. Henry, 'Initial Eastern Assessments of
the Seventh Oecumenical Council', *JTS* NS 25 (1974), 75–92; P. Speck, *Kaiser Konstantin VI*,
(Munich, 1978), 151, esp. n. 351; 557–9.

[100] Cf. *PC* 69. 181, on the occasion of 'celebrating the memory' of Plato.
[101] Cf. Dobroklonskij, *Prepodobnij Feodor*, i. 299; P. Lemerle, *Le Premier Humanisme byzantin*, 123.
[102] *Vita A*, 117C; *Vita B*, 237B: εἰσαγωγικαὶ καὶ στοιχειώδεις τῶν μαθημάτων
τέχναι.
[103] For background to the type of education available in this period, see A. Moffatt,
'Schooling in the Iconoclast Centuries', in Bryer and Herrin (eds.), *Iconoclasm*, 85–92;
Lemerle, *Le Premier Humanisme byzantin*, 100–4 and *passim*; Wilson, *Scholars of Byzantium*
(London, 1983), 1–27, 49 ff.; Mango, *Byzantium*, 125 ff.; F. Dvornik, *Les Légendes de Constantin
et de Méthode vues de Byzance* (Prague, 1933), 25–33; L. Bréhier, *La Civilisation byzantine* (Paris,
1950), 456–503; Alexander, *The Patriarch Nicephorus*, 57–9.
[104] Cf. Lemerle, *Le Premier Humanisme byzantin*, 100; but see Dobroklonskij, *Prepodobnij
Feodor*, i. 298. In reality, the *quadrivium* was probably studied more at the level of higher studies than of secondary education. Cf. Mango, *Byzantium*, 127.

allusions to numbers (their perfection and mystical significance) and to geometrical figures do indicate some familiarity with arithmetic and geometry.[105] Likewise, his ability to write hymns presupposes knowledge of the rules of music[106] and he shows some knowledge of the scientific causes of natural phenomena[107]—all of which point to study of the *quadrivium*. Of more importance, none the less, was the *trivium*.

Vita B states that Theodore learnt grammar, dialectic ('which specialists call philosophy'), and rhetoric.[108] Grammar also included study of pagan poetry.[109] Some of the authors Theodore studied are alluded to in his writings, especially in his letters addressed to the educated. These include Homer, Euripides, and Demosthenes (who were important authors during most of antiquity), Aristophanes, Aeschylus, Diogenes, Plato, and Aristotle.[110] Theodore's command of grammar, and especially dialectic, were to be of great importance in his polemic with the iconoclasts.[111] His expositions of iconophile theology demanded a keen understanding of Aristotelian dialectic, the detailed arguments for which could have been taken from a number of sources.[112] What is today

[105] Writing to Naukratios, ep. 186. 22–3, Theodore compares the perfection of the Holy Trinity to the perfection of number: εἴπερ ὁ μὲν τῆς τελειότητος, ὁ δὲ τῆς Τριάδος ἀναλογῶν ἐστιν ἀριθμός. On the mystical sense of numbers, see *Oratio in S. Bartholomaeum*, *PG* 99. 792C (= Westerbergh, *Sermo*, pp. 41, 15 ff.). Use of geometrical figures is illustrated in *Antirrheticus* 3. 1. 389C; 29. 404B; 45. 409D; *Refutatio Poem. Iconomach.*, 14. 460B; ep. 546 (to John the Grammarian), 20 ff.; cf. ep. 427. 45 ff.

[106] Cf. *Vita B*, 312D. In PK 85. 606 (= *MC* 98. 97) hymnography and tropar writing is mentioned as an activity of the monastery.

[107] e.g. in the *Laudatio S. Joannis Evang.* 782A, Theodore describes the accepted hypothesis of the origin of thunder and lightning. In PK 79. 550–1 (= *MC* 104. 117) he gives a rudimentary explanation of the physical causes of earthquakes.

[108] *PG* 99. 237B. Cf. *Vita C*, no. 6.

[109] *Vita A*, 117D, tells us that Theodore ignored the fables but focused only on what was useful. Likewise, with the classical models of rhetoric.

[110] References in Fatouros, *Theodori Studitae Epistulae*, ii. 973–8. J. Leroy makes an astonishing statement when he says, in 'La Vie quotidienne du moine Studite', *Irénikon*, 27 (1954), 42 n. 5, 'On ne trouve nulle part dans les œuvres de Théodore la moindre allusion à des auteurs profanes.' Leroy is surely thinking only of the Catecheses.

[111] Writing to John the Grammarian, ep. 546. 10–11, he argues, 'And if it is necessary to speak according to grammatical terms (κατὰ τὴν γραμματικὴν τεχνολογίαν) . . .' Cf. ep. 445.11 ff. (to Severianos).

[112] e.g. in the *Antirrhetici*, 329A, 337A–D, 341B–D, 345A, 360D, 368B, 389A, 433C etc.; epp. 427, 430, 445, 491, 528, 546. Aristotelian image theory had been developed by Byzantine schoolmen in the first decade after the Second Council of Nicaea: Alexander, *The Patriarch Nicephorus*, 196–7. See also idem 189 ff., on the use of Aristotelian logic and terminology by Theodore and Nikephoros. For further study, see G. Tsigaras, 'Philosophisches Instrumentarium der Christologie von Theodoros Studites über die Darstellung des

known as the *Dialectica* of John Damascene (the first part of the *Fons Scientiae*), may have been one such source.[113] The Greek Menaion for 11 November and the short Synaxarion *Vita* both claim that Theodore had achieved the 'highest level of knowledge'.[114] *Vita A*, besides, claims that he learnt from philosophers the whole of philosophy, ethics, dogmatics, dialectic, and demonstration.[115] Such claims, however, seem to have been dictated more by the canons of the hagiographical genre than by the evidence available.[116] Indeed, scholars have not been slow to point out that Theodore is not particularly distinguished by the rhetorical skill, classical background, or literary sophistication expected of one who has supposedly achieved the heights of learning.[117] A curious tale is told in the *Vita* which illustrates how some of Theodore's younger contemporaries shared these modern criticisms. Some disciples of Archbishop Gregory Asbestas of Syracuse had visited a certain man in Sardinia who was fond of Theodore's verses, especially those which were composed for the Lenten

menschgeworden Logos', *Annuarium Historiae Conciliorum*, 20 (1988, pub. 1989), 268–77; M.-J. Baudinet, 'La Relation iconique à Byzance au IXᵉ siècle d'après Nicéphore le Patriarche: Un destin de l'aristotélisme', *Les Études philosophiques*, 1 (1978), 85–106.

[113] This is suggested by the almost identical wording found in ep. 528. 56–8 and the *Dialectica*, B. Kotter (ed.), *Die Schriften des Johannes von Damaskos* (Berlin 1969), i. 102, 32, 5–7, and the chapter on περὶ τῶν πρός τι, ibid. 117–19. Compare also *Antirrheticus* 3. 433C and *Dialectica*, Kotter, 74–6. This relationship was also noted by Dobroklonskij, *Prepodobnij Feodor*, i. 301.

[114] *Ex Menaeis Graecorum*, PG 99. 100D: καὶ εἰς τὸ ἀκρότατον ὕφος τῆς γνώσεως ἀνήχθη; *Ex Synaxario*, ibid., 101C: πᾶσαν δὲ γνῶσιν τῶν μαθημάτων ἐκμαθών.

[115] PG 99. 117D–120A.

[116] B. Vidov, in *St Theodore the Studite*, Studite Spiritual Library (Toronto, 1985), 13, writes 'As a university student, Theodore frequented classes in Theology, Law and Philosophy . . . Theodore finished his studies in Constantinople.' Earlier, on p. 12, he also states, 'When Photino changed his beautiful clothes for monk's attire, he decided his sons Theodore, Joseph and Euthymius should remain in Constantinople to finish their studies. If they so desired, they could follow him when they were of age.' Both statements are groundless imaginative embellishments on the sources. Vidov's monograph, of a popular and edifying nature, is in fact fraught with errors of fact.

[117] S. Efthymiadis, 'The Vita Tarasii and the Hagiographical Work of Ignatios the Deacon', D.Phil. dissertation (Oxford, 1991), 24–9; Lemerle, *Le Premier Humanisme byzantin*, 123–4; P. Speck, *Theodoros Studites, Jamben auf verschiedene Gegenstände* (Berlin, 1968), 100 ff. R. Browning, 'The Language of Byzantine Literature', in S. Vryonis Jr. (ed.), *The 'Past' in Medieval and Modern Greek Culture*, Byzantina kai Metabyzantina (Malibu, 1978), i. 114–15. Lemerle writes, for example, 'Quant aux poésies, ïambes et épigrammes, elles sont de véritables pastiches ou, pour mieux dire, d'habiles exercises d'école, mais elles montrent au moins que leur auteur avait reçu de solides connaissances de métrique', *Le Premier Humanisme byzantin*. The Catecheses all have a simple direct style, as do very many of the letters.

Triodion. These disciples began to ridicule the poems and their author for not having been composed according to the rules of art. The guest, who was easily impressed, thereupon changed his own opinion about their literary merit. That same night the deceased Theodore appeared to his faithless admirer, causing him to be whipped.[118]

On the other hand, it is recognized that Theodore was a skilful wordsmith (as the great number of *hapax legomena* in his works indicate) and that his literary prowess could be expressed in the right circumstances with developed forms of Byzantine epistolography, and high-style rhetoric.[119]

As for his theological training, this would have been acquired, first informally during the time of his general education, and then from both private study and (presumably) formal guided tuition as a monk within the monastery. During his formative years he would probably have been exposed to the Psalms as a text for grammatical studies.[120] He may well have been given the homilies of Gregory of Nazianzus as a model for rhetorical composition,[121] or at the very least been exposed to them in church.[122] The *Vita* informs us that he had also, when in his teens, immersed himself in the reading and study of the lives of the saints.[123] Certainly in the early years of his life as a monk at the Sakkoudion monastery he studied the Scriptures and writings of the Fathers, in particular those of St Basil.[124] Manuscripts containing the works of the Fathers, past theologians, and spiritual writers were not particularly abundant during this period, and it was this, together with the research activities of the defenders and opponents of icons, that made calligraphy and copying such an important monastic

[118] *Vita B*, 312D–313A; *Vita C*, n. 68.

[119] Dobroklonskij, *Prepodobnij Feodor*, i. 301 and *passim*; Efthymiadis, 'Vita Tarasii', 24–9; idem, 'Le Panégyrique de S. Théophane le Confesseur', *AB* 111 (1993), 265–6; I. Ševčenko, 'Levels of Style in Byzantine Prose', *JÖB* 31/1 (1981), 292–4; G. Fatouros, 'Fehlendes in Lampes "Patristic Lexicon": Zum Wortschatz der Studites-Briefe', *JÖB* 33 (1983), 109–19; idem, 'Zur Sprache des Theodoros Studites', in *Lexicographica Byzantina*, ed. W. Hörander and E. Trapp (Vienna, 1991), 123–8 where the author explains why Theodore purposely uses simple style for the most part; also in *Theodori Studitae Epistulae*, 126*–8*. A list of *hapax legomena* and unusual forms appearing in the letters is also to be found in ibid. ii, 'Index Verborum Memorabilium', 921–55.

[120] Cf. A. Moffatt, 'Schooling in the Iconoclast Centuries', in Bryer and Herrin (eds.), *Iconclasm*, 92; N. G. Wilson, *Scholars of Byzantium*, 24.

[121] Cf. N. G. Wilson, ibid. 23.   [122] Cf. Alexander, *The Patriarch Nicephorus*, 58.

[123] *Vita B*, 237C. *Vita A*, 120B, speaks of his study of the Scriptures.

[124] *Vita A*, 128C.

activity.[125] Theodore's uncle Plato is credited with having provided monasteries with scores of personally copied books,[126] and Theodore himself developed the skills of the scribe, always taking a keen interest in books both for reading and for copying.[127] Probably as a result of the copying activity of his monastery Theodore could consider it to be in possession of an abundance of books.[128]

The lives of the saints, especially of the martyrs, were of great importance to Theodore as means of spiritual growth for himself and his monks and as models of resistance during times of trial.[129] The monastic Fathers also provided inspiration for his monastic reform.[130] The writings of the Fathers, along with Scripture, would have been the main sources for Theodore's theological education. It is difficult to say to what extent he had at hand the original works of those whom he quotes, and to what extent he quotes from secondary sources, especially the florilegia that abounded during the iconoclast period.[131] He had the works of Basil the Great (and the *Constitutions* of Pseudo-Basil) at hand, and from the diversity and frequency of citations from Gregory of Nazianzus and John Chrysostom,[132] who, besides, were extremely popular

---

[125] C. Mango, 'The Availability of Books in the Byzantine Empire, A.D. 750–850', in *Byzantine Books and Bookmen*, a Dumbarton Oaks Colloquium (Washington DC, 1975), 29–45, esp. 44–5; Lemerle, *Le Premier Humanisme byzantin*, 124–7.

[126] *Laudatio Platonis* 820A. Cf. Mango, 'Availability of Books', 44.

[127] Cf. ep. 103. 19–20, where Theodore asks Naukratios for books; ep. 150. 5 ff., where he complains to the same that all his books have been taken from him. On Theodore as a scribe, cf. *Vita B*, 264A; *Vita C*, no. 27; *De Obitu S. Theodori Studitae*, PG 99. 1848B. See Lemerle, *Le Premier Humanisme byzantin*, 124–5 and n. 55.

[128] PK 43. 308: καὶ γὰρ χάριτι Χριστοῦ πολλὴ ἡμῖν πάρεστι βίβλων περιουσία.

[129] In ep. 2. 68–9, Theodore tells Plato how he has read a 12-volume book where martyrdoms are listed: μαρτυρίων ἐν δώδεκα δέλτοις ἀπογεγραμμένων. This is the earliest recorded evidence for the *Menologion*, where the lives of martyrs and saints are recorded according to their day of commemoration. Cf. A. Ehrhard, *Überlieferung und Bestand der hagiographischen und homiletischen Literatur der griechischen Kirche* (Leipzig, 1937), i. 21 ff. In ep. 386. 62 ff. he speaks of μαρτυρογραφία—original accounts of martyrdoms upon which orators draw for their encomia.

[130] Cf. Leroy, 'La Réforme studite', 188 n. 58, and below.

[131] Cf. M. Richard, 'Florilèges spirituels grecs', *DS* 5 (Paris, 1964), 499–510. I. Hausherr, in *Saint Théodore Studite, l'homme et l'ascète*, Orientalia Christiana, 6 (1926), 16 n. 1, seems, however, to rather exaggerate when he states: 'La Bibliothèque du Stoudion consistait surtout en floriléges.' He bases this solely on a statement in the *Laudatio Platonis*, 820A, where Theodore says Plato copied texts ἐκ διαθόρων Θείων Πατέρων ἀνθολογηθέντα

[132] Citation of works in the letters are given in Fatouros, *Theodori Studitae Epistulae*, ii. 973 ff. Gregory is mentioned by name at least 23 times; Chrysostom, 25 times (cf. ibid. 866, 870, for references to the names).

authors at that time, one can presume that he may well have con-
sulted the full texts. His library also contained the *Instructions* of
Dorotheos of Gaza and the *Ladder of Divine Ascent* of John Klimakos,
both of which influenced his expositions of the monastic life.[133]
The immensely popular *Spiritual Meadow* of John Moschos was
almost certainly in his possession.[134] It is quite possible that
Theodore also had at hand the full texts of Dionysios the Pseudo-
Areopagite, given the influence the writings of the latter had on
Theodore.[135] He seems to have had a copy of the *Panarion* of
Epiphanios,[136] and had also read Gregory of Nyssa.[137] Other
authors such as Ignatios of Antioch and Athanasios of Alexandria
are quoted but it is impossible to know whether or not he had any
of their original works.[138] The fact that he composed epigrams in
their honour might suggest that he would have wanted more than
an anthology to represent their works.[139]

   Theodore's writings illustrate that he was by temperament a
practical person and a man of action rather than a speculative theologian.[140] He admits as much when he confesses that he needs

---

[133] J. Leroy, *Studitisches Mönchtum, Spiritualität und Lebensform* (Graz, 1969), 18.

[134] As can be inferred from the story given in ep. 462. 25 ff. concerning baptism using
sand, found in the *Pratum Spirituale*, *c.*176: *PG* 87. 3. 3044D–3045C. On this see below, Ch.
5.1. Cf. *Praefatio posthumae*, *PG* 99. 72D. A story from Moschos is also quoted in *PC* 93. 235.
The Spiritual Meadow (τὸ λειμωνάριον) is a collection of short edifying anecdotes about
monks and hermits in the tradition of the *Apophthegmata Patrum*. Moschos was a close associate of Sophronios the (future) patriarch of Jerusalem. English translation of his work:
J. Wortley, *The Spiritual Meadow of John Moschos* (Michigan, 1992). Theodore does not actually name this work, indicating how widely known its stories were in monastic milieux. Cf.
N. Baynes, 'The "Pratum Spirituale"', *OCP* 13 (1947), 404–14; H. Chadwick, 'John Moschus
and his friend Sophronius the Sophist', *JTS* NS 25 (1974), 41–74; B. Baldwin, 'Moschos,
John', in *ODB* ii. 1415.

[135] Dionysios featured in iconophile florilegia, quoted for example at the Second
Council of Nicaea and repeated by Theodore in his iconophile tracts (cf. E. J. Martin, *A
History of the Iconoclast Controversy*, (London, 1930), 187, 188, 194). But Theodore also uses him
as an authority in other instances, such as the famous passage on the 'list of mysteria' in ep.
489 (on this see below, Ch. 4.1). He is referred to 23 times in the letters (Fatouros, *Theodori
Studitae Epistulae*, 866–7). On Dionysian influence on Theodore, see below, Chs. 4–6, *passim*,
and E. Patlagean, 'Les Studites, l'empereur et Rome: Figure Byzantine d'un monachisme
réformateur', in *Bisanzio, Roma e l'Italia nell'alto Medioevo*, Settimane di studio nel centro
Italiano di studi sull'alto medioevo, 34, 3–9 April 1986 (Spoleto, 1988), 429–60, esp. 429–33.

[136] Ep. 40. 22–4. He seems also to have had the *De receptione haereticorum* of Timothy of
Constantinople (ibid. 56–7, and below, Ch. 5.2, n. 62).

[137] Cf. ep. 471. Gregory is cited 6 times in the letters.

[138] Ignatios is cited twice in the letters (Fatouros, *Theodori Studitae Epistulae*, 869);
Athanasios 10 times (ibid. 863).

[139] *PG* 99. 1797 ff.; P. Speck, *Theodoros Studites*, 226 ff.

[140] Cf. I. Hausherr, 'Barsanuphe', *DS* i. 1261.

recourse to authority when faced with questions of a speculative type, declaring ἀμύητος ἐγὼ τῶν δυσεφίκτων ('I have no understanding of difficult conceptual matters).[141] I. Hausherr, an authority on Theodore, believes this confession to be more than an exercise in humility, intimating that even if Theodore had studied texts of the Fathers *in extenso*, he seems to take little note of context and is interested only in the conclusions and the way they are expressed.[142] Certainly, this 'lazy' method of doing theology was commonplace during the period.[143] Theodore's writings in defence of icon veneration such as the three *Antirrhetici*, on the contrary, would prima facie seem to evidence critical and analytical powers and an ability to elaborate sophisticated argumentation when required to do so. However, these arguments were taken from a stockpile of Aristotelian arguments developed by iconophiles since the Second Council of Nicaea. To this author, they do not evidence any original *creative* thinking. Theodore's passion and his forte lay in the practical application of Christian theory. He was a highly intelligent practical theologian.

Theodore was 16 when Emperor Constantine V died (775), after a rule of thirty-four years.[144] He was succeeded by Leo IV, the son of the first of Constantine's three wives, and the designated heir. Although brought up an iconoclast, Leo did not have the same concern with the theological doctrine of iconoclasm as did his father, and he sought to court those of the 'indifferent class'—those committed neither to icons nor to their destruction—to build up popular support.[145] He set about to reverse the anti-monastic policy of Constantine by appointing monks to a number of important

---

[141] Ep. 219. 9. Cf. ep. 518. 8.

[142] I. Hausherr, *Saint Théodore Studite* (Rome, 1926), 16: 'Théodore court à la conclusion, et s'y cramponne sans examiner suffisamment les prémisses. Sa force est dans son tempérament plus que dans son esprit. Quand on lui pose une question trop spéculative, il se récuse à plus savant que lui . . .'

[143] In making his judgement Hausherr gives as sole example Theodore's use of St Basil in defence of icons: 'the honour given to an image goes to the prototype', which originally was a trinitarian argument about the divine nature of the Son (*De Spiritu Sanctu*, 18: *PG* 32. 1490C). Yet the Second Council of Nicaea used the argument in the same way, as did all other iconophiles. Theology in this period was heavily authority-based or 'florilegistic'— what one might call in contemporary Catholic circles 'Denzinger' theology.

[144] Theophanes, *Chronographia*, AM 6267, p. 448.

[145] P. Speck, *Kaiser Konstantin VI*, 54–5, 70–3, 99–101. Cf. Herrin, *The Formation of Christendom*, 409–10.

episcopal sees,[146] but stopped short of actually encouraging the
monastic vocation.[147] He did not, however, end the official ban on
icon veneration.[148] It was only after his premature death in 780
that his iconodule wife, Irene, could think about bringing about
the full restoration of the monastic institution and the restoration
of icons. During her first year in power, the *Chronicle* of Theophanes
records, 'The pious began to express themselves freely, the word of
God began to spread, those who sought salvation began to
renounce the world without hindrance, the glory of God began to
be exalted, the monasteries began to be restored, and every good
thing began to show itself.'[149]

Irene was from a prominent family in Athens and had been
married to Leo by Constantine V in 769. Their son Constantine
VI was crowned junior emperor in 776, when he was but 5 years
old, in order to exclude Leo IV's half-brothers (from Constantine
V's third marriage) from the throne.[150] When Constantine VI's
father died he was too young, at 10 years of age, to rule. His
mother, the Augusta Irene, therefore ruled as regent.[151]

It was around the end of Irene's first year as regent that
Theodore's whole family, encouraged by Plato, who was then
abbot of the Symboloi monastery, embraced the monastic life.[152]
Other wealthy and prominent men and women, including
Theophanes the Confessor, the editor of the *Chronicle*, also took
advantage of the change of political climate to do the same.[153]
According to the *Vita*, Theodore's parents sold their house, dis-
tributed gold to the poor, freed and rewarded their slaves, and then
left with the rest of the family for the family estate called Boskytion,

---

[146] *Chronographia*, AM 6268, p. 449.   [147] Cf. Treadgold, *The Byzantine Revival*, 63.

[148] The one recorded case of persecution of iconodules occurred at the end of Leo's
reign when he had certain civil officials flogged and imprisoned (including the court official
Theophanes, who died a confessor in prison) for venerating icons. Leo's wife, Irene, was
also implicated, *Chronographia*, AM 6272, p. 453; Treadgold, *The Byzantine Revival*, 6.

[149] *Chronographia*, AM 6273, p. 455.

[150] Treadgold, *The Byzantine Revival*, 9–11; Ostrogorsky, *History of the Byzantine State*, 176;
J. B. Bury, *A History of the Later Roman Empire from Arcadius to Irene* (London, 1889; repr.
Amsterdam, 1966), ii. 478.

[151] On the rule of Constantine VI and Irene, see Speck, *Kaiser Konstantin VI*; Treadgold,
The Byzantine Revival, 60–126; idem, 'The Unpublished Saint's Life of the Empress Irene',
BF 7 (1982), 237–51. For a more popular account of Irene, see C. Diehl, *Figures Byzantines*
(Paris, 1906), ch. 4 (also in translation: *Byzantine Empresses* (London, 1964), 65–93)).

[152] *Laudatio Platonis*, 824B; *Laudatio Funebris*, 889C ff.; *Vita A*, 121B; *Vita B*, 240D; *Vita C*,
no. 8.

[153] Treadgold, *The Byzantine Revival*, 63; Speck, *Kaiser Konstantin VI*, 113–14.

situated near Katabolos, in Bithynia, south of the Sea of Marmara.[154] This occurred in 781, when Theodore was 22, his cultivated life of piety making him well prepared for this move. 'What a marvellous event! What a wonderful conversion!' he would later recall with emotion.[155]

At the little monastic centre which the family group set up in Boskytion[156] Theodore was tonsured and received the monastic habit from his uncle Plato, who in the meanwhile had sacrificed the semi-reclusive life he had practised at the Symboloi monastery in order to devote himself to directing the group.[157] Theodore's monastic sponsor (ἀνάδοχος) was none other than Theophanes the Confessor.[158]

After some two years or more the group moved to another family property nearby, where they founded the Sakkoudion monastery, with Plato as its abbot.[159] This monastery would become the headquarters and educational centre of the 'Stoudite' confederation before the move to the capital in 799. A church dedicated to St John the Evangelist, and richly adorned with mosaics, was built here, which Theodore designed and helped construct.[160] One of Theodore's epigrams commemorates the occasion.[161]

---

[154] According to the *Vita* it was the whole family, males and females, that left the city. But in the *Laudatio Funebris in Matrem Suam* 892D, Theodore describes how Theoktista threatened personally to place Euthymios in the boat destined for Boskytion if he would not go willingly. This implies that she remained behind with her daughter in order to join a convent in Constantinople. It is known that Theoktista did begin her new life by living 'κελλιωτικῶς' (*Laudatio Funebris*, 893A), which she could have done somewhere in the region near the Symboloi had she moved there. Whatever the case, Theoktista did eventually settle in a convent in the city.

[155] *Laudatio Funebris* 889C.

[156] On Boskytion, see V. Ruggieri, *Byzantine Religious Architecture (582–867): Its History and Structural Elements*, OCA 237 (Rome, 1991), 215–16, cf. 122, 125.

[157] *Laudatio Platonis* 824BC, 813A, 816C; *Vita A*, 121D; *Vita B*, 241C; *Vita C*, no. 9. On the different types of monasticism practised during this time, see D. Papachryssanthou, 'La Vie monastique dans les campagnes Byzantines du VIIIᵉ au XIᵉ siècle. Ermitages, groupes, communautés', *Byzantion*, 43 (1973), 159–80; A. Kazhdan, 'Hermitic, cenobitic and secular ideals in Byzantine hagiography of the ninth century', *Greek Orthodox Theological Review*, 30 (1985), 473–87; R. Morris, *Monks and Laymen*, 31–5.

[158] S. Efthymiadis, *Le Panégyrique de S. Théophane le Confesseur*, AB 111 (1993), 262, 269, s. 2, 5–6. Cf. Pargoire, 'Saint Théophane le Chronographe et ses rapports avec Théodore Studite', *VizVrem.* 9 (1902), 56–61.

[159] *Vita C*, no. 9. On Sakkoudion, see Janin, *Les Églises et les monastères*, 177–81; Ruggieri, *Byzantine Architecture*, 107, 225–6.

[160] *Vita A*, 125B; *Vita B*, 244B; *Vita C*, no. 11. Cf. Ruggieri, *Byzantine Architecture*, 225–6.

[161] Epigram XC, Εἰς τὸ τετρακάμαρον. *PG* 99. 1801C; Speck, *Jamben*, 244–6; Ruggieri, *Byzantine Architecture*, 139.

The monastery, with its distinctive ethos and regime, prospered and flourished, attracting many new candidates.[162] It may even have been the beneficiary of imperial privileges.[163] After seven years or more as a lay monk Theodore received holy orders from the hands of Patriarch Tarasios (784–806), sometime after the Council of 787.[164] Plato remained the sole *hegoumenos* until 794 when, following a dangerous illness, Theodore was elected co-abbot (at the age of 35). They remained co-abbots for five years, until the move to Constantinople, after which Plato took a formal vow of obedience to his nephew and protégé in order to devote himself once again to a more reclusive monastic existence.[165]

1.4 THEODORE'S MONASTIC REFORM

The years spent at Sakkoudion, among the most tranquil of Theodore's career, gave rise to a renewed rule of monasticism that was to have a remarkable influence not only on the Byzantine monasticism of Theodore's day, but for centuries to come.[166]

---

[162] The *Vita* notes some of the more exceptional personalities in the monastery: Joseph (Theodore's brother), Athanasios, Naukratios, Euthymios, and Timotheos. Candidates also included those who transferred from other monasteries. In all cases they were accepted only with discernment: *Vita A*, 128B-D; *Vita B*, 245A–247C; *Vita C*, nos. 12 ff. Even before Theodore became abbot there were about 100 monks in the monastery: *Vita B*, 248D.

[163] Cf. Ruggieri, *Byzantine Architecture*, 115.

[164] *Vita A*, 129CD; *Vita B*, 248AB; *Vita C*, no. 15. The date of priestly ordination can be known only approximately from Theodore's statement that he was ordained after the Synod of Nicaea, in ep. 38. 75: χειροτονίαν ἐδεξάμεθα μετὰ τὴν σύνοδον παρὰ τοῦ κυροῦ Ταρασίου. On Theodore's possible presence at the Council as adviser to Plato, see Dobroklonskij, *Prepodobnij Feodor*, i. 337–8; Gardner, *Theodore of Studium*, 44.

[165] *Laudatio Platonis* 828C, 836A; *Vita B*, 248D ff.

[166] Theodore's monastic spirituality and his rule, even in its incipient form, may have well influenced part of the legislation of the Second Council of Nicaea through the presence of Plato. Cf. Ruggieri, *Byzantine Architecture*, 22 n. 46, 25. His rule or *Hypotyposis* and penitential were adopted by many monastic *Typika*, and his *Catecheses* were widely dispersed. On Theodore's influence in south Italy, Mount Athos, and Russia, see Leroy, 'La Réforme studite', 212–14; idem, 'La Vie quotidienne du moine Studite', 24–8; T. Minisci, 'Riflessi studitani nel monachesimo orientale', in *Il monachesimo orientale*, OCA 153 (1958), 215–33; M. Heppell, 'The Early History of the Kievan Monastery of Caves', in M. Mullett and A. Kirby (eds.), *The Theotokos Evergetis and Eleventh-Century Monasticism* (Belfast, 1994), 56–66; R. Taft, 'Stoudite Typika', in *ODB* (1961), iii. On the influence of Theodore on Paul of Evergetis, see J. Leroy, 'Un nouveau témoin de la Grande Catéchèse de S. Théodore Studite', *REB* 15 (1957), 73–88. On the general influence of Theodore on oriental coenobiticism, see Placide de Meester, *De monachico statu iuxta disciplinam byzantinam: Statuta selectis fontibus et commentariis instructa, fonti*, 2/10 (Rome, 1942), *passim*.

Theodore's role as a monastic reformer, expressed in the form of
the Stoudite Rule, is in fact as important for church history as his
role as a defender of the icons.[167] Although the idea for the reform
is credited by Theodore to Plato, it is generally acknowledged that
the real initiator was Theodore.[168]

In the ninth century various forms of Byzantine monasticism
existed: hermits who lived in isolation, anchorites who maintained contacts with other ascetics or allowed groups of disciples
to form around them, and Koinobia, which in reality were like
lavrai, with dependent anchorites.[169] Mount Olympos was popu-
lated by anchorites during this period, the most famous of whom,
during Theodore's time, being St Ioannikios.[170] According to
Leroy, the supreme ideal inculcated in the monasteries of the time
was not that proper to coenobitic life, namely the life of renunciation or ἀποταγή,[171] but ἡσυχία, proper to contemplative life.
Coenobitic life had, as a result, 'un style assez spécial'.[172] The

[167] Leroy, 'La Vie quotidienne', 23; idem, 'La Réforme studite', 214. The Roman
Church, not being so acquainted with or interested in Eastern monasticism, remembers
Theodore solely for his role as an icon defender. The *Martyrologium romanum, 12 Novembris*,
says simply of Theodore's life: 'qui pro fide catholica adversus Iconoclastas strenue pug-
nans, factus est in universa ecclesia catholica celebris.'

[168] *Laudatio Platonis* 824D. According to the *Vita*, however, it was Theodore who put
before his uncle the need for changes: *Vita A*, 129A; *Vita B*, 245B-C; *Vita C*, no. 14. Cf.
Dobroklonskij, *Prepodobnij Feodor*, i. 332–4; Leroy, 'La Réforme studite', 191–2; idem, 'Études
sur les "Grandes Catéchèses"', 2. The reform has been thoroughly analysed by Leroy, who
remains the greatest authority on the subject. His most notable studies are 'La Réforme studite', OCA 153 (1958), 181–214; 'La Vie quotidienne du moine studite', *Irénikon*, 27 (1954),
21–50; 'Le Cursus canonique chez s. Théodore Studite', *EL* 68 (1954), 5–19; 'S. Théodore
Studite', *Théologie de la vie monastique* (Paris, 1961), 423–36; *Studitisches Mönchtum. Spiritualität und
Lebensform* (Graz, 1969).

[169] Cf. Papachryssanthou, 'La Vie monastique', 160–6; Morris, *Monks and Laymen*, 33–4.
The Symboloi monastery appears to have belonged to the third type. Traditionally, a *lavra*
was formed of a group of monastic cells (*Kellia*), where monks lived as solitaries during the
week (but still owing obedience to a *hegoumenos*), and central facilities where there was common life at weekends.

[170] For his life, see *AA.SS. Novembris. II*, i. 332–435; *PG* 116. 35–92. BHG 935–7;
S. Vryonis, 'St Ioannicius the Great (754–846) and the "Slavs" of Bythynia', *Byzantion*, 31
(1961), 245–8; A. Kazhdan and N. P. Ševčenko, 'Ioannikios', in *ODB* ii. 1005–6; Ruggieri,
Byzantine Architecture, 101–3.

[171] Leroy neglects, however, to stress ὑποταγή, which was specific to the coenobites. On
this, see below, Ch. 2 and M. Wawryk, *Initiatio Monastica in Liturgia Byzantina*, OCA 180
(Rome, 1968), 5 ff. (on *apotage* as fundamental to all forms of monasticism).

[172] Leroy, 'La Réforme studite', 183, 185. Cf. C. Frazee, 'St Theodore of Studios and
Ninth-Century Monasticism in Constantinople', *Studia Monastica*, 23 (1981), 31. But see the
comments of Papachryssanthou, 'La Vie monastique', 179–80, who disagrees with Leroy's
conclusions that the lack of separation between *koinobia* and hesychasts was detrimental to
Byzantine monasticism.

task of reasserting the ideals proper to the coenobite was taken on by Theodore, and it remained a constant concern.[173] This concern was so much the greater because precisely in those times, due to favourable political and economic conditions, many new coenobitic foundations were being made. Theodore launches an attack on the *hegoumenoi* of some of these monasteries in words that echo those of Gregory of Nazianzus.[174] According to Ruggieri, Theodore has in mind those who had founded monasteries, and appointed themselves *hegoumenoi*, for the sole purpose of investing and increasing their own property. The nature of their estates would be juridically altered such that as 'monasteries' they would enjoy the religious privileges for their development.[175] These *hegoumenoi*, Theodore laments, claim to have renounced the world, yet they take their worldly goods and servants with them into the cloister. 'Yesterday they knew nothing of monastic profession', he further notes with irony, 'today they are hegoumenoi.'[176] Monasticism was in a true state of decadence and needed a return to its authentic sources.[177]

Theodore conceived his reform as a simple return to the original spirit of coenobiticism, rather than as an updating and adaptation of the monastic institution as such.[178] In practice it turned

[173] The distinction between the life of the hesychast and that of the coenobite is nowhere described more clearly than in *PC* 38, 108–10. Theodore explains that monks must live according to the vocation to which they are called, giving examples of failed hermits. Ruggieri, *Byzantine Architecture*, 102 n. 89, seems to suggest that Ioannikios, the famous hermit, is on this list. If I have read him correctly then this is a misreading of the Catechesis. Elsewhere Theodore shows the greatest of respect towards him (ep. 461: Sirmond's edition, Bk. II, ep. 116, *PG* 99, 1385a, gives the title incorrectly as Ἰωάννῃ ἐρημίτῃ in place of Ἰωαννίκῃ]; ep. 490. 80, where he is called 'our spiritual father'). In *PC* 38, however, Ioannikios is indirectly criticized in the sense that Theodore makes clear it is the coenobites who have suffered most from the iconoclast persecution (of Leo V), thereby deserving greater reward than the desert dwellers. In turn, the hesychast Peter the Monk is critical of the Stoudite monks in his *Vita* of Ioannikios (BHG 936).

[174] *Laudatio Platonis* 812A–C, cf. 825B. For Gregory: *PG* 35. 1091A. Cf. Ruggieri, *Byzantine Architecture*, 109; idem, 'Anthusa di Mantineon ed il canone XX del concilio di Nicea II (Anno 787)', *JÖB* 35 (1985), 133–4.

[175] Ruggieri, *Byzantine Architecture*, 109–10. In other cases, where the founder appointed a *hegoumenos* for the newly built monastery, ownership would be retained with taxes paid to the landowner on a lease contract basis: ibid.

[176] *Laudatio Platonis* 812BC.

[177] Cf. PK 25. 173; *Vita B*, 245BC; *Laudatio Platonis* 824D.

[178] Cf. PK 78. 545 (from many possible examples): τῷ κανόνι τῆς παραδεδομένης ἡμῖν παρὰ τῶν ἁγίων πατέρων ἡμῶν διδασκαλίας καὶ νομοθεσίας.

out to be 'an ingenious renovation of Byzantine monasticism, rather than a pure "return to the Fathers" '.[179]

Early in his monastic career Theodore had brought to the attention of Plato that the then widespread practice of breeding livestock, with all that it entailed, namely keeping domestics and trading, was quite contrary to the authentic coenobitic spirit of poverty. A true monk had to live by the work of his own hands.[180] Theodore's prescriptions on poverty, which were the expression of the total detachment required of a monk, went as far as demanding that each week one's clothes be exchanged for those that had been worn by another.[181] The quality of a monk's clothes, according to Theodore, should be such that nobody, seeing it lying in a public highway, would want to pick it up. If after three days it were still there, only then would it be suitable for the monk.[182]

Theodore's monastic system was highly regimented. It had a hierarchy of officers, beginning, after the abbot, with the second-in-command, the *Deuteros*. These officers were responsible for the discipline of the monastery and had to be obeyed.[183] All the monks, in fact, had a specific office or ministry to fulfil for the benefit of the whole community. Child members of the community would be under the tuition of nominated teachers.[184] Young

---

[179] Ruggieri, *Byzantine Architecture*, 111. Ruggieri's comment is true with regard to the structuring of coenobitic life. The ideals inculcated by Theodore, however, corresponded exactly to those of the Fathers and as found in the liturgical texts of coenobitic monastic profession. On this, see Ch. 6.

[180] TC I. 63. 614 (quoting St Basil); *PC* 54. 149; *Laudatio Platonis* 825A; *Vita B*, 245C. The resulting prohibition of keeping female animals (cf. *Testamentum* 1816D, 1820A, and ep. 10. 21–4 (this letter to Naukratios, 801–6?, contains an early version of the Testament)) has most commonly been interpreted as being due to 'scrupulum atque pudor monasticus erga femineum sexus': P. de Meester, *De monachico statu iuxta disciplinam byzantinam*, 168 n. 7. Cf. J. Pargoire, 'Une loi monastique de S. Platon', *BZ* 8 (1899), 98–106; Dobroklonskij, *Prepodobnij Feodor*, i. 334 ff. In this matter I prefer to follow, at least for the discipline's primary sense, the reading of Leroy: 'La Reforme studite', 191–2; 'Études sur les "Grandes Catéchèses" ', 2 n. 8, who argues that Theodore was returning to the spirit of St Basil, who prohibited καπηλικὰ κέρδη to his confraternities (*Regulae Fusius Tractatae*, 44: *PG* 31. 1032B).

[181] *Vita B*, 261CD; TC I. 66. 624; PK 97. 699; PK 105. 776; *Epitimia*, no. 29, *PG* 99. 1736D. Cf. Leroy, 'La Réforme studite', 193.

[182] *MC* 84. 34. Cf. TC I. 63. 615, *MC* 64. 179, *MC* 66. 184, *MC* 68. 191.

[183] On obedience, see Ch. 2.

[184] At the Stoudios monastery there was a small school where children destined to become monks were given an elementary education based on the study of Scripture (they could be tonsured at the age of 16: ep. 489. 48, although Trullo ch. 40 permitted this at the age of 10). Mention of teachers and pupils is made in TC I. 57. 599 and *MC* 53. 48. The school was separated from the monastery: *Vita Nicolai Studitae*, *PG* 105, 869C. On the

monks could very well find themselves as apprentices to a senior craftsman. Several crafts were practised at the monastery, making it take on the physiognomy of a medieval village.[185] Ministries listed by Theodore include those of the cook or baker, gardener, cattle-driver, fisherman, hook-maker, weaver, cobbler, tailor, and basket-maker. Some monks devoted themselves to the finer arts or to more intellectual occupations. There were goldsmiths and bookbinders,[186] parchment-makers (for codices),[187] painters or ζωγράφοι (for the production of icons),[188] hymnographers, and calligraphers.[189] Physical work was important not just as a means of self-support; it was an integral part of coenobitic spirituality. Not just φιλεργία, but πολυεργία, was a virtue in the same way as obedience and humility.[190]

Intellectual work was regarded as an exceptional occupation.[191] Although the monastery was indeed a centre for learning, education or the pursuit of academic excellence was not an end in itself: 'We did not leave the world to enjoy pleasures, nor to be learned, or wise, or to be a calligrapher. We came here to be cleansed of sin,

children of the Stoudite monastery, see Hausherr, *Saint Théodore Studite*, 76–7 (where it is argued that the τέκνα in the introductory words of the Great Catecheses refer truly to children). Other texts with mention of children: TC I. 35. 541; *MC* 62. 173 (τὰ νήπια); PK 21. 150, PK 120. 896. Pastoral provisions had to be made by Theodore to prevent homosexual relations with 'beardless youths': PK 65. 458 (the young to sleep together, not with older monks); *MC* 39. 110, *MC* 43. 122, PK 15. 101 (= *MC* 54. 150) (on the danger of gloating on τὰ παιδία καὶ τὰ μαλάκια); *MC* 56. 156.

[185] Lists of officers, tasks, and crafts are found in several texts of the Catecheses: TC I. 13. 390, TC I. 35. 541, TC I. 57. 598, TC I. 70. 632, TC III. 31. 63, PK 36. 266–9, PK 46. 335–6, PK 50. 365, PK 81. 568, PK 94. 675, PK 97. 700, PK 101. 733, PK 102. 744–9 (perhaps the best text with discussion of the ministries). Cf. *Vita B*, 260D–261B. Theodore even composed iambs for the various officers, including for the cook, describing their responsibilities. Cf. Leroy, *Studitisches Mönchtum*, 44 ff. Detailed penances were also prescribed for each officer if he neglected to perform his duty competently and virtuously. These can be seen in the first part of the *Epitimia*, *PG* 99. 1733–48.

[186] PK 46. 336.

[187] PK 28. 195 ἢ τοῦ μεμβρανοποιοῦντος); PK 36, 269 (ὁ . . . μεμβρανᾶς).

[188] PK 117. 871.

[189] PK 85. 606 (= *MC* 98. 97). Calligraphy was as much a manual as an intellectual labour. On the practical aspects of this labour, see J. Featherstone and M. Holland, 'A Note on Penances Prescribed for Negligent Scribes and Librarians in the Monastery of Stoudios', *Scriptorium*, 36 (1982), 258–60.

[190] TC I. 4. 464, TC I. 9. 479, TC I. 63. 613, *MC* 82. 26, PK 15. 100 (= *MC* 54. 149), PK 56. 401, PK 58. 411 (ἐργασία); *PC* 4. 19, *PC* 37. 107, *PC* 39. 282. Cf. Leroy, 'La Réforme studite', 195.

[191] Cf. Leroy, 'La Réforme studite', 194 ff.; 'La Vie quotidienne', 36 ff.; C. Frazee, 'St Theodore of Stoudios', 38 ff. Some monks did engage in intellectual tasks (cf. PK 119. 891) but only as a matter of obedience.

to learn the fear of God and to humble ourselves to the point of death.'[192] None the less, a good education in the doctrine of icons, for example, was something Theodore expected of all his monks once icon theology became an urgent issue.[193] He approved of his monks being erudite, and even took personal pleasure in helping with their education. But he also warned them of the dangers of pride through knowledge.[194] Wisdom did not come through book-knowledge.[195] In an early Catechesis he makes this very clear:

At the tribunal of Christ it will be of no avail being well-learnt, well-spoken, knowing texts by heart, being well-read. The Fathers in the *Gerontikon* were wise not because they knew much—some were quite uneducated. You can have studied much and yet still be eternally condemned. You can be saved even if you cannot distinguish α from β. But if you search out your own will (τὸ οἰκεῖον θέλημα) and have learnt everything and know everything, perhaps even the Egyptian alphabet, you will still feel fire consuming you for all eternity.[196]

Theodore's monks were expected to nourish their interior lives with the reading of Scripture and holy books.[197] These books would be borrowed from the monastic library and were to be cared for 'as if received from God'.[198] They were to study and learn by heart the rules of monastic living.[199]

The liturgical life of the monastery was its central activity.[200] Work was always to take second place to liturgy and psalmody.[201] Stoudite liturgical usages owed much to Palestinian monasticism as well as to the usages of the church of Constantinople. The *typika* that developed after Theodore's reform, and which codified this

---

[192] *MC* 45. 125.

[193] *PC* 15. 49. Cf. *PC* 29. 86 ('there is to be no excuse for ignorance').

[194] Cf. ep. 81. 26–8 (Theodore commends the desire of two of his monks to be erudite (πεπαιδευμένους), while warning them that humility must grow as knowledge grows); *MC* 61. 171; PK 43. 308 (Theodore taught the monks Petronios and Eulalios to read and write, lending them books to help them improve their writing style); *PC* 118. 299 ('For those occupied with studies, be careful not to irritate God with these studies.')

[195] TC I. 84. 659: 'Wise is he who leads a pure and blameless life, even though he knows no γράμματα or has no Greek studies.' Cf. PK 1. 4; *PC* 43. 421–2.

[196] TC I. 60. 609.

[197] Cf. *PC* 89. 226: 'learn to know by reading the exploits of the holy Fathers, how great was their enthusiasm, how great was the bubbling of their spirit, what their struggles were and how, for these reasons, our good God glorified them'.

[198] *MC* 93. 72. Librarians were also warned to be careful about greasy fingers when handling books: TC I. 49. 575.

[199] PK 54. 387 etc.   [200] See Leroy, 'La Vie quotidienne'.

[201] PK 67. 471.

new synthesis, dominated Byzantine monasteries until at least the twelfth century.[202]

An important aspect of Theodore's reform was the reintroduction of the ancient custom, which had largely fallen into disuse, of providing a carefully prepared regular teaching or Catechesis for the whole community, which he would pronounce, whenever possible, three times a week in the early morning.[203] In these Catecheses he would 'discuss and examine the commandments of the Lord, in order to excite, persuade, threaten and enlighten' his monks.[204] Reviving this ancient tradition[205] was extremely beneficial 'because it is part of human nature to remember for a time and then to forget . . . [the soul] is like the body which needs food and drink again and again'.[206] His reflections were the fruit of his reading of and meditation on Scripture and the writings of

---

[202] R. Taft, *The Liturgy of the Hours in East and West* (Collegeville, 1986), 276. Thus, for example, together with adapting the Palestinian office the Stoudion produced much new ecclesiastical poetry which was subsequently taken up in the Byzantine Sunday and Lenten-paschal anthologies, the *Oktoechos*, *Triodion*, and *Pentekostarion*.

[203] In Theodore's letter to Naukratios, ep. 10. 44–6, also found similarly phrased in the *Testamentum*, *PG* 99. 1820C, no. 11, he says: Παραφυλάξεις πάντως τὸ ποιεῖσθαι τρισσάκις τὴν κατήχησιν τῇ ἑβδομάδι καὶ καθ᾽ ἑσπέραν, which Sirmond's Latin translation, taken up by Migne in *PG* 99, 942B (and 1820C), renders as 'Cura prorsus ut catechesim qualibet hebdomadae ter facias ad vesperum.' Julien Leroy, however, has argued convincingly that this is an erroneous rendering, the καί having been ignored by the translator, and referring in fact to a second series of Catecheses that took place each evening, and taking the form of an informal allocution (in PK 18. 126 (= *MC* 44. 123) there is a similar juxtaposition: καθ᾽ ἑβδομάδα συνερχόμενοι τρίς, ἀλλ᾽οὖν καὶ καθ᾽ ἑσπέραν συνερχόμενοι). This practice corresponded to the Pachomian monastic tradition (from which, it seems, Theodore adopted the term κατήχησις). They were pronounced probably at the end of Orthros (matins) on Sunday, Wednesday, and Friday, as is recommended to abbots in the *Hypotyposis* (which post-dates Theodore) as given in *PG* 99. 1709C. See Leroy, 'Les Petites Catèchèses de S. Théodore Studite', *Le Muséon*, 71 (1958), 354–6; 'Études sur les "Grand Catéchèses" de S. Théodore Studite', 3–13. On p. 13 of the 'Études', Leroy also states, 'Il paraît . . . que les textes qui ont été conservés sont, tous, ceux de catéchèses matinales.' This corrects the statement of Fatouros, in *Theodori Studitae Epistulae*, 33, note on ep. 10. 44, 'κατήχησιν: intellige catechesin parvam.' Texts which may be brought forward to prove Leroy's argument include *MC* 67. 188 ('the night has been brief'); *MC* 107. 133 (the monks are tired after the morning *kanon*); PK 15. 102 (=*MC* 54. 151) (Theodore will not prolong the Catechesis because it is dawn: καὶ ἵνα μὴ εἰς μακρὸν ἐκτείνω τὴν κατήχησιν διὰ τὸ αὖγος . . .); *PC* 18. 55 (it is summer time and through lack of sleep the monks find it difficult to listen to a Catechesis).

[204] *MC* 84. 30.

[205] This regular catechesis was κατὰ τὴν διατυπωθεῖσαν ἐξ ἀρχῆς παράδοσιν: *PC* 53. 146. Cf. PK 78. 542 ('a custom of the Fathers').

[206] PK 108. 789–90. Cf. PK 115. 847 (= *MC* 73. 203) (Catechesis is spiritual food); *PC* 85. 217: 'Our nature is lazy . . . it is forgetful of instructions and needs the shock of language to stimulate it.'

the Fathers, along with his own personal experience.²⁰⁷ These Catecheses, which have been under-studied by scholars, provide valuable insights into the everyday life of a ninth-century Byzantine monk and of contemporary customs and events.²⁰⁸

Another key feature of Theodore's spirituality is his emphasis on frequent ἐξαγόρευσις, the manifestation to the abbot or spiritual father of 'thoughts'.²⁰⁹ This observance was one of the πατροπαράδοτοι (traditions of the Fathers) which, if strictly followed, would be a true imitation of the Fathers, and a true following of the 'archetypal image of the apostolic life' which they provide.²¹⁰ The teaching and example of the Fathers were to be followed as literally as possible.²¹¹

St Basil, ὁ μέγας νομοθέτης ἡμῶν Βασίλειος ὁ θεῖος ('Our Great Lawgiver, the Divine Basil'),²¹² who had enormous stature in the Greek Church, was Theodore's most frequent cited authority,²¹³ but a careful reading of his works shows that he was actually

---

²⁰⁷ *MC* 56. 154, PK 22. 159 (= *MC* 100. 103) (ἐκ τῶν θεοπνεύστων ἀναγνωσμάτων).

²⁰⁸ The Catecheses provide information ranging from the mortality of monks (death at 70 or 80: TC III. 40. 80, *MC* 16. 45), diet (on non-fast days: grilled or baked fish, cheese, cabbage, beans with butter, other greens, seasoning, fruit, one or two glasses of wine a day: PK 7. 43 (an excellent picture of every day life is given on 45–6)), medical myths (too much sleep makes the body fat: *PC* 27. 80), Arab incursions (TC I. 87. 665 ('many have been killed, the blood of innocents spilt without mercy—men, women, children, the aged—others are put into iron chains and taken into slavery'); PK 121. 905 (those scattered are dying from hunger and thirst); *PC* 124. 315), illnesses (caused by the weather: *MC* 64. 180), an earthquake (PK 79. 550), a panther roaming around Mt. Olympos (*PC* 117. 295), devotions (to the silver keys of St Peter in Rome: *PC* 15. 49), etc. On the Catecheses see below, Ch. 1.10.1–2.

²⁰⁹ Leroy, 'La Vie quotidienne', 33; Hausherr, *Saint Théodore Studite*, 34–6. The monk was even defined as τὸ ἐξαγορευτικόν: *MC* 82. 26. Epitimia were prescribed for those negligent in confessing their faults and imperfections: *Epitimia* 1736C no. 25, 1749A n. 2. Cf. *De confessione* (Περὶ ἐξαγορεύσεως), 1721AB; *Responsiones ad interrogata (Questions and Answers on Penance* = Περὶ ἐρωτήσεως), 1732D. On penance and confession of thoughts, see below, Ch. 4.7.

²¹⁰ *Testamentum* 1816B, no. 11, 1820AC; PK 113. 836: κατὰ μίμησιν τῶν ὁσίων πατέρων ἡμῶν; *Laudatio Platonis*, 824D: πρὸς δὲ τὴν ἀρχέτυπον εἰκόνα τῆς ἀποστολικῆς ζωῆς.

²¹¹ Cf. *Testamentum* 1816C, where Theodore states the ascetical laws of St Basil are not to be taken in 'half measure'. On imitation of the Fathers, see below, Ch. 2.4.

²¹² PK 17. 121.

²¹³ *Vita B*, 245B, says Theodore had a particular predilection for the works of St Basil, including his *Monastic Constitutions*: ταῖς ἀσκη τικαῖς νομοθεσίαις. Although Theodore cites or paraphrases these Constitutions (e.g. PK 10. 66, PK 45. 327, etc.), they do not in fact belong to the authentic Basil. Cf. Leroy, 'La Réforme studite', 189. The *Scholion in S. Basilii Ascetica* 1685–8, which seeks to defend the authenticity of the *Constitutions*, is almost certainly not a work of Theodore's. Cf. Leroy, 'L'Influence de saint Basile sur la réforme Studite d'après les Catéchèses', *Irénikon*, 52 (1979), 494. Basil is cited by name numerous times throughout Theodore's writings (81 times in the letters alone: Fatouros, *Theodori Studitae Epistulae*, 865), and is always given a pre-eminent place among the Fathers.

influenced, at least in matters of terminology and monastic orga-
nization, more by other Fathers. This is especially true of
Dorotheos of Gaza,[214] to whom Theodore seems to be most
indebted.[215] In fact, it is because of Theodore's enthusiasm for
Dorotheos, whose thought was in perfect harmony with that of
Basil (although in more developed form), that Dorotheos found his
way into the canon of Orthodox Byzantine monastic authorities.[216] His disciple Dositheos is also mentioned often as an example to be followed.[217] The influence of John Klimakos can also be
readily detected in Theodore's works,[218] as well as, although to a
lesser extent, John Cassian[219] and Mark the Hermit.[220] He was

---

[214] Dorotheos was born in Antioch *c*.500 and died between 560 and 580. He came under
the influence of the recluse Barsanouphios and the prophet John. He later founded his own
coenobitic monastery, near Gaza. His spiritual instructions (Διδασκαλίαι) survive in an
abridged version of the mid-9th cent., probably compiled by a disciple of Theodore. These
were then translated into various oriental languages. Cf. B. Baldwin, 'Dorotheos of Gaza',
ODB i. 654.

[215] Leroy, 'La Réforme studite', 190; idem, 'L'Influence de saint Basile', 491–506; J. M.
Szymusiak and J. Leroy, 'Dorothée (saint)', in *DS* iii. 1663; I. Hausherr, 'Les Grands
Courants de la spiritualité orientale', *OCP* 1 (1935), 131. The example or teaching of
Dorotheos is found in, for example, TC I. 33. 535, TC I. 61. 610, TC III. 40. 80, *MC* 25. 71,
MC 41. 114, *MC* 42. 117, PK 20. 147, PK 44. 320. Leroy, in fact, believes that Basil's direct
influence on Theodore is very much less than the latter makes out. My own conviction is
that the central themes of Basilian spirituality could well have been taken directly from
Basil. Theodore regards Basil as the great 'lawgiver' (cf. ep. 489. 16, where Christ, too, is ὁ
θεσμοθετήσας). This term should be understood to include not just the (supposed) author
of the *Constitutions* but the original author of Basilian spiritual and doctrinal themes. On
these themes and the meaning of law, see below, Ch. 2 and *passim*.

[216] Cf. *Dorothée de Gaza. Œuvres Spirituelles*, ed. L. Regnault and J. de Préville, *SC* 92 (Paris,
1963), Introduction, 91: 'C'est à notre connaissance, saint Théodore Studite qui a été le premier et le plus grand de tous ses [of Dorotheos] disciples. En prenant sa défense et en fais-
sant son éloge dans son testament, il lui a acquis d'emblée une popularité et un crédit
considérable dans le monachisme byzantin.' Theodore had been accused by his detractors
of heresy for upholding the teaching of Dorotheos (also of Barsanuphios and Dositheos): ep.
34. 126 ff. But as he explained in this same letter, and especially in his *Testamentum* 1816BC,
there were others of the same name who had been condemned as 'monophysite' heretics by
Patriarch Sophronios (*Epistola Synodica ad Sergius cp.*, *PG* 87. 3193CD). The most numerous
MSS with the works of Dorotheos are of Stoudite origin. These have a prologue that
explains, in the words of Theodore's *Testament*, the orthodoxy of Dorotheos and Dositheos:
text in *SC* 92 (1963), 106–9.

[217] e.g. in ep. 8. 31–2, TC I. 9. 480, TC I. 33. 537, *MC* I. 3, *MC* 25. 70, *MC* 69. 194, *MC*
75. 212, *MC* 79. 12, PK 5. 31, PK 110. 815. For Dorotheos' mentor Barsanouphios, cf. TC I.
5. 468.

[218] *Testamentum* 1816D, ep. 303. 25, TC I. 15. 496, TC I. 27. 523, TC I. 49. 572, PK 5. 32,
PK 73. 505, PK 98. 706 (= *MC* 101. 107), PK 122. 913, *PC* 29. 84, *PC* 47. 132.

[219] TC I. 53. 585, *MC* 66. 184. Greek résumés of Cassian may have been available to
Theodore. For a discussion of Cassian's influence, see J. Leroy, 'Saint Théodore Studite',
in *Théologie de la vie monastique* (Paris, 1961), 424 and n. 6.

[220] TC I. 53. 585, TC I. 55. 591; *MC* I. 3.

also familiar with the lives of the founders of monasticism and often presented them, their immediate disciples, and other outstanding coenobitic saints from Egypt and Palestine as models to be imitated by the Stoudites: Anthony[221] and Pachomios,[222] Theodosios the Cenobiarch,[223] Arsenios,[224] Hilarion,[225] Silvanos,[226] Euthymios,[227] Sabas,[228] and several others whose names were to be found in the *Gerontikon*,[229] and who were true witnesses to authentic primitive monasticism.[230] It was from these saints and their monasteries that Theodore's monks drew inspiration.[231] Theodore's *epitimia* were based on the practices of such monasteries.[232]

---

[221] Ep. 490. 30, TC I. 8. 476, TC I. 28. 525, TC I. 33. 537, TC I. 78. 648; *MC* 2. 6, *MC* 69. 194; PK 13. 88, PK 50. 362, PK 96. 691, PK 110. 814; *PC* 28. 83, *PC* 43. 121, *PC* 49. 137 ('whose life we have [just] read'), *PC* 102. 259, *PC* 126. 322.

[222] TC I. 8. 476, TC I. 33. 537; *MC* 1. 3, *MC* 60. 169; *PC* 7. 28 etc.

[223] Ep. 149. 25; TC I. 33. 537, TC I. 50. 578; *MC* 1. 3; PK 23. 165 etc. In TC I. 53. 585 and TC III. 40. 80, Theodore refers to the rule or διατύπωσις of Theodosios which he may have made his monks follow initially. See Leroy, 'La Réforme studite', 209.

[224] *PC* 4. 19. See especially *Oratio XII. Laudatio S. Arsenii Anachoretae*, *PG* 99. 849–81 (T. Nissen, *Byzantinisch-neugriechische Jahrbücher*, 1 (1920), 246–62).

[225] TC I. 8. 476; *MC* 1. 3, *MC* 69. 194; PK 110. 814.　　　　　　[226] PK 5. 31.

[227] Ep. 500. 35; TC I. 33. 537, TC III. 31. 63; *MC* 1. 3; PK 23. 165, etc.

[228] Ep. 149. 25, ep. 555. 105; TC I. 8. 476, TC I. 33. 537; *MC* 1. 3, *MC* 75. 212, *MC* 79. 13; PK 17. 122, etc.

[229] The *Gerontikon* is referred to in e.g. TC I. 60. 607, TC I. 63. 615, TC I. 67. 626.

[230] Cf. Leroy, 'La Réforme studite', 188–9 and n. 58; idem, *Studitisches Mönchtum*, 18. The *Ladder* of John Klimakos is also replete with allusions to the Desert Fathers whom Theodore mentions. Other saints names include Akakios, Zacharias, Makarios, Horsisios, Petronios, Abbakyros, Domitianos, Menas, Zosimos (e.g. in TC I. 33. 537, TC I. 53. 586; *MC* 69. 194, *MC* 75. 212, *MC* 95. 79). It is to these saints who 'shone in obedience' and not to virtuous and saintly solitaries that Theodore drew attention (*PC* 38. 109). On the saints of early monasticism see, as an introduction, D. J. Chitty, *The Desert a City. An introduction to the Study of Egyptian and Palestinian Monasticism under the Christian Empire* (Crestwood, 1995; 1st printing: Oxford, 1966).

[231] Cf. PK 23, 165 (=MC 31, 87): Δράμωμεν ταῖς ἐννοίαις, τέκνα, ἐπὶ τὸ ἐκείνου μοναστήριον. ἴωμεν ἐπὶ τὰ τοῦ μεγάλου Παχωμίου συστήματα· βλέψωμεν ἐκεῖ τὸν ἀοίδιμον Ἰωνᾶν, Πετρώνιον τὸν τρισόλβιον, Θεόδωρον τὸν ἡγιασμένον. εἶτα πορευσώμεθα ἐπὶ τὸ τοῦ ἀοιδίμου Θεοδοσίου ἀγνιστήριον, ὀψώμεθα κἀκεῖσε Βασίλειον τὸν ἀείζωον, Ἀέτιον τὸν θαυμάσιον, τὸν ὁδεῖνα καὶ τὸν ὁδεῖνα. κἀκεῖθεν ἀπελευσώμεθα πρὸς τὸ τοῦ θεσπεσίου Θεοκτίστου σεμνεῖον, πρὸς τὸ τοῦ παναγίου Εὐθυμίου καὶ Σάββα ἐργαστήριον· καὶ ἁπλῶς συντομολογῶ τὰ ἐν τοῖς ἄνω χρόνοις καὶ μέσοις καὶ τελευταίοις, πῶς καὶ πόσον καὶ ποταπῶς ἠγωνίσατο εἰς ἕκαστος τὸν ἀγαθὸν αὐτοῦ δρόμον.

[232] A study of Theodore's sources has been made by Dobroklonskij, *Prepodobnij Feodor*, i. 534–47.

1.5 BEGINNING OF DIFFICULTIES: THE MOECHIAN AFFAIR

While Theodore was laying the foundations of his reform in the quiet of Sakkoudion, life elsewhere was anything but quiet. Tarasios the *Protoasecretis* had been elected patriarch in 784 and immediately set about to restore unity within the church and to reconcile Constantinople with the other four patriarchates. With Irene's backing he set in motion the idea of an ecumenical Council which, apart from condemning iconoclasm and annulling the Synod of Hieria, would reconcile iconophile and iconoclast bishops. Furthermore, it would deal with the problem of simony, which had infested the Byzantine church. When the Council finally concluded its proceedings, in October 787, Tarasios had acquitted himself well on the first two counts, with the emperor and empress being acclaimed as the 'New Constantine and New Helen' for their role in re-establishing Orthodoxy.[233] His handling of the simoniacs (bishops who had performed ordinations for money), however, was controversial and was to cause embarrassment to Theodore in later years.[234]

The piety of the Empress Irene, who had so skilfully neutralized initial opposition to the Council,[235] may have been strong, but her

---

[233] For a synthetic historical account of the Council, the initial opposition, the proceedings, and the outcome, see, among other studies, G. Dumeige, *Nicée II*, Histoire des conciles oecuméniques, 4 (Paris, 1978); J. M. Hussey, *The Orthodox Church in the Byzantine Empire* (Oxford, 1984), 45–50; Herrin, *The Formation of Christendom*, 417–24; Treadgold, *The Byzantine Revival*, 82–9; P. Henry, 'Initial Eastern Assessments of the Seventh Oecumenical Council', *JTS* NS 25 (1974), 75–92.

[234] Theodore's views concerning the way Tarasios dealt with the simoniacs are expressed in his letter to Arsenios, ep. 38 (*ann.* 809). 44–54; to Stephan the Lector, ep. 53. 30 ff. Both these letters have been studied closely by Speck, *Kaiser Konstantin VI*, 193–8. See also M.-Z. Auzépy, 'La Place des moines à Nicée II (787)' *Byzantion*, 58 (1988), 18–19. Contrary to the stipulation of canon 5 of the Council, which decreed deposition of simoniacs, Tarasios, under pressure from Irene, subsequently decreed that an exception be made for iconoclast simoniacs, after completing a period of penance lasting for at least one year. The monks led by the Stoudite Sabbas were obstinately opposed to this. Tarasios vacillated until after the deposition of Irene. Theodore claims that the Sakkoudion monks, who gave Tarasios support at the Council, were deceived into believing that Tarasios would never hold communion with the simoniacs. For documentation and discussion of the development of Tarasios' views, see V. Grumel, *Les Regestes des actes du patriarcat de Constantinople*, i. *Les Actes des patriarches*, pt. 2 *Les Regestes de 715 à 1043*, Le Patriarcat byzantin, 1 (Paris, 1936), nos. 360–4.

[235] Cf. Treadgold, *The Byzantine Revival*, 81–2.

political ambitions were much stronger. She had established herself
as much more than a regent for Constantine, the legitimate heir to
the throne; she regarded herself as co-ruler. Indeed, on the coinage
issued at this time, where both she and her son are depicted, it is she
and not her son who holds the orb, the symbol of rule.[236] When
Constantine was still but a child, in 781, she had arranged a political alliance with the Franks by agreeing for him, when he came of
age, to marry Rotrud, the still-younger daughter of Charlemagne.
By early 787 the agreement had been broken. Constantine was 16
and still a boy, but there was no constitutional reason why he should
not rule without his mother,[237] and still less why he should not
decide his own future. None the less, his mother arranged a bridal
show and compelled her son, in November 788, to take as wife the
pretty Armenian Maria of Amnia.[238] The marriage, however, did
not work. Although Maria bore Constantine two daughters, Irene
and Euphrosyne,[239] he seems always to have resented his forced
wedding and bided his time to do something about it. An army
revolt in November 790 established Constantine as sole ruler—his
mother had steadfastly refused to step down for him, even though
he was now 19—and he banished Irene to her palace of
Eleutherios. Unfortunately for him, though, he was indecisive in his
rule and by January 792 he recalled Irene and reconfirmed her as
co-ruler. The joint rule lasted till 797. It is no credit to Irene that she
led a conspiracy against her son and ordered that he be blinded in
the very room of the Imperial Palace where she had given birth to
him. This occurred on 15 August 797. Irene became sole ruler. The
hapless young Constantine died of his wounds.[240]

It was during the second period of joint rule that the
Sakkoudion monastery found itself in conflict with the throne.

[236] Ibid. 60.

[237] Justinian II, just over a century before, ruled alone when he was only 15.

[238] Theophanes, *Chronographia*, AM 6281, p. 463; Treadgold, *The Byzantine Revival*, 90–1;
Speck, *Kaiser Konstantin VI*, 203–10.

[239] Treadgold, *The Byzantine Revival*, 402 n. 128. This author identifies the daughters with
the nuns Irene and Euphrosyne of Theodore's ep. 62. Although I have followed Treadgold
in his account of there being two daughters, other authors recognize only one, Euphrosyne,
who would eventually marry Emperor Michael I.

[240] Theophanes, *Chronographia*, AM 6284, p. 468; AM 6289, p. 472. Treadgold, *The
Byzantine Revival*, 96–110; G. Ostrogorsky, *History of the Byzantine State*, 180–1. Speck, *Kaiser
Konstantin VI*, 308–21, argues that Constantine's death was effectively concealed from the
populace, which explains the later reports that he was still alive. This thesis is adopted by
Treadgold, *The Byzantine Revival*, 403 n. 138.

Constantine had fallen in love with one of his mother's ladies-in-waiting, Theodote, who happened to be a relative of Plato and Theodore. There were rumours that she was not the first to be the object of his extramarital affairs.[241] A trumped-up charge of conspiring to poison him was the way Constantine chose to secure a divorce.[242] Since this also amounted to treason, the penalty for which, if proved to be true, was execution, it may have been Tarasios who negotiated that instead Maria be sent to a monastery to be tonsured.[243] This in itself, if it were a free choice, would have been a ground for divorce.[244] Maria entered the monastery in January 795, never to return.[245]

In August of the same year, fortified by a moderate military success against the Arabs, Constantine announced his betrothal to Theodote, crowned her Augusta (a title which Maria never enjoyed), and married her at the suburban Palace of St Mamas forty days later in September. The patriarch himself had refused to bless the union, knowing that the grounds for the divorce had been contrived and that a new union was contrary to church law.[246] He did permit, however, or at least tolerate, that it be blessed by the priest Joseph, steward of St Sophia and abbot of the monastery of Kathara in Bithynia.[247] Nor did the patriarch, for reasons of

---

[241] The only source of this is Theodore's letter to Patriarch Nikephoros, ep. 25. 45–6, written in 808, some 15–20 years after the supposed events. Cf. the disparaging character portrayals in *Laudatio Platonis* 829A, and the comment by Michael, Theodore's biographer, *Vita B*, 256D. All these statements may be simply the product of *Tendenzliteratur*.

[242] Permitted by the laws of Justinian (*Novella* 117. 8) and Leo III (*Ekloga* 2. 12–13). On the charge of attempted poisoning: *Vita Tarasii* (BHG 1698), *PG* 98. 1406BC.

[243] The *Vita Tarasii* gives the initiative to Constantine: ibid, 1408A–C. As a historical source this document needs to be read with caution: see Speck, 252–3 and 255–9 *passim*.

[244] *Novella* 117, s. 9 pt. 4.

[245] Theodore writes to Maria in ep. 514 (*ann.* 823/4). On this letter, see Fatouros, *Prolegomena*, 461*–2*.

[246] For the legal aspects of the marriage, see A. Fuentes, *El divorcio de Constantino VI y la doctrina matrimonial de San Teodoro Estudita* (Pamplona, 1984); D. Gemmiti, *Teodoro Studita e la questione Moicheiana* (Naples, 1993) (this work reproduces, almost verbatim, substantial parts of Fuentes's study but without giving any acknowledgement.) For a different perspective, see P. Karlin-Hayter, 'A Byzantine Politician Monk: Saint Theodore Studite', *JÖB* 44 (1994), 220–1.

[247] On the Kathara monastery, see R. Janin, *Les Églises et les monastères*, 158–60. On the patriarch's involvement, Theodore writes, in ep. 22. 99–103, 'It is clear that he [Tarasios] saw himself in danger of being ejected from the Patriarchate. So when he found this person who was eager to do it—someone found at court—he transferred the danger to him. Now if it is true that he gave an order—but, enough of this; we do not believe he did. He fully satisfied us and many others on that count.'

oikonomia, refuse communion to the emperor.[248] The marriage caused some shock to the populace, despite the unusually grand festivity that accompanied the wedding,[249] a fact that his mother Irene used to her advantage when planning his downfall.[250]

Theodore, who at this time was completing his first year as abbot, broke communion with the patriarch on hearing of his complicity in what he considered to be an adulterous ('moechian') second marriage.[251] Emperor or not, Constantine was still subject to God's laws which forbade putting away one's legal wife to take another.[252] Although conscious of the gravity of breaking communion with the head of his church, his decision, which soon reached the attention of the emperor himself, was fully consonant with his own life project of combatting the decadence in which monastic life had fallen by insisting on the exact obedience of the laws of

---

[248] These events are reported by Theophanes, *Chronographia*, AM 6288, pp. 469–70. Other sources include the *Vita Tarasii*, 1406–10; *De schismate Studitarum* (also cited as *Narratio de sanctis Patriarchis Tarasio et Nicephoro*), *PG* 99. 1852A; Michael the Monk, *Vita B*, 252CD (cf. *Vita A*, 136D–137B; *Vita C*, no. 18); *Laudatio Platonis* 844B. A full narration with discussion is to be found in P. Henry, 'Theodore of Studios: Byzantine Churchman', 38–42; idem, 'The Moechian Controversy and the Constantinopolitan Synod of January A.D. 809' *JTS* NS 20 (1969), 500–1; Speck, *Kaiser Konstantin VI*, 255–67; Treadgold, *The Byzantine Revival*, 104. Although pressure by the emperor was certainly applied to the patriarch not to block the marriage, modern scholars believe that the alleged threat against Tarasios, failing co-operation, to reintroduce iconoclasm (reported in the *De schismate Studitarum*, 1852D), is a mid-9th cent. fiction. Cf. Speck, *Kaiser Konstantin VI*, 280–1; Treadgold, *The Byzantine Revival*, 402 n. 129; Hatlie, 'Abbot Theodore', 118 n. 24. A discussion of *oikonomia* is found below, Ch. 2.6.

[249] There were forty days of celebration, according to Theophanes: *Chronographia*, AM 6288, p. 470.

[250] Treadgold, *The Byzantine Revival*, 105. Theophanes reports, in *Chronographia* AM 6287, p. 469, that it was on Irene's advice that Constantine went ahead with his plan, knowing the adverse consequences that were bound to follow. Cf. idem, AM 6288, p. 471. Speck, *Kaiser Konstantin VI*, 252–3, however, contests that Irene could have had this influence.

[251] For a thorough account of Theodore's concerns, see Hatlie, 'Abbot Theodore', 110–50. See also Pratsch, *Theodoros Studites*, 92–107.

[252] Five letters (epp. 1–5) are contemporary with this conflict, although there may have been six others that are now lost (Dobroklonskij, *Prepodobnij Feodor*, 384, 387–8). In these letters, written in exile, Theodore only refers to the 'truth', 'law', or 'commandments' of God that need to be upheld, and are worth suffering for (ep. 1. 7, 10, 24, 57, 73, ep. 3. 25, 33, 43, ep. 4. 23–4). There is no mention as such of the emperor's illegal action or of his 'adulterous' marriage. Indeed, Theodore expressly states he commemorates him in the Divine Liturgy and prays for him in private and in public (ep. 4. 42–3). However, when he reflects on these events later (starting with epp. 21 and 22, AD 808)) he is much more forthright in accusing the deceased emperor of adultery and breaking God's laws. Although the precautions dictated by methodology are needed in interpolating Theodore's later comments to this particular period, there seems to be no reason to assume that his basic concerns appreciably changed. On this, see Hatlie, 'Abbot Theodore', 122 n. 30; 124, n. 33. Also see below, Chs. 2–3.

authentic coenobitic and, by implication, truly Christian life.[253]
The emperor tried various means to break the Sakkoudion opposition, even, reportedly, hoping that a late summer holiday at the
nearby spring-baths of Prousa would bring Theodore and Plato to
his presence, but all to no avail. In February 797 Constantine
decided on stronger measures, ordering the arrest of Plato,
Theodore, and a few other monks. The rest of the Sakkoudion
community (numbering about a hundred) were dispersed. Plato
was conducted to Constantinople where he was incarcerated in the
Imperial Palace. Theodore was flogged, placed under arrest at the
Kathara monastery (his jailer being none other than the steward
Joseph), and then sent into exile with his brother Joseph and a few
others to Thessalonica, where they arrived on 25 March.[254]

This exile, the first of three, lasted five months. Theodore's first
extant letters date from this period.[255] Unbeknown to Theodore,
Irene had been scheming since the time of the Prousa holiday to
dethrone her son.[256] When she finally succeeded one of her first
acts as new sole ruler was to recall the Sakkoudites.[257] The steward Joseph was also deposed, and with this relations between the
monks and the patriarch were restored.[258] The debt of the monks

---

[253] This fact does not seem to have been sufficiently taken into account by those historians who see a disproportion between the Sakkoudion protests, especially as they developed,
and the actual issue at hand (Henry, *Theodore of Studios*, is an exception). As a result some
authors (e.g. Speck) suspect that other concerns, of a more personal nature, were at play.
For a discussion, see Hatlie, 'Abbot Theodore', 122 ff. Defending his right to criticize the
patriarch, Theodore refers to precedents in Scripture and to sayings of St Basil, permitting
a monk to correct a superior: ep. 5. 18–43, 59–75. In ep. 4. 25, 35, the authority of the
Fathers, and St Basil in particular, is invoked to support his uncompromising stand.

[254] Theophanes, *Chronographia*, AM 6288, p. 471; *Vita B*, 253A–256D; *Laudatio Platonis*
829D–833A; ep. 3 (which gives a detailed account of Theodore's journey); *Laudatio Funebris*
893B–896A.

[255] Five letters date from this early period, two of which (epp. 4 and 5) were written just
before the exile. According to *Vita B*, 256C, Theodore also wrote to the pope of Rome. This,
however, is almost certainly an error of chronology. According to Henry, *Theodore of Studios*,
67, the error was intentional so that the conflict could be seen by later generations as
Theodore *v.* emperor and not Theodore *v.* patriarch.

[256] Theophanes, AM 6289, pp. 471–2; Treadgold, *The Byzantine Revival*, 107.

[257] Theodote, in the meanwhile, experienced the fate of other hapless regal women:
retirement to a monastery. See Symeon the Logothete (Georgius Interpolatus), in
Theophanes Continuatus, *Chronographia*, ed. I. Bekker (Bonn, 1838), 809; Pseudo-Symeon
(Symeon Magister), ibid. 645–6.

[258] *Vita B*, 256D; *Laudatio Platonis* 833C. Grumel, *Regestes*, nos. 368–9. Grumel speaks of
a 'jugement synodal excommuniant et déposant le prêtre Joseph.' Henry, *Theodore of Studios*,
45–6, has argued that it is more probable that the deposition and temporary exclusion from
communion (a 'minor' excommunication) was a patriarchal act, but not synodal.

to the empress is expressed by the total absence of any adverse comment about her cruelty to her own child.[259] Theodore's sole extant letter to Irene, written in 801 after she had granted sweeping tax exemptions to the people of Constantinople, is, as Henry notes, 'fulsome even by Byzantine standards'.[260] Theodore's biographer describes Irene with the (conventional) epithet of 'Christ-loving' in the very same sentence as he describes Constantine's loss of both eyes.[261]

1.6 THE MOVE TO THE MONASTERY OF STOUDIOS

During the period immediately following re-establishment of monastic life at the Sakkoudion, the newly acquired fame of Theodore drew many visitors and monastic candidates.[262] According to Theodore's biographer, Patriarch Tarasios and the Empress Irene offered Theodore and his monks the old monastery of Stoudios on the south-west edge of Constantinople as an alternative to Sakkoudion because Arab incursions made the area unsafe.[263] Theodore moved to this monastery in 798/9. Perhaps an equally pressing reason for this move was the expanding

[259] An exception is Theophanes (who did not belong to Theodore's group) who writes (AM 6289, p. 472), 'By the will of his mother and her advisors, at around the ninth hour he was terribly and incurably blinded with the intention of killing him. For seventeen days the sun grew dark, making ships wander and go astray. Everyone agreed the sun stored up its rays because the Emperor had been blinded. In this way his mother Irene took power.' Two years later Irene did the same to the sons of Constantine V in order to thwart a plot to dethrone her: Theophanes, AM 6291, p. 474. Elsewhere, however, he forgets these events and refers to the empress as 'the most pious Irene'.

[260] *Theodore of Studios*, 505 n. 1. The letter in question is ep. 7. On the tax exemptions, see Theophanes, AM 6293, p. 475; J. B. Bury, *A History of the Eastern Roman Empire (A.D. 802–867)*, (London, 1912; repr. New York, 1965), 3–4; J. F. Haldon, *Byzantium in the Seventh Century. The Transformation of a Culture* (Cambridge, 1990), 149–50; Fatouros, *Prolegomena*, 150*; Treadgold, *The Byzantine Revival*, 117–18, who notes that this may have been a measure of desperation on Irene's part to stem her sinking popularity, thereby warding off conspiracies.

[261] *Vita B*, 256D. *Vita A*, 141B, describes the blinding as divine retribution, implying that Irene was God's instrument.

[262] *Vita B*, 257CD; *Vita A*, 144BC; *Vita C*, no. 23. In TC III. 16. 34, Theodore says many of the new monks are from undistinguished backgrounds, from poor families and even from foreign races—barbarian and Scythian (such as the future martyr Thaddeos).

[263] *Vita B*, 257D–260A; cf Theophanes, *Chronographia*, AM 6291, p. 473; Treadgold, *The Byzantine Revival*, 113. According to Anastasius the monastery was governed by imperial statute: *Anastasius Bibliothecarii. Episolae sive Praefationes* 18, in *MGH Epistolarum*, vii. 441–2.

number of monks and the desire to extend the Sakkoudion confederation.[264] At any rate, even after the move Sakkoudion had its
monks (reassembled after the Arab threat had passed?), remaining
for a time the mother-house, and Theodore (and other brethren)
commuted between the two monasteries.[265] Plato, in the meanwhile, had given up his co-abbacy in favour of his energetic
nephew.[266]

The Stoudios monastery was founded by a certain Studius who
was eastern consul in 454.[267] Just before assuming this position he
had built a church dedicated to Saint John the Baptist (the
'Forerunner'), perhaps hoping to have placed there the relic of
the head of the saint which had reportedly just been found at
Emesa. Not having succeeded in this he turned the church over to
the Akoimetoi ('sleepless') monks, named because of their uninter-
rupted choir services, who then made a foundation there (c.460?).[268]
When Theodore, himself the 'imitator of the Forerunner',[269]
arrived there were but a handful of monks, the result of the persecutions of Constantine V.[270] Numbers grew rapidly, and before long
Theodore could speak of having 'more than three hundred broth-

---

[264] As Leroy has convincingly argued: 'La Réforme studite', 201–7. The only reference
in Theodore's writings to the move is in *Laudatio Platonis* 833D, where the reason for the
move is described enigmatically as διὰ τὸ ἔθνος, which may simply imply a request from
the capital. Cf. Ruggieri, *Byzantine Architecture*, 225 n. 203; Leroy, 'La Réforme studite', 202
n. 166.

[265] Leroy, ibid. 204–5. On the confederation, see also Fatouros, *Prolegomena*, 11*;
G. Režač, 'Le diverse forme di unione fra i monasteri orientali', in *Monachesimo Orientale*,
OCA 153 (Rome, 1958), 118–25.

[266] *Laudatio Platonis* 836A.

[267] Nothing is known about the man or his career. Because of his Latin name he was traditionally thought to have come from Rome (cf. *Vita A*, 145A).

[268] C. Mango, 'The Date of the Studius Basilica at Istanbul', *BMGS* 4 (1978), 115–22;
A. Kazhdan, A.-M. Talbot, and A. Cutler, 'Stoudios Monastery', *ODB* 3 (1960): 'Brick
stamps uncovered in recent excavations suggest that the church was begun in 450
(U. Peschlow, *JÖB* 32.4 (1982) 429–33).' On the *inventio* of the head of John the Baptist, see,
Chronicon Paschale 284–628 AD, trans. with notes and introduction by Michael Whitby and
Mary Whitby (Liverpool, 1989), 82 and n. 270.

[269] *Vita B*, 260B. The allusion is to Theodore's opposition to Constantine's marriage,
much as St John had stood up to Herod Antipas over his illegal marriage to Herodias, his
brother's wife (Matt. 14: 1–12).

[270] *Vita B*, 259A, says there were not quite ten monks. *Vita A*, 145B, says there were not
more than twelve. The abbot had been Sabas, who resigned his abbacy in favour of
Theodore. There is no evidence, however, that Sabas had followed the rule and spirituality of the Akoimetoi. Cf. Leroy, 'La Réforme studite', 204 and n. 183; idem, 'La Vie quotidienne', 27.

ers'.[271] With time this number reached several hundred more.[272] Theodore's skills as an administrator and organizer were tested to the full, and he continued to refine the details of his rule.[273] The Stoudios monastery became the main monastery of the confederation, Theodore himself and his followers becoming known as Stoudites.[274] Their special heavenly patrons were the holy Theotokos and 'the Forerunner and the Theologian [i.e. Evangelist]'.[275] The ruins of the monastery still stand.

1.7 SECOND PHASE OF THE MOECHIAN CONFLICT: THE JOSEPH AFFAIR

In the city of Constantinople, and even less so in the seclusion of the Stoudios monastery, few could have been immediately aware

---

[271] TC I. 70. 632: ἐν ἐν τοῖς τοσούτοις προσώποις τῶν ὑπὲρ τριακοσίων ἀδελφῶν ἡμῶν θέλημα . . . See also Leroy, 'La Vie quotidienne', 27 n. 27. Other allusions to the growing numbers of monks can be found in TC I. 33. 535, TC I. 47. 567, TC I. 55, TC I. 73; *MC* 74. 208, *MC* 75. 210, *MC* 82. 25 (some monks took the habit on this day); *MC* 92. 67–8 (Theodore complains that the monastery has so many monks that he is unable to have personal contact with each one: 'You are a large group; my corporal eye cannot always see all of you, but my internal eye invigilates over you'); *MC* 99. 98; PK 25. 172, PK 47. 338 (Theodore has given the habit to 27 postulants on the same day (= *MC* 29, but without the detail of this number)); PK 75. 516 (so many coming to the monastery that there is not enough room to live in); PK 77. 536, 538 (the community is growing at such a pace that there is sometimes a crush when all leave common rooms at the same time); PK 86. 609, PK 93. 664, PK 119. 889.

[272] Theophanes, *Chronographia*, AM 6298, p. 481, writes of 'perhaps seven hundred monks'; Stoudite sources give the number one thousand: *Vita B*, 259; *Vita A*, 148C. Even though there were other churches within the same monastic area (Ruggieri, *Byzantine Architecture*, 196), it is difficult to imagine how such a large number could be brought together for liturgical services. It seems likely that the numbers refer to the whole Stoudite confederation.

[273] Cf. *Vita B*, 261A–D.

[274] Before 814, the main monasteries of the confederation seem to have been the Sakkoudion, the Theotokos of (Ta) Kathara, and the monasteries of Hagios Christophoros and Trypyliana, both of which seem to have been situated near the Sakkoudion. A number of Theodore's early Catecheses were given in letter form for these young monasteries, from which the names of the latter are known: PK 55. 390, PK 56. 398, PK 57. 404, PK 58. 409, PK 59. 416, PK 64. 446, etc. For details on these monasteries see, Janin, *Les Églises et les monastères*, 158–60, 179, 187–8; Ruggieri, *Byzantine Architecture*, 107–8 and *passim*. Other monasteries beyond this date are known to have been part of the Stoudite circle: ibid. 108. Mention in the Catecheses of Theodore's trips away from the Stoudios monastery indicates that he was active outside his monastery, including, probably, visits to these confederated monasteries: TC I. 8. 470 (Theodore cannot always be with his monks); TC I. 63. 614 (sends a Catechesis by letter from another monastery to the Stoudios monastery); PK 21. 149 (he has been away); PK 112. 826 (he has been visiting another monastery).

[275] The Sakkoudion was under the patronage of John the Evangelist. Invocation of patrons in: TC I. 81. 653; PK 34. 252, PK 57. 404, PK 101. 730, PK 112. 825, etc.

of the momentous significance of the event that occurred in Rome
on 25 December 800. Pope Leo III had crowned Charlemagne
emperor of the Romans.[276] But its effect on the politics of the day
was to be revolutionary: it constituted an act of rebellion against
the imperial government that would have as a long-term consequence the total separation of East and West as political and ecclesial entities. At the time, however, the concept of a united empire
still prevailed.[277] The solution sought to end the crisis, which did
nothing to enhance the reputation of Irene (who was in no position
to intervene militarily), was the time-honoured alliance-maker: a
marriage pact. Charlemagne would marry the widow Irene.[278]
Even the denunciation of Irene's Nicene Synod by Charlemagne's
theologians was not seen as a serious obstacle to this proposed
union.[279] Dissatisfaction at Irene's policies and, especially, real
fears of the implications of this alliance led to a successful (and
bloodless) coup. On 1 November 802 Irene was arrested and
deposed. Nikephoros, patrician and general logothete, acceded to
the throne and was immediately crowned emperor (802–11) by
Patriarch Tarasios. Irene was soon to be exiled to a convent she
herself had founded on the nearby island of Prinkipo. From there
she was sent to Lesbos where she died, on 9 August 803.[280] The
transference of power passed without comment in the writings of
Theodore, who felt less nostalgia for the reign of Irene than others,
such as Theophanes, did.[281]

Nikephoros proved to be a capable and energetic ruler, and willing to risk unpopular measures in order to strengthen the economic base and the external security of the Empire. This he did by
sweeping tax reforms, including the abolition of the exemptions
made by Irene (which were proving to be too costly to the state),

[276] Herrin, *The Formation of Christendom*, 464: 'In the East, no formal notification of the
ceremony of 800 was received, and its precise import remained unknown.'

[277] PK 3. 17 seems to be referring to these events when Theodore states, 'here we proclaim one Emperor, and elsewhere our brothers [i.e. Christians] proclaim another . . .
There is no reason for there to be two heads in a single empire.'

[278] A good account of these events is found in Herrin, *The Formation of Christendom*, 454–62;
464–6. On the marriage proposal, see Theophanes, *Chronographia*, AM 6293–4, p. 475.

[279] This occurred at the Synod of Frankfurt (794). Discussion in Herrin, *The Formation of
Christendom*, 434–44.

[280] Theophanes, *Chronographia*, AM 6295, pp. 476–80; Treadgold, *The Byzantine Revival*,
119–20, 129.

[281] Cf. Henry, *Theodore of Studios*, 505. Theodore recognized Nikephoros' more efficient
rule. Theophanes' account of Nikephoros' reign is highly prejudiced.

the rooting out of corruption in the fiscal chain, and the strength-ening of the Western frontiers, made possible largely through a mass recolonization programme.[282] The imperial treasury was massively increased, including at the expense of the church, earn-ing from Theophanes the accusation that Nikephoros 'loved gold, not Christ' (χρυσὸν οὐ Χριστόν).[283] Theodore, on the other hand, recognized the ruling skills of the emperor and respected him for that.[284]

The emperor also acquired a reputation for his personal piety (having as spiritual father George of Amastris), and for being a pro-tector of the poor.[285] Theophanes, the main chronicler of these years, despised the emperor, none the less, also because of the lat-ter's policy of religious toleration, accusing him of being the worst sort of heretic himself: an iconoclast[286]—a manifestly false charge contradicted even by Theodore.[287] Yet Theodore was to suffer at the hands of the emperor.

On 18 February 806 the elderly patriarch died. As no immedi-ately suitable candidate, who was both intelligent and pragmatic, could be named by the emperor to succeed him, a free election to the patriarchate was to be held. Theodore was an obvious con-tender—being a reformer of respected authority and the head of a large group of monks—but he was probably considered too inflex-ible for the emperor to want to work alongside him. None the less, both he and Plato were consulted (with the latter declaring for his

[282] On the reforms of Nikephoros, see Treadgold, *The Byzantine Revival*, 128–95; Ostrogorsky, *History of the Byzantine State*, 186–97.

[283] Theophanes, *Chronographia*, AM 6299. 483. 1–2. It is possible that the real author of these and other derogatory remarks was George Synkellos, subsequently edited by Theophanes who, none the less, must have been in agreement with them. See, C. Mango, 'Who wrote the Chronicle of Theophanes?', *Zbornik radova Vizantološkog Instituta*, 18 (1978), 9–17. George seems to have been implicated in a plot against the emperor in 808: Treadgold, *The Byzantine Revival*, 153.

[284] In ep. 16. 4–5, written in 806, Theodore praises the emperor for 'setting the empire right when it was in a bad state'.

[285] On the asceticism of Nikephoros, which included prayer, fasting, and sleeping on the floor, see *Vita Georgii Amastridos* (BHG 668), in V. Vasilievskij, *Trudy*, 3 (Petrograd, 1915), 53–4. On favouring the poor, see *Vita Nicetae Mediciensis* (BHG 1341) in *AA.SS Aprilis I*, xxiv. Theophanes, *Chronographia*, AM 6295, p. 479. Cf. Treadgold, *The Byzantine Revival*, 131.

[286] Theophanes, *Chronographia*, AM 6303, p. 489. The charge arises because the emperor did not prevent the hermit Nicholas, who had been an iconoclast, from preaching publicly against icons. On toleration of the Paulicians and Athinganoi (a Phrygian sect), see ibid. 488 and Treadgold, *The Byzantine Revival*, 169.

[287] Cf. ep. 443. 56–8 (written ann. 821–6), where he states whatever may have been his other crimes, including being avaricious, Nikephoros cannot be faulted for his orthodoxy.

nephew),[288] but the emperor eventually made the choice of a layman, also a Nikephoros, who had worked as an imperial secretary
under the then protoasecretis Tarasios and had worked in the
administration of the Nicene Council.[289] He was also a man of
learning, having composed a short history of the seventh and
eighth centuries in classicizing Greek.[290] Anticipating Stoudite
opposition to the enthronement, the emperor had Plato and
Theodore placed under arrest, an imprisonment that lasted
twenty-four days, giving enough time for the patriarch-elect to be
tonsured, to receive all orders, and be consecrated as archbishop
and patriarch on Easter Sunday, 12 April 806.[291] After their release
Theodore and Plato decided to accept their new patriarch without
protest. Indeed, it may have been a conscious act of *rapprochement*
on the part of the patriarch, with the emperor's agreement, to
invite Theodore to take part in an election of the new abbot of the
monastery Τὰ Δαλμάτου.[292] An even more obvious attempt to
win him over was the appointment of Theodore's brother Joseph
to the archbishopric of Thessalonica.[293] The nomination followed
a turn of events that had suddenly put a great strain on the relations between the Stoudite monks and the patriarchate. This
occurred over the Joseph affair, the second phase of the moechian
controversy.

---

[288] Cf. ep. 16 (Theodore's letter to the emperor); *Laudatio Platonis* 837BC (where Plato's candidate, whom Theodore refuses to name, seems to be himself). Cf. Alexander, *The Patriarch Nicephorus*, 67. For a detailed analysis of ep. 16, see Henry, *Theodore of Studios*, 50–5.

[289] *Vita Nicephori*, in *Nicephori Opuscula Historica*, ed. de Boor, 142–52. On his career before 806, see Alexander, *Patriarch Nicephorus*, 54–64; Treadgold, *The Byzantine Revival*, 141–2. On the relationship of emperor to church, in matters of appointments etc., see Ch. 3 below.

[290] The Ἱστορία Σύντομος or *Breviarium*. See Alexander, *The Patriarch Nicephorus*, 157–62; C. Mango, 'The *Breviarium* of the Patriarch Nicephorus', in *Byzantium: Tribute to Andreas N. Stratos* (Athens, 1986), 539–52.

[291] *Laudatio Platonis*, 837C. Theophanes, *Chronographia*, AM 6298, p. 481, notes how the Stoudite opposition was due to the fact that Nikephoros was a layman when appointed, and that the emperor initially threatened to break up the Stoudios monastery when cognizant of this resistance to his choice. Although such an appointment was technically against church law (Sardica, canon 10), there is no record of Stoudite opposition to the election of Tarasios, who had been similarly appointed by Irene. For a detailed account of the events surrounding the election of Nikephoros, see Alexander, *The Patriarch Nicephorus*, 65–71. Fatouros, in *Prolegomena*, 13*, neglects the testimony of Theophanes, and states the 24-day arrest was due to the 806 synod. It is possible that PK 122. 916 refers to this imprisonment (and PK 57 to Theodore's release): I. Hausherr, *Saint Théodore Studite*, 83 n. 57.

[292] PK 89. 631–2; Grumel, *Regestes*, no. 375. Cf. Alexander, *The Patriarch Nicephonis*, 84–5; Treadgold, *The Byzantine Revival*, 143 and n. 188 (p. 408).

[293] Cf. ep. 23 (in which Joseph explains why he accepted the nomination).

In that same year of 806 Emperor Nikephoros decided he would reopen the Joseph case, convoking a synod of fifteen bishops with the purpose of restoring the former steward to his office and to an active priesthood. It had been nine years since his deposition under Irene. Theodore was also asked to attend, but as a monk he had no active voice, indeed choosing to remain silent during the proceedings.[294] The motives of the emperor in all this are not altogether clear, but it seems quite likely that this was a political reward to Joseph for the essential part he had played in defusing a plot against the throne led by Bardanes Turcus.[295] Theodore's response to Joseph's reinstatement was much like his response to the first crisis in 795/6. He broke communion with Joseph and all who concelebrated with him, keeping away from imperial and patriarchal circles. This passive protest, which avoided outright condemnation of the synodal decision, was justified by Theodore on the basis of *oikonomia*.[296]

It does not seem that the emperor was aware of Theodore's position until early in 808.[297] Suspicions were aroused when Joseph, on an extended visit to his brother at Stoudios, persistently avoided presenting himself to the emperor or to concelebrate with the patriarch on the feast days that occurred during his visit. An imperial agent, the logothete of the course, was sent to Joseph to demand an explanation. He replied that his opposition was to the reinstated steward Joseph but not to the patriarch nor to the emperors. The logothete, in turn, replied, 'Our pious Emperors have no need for you, neither at Thessalonica nor elsewhere.'[298] In

---

[294] Grumel, *Regestes*, no. 377; ep. 555. 42–8. On Theodore's presence at the Synod, see Dobroklonskij, *Prepodobnij Feodor*, 607; Henry, *Theodore of Studios*, 57–8; Niavis, *The Reign of the Byzantine Emperor Nicephorus I (AD 802–811)* (Athens, 1987), 152–3; Treadgold, *The Byzantine Revival*, 143; Hatlie, 'Abbot Theodore', 153.

[295] Theophanes, *Chronographia*, AM 6295, pp. 479–80; *Synodicon Vetus*, ed. J. A. Fabricius and G. C. Harles, *Bibliotheca Graeca* (Hamburg, 1809), xii. 415. On the revolt, see also Treadgold, *The Byzantine Revival*, 131–3 and Bury, *Eastern Roman Empire*, 10–14. For a discussion of the emperor's motives, see Hatlie, 'Abbot Theodore', 152 n. 83.

[296] For an analysis of Theodore's understanding of *oikonomia*, see Ch. 2.6 below.

[297] If the patriarch had known, he perhaps would not have made Joseph archbishop. On the other hand, being aware of it he may have used this as a way of healing the rift. In fact, Joseph did seem to drift from Theodore's intransigent stance after the events of 809, judging by the tone and content of ep. 43 (written between 809 and 811).

[298] ep. 31. 20–1. On this whole episode, see Dobroklonskij, *Prepodobnij Feodor*, 613–14; Alexander, *Patriarch Nicephorus*, 90–1; Henry, *Theodore of Studios*, 59–61; Pratsch, *Theodorus Studites*, 147 ff. (The reference to 'Emperors', in the plural, is due to the fact that Nikephoros had crowned his son Stauracius junior emperor and successor in 803.) It is not certain

the following months Theodore engaged in a campaign to explain his views, which had now been revealed by his brother.[299] By the end of the year the emperor, dissatisfied with the Stoudites, had Theodore, Plato, Archbishop Joseph, and a monk Kalogeros, placed in custody at the monastery of Sergios and Bakchos where further unsuccessful attempts were made to persuade them to soften their intransigence.[300] In January 809 they were given another chance before a synod of assorted bishops, abbots, and imperial officials. This synod, which Theodore would call μοιχοσύνοδος (the adulterous synod),[301] determined (1) confirmation of the restoration to priestly dignity of Joseph of Kathara; (2) anathema to anyone not accepting the principle of *oikonomia* as used by the saints; (3) the removal from his see and the demotion to the rank of priesthood of the Archbishop Joseph of Thessalonica.[302]

Theodore's reading of the synodal decisions, which he understood in terms of their ultimate implications, was that, unlike the first moechian controversy, which was essentially a compromise on the part of some individuals with sinful action, official church sanction had now been given to aberrant doctrine. Indeed, he would now accuse the synod of teaching heresy.[303] It was the synodal use

whether this formula actually decreed deposition or not. The interview occurred at a time when another conspiracy against the throne had been uncovered, in which church officials had also been implicated. Treadgold suggests that one of the reasons for ecclesiastical discontent was the Joseph affair (Treadgold, *The Byzantine Revival*, 153–4). There is no suggestion that the Stoudites were directly involved but Archbishop Joseph's visit to the capital just at this time seems unfortunate for him.

[299] Epp. 21–8, 30, 31, 32 are datable to this period of *apologia* (808 to the beginning of 809). The letters are conciliatory in tone, with some compromise suggested, except for the insistence that Joseph be barred from sacramental functions.

[300] Recounted in ep. 48 and *Laudatio Platonis* 840D. The emperor's dissatisfaction before the incarceration is shown in the fact that he had refused an audience to Theodore and Joseph and had refused to permit Joseph to be present at the customary salutations given by church officials before leaving on a military campaign. See epp. 23 and 26. The patriarch, during the emperor's absence, also refused to see the Stoudites. 'What is there to say about the Patriarch?' Theodore laments, 'He will neither send any answer nor even hear an appeal; he is Caesar's Steward in every respect' (ep. 26. 24–6).

[301] The first use is in ep. 33, 68, written to Pope Leo after Theodore's condemnation.

[302] On the *acta* of the synod, see Dobroklonskij, *Prepodobnij Feodor*, 631–3; Grumel, *Regestes*, nos. 378–81. The synod has been extensively studied by Henry, *Theodore of Studios*, 63–4 and esp. Appendix A, 266–72; idem, 'The Moechian Controversy', 509–18. See also the comments made in Hatlie, 'Abbot Theodore', 159 n. 89.

[303] Ep. 33, to Pope Leo, is the first instance of the charge of heresy. 'Stretch out your hand to our Church . . . which has already sunk into the depths of heresy (ἐν τῷ τῆς αἱρέσεως βάθει)' . . . 'Now you . . . thunder forth the things that need to be said against

of an anathema that suggested to him that the issues were not just about discipline.[304] In his letter from exile to Pope Leo, Theodore writes:

> They dogmatise the adulterous union to be an economy (οἰκονομίαν οὖν τὴν ζευξιμοιχείαν δογματίζουσιν). They determine that the divine laws do not apply to Emperors. They prohibit imitation of such people as the Forerunner and Chrysostom, who stood firm even to the point of shedding blood for the sake of justice and truth. They proclaim that any bishop has authority in matters of the divine canons, no matter what is in fact set down in them.[305]

Ultimately, the synod had declared itself against the Gospel, and as such this was no less serious than the heresy of iconoclasm.[306]

Theodore's attitude was probably quite incomprehensible to the emperor.[307] That the issue was clearly not about authorizing adultery seems to be evidenced by the fact that around that same time, perhaps before the synod, Nikephoros had officially declared the retroactive invalidity of the adulterous union between Constantine VI and Theodote, and therefore the disqualification of the progeny to Constantine's inheritance.[308] It seems that the emperor still attempted to break Theodore's resistance for a time after the synod, but when this failed he issued an imperial edict which banished the Stoudite leadership into exile.[309] The Stoudite brotherhood

the current heresy (κατὰ τῆς παρούσης κακοδοξίας). These men [the synodal fathers], arrogating authority to themselves, were not afraid to convoke an heretical synod (αἱρετικὴν σύνοδον)' (lines 53–5, 60–3). An analysis and discussion of heresy is found below, Ch. 5.

[304] The real issue was not about the principle of *oikonomia*, which the Fathers of the church—and Theodore too—accepted, but of its application and its limits.

[305] Ep. 33. 31–6. These arguments are also summarized well in ep. 34 (also to Pope Leo) and ep. 555, to the *lavra* of St Sabas in Palestine.

[306] Ep. 53, 107–9, 112–13: 'But now a dogma against the Gospel, against the Forerunner and against the canons has been synodically promulgated through the reception of the joiner of adulterers' 'Which, even though coming after the heresy of the iconomachs, is no less than the latter for those who look at the matter piously.'

[307] As it was also to many churchmen, monks, and even some of his own brethren: ep. 556. 23–5. References to defectors are found in epp. 28. 48 and 51. Cf. R. Devreesse, *Une lettre de S. Théodore Studite relative au synode moechien (809)*, AB 68 (1950), 51–2; Henry, *Theodore of Studios*, 168–9.

[308] The only source for this is Theodore's own report in ep. 31. 52–8. See, Alexander, *Patriarch Nicephorus*, 92.

[309] Henry, 'The Moechian Controversy', 511–12, 518–19. After the synod Theodore and the others were held at the Agathos monastery, in Constantinople, where they received notification from the *spatharios* of having been anathematized. From there they were taken to the Hagios Mamas monastery, likewise in the capital. See ep. 48. 62–8.

52

Biography

remained, for the most part, in solidarity with Theodore, and as a result the Stoudios monastery was closed and the monks dispersed, some of them also being sent into exile.[310] Places such as Cherson, Thessalonica, and Lipara, beyond Sicily, became the new homes of the monks.[311] Theodore, Plato, and Joseph were exiled to separate locations on the nearby Princes' Islands.[312] Here they remained for two years and some months until recalled by the emperor in 811.[313] Nikephoros planned to lead what was to turn out to be a fatal expedition against the Bulgars.[314] Before he left he seems to have attempted a reconciliation with the Stoudites, bringing them back on the occasion of the serious illness of Plato. It also seems that the emperor had even intended after his campaign to restore the Stoudios monastery. But this was left for another to do.[315] Nikephoros fell in battle on 26 July 811 against Krum, the Bulgarian Khan.[316] The latter had the skull of the Byzantine emperor plated in silver so that toasts could be drunk from it.[317]

Nikephoros' successor was his son Staurakios. But as he had been seriously wounded at the same battle as his father had died, his reign could not last long. Not having any children, the succession became an urgent issue. The throne passed, after just two months, on 2 October, to Michael Rhangabe, the husband

[310] *Vita B*, 269B–D and ep. 48. 116–24, where a meeting between the emperor and the community is reported before its dissolution.

[311] Ep. 48. 40–61.

[312] *Laudatio Platonis* 840C; *Vita B*, 269B; ep. 33. 81. On the Princes Islands, see Janin, *L'Églises et les monastères*, 61–76. Theodore was imprisoned on the island of Chalke: epigrams 98–101 (Speck, *Theodores Studites*, 261 ff.) Joseph was imprisoned on Oxia, Plato on Prote: Fatouros, *Prolegomena*, 14*.

[313] From Chalke Theodore wrote, by my counting, 22 extant letters which can definitely be dated: epp. 33–44, 48–51, 53, 54, 553–556. Two are to the pope, and most of the others are also about the 809 synod.

[314] The menace of the Bulgars is revealed in a story about Christian martyrs in *PC* 63 (discussed at Ch. 2.4 below).

[315] *Laudatio Platonis*, 841D–844A; ep. 453. 8–9: ὑποστροφὴ τῆς ἐξορίας ἐπὶ τοῦ Νικηφόρου. On the basis of a passage in Theophanes, *Chronographia*, AM 6304, p. 494, which speaks of Michael I's desire to reconcile the patriarch with Theodore, Plato, and Archbishop Joseph, 'who had been held in bitter imprisonment. Michael was eager to unite them, and he did so', Bury, *Eastern Roman Empire*, 41, and others following him, place the recall from exile under this reign. *Vita B*, 272D also places the recall from exile under Michael I. The evidence from Theodore's own writings, however, is more compelling. See, Alexander, *Patriarch Nicephorus*, 96; Treadgold, *The Byzantine Revival*, 169.

[316] Supposedly, this had been prophesied by Theodore: *Vita B*, 272A–C. Nikephoros was the first emperor to die in battle with a foreign power since the 4th cent.

[317] Theophanes, *Chronographia*, AM 6303, p. 491.

of his sister Prokopia. Staurakios died three months later as a monk.[318]

One of Michael's first acts was to restore the Stoudites to their monastery and to reinstate Joseph as archbishop of Thessalonica. Being eager for ecclesiastical peace he instructed the patriarch to look again at the issue of the 809 synod and Joseph of Kathara. The intervention of Pope Leo III (795–816) was sought, who was well acquainted with the affair.[319] The result was that Joseph was once again deposed, and Patriarch Nikephoros apologized for his attitude which he put down to the late emperor's oppression.[320] At the same time Michael I sought peace with Charlemagne by recognizing him as emperor, and Patriarch Nikephoros sent his Συνοδικὰ γράμματα (synodal letters), with the customary confession of Orthodox belief of a newly elected patriarch, delayed by five years because of the late emperor's anger at Charlemagne's coronation.[321] The moechian controversy was now over, peace was restored within the church and between Churches.

1.8 THE RETURN OF ICONOCLASM

Theodore had three years of trouble-free monastic life, where he was able to resume his role of *hegoumenos* and give a regular Catechesis, before a much more serious disturbance within the church led him to be exiled from the Stoudios monastery for good. This was the revival of iconoclasm.

---

[318] Ibid. AM 6303, pp. 492–3, AM 6304, p. 495; *Vita B*, 272C. On the reign of Staurakios, see Treadgold, *The Byzantine Revival*, 174–7.

[319] Theodore had sent messages and two letters (epp. 33 and 34) to the pope. Theodore's detractors were also active in Rome. Cf. C. van de Vorst, *Les Relations de S. Théodore Studite avec Rome, AB* 32 (1913), 440–1; P. Hatlie, *Theodore of Stoudios, Pope Leo III and the Joseph Affair (808–812): New Light on an Obscure Negotiation*, in OCP 61 (1995), 407–23.

[320] *Laudatio Platonis* 844AB; *Vita B*, 273A; ep. 56. 40–1. Cf. Grumel, *Regestes*, nos. 387–8; Alexander, *The Patriarch Nicephorus*, 97.

[321] Grumel, *Regestes*, no. 382; Theophanes, *Chronographia*, AM 6304, p. 494. See also Treadgold, *The Byzantine Revival*, 178–9. Herrin, *The Formation of Christendom*, 465, overstates her case when she writes that Emperor Nikephoros had prevented the patriarch from sending his synodical letter because Pope Leo had crowned Charlemagne and had 'supported the Byzantine monastic party led by Theodore Stoudites in its criticism of the Emperor and the Patriarch'. Since the Joseph affair did not reach a critical point until two years after the patriarch's installation, and the pope was not involved until after the 809 synod, this could not have had much to do with the break in relations between emperor and pope.

Michael I Rhangabe's reign did not prove to be a success. By disposition he was mild-mannered, pious, generous, and courted popularity, especially with the clergy.[322] However, he was indecisive, being 'honest and fair, but unfit to administer affairs',[323] and was a poor military leader. With the crushing defeat of the Byzantine forces and the death of Emperor Nikephoros in recent memory, the army needed effective leadership. Krum had offered a peace treaty to Michael, involving loss to the Bulgars of some territories, a tribute to be paid, and mutual extradition of each other's subjects. Among Michael's advisers were senior churchmen, including Theodore. It was he, from among the clergy, who insisted that the peace plan not be adopted for fear of what would happen to the Bulgars who had joined the Byzantines and had adopted Christianity. Other advisers from the civil service counselled the same, but for different reasons.[324] The result was a renewal of hostilities leading to a decisive Byzantine defeat. Michael knew he now had to abdicate, which he did on 11 July after returning to Constantinople. He and all his family were tonsured and were made to leave the city. The new emperor, crowned the following day, was Leo the strategos of the Anatolikon theme (Leo V, 813–20), who had almost certainly orchestrated the Byzantine defeat by an act of treachery in hope of gaining the throne.[325]

Leo proved himself to be an able emperor. Scarcely had he been crowned when he was confronted by a siege on the capital by the Bulgar Khan Krum, who devastated the surrounding countryside.

[322] Cf. Treadgold, *The Byzantine Revival*, 177–80. At his coronation Patriarch Nikephoros obtained from him a written statement in which he pledged to preserve the Orthodox faith, not to stain his hands with the blood of Christians, and not to scourge ecclesiastics, whether priests or monks. Theophanes, *Chronographia*, AM 6303, p. 493.

[323] Theophanes, *Chronographia*, AM 6305, p. 500.

[324] Theophanes attacks the 'evil advisers and Theodore of Stoudios' for their 'stupidity and lack of care for public affairs' in not accepting the peace plan: ibid. AM 6305, p. 498. Theodore had been involved in another affair of state, when he insisted that Michael halt his policy, agreed to by the patriarch, of condemning Paulician and Athinganoi heretics to death. Cf. ibid. AM 6304, p. 495 (where Theodore is not expressly named); ep. 94. 11 ff., ep. 455. 73 ff.

[325] Cf. Treadgold, *The Byzantine Revival*, 188; Bury, *Eastern Roman Empire*, 351–2. Theophanes seems to place the blame for the defeat, once again, on 'counsellors inexperienced at war', 'evil advisers'. There is no intimation of Leo's treachery. Indeed, he is described as being 'pious and brave', who 'had totally supported Michael's ruling the Empire'. Theophanes, *Chronologia*, AM 6305, pp. 500–2. This chronicle was completed before Leo declared his iconoclasm.

In fact, for his first three years as emperor he was to witness a serious of humiliating defeats which only stopped through Krum's
sudden death from a brain haemorrhage. In the meanwhile, the
emperor, like every Byzantine of that age, had wondered what had
been the cause for God's anger in allowing so many military
defeats. He deduced that since iconophile rulers had all had a bad
end, whereas iconoclast emperors had had glorious burials, icon
veneration, despite official church teaching, was at fault.[326] Not
having committed himself to upholding church doctrine at his
coronation,[327] he felt free to summon free-thinking theologians to
reinvestigate early tradition with regard to this question. Perhaps
as a portent of things to come, the previous year, at Christmas of
813, on the occasion of the coronation as junior emperor of his son,
he changed the latter's name to Constantine. The two would be
acclaimed as 'Leo and Constantine'. He appointed John
Morocharzanios, later known as the 'grammarian', abbot of the
monastery of Sts Sergios and Bakchos, to head a commission, in
June 814, to study the question. The commission was subsequently
expanded, and, on John's own advice, was placed under a learned
bishop, Anthony Sassimates.[328] In December 814, a well-docu-
mented report, which included references to the acts of the Synod
of Hieria, was presented to the emperor, who in turn presented it
for consideration to Patriarch Nikephoros. Leo's contention was
that the military, which still had a core of iconoclast sympathizers,
was blaming icon veneration for its defeats, and that a good compromise would be to remove from churches those portable icons
that could be kissed and venerated.[329] Leo's mind was set, despite
Nikephoros' opposition which included refusal to enter into any
discussion with the emperor's theologians. The patriarch's argument, and that of the other iconophiles whom he assembled to try
and dissuade the emperor from reintroducing iconoclasm, was
that the issue had been settled definitively by the Second Council

---

[326] Scriptor Incertus, in Leo Grammaticus, *Chronographia* 349.

[327] Cf. Bury, *Eastern Roman Empire*, 56–7.

[328] On John the Grammarian, see Lemerle, *Le Premier Humanisme byzantin*, 135–46. John
was initially iconophile, and apparently even a painter of icons himself, but for an unknown
reason he secretly turned against them. Theodore writes to John during the 821–6 period,
showing great respect for his learning (epp. 492, 528, 545). The letters are to be found in
French translation in V. Grumel, 'Jean Grammaticos et saint Théodore Studite', *EO* 36
(1937), 183–8.

[329] Scriptor Incertus, in Leo Grammaticus, *Chronographia* 352–3.

of Nicaea and was therefore not open to discussion.[330] Theodore
was one of these iconophiles, telling the emperor to his face to leave
church affairs to the clergy.[331] Everything came to a head at the
beginning of Lent of the following year (13 March 815). Patriarch
Nikephoros felt compelled to resign, and was exiled to a monastery
he himself had founded at Chrysopolis, across the Bosporos.[332] A
lay court official, Theodotos Melissenos, was appointed in his
place, rushed through orders, and consecrated patriarch on Easter
Day. The week before, on Palm Sunday, Theodore had organized
a public procession of icons—by way of protest—around the
Stoudios monastery.[333] The new patriarch hastily convened a
synod, to which Theodore was invited but refused to attend, at
which iconoclasm was officially endorsed.[334] The Council of
Hieria of 754 was proclaimed the Seventh Ecumenical Council,
and that which met in 787 was annulled. Monks and clergy were
required to sign an iconoclastic statement to prove their allegiance
to the church, a requirement that seems to have been commuted
early on to receiving communion from an iconoclast priest.[335]
Recalcitrant Orthodox bishops were anathematized, deposed, and
handed to the secular authorities for imprisonment and eventual
exile. Iconoclasm was officially restored.[336]

[330] For Nikephoros' theology, see Alexander, *The Patriarch Nicephorus*, 189–215; J. Travis, *In Defence of the Faith: The Theology of Patriarch Nikephoros of Constantinople* (Massachusetts, 1984); J. Featherstone, 'The Refutation of the Council of 815 by the Patriarch Nicephoros', Ph.D. thesis (Harvard, 1984); K. Parry, 'Theodore Studites and the Patriarch Nicephoros on Image-Making as a Christian Imperative', *Byzantion*, 59 (1989), 164–83. (In Theodore's own writings more importance was actually given to the council in Trullo than to the Second Council of Nicaea in defence of the icons.)

[331] *Vita B*, 280C–284B; *Vita A*, 181D–184A; *Vita C*, nos. 37–8; *Vita Nicetae Mediciensis* 35. xxx; *Vita Nicephori*, ed. de Boor, 187. Cf. Scriptor Incertus, in Leo Grammaticus, *Chronographica* 355–7. See also below, 3. 5.

[332] Cf. *Vita B*, 285A.

[333] *Vita B*, 285B; *Vita A*, 186BC. This was in contrast to Leo V's removal of the icon of the Chalce, just before Christmas, under the pretext of protecting it from a mob. See Alexander, *The Patriarch Nicephorus*, 129.

[334] Theodore wrote to the synod in the name of all the abbots of the city, giving their reasons for considering the assembly utterly illegal: ep. 71 (April, 815). In this letter (line 14) Theodore for the first time refers to the Second Council of Nicaea as 'holy' and thereby, by implication, ecumenical: τῆς ἐν Νικαίᾳ τὸ δεύτερον ἁγίας συνόδου.

[335] Signing a formula: ep. 60, 13 (ὅτι δὲ καὶ ὑπογράψαι ἔφης); ep. 215, 5 (ἐκ πιττακίου); ep. 225, 99 (πρεσβύτερος εἴτε ὑπογράψας εἴτε κοινωνήσας . . .); ep. 294, 14 (ὑπογράψας πρεσβύτερος) etc.

[336] The most modern account of all the events that led up to this council is found in Pratsch, *Theodoros Studites*, 204–43. Other accounts in: Alexander, *The Patriarch Nicephorus*, 125–40; 'The Iconoclastic Council of St Sophia (815) and Its Definition (*Horos*)', *DOP* 7

The persecution that followed was not intended to make martyrs, but to break the resistance of the recalcitrant. As with the
persecution under Constantine V, it was selective, allowing many
iconophiles to remain relatively unmolested.[337] None the less,
martyrdoms did still occur.[338] Some of the details in Theodore's
descriptions of the persecution have been thought exaggerated by
historians,[339] but there is no reason to doubt the truth of his reports
of its general ferocity.[340] According to him, icons were destroyed
on a wide scale.[341] In one Catechesis Theodore states that 'there
are up to one hundred and beyond' of the brethren from various
communities who died as confessors of the faith during these persecutions.[342] He asks in a different Catechesis: 'Is it not on account
of and witness to the Word of God that you have undergone exile
and persecution? Have you not had, previously, the experience of
prison? Have you not shed your blood through the harsh treatment

---

X(1953), 35–66; Treadgold, *The Byzantine Revival*, 207–14; Hussey, *The Orthodox Church in the Byzantine Empire*, 55–8.

[337] Leo's own wife, Theodosia, was a known iconophile (cf. ep. 538 (*ann.* 821–4), written to her and her son Basil), as were a number of court officials (some being friends of Theodore) whom Leo tolerated: Treadgold, *The Byzantine Revival*, 221–2.

[338] The only Stoudite martyr named by Theodore for emulation by others is St Thaddeos (in ep. 186; *PC* 29, *PC* 43, etc.). He died after being sentenced to 130 strokes of the lash. On this martyr, see C. van de Vorst, *S. Thaddée Studite*, *AB* 31 (1912), 157–60.

[339] Martin, *A History of the Iconoclast Controversy*, 177 and n.13, e.g., writes: 'It is difficult to interpret otherwise than as exaggeration the statement Theodore makes to the Patriarch of Alexandria: "Some have departed, martyrs to the Lord, after being beaten with rods. Some have been sewn in sacks and drowned, as has been related by those who saw them" [ep. 275, 52–4]. The simple facts seem to be that the only lives lost in the attack of Leo V were the monks who died under the lash.'

[340] On the persecution, see Alexander, *The Patriarch Nicephorus*, 140–1; idem, 'Religious Persecution and Resistance in the Byzantine Empire of the Eighth and Ninth Centuries: Methods and Justifications' *Speculum* 52/2 (1977), 245–52 and *passim*; Martin, *A History of the Iconoclastic Controversy*, 174–83; Bury, *Eastern Roman Empire*, 71–6; A. Tougard, 'La Persécution iconoclaste d'après la correspondance de Saint Théodore Studite', *Revue des questions historiques*, NS 6 (1891), 80–118.

[341] See epp. 275, 278, 425.

[342] *PC* 36. 102–3: 'And now our brother Theodoulos has departed. He was one of the best: proven in obedience, firm in the confession [of faith], having endured blows and prison in the cause of Christ, having fulfilled his life in persecution. What is more lovable than this: that so many of our brethren—up to one hundred and beyond (μέχρι γὰρ ἑκατοντάδος καὶ πρὸς ὁ ἀριθμὸς πρόεισι)—who, after having shone brightly after the manner of the stars in the places where they were banished, left their sacred bodies as a witness to Orthodoxy (εἰς μαρτύριον ὀρθοδοξίας) for our contemporaries and for posterity? And I am not just speaking of those of our community, but also of the brothers of other monasteries who have undergone persecution until the end.'

you received? Have not certain of our brothers died like martyrs (ἀθλητικῶς)?'[343]

Those particularly targeted in the persecution were the iconophiles who spoke out against the synod. Primary among those leaders who refused to remain silent was Theodore, who, in Nikephoros' absence, became the leader of the opposition, organizing it into an effective resistance movement. He believed it was not only his duty, but the duty of all true Orthodox Christians to be constant in their confession of the true faith and to speak out (παρρησιάζεσθαι) in time of persecution.[344] As a result Leo was particularly severe towards Theodore. He was arrested in April 815 and imprisoned, together with one of his brethren, Nicholas, in a fort named Metopa, on the eastern bank of the Apollonian Sea.[345] Plato was spared this persecution, having died the previous year, on 4 April 814. Theodore remained here until the spring of the following year. In the meantime the emperor, instead of closing down the Stoudios monastery, appointed the monk Leontios, who had broken with Theodore over the moechian affair, as new *hegoumenos*.[346] From Metopa Theodore and Nicholas were taken to Bonita, in the Anatolikon theme of Asia Minor, where they remained for three years, to May/June 819. Theodore's biographer records how Theodore suffered particularly intensely here. Having been caught sending letters, the emperor ordered that he be stripped naked and given one hundred strokes of the lash. The wounds he received, on 23 February 819, festered to such an extent that he could have died; however, they healed by Pentecost of that year.[347] From Bonita Theodore was transferred, more dead than alive, to the city of Smyrna in the Thracesian theme where he was thrown into a dungeon, kept under close guard, and severely mistreated. His daily diet was bread and water, and on this he seems

[343] *PC* 72. 188. Cf. *PC* 121. 307 where Theodore describes an unnamed confessor of the faith who had been imprisoned under Leo, receiving 300 lashes on his back and chest, his face having been broken with fist blows and a rod, and losing two teeth in the process. He died some years later.

[344] Alexander, 'Religious Persecution', 248, 252. P. Hatlie, 'The Politics of Salvation: Theodore of Stoudios on Martyrdom (*Martyrion*) and Speaking Out (*Parrhesia*)', *DOP* 50 (1996), 263–87.

[345] *Vita B*, 288BC. The Apollonian sea is an inland sea in the Opsikian Theme, Bithynia, and east of Olympos.

[346] Ep. 333. 41–5; ep. 381. 114–27. Joseph of Kathara, incidentally, was reinstated by the emperor: Treadgold, *The Byzantine Revival*, 215.

[347] *Vita B*, 296A–297C.

to have managed to survive for twenty months until his release in the new year of 821, following the accession of a new emperor, Michael II.[348]

From exile Theodore wrote extensively,[349] not only to his own monks, encouraging them to persevere, but to bishops, clergy, monks of other monasteries, prominent and more ordinary lay people, and the heads of other patriarchal Churches, including the pope.[350] To his own monks, through fear of interception by imperial agents, he used codes for names, adopting a similar system to that developed during his second exile.[351] Emperor Leo V, in the meantime, had had some military successes, concluding a favourable peace treaty with the Bulgars and securing the eastern Arab front. With this he justified his iconoclastic policy.[352] To Theodore, on the other hand, nothing could justify iconoclasm. According to his theology, the prototype was in the image itself, truly if not consubstantially. Thus the rejection of Christ's image was a heresy that rejected Christ himself.[353]

Whoever does not confess that our Lord Jesus Christ is represented in a picture does not confess that he lived in the flesh. For to have lived in the flesh and to have been represented in a picture is the same thing. Whoever does not venerate his holy image does not venerate the Lord (Ὅστις οὐ προσκυνεῖ τὴν ἁγίαν αὐτοῦ εἰκόνα, οὐ προσκυνεῖ τὸν Κύριον); in the image, in effect, is the prototype, and the image is exposed and venerated according to the prototype of whoever is represented. Even if the adversaries of images say that they venerate him, they lie . . . such is the teaching of the Apostles that we have received from our holy Fathers.[354]

[348] *Vita B*, 297C–299B, 304C. On Theodore's places of exile, see also J. Pargoire, 'S. Théophane le Chronographe et ses rapports avec S. Théodore Studite'. *VizVrem.* 9 (1902), 69–71.

[349] The majority of his extant letters date from this period (815–20): around 340.

[350] On his correspondence with the pope, see C. van de Vorst, 'Les Relations de S. Théodore Studite avec Rome', 439–47; cf. V. Grumel, 'Les Relations politico-religieuses entre Byzance et Rome sous le règne de Léon V l'Arménien', *REB* 18 (1960), 19–44. Pope Paschal I (817–24) showed himself to be favourable to Theodore's cause, refusing to give an audience to Patriarch Theodotos' envoys, and sending a remonstrative letter to the emperor: Grumel, 'Les Relations', 26 ff.; ep. 272. 14–15.

[351] During the moechian controversy he developed a system whereby the 24 letters of the Greek alphabet corresponded to the more prominent members of his community: ep. 41 (*ann.* 809–11).

[352] Treadgold, *The Byzantine Revival*, 219–20.

[353] Cf. ep. 303, 20–1, 24: πλὴν ἡ παροῦσα αἵρεσις ἄρνησις Χριστοῦ ἐστιν ἀσφαλῶς· . . . ὥστε οὐχ ἡ τυχοῦσα αἵρεσις, ἀλλα ἀρνησίχριστος.

[354] *PC* 51. 142.

Iconoclasts reduced Christ to a mere φάντασμα (ghost).[355] They
denied his incarnation, for if Christ's body was material it was cir-
cumscribed and therefore could be depicted. No one could be an
iconoclast and claim to be a Christian.[356]

The brutal murder of Leo, on Christmas morning of 820, came
as joyful news to Theodore. When the exiled Patriarch Nikephoros
heard the news, he supposedly calmly remarked, 'Then the
Roman Empire has lost a great, although impious, protector.'[357]
Theodore, on the other hand, was less restrained: 'He lacerated
the body of Christ—the great dragon, the apostate, the twisted serpent, the prelude to the Antichrist, the polluted and blasphemous
mouth . . . the God-accursed man, the embodiment of Satan's servant. I'm not sure if what I say is sufficiently derisive of the guilty
one, since the impiety of the accursed one goes by many names.'[358]

1.9 THE LAST YEARS

When Theodore, under the amnesty granted by the new emperor,
Michael II the Amorian (820–9), was recalled from Smyrna his
hopes were high that the iconoclasm of the previous emperor
would be denounced. He immediately wrote to Michael, encouraging and imploring him to end the heresy and to reconcile the
patriarchate with Rome and the other three ancient patriarchates,
from whom Byzantium was in schism.[359] Theodore was to be dis-

[355] Ep. 425. 41.
[356] For Theodore's theology of the icon, see, among other studies, V. Grumel,
'L'Iconologie de saint Théodore Studite', *EO* 20 (1921), 251–68; Martin, *A History of the
Iconoclastic Controversy*, 184–98; P.J. Alexander, *The Patriarch Nicephorus*, 191–8; K. Parry,
'Theodore Studites and the Patriarch Nicephoros on Image-Making as a Christian
Imperative', *Byzantion*, 59 (1989), 164–83; Theodor Damian, 'The Icons: Theological and
Spiritual Dimensions According to St Theodore of Studion', Ph.D. Dissertation (Fordham
University, 1993).
[357] Genesius, *Regum Libri Quattuor* 14.
[358] Ep. 419. 12–18. Cf. Theodore's expressions of contentment at Leo's death in epp. 58,
417, 419, 435.
[359] Ep. 417. Theodore also wrote letters to high officials of the imperial court, hoping
they could bring to bear influence on Michael: epp. 419, 420, 424–6. Theodore may have
written these letters from Pteleae, where he had stayed some while, after having travelled
there from Smyrna via Xerolopha and Λάκκου Μιτάτα: *Vita B*, 304D. From Pteleae he
journeyed to the region around Prusa, namely Bithynian Olympos, and then on to
Chalcedon where he met the old exiled patriarch: *Vita B*, 316BC. Theodore seems to have
travelled along the coastal road from Smyrna. Cf. Bury, *Eastern Roman Empire*, 112 and
Fatouros, *Prolegomena*, 18*.

appointed. Michael was claiming to be Leo's legitimate successor and it would not have been politically expedient suddenly to reverse his policies. Besides, it is quite possible that he himself, although outwardly a Christian, held Athingan sympathies, having perhaps even belonged to this puritanical sect, which held much in common with Judaism, including an antipathy to religious images.[360] Michael's declared policy was to have no policy. He suggested, by way of compromise to the deposed Patriarch Nikephoros,[361] that all three synods of 754, 787, and 815 be put out of mind and that there should be no open discussion for or against images.[362] Previously he had suggested that a compromise be reached through an open discussion between the returned exiles, including both bishops and abbots, and the iconoclast hierarchy. Theodore wrote on behalf of the returned exiles respectfully refusing a debate, but suggesting that the pope be asked to arbitrate.[363] He also attended a meeting with the emperor, where he represented Patriarch Nikephoros, and once again refused on principle to meet the heretics or to have a compromise imposed from without. Instead, detailed arguments refuting, point by point, the iconoclast position were presented. At this the emperor, unimpressed, declared that he himself had never venerated icons and that he intended to leave things as they were. Iconophiles would be tolerated, but only outside the city of Constantinople. Dismayed, Theodore and his group left the city and headed for Bithynia. They were to remain exiles.[364] 'The winter is past,' he commented, 'but spring has yet to come.'[365] 'Those who don't accept images don't accept Christ . . . the truth is clear but only one in a thousand understands it.'[366] He and his Stoudite monks settled temporarily at a monastery in the Crescens (Kreskentiu) region on

---

[360] Treadgold, *The Byzantium Revival*, 225, 229, 230.

[361] The iconoclast Patriarch Theodotos had died at about the same time as Michael's accession to the throne and the emperor was now willing to negotiate a return of the former patriarch, but on his own terms.

[362] *Vita Nicephori*, ed. de Boor, 209–10; *Theophanes Continuatus*, ed I. Bekker, 47–8.

[363] Ep. 429. Cf. *PC* 116, *PC* 127.

[364] *PC* 19. 59, *PC* 48. 133, *PC* 75. 195, *PC* 83. 212. Theodore notes with intense disapproval how other monasteries went along with Emperor Michael's compromise: *PC* 92. 233–4.

[365] Ep. 469. 35–6.

[366] *PC* 15. 48. He continues by commenting on how the iconoclasts of the period could be divided into two categories: 'one category never puts the image of Christ up on a stand; the other category does, but like a trophy of war or of a hunt'.

the Gulf of Nikomedia, where he had been prior to his trip to Constantinople.[367] They were to remain in constant fear of persecution.[368]

When Michael became emperor a rival contender, with equal claim to the throne, was simultaneously acclaimed. This was Thomas the Slav, an old friend of Leo V from the Anatolikon theme, who presented himself as Leo's avenger. Civil war ensued, dividing the empire practically in two, and lasting until spring 824, with Michael successfully gaining control of the whole Empire.[369] Theodore, who did not show any particular sympathy for Thomas's cause, was none the less recalled to the capital in the spring of 822, along with other iconophile abbots and bishops, as a measure of precaution to prevent them from rallying to the enemy.[370] Thomas had control of the areas surrounding the capital and now laid siege to the capital itself. By winter of that year the siege was raised, although the war continued, and Theodore was permitted to return to Crescens, where he remained until the summer. Once again he was forced to transfer elsewhere, this time because of an invasion by Arabs in alliance with Thomas.[371] He sailed to the isle of Prinkipo, where other refugees had gathered, and remained until the autumn, whence he embarked for the Tryphon monastery on Cape Akritas, situated between Nikomedia

---

[367] *Vita B*, 316D–318D.

[368] *PC* 14. 46–7, *PC* 49. 138, *PC* 51. 140, *PC* 61. 162, *PC* 86. 218. It would appear from *PC* 84 that Theodore did not commemorate the emperor in the liturgy; he recognizes that this omission, especially if done in the city, was dangerous.

[369] Treadgold, *The Byzantium Revival*, 228–44; Bury, *Eastern Roman Empire*, 84–110. An imperial propaganda machine was put into motion after Thomas and his supporters had been defeated. Thomas was portrayed as a rebel and his cause as a rebellion against the legitimate ruler. A long iambic poem, *Against Thomas*, was written by Ignatios the Deacon, and this helped propagate the distortion of fact. Cf. Treadgold, *The Byzantium Revival*, 244–5; P. Lemerle, 'Thomas le Slave'. *TM* 1 (1965), 255–97. References to the civil war are found in *PC* 94 and *PC* 97.

[370] *Vita B*, 317D–320A; ep. 478. 26–46 (for Theodore's opinion of the civil war). Although a friend of Leo's, Thomas promised to be all things to all men. Michael had appointed Bishop Anthony Cassimates, who had led the second iconoclast commission in 814, to the vacant patriarchal throne (spring, 821). Iconophile defection to Thomas was therefore a real fear.

[371] Ep. 475. 3 ff.; ep. 512. 2–8. Allusions to the Arab raid are also to be found in *PC* 43, *PC* 99, and *PC* 124. Cf. C. van de Vorst, 'La Petite Catéchèse de S. Théodore Studite', *AB* 33 (1919), 40–1; Treadgold, *The Byzantium Revival*, 241. M.-H. Congourdeau, *Théodore Stoudite: Petites Catéchèses* (Paris, 1993), 106 n. 62, is mistaken in assuming the reference in *PC* 43 is to the Arab raid of 798. Theodore's biographer does not mention this raid at all.

and Chalcedon.[372] The civil war had now effectively ended, with the surrender and execution of Thomas. It would take the emperor just a few more months to secure a total victory. It seems the emperor also wished to come to a conciliatory agreement with Theodore, but once again this was refused on the grounds that to decide issues of doctrine either a legitimate local synod, with Nikephoros as head, would have to be summoned, or an ecumenical synod with all patriarchates represented.[373]

One other issue led Theodore to be dismayed at the unorthodoxy of his ruler. Late in the civil war Thekla, Michael's wife, died. Pressure was put on him by his imperial entourage to take another wife. For political reasons Michael chose Euphrosyne, a child of the first marriage of Constantine VI to Maria of Amnia. Risking confrontation with the church, he removed her from her monastery on Prinkipo where she had been a nun for several years. Theodore seems to have been alone among iconophiles to have condemned this act of sacrilege.[374]

By the middle of the year 826 the health of the 66-year-old Theodore had rapidly deteriorated. For many years he had suffered periodically from illnesses; even before the revival of iconoclasm and his long imprisonment he had almost died through sickness.[375] He dictated his last Catechesis on 4 November 826.[376] It is not known when he left his monastery of St Tryphon, but on Sunday 11 November, on the feast day of St Menas, he died whilst

---

[372] On the Tryphon monastery, see Janin, *Les Églises et les monastères*, 55–6. Before moving to his new destination Theodore travelled to Chalcedon where, after a brief illness, he paid another visit to the aged Patriarch Nikephoros: ep. 475. 7 ff.; *Vita B*, 320B.

[373] The only source for this is ep. 478 (*ann.* 823) to Leo Sakellarios. The latter was charged by the emperor with negotiations, and this letter could be interpreted as Theodore's rejection of a new offer to meet with the iconoclasts. See Bury, *Eastern Roman Empire*, 116. Another letter was written by Theodore, explaining iconophile doctrine, to the emperor and his junior emperor Theophilos in 826: ep. 532.

[374] *PC* 74. 192–3 (Theodore recalls the upheaval and persecution that followed on Constantine VI's illegal wedding, and prepares his monks for another time of persecution.) Cf. ep. 514, to Euphrosyne's mother, Maria, urging her not to attend the imperial wedding. The letter dates from the end of 823 to the beginning of 824.

[375] PK 118. 882–3. References to ill-health are to be found in TC I. 44. 558; *MC* 33. 91 (Theodore is ill 'again'); *MC* 41. 113 (he is suffering 'intolerable pains'); PK 7. 39 (could not give Catechesis due to illness). In this last period of his life references to old age and illness are found in *PC* 37 (sudden illness), *PC* 90, *PC* 111, *PC* 126. In *PC* 31. 90 Theodore states that he is feverish. This was his last Catechesis.

[376] *PC* 31 was reproduced in part by Naukratios in his encyclical: *PG* 99. 1841A.

at a monastery on Prinkipo.[377] Naukratios, his close disciple and successor as elected *hegoumenos*, described his last words in an encyclical letter written perhaps just a few weeks after the event: 'Give heed to the Testament which I have left you. Keep your faith unshaken and your life pure.'[378]

Theodore the Stoudite had lived through eight imperial reigns and had reached his ninth; he had been a monk for some forty-five years and abbot for thirty-two. He had been in exile for more than fifteen years—a third of all his years as a monk. Accepted by his own as a confessor of the faith, Theodore inspired many others to follow his example. His stature within monastic circles as a leader, as a teacher and as a defender of Gospel values was enormous. As a monastic reformer, his contribution to the Byzantine Church was unique and long-lasting.[379] He did not live to see the solemn restoration of icon veneration,[380] but his remains were given a triumphant translation to the Stoudios monastery on 26 January 844 as a symbol of gratitude for having valiantly championed the iconophile cause. There he was buried next to his spiritual father Plato and his brother Joseph.[381]

---

[377] *Vita B*, 325D–328A, followed by the other *Vitae*, states that Theodore died at the Tryphon monastery and that his body was then immediately taken to Prinkipo. The encyclical written by Naukratios, on the other hand, which was written immediately after the death, and which was witnessed by its author, says nothing of a transferral to Prinkipo. Van de Vorst has argued convincingly that Theodore's biographer, Michael, was mistaken: 'La Translation de S. Théodore Studite', 30–4. On the date of Theodore's death, cf. ibid. 31. Theodore was not quite 67 when he died: *Vita B*, 321D.

[378] *Naucratii Confessoris Encyclica* 1844B; *Vita B*, 325A.

[379] See above. His defence of the inviolability of the marriage bond, however, was not hailed in later tradition. Can this be associated with the later ecclesiastical sanction of divorce and remarriage and/or an acceptance of an interpretation of *oikonomia* that would have been foreign to Theodore?

[380] The Triumph of Orthodoxy, First Sunday of Lent, 843. On this day the *Synodicon of Orthodoxy* was read for the first time. Starting with iconoclasm, this document lists and condemns heresies and their propagators and praises the defenders of Orthodoxy. Theodore is one of the many who are listed for defending the true doctrine of icons: Θεοδώρου τοῦ πανοσίου ἡγουμένου τῶν Στουδίου αἰωνία ἡ μνήμη. Text in J. Gouillard, 'Le synodikon de l'Orthodoxie', in *TM* 2 (1967), 53, line 127. It is significant that in the text of the Synodikon Theodore's rather strong doctrine of the presence of the archetype *in* the material image, and therefore the presence of sanctifying grace *in* the image, is absent. Theodore's contribution to Orthodoxy, therefore, was not so much a theological contribution as a valiant defence of the principles established at the Second Council of Nicaea. Cf. ibid. 181.

[381] *Vita B*, 328A; *Vita Nicolai Studitae*, PG 105. 904B; van de Vorst, 'La Translation de Théodore Studite', 27.

1.10 THEODORE'S WRITINGS

Theodore's writings were assembled into a corpus in the years following his death. Of early ninth-century authors he is the most prolific and, because of his concern with day-to-day matters and the political and ecclesiastical events of his time, of the greatest importance to the ninth-century historian. His style was highly personal. It was direct and, for the most part, simple and he was not afraid to express his feelings as well as his thought. The purpose of his writing was usually practical, not literary, and he knew that he was often dealing with monks with little education. The most important and influential of Theodore's writings were his Catecheses and letters. He also composed homilies and orations, dogmatic, poetic, and liturgical works and shorter pieces directly to do with his monastic reform.

1.10.1 *The Parva Catechesis (Μικρὰ Κατήχησις).*

The first work commented on by Michael, Theodore's biographer, is a collection composed of 134 pieces, τῶν Μικρῶν Κατηχήσεων. At the time he wrote (after 868) extracts from this book were read three times a week to the Stoudite community.[382] The modern designation μικρὰ κατήχησις was unknown to Michael, but oral tradition designated the volume in this way as a matter of convenience.[383] Neither is this title to the collection to be found in the manuscript tradition.[384] Indeed, it may be that Theodore himself used the term κατηχητική for each of his monastic allocutions,[385] but whatever the case, contrary to what is stated in his biography, he did not collect them into volumes.[386]

---

[382] *Vita B*, 264A. Cf. *Hypotyposis* 1709C, where it states that the reading is done after Orthros on Sunday, Wednesday, and Friday.

[383] Cf. *Vita A*, 152C.

[384] Leroy, 'Les Petites Catèchèses de S. Théodore Studite', *Le Muséon*, 71 (1958), 329–37; idem, *Études sur les 'Grand Catéchèses' de S. Théodore Studite*, 24. Even 'small Catecheses', in the plural form, is unknown to the early MS tradition, appearing first in a MS of the 14th cent.

[385] As can be argued from the titles of his Catecheses found in the collection of his letters (epp. 381, 382, 433, 457, 473, 480, 488, 503).

[386] Leroy, 'Les Petites Catéchèses', 352 and *passim*; idem, 'Études', 23. The fact that *PC* 31 was dictated on Theodore's deathbed is proof enough that the collection could not have been put together by Theodore himself.

The modern title used in a critical edition is thus somewhat of an anomaly.

Michael also tells us that these Catecheses differ from the collections τῶν Μεγάλων Κατηχήσεων in that they were delivered hastily and were dictated, whereas the latter were written and more carefully composed.[387] Yet there is no evidence for such an assertion. Indeed, as Hausherr and Leroy have pointed out, the *Parva Catechesis* is distinguished by its more careful composition and its more refined and *recherché* style.[388] Nor is there any evidence in Theodore's writings for an office or ministry of a personal secretary, which surely would otherwise have been essential.[389] Furthermore, the adjective 'small' as opposed to 'great' is not a true reflection of the length of the individual Catecheses, which cannot be adequately differentiated using this criterion. Rather, it reflects that this collection of 134 pieces was smaller in size than the combined three-volume collection of the *Magna Catechesis*.[390] The selection making up the *Parva Catechesis* was dictated by its liturgical use, and it achieved great popularity as a result. Its popularity also explains why Michael speaks of it as the 'first' book of the Catecheses, despite its later composition, between 821 and 826.[391]

Volume 99 of Migne, devoted to the works of Theodore, gives an almost exclusively Latin translation of this work (509–688), which was prepared by J. Livineius in 1602.[392] The Greek text (with a new Latin translation) was edited by J. Cozza-Luzi in 1882,[393] but a better edition, using a much broader manuscript

[387] Leroy, 'Les Petites Catéchèses' ibid.

[388] Hausherr, *S. Théodore Studite*, 82; Leroy, 'Études', 15 n. 32.

[389] Theodore is otherwise exhaustive in his list of major ministries. The one exception we know of is when, on his deathbed, he dictated his last Catechesis: *Vita B*, 324A; *Naucratii Confessoris Encyclica*, 1836C. Cf. Leroy, 'Études', 19.

[390] Cf. Leroy, 'Études', 25, and idem', Les Petites Catéchèses', 136. The Great Catechesis often does have longer pieces but there are too many exceptions to warrant a rigid division along these lines. In the 'Études', Leroy emphasizes this fact more than in his earlier work. The true difference between the *PC* and the Great Catechesis lies in chronology. See below.

[391] *Vita B*, 264A. Whereas the MSS for the Great Catechesis are relatively rare, there are more than 70 pre–16th cent. MSS of the *PC*, most dating to the 12th cent., and some 160 in total: Leroy, 'Les Petites Catéchèses', 336 n. 35; M.-H. Congourdeau, 'Théodore Stoudite', in *DS* 15 (1990), 403. For the date of composition, see C. van de Vorst, *La Petite Catéchèse de S. Théodore Studite*, *AB* 32 (1914), 31–51. For the liturgical use, see Leroy, 'Les Petites Catéchèses', 345–53.

[392] The title is *Ad Discipulos Catechesis*. Greek texts are given with sermones 65, 114, and 125, and fragments with nos. 2, 9, and 69.

[393] *Sancti Theodori Studitae sermones parvae catecheseos*, in A. Mai, NPB 9/1 (Rome, 1888).

base, was produced by E. Auvray in 1891.[394] A reprint of this rare
Auvray text was made in Thessalonica in 1984,[395] and it is this that
is being used for this study.[396] A French translation based on the
Auvray text was produced in 1993.[397]

1.10.2 The Magna Catechesis (Μεγάλη Κατήχησις)

As with the *Parva Catechesis*, this title is unknown to the manuscript
tradition and is shorthand, developed through oral tradition, for
the greater or larger collection of Theodore's Catecheses.[398] The
Vita speaks of three such volumes written by Theodore, implying
that they were to be read privately rather than being delivered
orally.[399] It seems that in the second half of the ninth century these
works, unlike the *Parva Catechesis*, were consulted privately by
monks in the library, but they were rarely made public.[400] The
style of these Catecheses is closer to the spoken language than the
Parva Catechesis, and were in fact pronounced,[401] but by a younger
and more hurried abbot than that of the *Parva Catechesis*, leaving a
'décousu ordinaire' in the allocutions.[402] The *Magna Catechesis* differs fundamentally from the *Parva Catechesis* only in belonging to an

---

[394] Τοῦ ὁσίου πατρὸς ἡμῶν καὶ ὁμολογητοῦ Θεοδώρου ἡγουμένου τῶν
Στουδίου μικρὰ κατήχησις. *Sancti patris nostri confessoris Theodori Studitis praepositi parva catechesis* (Paris, 1891).

[395] Τοῦ ὁσίου πατρὸς ἡμῶν καὶ ὁμολογητοῦ Θεοδώρου ἡγουμένου τῶν
Στουδίου μικρὰ κατήχησις, ed. Nikodimos Skretta, ᾿Ορθόδοξος Κυψέλη, II
(Thessalonica, 1984).

[396] Unfortunately the pagination does not correspond to Auvray's printed edition, nor
are there line numbers. There are occasional omissions (e.g. some lines missing in *PC* 15 and
PC 18). With these caveats I have judged it acceptable to use this Thessalonica edition,
although keeping the Auvray Latin designation of *PC* (*Parva Catechesis*) when quoting from
the text. For a more detailed account of the editions of the *PC*, see Fatouros, *Prolegomena*,
21*–4*.

[397] *Théodore Stoudite: Petites catéchèses* trans. Anne-Marie Mohr. Introduction, notes, bibliography, thematic index, and glossary by Marie-Hélène Congourdeau, 'Les Pères dans la
foi' (Paris, 1993). Note the more correct plural form in the title.

[398] Vita *A*, 152D speaks of the Μεγάλη Κατηχητική. Vita *B*, 264B refers to the more
correct Μεγάλαι Κατηχήσεις. The Latin form Magna Catechesis (MC) is my own
designation; it translates the Greek singular form exactly and complements Auvray's
terminology.

[399] *Vita B*, 264A.

[400] This is reflected in the very poor MS tradition. For a discussion, see J. Leroy, 'Un
nouveau témoin de la Grande Catéchèse', 73–5; 'Études', *passim*.

[401] Cf. TC I. 63. 614 (Theodore normally pronounces his Catechesis but on this occasion he sends a letter); PK 38. 276 (= *MC* 40. 112) (Theodore reads his Catechesis).

[402] Hausherr, *S. Théodore Studite*, 81–2.

earlier period of Theodore's abbacy. The three books of the manuscript tradition (which do not necessarily correspond to the ninth-
century archetype), each with selections made from a greater
number of original texts, were written between 795 and 814, and
between periods of exile when Theodore could be with his
monks.[403] The style and contents of the Catecheses did not always
commend wider diffusion, certain intimate details of monastic life
being unsuitable for general disclosure.[404] This undoubtedly contributed to its poor manuscript tradition.

According to Leroy's analysis, Book I comprises 87 Catecheses,
dating from 795 to 799/800; Book II, 128 Catecheses, of which 125
are extant, dating from 799/800 to 808/11; Book III, 40
Catecheses, dating from 812 to 813/14. There are 9 additional
Catecheses which are undatable and which Leroy calls *extravagantes*. Furthermore, a few do not seem to fit the chronological context of their particular book.[405] There are therefore 261 extant
sermons from this three-book manuscript tradition. Only one
manuscript, *Patmiacus 111*, from the end of the tenth century, pre-
serves the integral text of Book I.[406] Book II is found in almost
complete form in the same manuscript.[407] Book III is found in
only two manuscripts, *Patmiacus 112*, from the end of the tenth century, and *Ambrosianus E 101 sup.* from the twelfth century. The small
number of Catecheses in this third book suggest that only a selection from this book has been preserved. The *extravagantes*, eight of
which are found in only one manuscript, the *Parisinus graecus 891*,
from the twelfth century, suggests that the other books are also
incomplete. It is impossible to know exactly the original number in
these books, let alone the original number of Theodore's
Catecheses. It is known that he gave a Catechesis three times a

---

[403] Hausherr, *S. Théodore Studite*, 76–86; Leroy, 'Études', 85 and *passim*.

[404] For example, what Theodore says on particular friendships and παρρησία, or exces-
sive familiarity, which may lead to homosexuality. The style is improvised and expressions
can also be coarse. There are also errors present which may not be due to scribal negli-
gence. See Leroy, 'Études', 15–17.

[405] Ibid. 22–9, 86–100. Cf. Hatlie, 'Abbot Theodore', 499–500, who also had access to
this unpublished text.

[406] Catechesis 1, however, is missing but is supplied by other MSS.

[407] The most complete MS is the 12th-cent. Baroccianus 130 of the Bodleian Library. It
was copied from a mutilated copy, probably the same as the model used for Patmiacus 111.
In the Baroccianus MS n. 14 is incomplete and the next three are missing. Patm. 111 ignored
nos. 14–17 and gave a continuous numbering, making 124. The model had 128.

week, once his reforms had been fully accepted,[408] but it is also
known that some fifteen years of his thirty-two years of abbacy
were spent outside his normal community. This leaves more than
fifteen years within his community.[409] Making various allowances
for illness, absences, etc., a quick mental calculation reveals that
the number of morning Catecheses must have been very high.
Leroy gives a conservative estimate of at least 1,500.[410] This means
that, even with the *Parva Catechesis* included, only about 26 per cent
of the original number remains today.

The only satisfactory edition of the *Magna Catechesis* is of Book II,
undertaken by A. Papadopoulos-Kerameus in 1904.[411] Basing
himself primarily on *Patmiacus 111*, he edited 124 Catecheses.[412]
Like Auvray's text, this edition is extremely rare.[413] A reprint of the
text, although with more economical spacing (523 pages compared
to the original 991!), was made in 1987 in Thessalonica.[414] The
reprinting has so many errors, however, that its use as a critical text
is hazardous.[415]

Cozza-Luzi had also produced an edition of 111 Great
Catecheses, based entirely on one manuscript, the twelfth-century

[408] Leroy, 'Études', 7–13. Cf. above, n. 203.

[409] Not including his time at the Tryphon monastery where he gave his Parva
Catechesis.

[410] Leroy, 'Études', 13–15.

[411] Designated as *PK*: Τοῦ ὁσίου Θεοδώρου τοῦ Στουδίτου Μεγάλη Κατήχησις.
Βιβλίον δεύτερον, ἐκδοθὲν ὑπὸ τῆς Αὐτοκρατορικῆς Ἀρχαιογραφικῆς Ἐπιτροπῆς
(St Petersburg, 1904). No mention of the editor is actually made either on the cover or
within the book. Catecheses 52–74 are in fact letters, demonstrating that it was chronology
rather than literary genre that determined the content of the book. See also below, on the
letters.

[412] The other extant Catechesis of this book, the incomplete no. 14 of Barrocianus 130,
remains unedited. Papadopoulos-Kerameus worked, in fact, with a copy of the Patmos MS
made by the monk Amphilochios of the monastery of St Panteleimon on Mt. Athos, and
with the notes made by Alexander Thadeev of the Imperial Russian Archeological Institute
of Constantinople who went to Patmos to consult the original MS. As a result of not having consulted the original himself, some errors, transmitted by these two sources, crept into
his text. Nine omissions from the original text have been noted by Leroy. For details, see
Leroy, *Les Petites Catecheses*, 338–43.

[413] I have been fortunate to obtain a photycopy from the Pontifical Oriental Institute in
Rome. When Paul J. Alexander wrote *The Patriarch Nicephorus* in 1958, he was constrained to
use the Russian translation in Makarius' *Velikia Minei Chetii*, first published in St Peterburg,
1897, repr. 1904. See Alexander, *The Patriarch Nicephorus*, 84 n. 84. Alexander seems to suggest that it is Papadopoulos-Kerameus' text that he is citing, which is thoroughly misleading.

[414] Τοῦ ὁσίου Θεοδώρου τοῦ Στουδίτου Μεγάλη Κατήχησις. Βιβλίον δεύτερον.
ed. Nikodimos Skretta, Ὀρθόδοξος Κυψέλη, I (Thessalonica, 1987).

[415] Cf. the observations made by Leroy, *Les Petites Catecheses*, 343–5. Twenty-nine omissions from the PK edition are noted. In this study PK is used.

Parisinus graecus 891. It was published in two parts, 1–77 in 1888, 78–111 in 1905.[416] Papadopoulos-Kerameus had been aware of the first volume where he found twenty-four corresponding Catecheses. The second volume, which appeared after his own work, contained another sixteen overlapping Catecheses, making a total of forty.[417] Catechesis 26 is in fact identical to *Parva Catechesis* 100. The remaining Catecheses (111–41 = 70) are taken from Books I and III, eight being *extravagantes*. These books remain unedited, although a complete new edition of the entire collection of Great Catecheses has been announced.[418] Therefore, of 261 extant Catecheses 194 have been published (124+70), leaving sixty-seven unedited. One of these is an *extravagans* and one other is from Book II. Of the remaining sixty-five, sixty-two have been published in Russian translation, in the *Tvorenija prepodobnago otsa nashego i ispovidnyka Feodorja Studitja v russkom perevod*, 2 vols. (St Petersburg, 1907). This translation was based on *Patmiacus 111* and *Patmiacus 112*, as copied by the monk Amphilochios and kept at the Russian monastery of Saint Pantelomeion on Mt. Athos.[419] Because this is the only complete published version of Books I and III, albeit in translation, it is of some value to scholars.[420] For this reason Table 1 indicates where the texts correspond to Cozza-Luzi, thus enabling the determination of the unedited texts.

Thirty-eight texts of Book I have therefore been edited by Cozza-Luzi. The remaining forty-nine are unedited. These are 2, 3, 4, 5, 8, 9, 11, 12, 13, 15, 23, 26, 27, 28, 30, 31, 33, 35, 36, 38, 41, 44, 45, 47, 49, 50, 51, 52, 53, 54, 55, 57, 58, 59, 60, 61, 63, 64, 65, 66, 67, 70, 73, 74, 78, 80, 81, 84, 87. These unedited texts are in volume i of the *Tvorenija* and correspond exactly with Leroy's own unpublished

[416] A. Mai, NPB 9/2 (Rome, 1888); NPB 10/1 (Rome, 1905).

[417] Cf. P. O'Connell, 'The Letters and Catecheses of St Theodore Studites', *OCP* 38 (1972), 257–9. The 40 identical Catecheses are given in table form.

[418] By A. Kambylis and G. Fatouros. Cf. M.-H. Congourdeau, *Théodore Stoudite, DS* 15 (1990), 404.

[419] Cf. above, n. 412. *Tvorenija*, i. pp. vii–viii. At *Tvorenija* ii. p. iii the editor states that Book III (which in this translation has 46 Catecheses, 7 of which are Leroy's *extravagantes*) is based on *Patm.* 111. This must be a printing error. *Patm.* 111 contains only books I and II. *Patm.* 112 contains Book III.

[420] Although rare, copies are held by e.g. the libraries of St Vladimir's Russian Orthodox Seminary in Crestwood, New York, and the Pontifical Oriental Institute in Rome. The translation is reliable. Another Russian work, *Dobrotolubie v russkom perevod* (Philokalia in Russian translation), vol. iv (Moscow, 1889; repr.: 1901), a work kindly lent to me by Bishop Kallistos Ware, also has unedited texts. A cursory examination revealed 44 identifiable unedited Catecheses of Book I.

Table 1. *Relationship of Cozza-Luzi texts to Book I of the Great Catecheses*

Book I	Cozza-Luzi
1	102
6	49
7	85
10	106
14	17
16	80
17	79
18	60
19	45
20	48
21	47
22	61
24	74
25	62
29	68
32	108
34	89
37	95
39	52
40	72
42	16
43	41
46	2
48	39
56	42
62	15
68	58
69	22
71	43
72	1
75	77
76	67
77	38 (= PK 26)
79	12
82	64
83	78
85	83
86	25

critical Greek text (which was in its early stages before the
author died). In volume ii of the *Tvorenija* only thirty-eight of the
forty Catecheses of Book III are given. The editors published forty-
six, but one is a duplicate of Book I and seven are *extravagantes*.
Table 2 is an analysis of *Tvorenija* Book III (*extravagantes* given with
asterisk).

Table 2. *Analysis of* Tvorenija *Catecheses Book III*

Tvorenija Catecheses Book III	Cozza-Luzi
1	50
2	35
4*	84*
5	90
6*	96*
7	92
9	16 (= Book I, 42)
10	99
11*	7*
12*	28*
13	71
14	65
15	93
17	46
22	59
23	21
25	30
26*	33*
27	34
28	36
29	53
30	82
32	81
33	18
35	9
36	66
37	6
38	75
41	51
42*	56*
43	63
44*	69*
45	76

Thus there are thirteen unedited texts, namely 3, 8, 16, 18, 19, 20, 21, 24, 31, 34, 39, 40, 46. With this analysis all Cozza-Luzi's texts have also been accounted for.[421]

1.10.3 The Letters of Theodore

Theodore's letters are without doubt the most important part of his corpus of literary works. In them he displays his character and personality, his literary ability, his theological ideas, and his relations with a wide range of people, ranging from disciples and friends to emperors and patriarchs. He wrote a great number of letters over a period of thirty years, often writing and receiving several letters each day. Over half of these are now lost. He considered it a duty to write frequently, especially in times of persecution and difficulty, in order—in the words of his biographer—to sustain others in their faith, thereby living out the divine commandment to love others.[422] He looked on St Cyprian, St Basil the Great, and especially the Apostle Paul as models for this epistolary activity.[423] His letters can be divided into six categories, according to theme and tone. One group of about forty consists of open letters to iconoclasts and to monasteries. Ten of these are actually Catecheses.[424] Another group is devoted to dogmatic and moral issues. A third and fourth group, where the influence of the epistolary style of St Basil is apparent, consist of letters of consolation and letters to monks who have abandoned their vocation. A fifth group, of most interest to historians, is of letters to individuals of high authority, including the emperor and pope. Finally, the largest part of the collection consists of letters to friends and acquaintances, disciples, and fellow-sufferers.[425]

---

[421] Cozza-Luzi 70 is an *extravagans*. I have not reproduced the PK–Cozza-Luzi correspondence as this is not pertinent to the subject at hand. Tables in O'Connell, 'Letters and Catecheses', 259.

[422] Cf. *Naucratii Confessoris Encyclica* 1829A; ep. 104. 18 ff.

[423] Fatouros, *Prolegomena*, 39*.

[424] Epp. 381, 382, 406, 410, 433, 457, 473, 480, 488, 503 (ep. 69, which is entitled a catechesis, is not one in the monastic sense of the *PC* and *MC*). The incorporation of these Catecheses in this collection of letters, much as the incorporation of letters in the collection of Catecheses, indicates that the collections were made on chronological criteria, more than on literary form.

[425] Fatouros, *Prolegomena*, 39*–41*.

Copies of letters were made before they were sent out, being then collected into five books.[426] These volumes were recopied, the latter being the archetype for an anthology made after Theodore's death which selected from each book.[427] The volumes that we have today were preserved as a legacy in Stoudite monastery libraries. G. Fatouros has produced an excellent critical edition of the letters, with thorough notes, summaries of the letters, commentaries, and analyses.[428] Prior to the appearance of this edition scholars were required to consult the editions of Cozza-Luzi, in Angelo Mai, and Sirmond, reproduced in Migne.[429] An analysis of these works would now be of only historical interest.[430]

Fatouros provides the text of 557 letters, three of which are of doubtful authenticity.[431] Among the letters he includes one, of probable authenticity, overlooked by previous students of Theodore.[432] The titles and probable titles of seven lost letters are also given.[433]

1.10.4 Other Writings

Apart from the Catecheses and letters Theodore composed a number of other works which have survived. In the introduction to

[426] Cf. *Vita B*, 264D. ep. 26. 42; Fatouros, *Prolegomena*, 42* and n. 8.

[427] The *Codex Parisinus Coislinianus 269*, from the 9th-cent., is directly dependent on the original Stoudite corpus and anthology. See Fatouros, *Prolegomena*, 42*; 43*–6*, and 119* where he shows the Stemma Codicum.

[428] *Theodori Studitae Epistulae, Corpus Fontium Historiae Byzantinae*, Series Berolinensis, 31/1, 31/2 (Berlin, 1992).

[429] A. Mai, NPB 8/1 (1871); *PG* 99. 903–1669. Also R. Devreesse, 'Une lettre de S. Théodore Studite', 54–7 (which provided the full text of an incomplete letter in *PG* 99. 2. 221); J. Gill, 'An Unpublished Letter of St Theodore Studite', *OCP* 34 (1968), 66–7.

[430] Dobroklonskij, *Prepodobnij Feodor*, is the real pioneer of work on the letters, together with B. Melioranski: *Perechen vizantiiskikh gramot i pisem I. Dokumenti 784–850 godov. Vedenie. Nieskolko slov o rukopisakh i izdaniakh pisem prepodnago Feodora Studita* (records of the Imperial Academy of Sciences, IV. 5) (St Petersburg, 1899). A useful short account (although now dated) is Bury, *Eastern Roman Empire*, Appx. 1, 451–2; O'Connell, 'Letters and Catecheses', 256–7; Hatlie, 'Abbot Theodore', 492–8; M.-H. Congourdeau, *Théodore Stoudite*, 404. The 2-book arrangement of Sirmond and Migne is based on *Vat. gr. 1432*, 12th cent., which does not correspond to the original. Sirmond also consulted *Paris gr. 894*, 14th cent., which has an anthology of four books. This 4-book division is noted in Fatouros' text: ep. 71–380 (Bk. I), 381–429 (Bk. II), 430–506 (Bk. III), 507–64 (Bk. IV). [431] Epp. 557–9.

[432] Ep. 560, extracted from V. Laurent, 'La Vie merveilleuse de Saint Pierre d'Atroa (+837)', *Subsidia Hagiographica*, 29 (Brussels, 1956), 147–9.

[433] Epp. 45–7, 561–4. There are thus 564 known letters (557 + 7 titles). In this collection Fatouros also adds the *Epistola ad Platonem*, *PG* 99. 500–5 (= ep. 57), which stood separate from Sirmond's edition. Comparative tables of the new with previous editions are provided by Fatouros, *Prolegomena*, 985–93.

his edition of Theodore's letters, Fatouros has also given an exhaustive list, with bibliography, of these other works.[434] From various indications in his extant works we know that some works have not survived. From the era of the moechian controversy the *Tetrades* (Τετράδες),[435] *Pentalogos* (Πεντάλογος),[436] *Considerations on Universal Economy* (Περὶ τῆς καθόλου οἰκονομίας),[437] and another work of *Questions and Answers*[438] have been lost. Likewise from the era of iconoclasm: the *Steliteutikos* (Στηλιτευτικός),[439] *Tetradia* (Τετράδια),[440] a Treatise (Βιβλιδάκιον καὶ τετράδες δεκατέσσαρες),[441] and a book against heresy written in trimetric verse.[442] Theodore's biographer also mentions that he had written a poetic version of parts of the book of Genesis.[443]

Only some homilies and panegyrics, from an original collection (πανηγυρικὴ βίβλος), have survived.[444] Eleven of these have been republished in Migne.[445] Three others have been published elsewhere, and two remain unedited.[446] Theodore's extant dogmatic or polemical works are from the iconoclastic period: *Arguments*

---

[434] Fatouros, *Prolegomena*, 21*–38*. A more succint list, with bibliography, is given by Congourdeau, *Théodore Stoudite*, 403–5.

[435] See ep. 43. 12 ff.　　　[436] Ep. 48. 6.　　　[437] Ep. 49. 63 ff.

[438] Ep. 556. 41.　　　[439] See *PG* 99. 329A.

[440] Epp. 275. 75, 276. 94, 277. 76, 278. 92, 279. 28.　　　[441] Ep. 405. 28 ff.

[442] *Vita A*, 153A.

[443] *Vita B*, 264C. For other lost works, see Fatouros, *Prolegomena*, 38*, nos. 31, 33.

[444] *Vita B*, 264B; *Vita A*, 152D. Homilies delivered on feasts of the Lord and his mother, of John the Forerunner, and other saints were collected in this book.

[445] *PG* 99, 692–901. The first oration of this series, *De Delectu Ciborum*, 688B–692B is in fact a catechesis: PK 31. The homilies in this series are on the adoration of the cross, on the vigil of Theophany (similar in content to PK 27 (= *MC* 32)), on Easter (with an introduction from Pseudo-Chrysostom), on the dormition of the Theotokos (trans. into Italian by M. de Rosa, *La dormizione vitale della Madonna. Panegirici di S. Teodoro Studita . . . Trad. e commentario* (Atessa, 1976), 11–20), on the angels, on the birth of John the Forerunner, on the beheading of John the Forerunner, on John the Evangelist, on the Apostle Saint Bartholomew, eulogy of the Abbot Plato, eulogy of Saint Arsenios the Anchorite, a funeral oration on his mother Theoktista. For bibliography and editions, see Fatouros, *Prolegomena*, 25*–8*.

[446] Unedited texts: BHG 2349t; 2356t. Cf. Fatouros, *Prolegomena*, 28*, nos. xvi, xvii. The other edited homilies are on Theophanes the Confessor, in *AB* 31 (1912), 19–23 (BHG 1792b) and *AB* 111 (1993), 268–84; on the third finding of the head of John the Forerunner, in *PG* 67. 448A–454A; on the birthday of the Theotokos (once attributed to John Damascene), *PG* 96. 680C–697A. See Fatouros, 28*–9*, nos. xiv, xv, xix. Fatouros also lists the speech given to Leo V in *Vita B*, 280C–281B, 284A, and *Vita A*, 173D–181A (no. xviii). For another possible homily from Theodore, but not listed by Fatouros, see M. van Esbroeck, 'Un Panegyrique de Théodore Studite pour la fête liturgique des sièges de Constantinople', *Studia Anselmiana*, 110 (1993), 525–36. The author argues that Theodore was the author of the lost Greek model of an early Georgian translation. The homily is for Akathistos Saturday, part of which is given in French translation.

against the Iconoclasts (Ἀντιρρητικοὶ κατὰ εἰκονομάχων),[447]
Refutation and Overturning of the Godless Poems (Ἔλεγχος καὶ
ἀνατροπὴ τῶν ἀσεβῶν ποιημάτων),[448] Certain Problems of the
Iconoclasts (Προβλήματά τινα πρὸς εἰκονομάχους),[449] Seven
Chapters against the Iconoclasts (Κατὰ εἰκονομάχων κεφάλαια
ἑπτά).[450]

Theodore's Testament (Διαθήκη) is a rather interesting document.[451] Although it was given to his monks at the end of his life,
it was the product of a document prepared at least twenty years
previously which had undergone subsequent redactions. The main
body of instructions to the *hegoumenos*, for example, is identical to
instructions written in 801–6, ep. 6, to the newly elected *hegoumenos*
Nikolaos. Part of the Testament is a confession of faith that had been
made to Pope Leo III in 809 when Theodore was under attack
from the moechian heretics.[452] Another part of the confession of
faith in the Testament probably dates to between 809 and 815.[453]
There is little that was added after this date and this must have
been the Testament Theodore refers to in a Catechesis prior to
815.[454]

Besides these works there are a number of writings attributed to
Theodore but which are inauthentic, of doubtful authenticity, or

---

[447] *PG* 99. 328–436 (*Antirrhetici adversus iconomachos*). English trans.: C. Roth, *St Theodore the
Studite on the Holy Icons* (New York, 1981).

[448] *PG* 99. 438C–441C (*Refutatio et subversio impiorum poematum*). In this work rare poems of
iconoclasts have been preserved.

[449] *PG* 99. 477–85 (*Quaestiones aliquae propositae iconomachis = Problemata ad iconomachos*).
Iconophile doctrine is given in question and answer form.

[450] *PG* 99. 485–97 (*Adversus iconomachos capita septem*). See ep. 177. 62.

[451] *PG* 99. 1813–24. English trans. (with some errors): N. P. Constas, *Saint Theodore the
Studite: The Testament* (Washington DC, 1991).

[452] *PG* 99. 1816AC; ep. 34. 126–40.

[453] *PG* 99, 1816A: 'I abhor and turn away from every deception of heretical communion,
accepting the six holy ecumenical councils (ταῖς ἁγίαις καὶ οἰκουμενικαῖς ἓξ συνόδοις),
also that which was recently convened for a second time in Nicaea against the accusers of
Christians (ἔτι τε καὶ τὴν ἔναγχος συναθροισθεῖσαν ἐν Νικαίᾳ τὸ δεύτερον κατὰ τῶν
Χριστιανοκατηγόρων).' By 815 Theodore began to refer to the Second Council of Nicaea
as 'holy' (and by implication ecumenical): ep. 71, 14: τῆς ἐν Νικαίᾳ τὸ δεύτερον ἁγίας
συνόδου. In 809, on the other hand, this was not his view (cf. ep. 38, 63–4: ἡ δὲ 'Ρώμη
ταῦτα οὐ προσήκατο [μὴ γένοιτο], ἀλλ' οὐδὲ αὐτὴν τὴν σύνοδον ὡς οἰκουμενικήν,
ἀλλ' ὡς τοπικὴν καὶ τὸ ἴδιον πτῶμα τῶν τῆδε ἀνορθώσασαν). The statement in the
Testament almost certainly reflects this earlier view, otherwise there would be no sense in distinguishing the Nicene Council from the other six in a formal confession of faith.

[454] PK 118. 877. In this Catechesis Plato is still alive (referred to as 'my father and yours')
and therefore it dates to before 4 April 814. Theodore speaks of his grave sickness and
expected death and mentions his *Testament*.

possibly authentic. Those which fall within the first category include the scholion on the Monastic Constitutions, which (erroneously) defends St Basil's authorship, and the explanation of the Liturgy of the Presanctified.[455] Among the works which are posterior to Theodore, or probably so, but which are faithful to his spirit are the *Constitutions* ('Υποτύπωσις),[456] *On Confession (Περὶ ἐξαγορεύσεως)*,[457] *Questions and Answers on Penance (Περὶ ἐρωτήσεως)*,[458] the *Four Chapters (Κεφάλαια τέσσαρα)*[459] and the *Epitimia ('Επιτίμια)*.[460] The *Didascalia (Διδασκαλία χρονική)* is of doubtful authenticity.[461] Finally, there is an abundant quantity of monastic and liturgical poetry attributed to Theodore.[462]

[455] *PG* 99. 1688–90, *PG* 99. 1685–8 (and *PG* 31. 1319–20). See J. Leroy, *Irénikon*, 52 (1979), 494; R. Taft, *ODB* (1961) iii. 1715.

[456] *PG* 99. 1704–20 (*Constitutiones Studitanae*). Ed. A. A. Dmitrievskij, *Opisanie liturgičeskich rukopisej*, 3 vols. (Kiev, 1915–17), i. 224–38. The preamble expressly states that the *Hypotyposis* forms part of the παράδοσις of Theodore (1704B). Theodore refers to an already developed *hypotyposis* in his own life-time: e.g. in PC 133, 341: καὶ πάντα καθ' ὑπατύπωσιν τῆς ἐκείνου πολιτείας ἐπειχθῶμεν διαπράττεσθαι.

[457] *PG* 99. 1721–9 (*De confessione et pro peccatis satisfactione*). The *De confessione*, as E. Herman has shown ('Il più antico penitenziale greco', *OCP* 19 (1953), 71–127), is a compilation from the first century after Theodore's death (mid–9th cent.—beginning of 10th cent.). It shows dependence on the earliest known Byzantine penitential, the κανονάριον, attributed in one MS tradition to Patriarch John the Faster but more likely to be the work of a certain deacon and monk John. Its *terminus ante quem* is the mid-9th cent. Cf., for text and commentary, M. Arranz, *I Penitenziali Bizantini. Il Protokanonarion o Kanonarion Primitivo di Giovanni Monaco e Diacono e il Deuterokanonarion o 'Secondo Kanonarion' di Basilio Monaco*, Kanonika, 3 (Rome, 1993), 15–129.

[458] *PG* 99. 1729–33 (*Responsiones ad interrogata quaedam*). The authenticity of this tract has not been established as certain. E. Herman, in *Textus selecti ex operibus commentatorum byzantinorum iuris ecclesiastici*, 11 n. 7, suggests that it may be authentic.

[459] *PG* 99. 1681–4 (*Capitula quatuor*). This short work is a compilation of various extracts from the Parva Catechesis. Cf. J. Leroy, 'Les capitula ascetica de S. Théodore Studite', *Revue d'ascétique et de mystique* 27 (1951), 175 ff.

[460] *PG* 99. 1733–57 (*Poenae monasteriales*) (= 110 ἐπιτίμια κοινὰ + 65 καθημερινὰ ἐπιτίμια). Herman, *Textus selecti*, 11, believes that the first part of the *Epitimia* is probably authentic, the second part being a later compilation. Leroy, in 'La Réforme studite', 210–12, with better foundation believes both parts to be posterior to Theodore, although admitting they do substantially reflect what can be found in his writings. He affirms that there are many variants in the MSS.

[461] *PG* 99. 1693–704 (*Catechesis Chronica*). Leroy, 'Études', 57, notes that the Didascalia, which is a Catechesis, is not found in any collection of Catecheses and is transmitted independently in only a few relatively late MSS. See also Herman, *Textus selecti*, 11 n. 5.

[462] Liturgical canons, in *PG* 99. 1757–68 (on the adoration of the cross); 1768–80 (on holy images); J. B. Pitra, *Analecta sacra spicilegio solesmensi parata* (Paris, 1876), i. 336–80. Epigrams or iambs, in *PG* 99. 1780–1812; P. Speck, *Theodoros Studites*. For a more complete list and bibliography, see Fatouros, *Prolegomena*, 32*–6*; Congourdeau, *Théodore Stoudite*, 405; C. Émereau, 'Hymnographi byzantini', *EO* 24 (1925), 177–9, *EO* 25 (1926), 178; H.-G. Beck, *Kirche und theologische Literatur im byzantinischen Reich* (Munich, 1959), 494–5.

With Theodore's biography clarified and placed in full context, and his writings described and classified, his thought can now be examined. The Principles of Order which can be extracted from his writings will form the subject of Part II of this work.

PART II

Principles of Order

2

Obedience and Authority

2.1 INTRODUCTION

The rigorism and intransigence of Theodore of Stoudios are characteristics often described by authors who find it difficult to come to terms with a man who was professedly a genuine monk and yet who was willing to engage in battle with his own superiors and indeed with the highest authorities, ecclesiastical and secular, in the whole empire. Surely this was a sign of arrogance that expressed rigid personality traits, especially in the context of issues that could be resolved by sensible compromise? Undeniably Theodore had a forceful character—even a cursory examination of Theodore's writings reveals this. And yet a fundamental question remains unexamined. Could not this so-called personal rigorism and intransigence be based on religious, specifically monastic, convictions, that formed the rock-solid basis of Theodore's monastic life and monastic reform and therefore were to him unassailable? For if this were the case, and if Theodore understood the issues of his time in genuinely religious terms, then Theodore's rigorism would have been shared in principle by others who were party to these same ideals. This question needs to be examined even for another reason. How, psychologically, could a man who revealed such arrogance and 'disobedience' towards authority, at the same time preach the absolute necessity of obedience to his own monks? Also, how could a rigid and/or politically self-seeking individual at the same time reveal—especially in the Catecheses—the very opposite traits of caring, tenderness, and 'maternal' concern towards his monks and friends? Were the two opposite personality tendencies found in Theodore, making him a hugely complex person?

In the pages to follow it will be argued that there is a consistent logic in Theodore's 'intransigence' and that, furthermore, this intransigence was nothing more than Theodore's interpretation of the exigencies of the Gospel as passed down by the Fathers of the church, especially St Basil. These convictions of faith were at the very heart of Theodore's own reorganization and reform of his monastic followers and can be expressed in the very short formula: 'Obey the commandments.' This in turn ensured the maintenance of that overriding principle—order in the universe.

Byzantine society was a society founded on the principle of order. Secular and ecclesiastical affairs were to be managed in a way that would reflect the order in heaven: 'God compacted the universe in an orderly manner and it was His wish that human life should be led in the same spirit.'[1] Obedience to authority, at the heart of good order, was divinely ordained: 'Let every person be subject to the governing authorities. For there is no authority (ἐξουσία) except from God, and those that exist have been instituted by God' (Rom. 13: 1). It was believed that such obedience to authority led to harmony, well-being, and unity.[2] These were very much the concerns of Theodore the Stoudite throughout the whole of his life. Just as there is unity in the Godhead and one divine authority, he states in an early Catechesis before a situation of disunity in his monastery in which his own authority was being threatened, so should there be a single earthly counterpart to provide unity in church and civil affairs. 'There is one Lord and lawgiver, as it is written, and one rule, one power—the Godhead of all things who is the source of all wisdom, goodness and order (εὐταξίας).' Theodore then goes further, invoking Genesis 1: 26: 'Let us make man in our image and likeness' in order to arrive at the conclusion that authority cannot be divided. As God's creation man also shares his authority, and for this reason there is, 'in the Churches, just one patriarch, one metropolitan in a single metropolis, one bishop in a single bishopric, one hegoumenos in a monastery'. In the secular sphere, he adds, 'there is but one emperor, but one commander of an army, one captain of a ship'.[3]

---

[1] Cyril Mango, *Byzantium. The Empire of the New Rome* (London, 1980), 218 (this is a paraphrased quote taken from the 10th-cent. *Book of the Eparch*). For bibliography on the Byzantine concept of order, see ibid. 319.

[2] Cf. the later formulation of Constantine Porphyrogenitos: '[may] the imperial power, exercising itself with order and measure, reproduce the harmonious movement that the Creator gives to the Universe and Empire' (ὑφ᾽ ὧν τοῦ βασιλείου κράτους ῥυθμῷ καὶ τάξει φερομένου εἰκονίζοι μὲν τοῦ δημιουργοῦ τὴν περὶ τόδε τὸ πᾶν ἁρμονίαν καὶ κίνησιν . . .): A. Vogt (ed.), *Constantin VII Porphyrogénète: Le Livre des Cérémonies* (Paris, 1967), i. Prologue, 1–2.

[3] TC I. 45. 562. Cf. Basil the Great who, concerned about the discord among the leaders of the church of his day, had expressed similar thoughts in the Preface of *De Iudicio Dei*,

The ideal world order, therefore, was monarchic, founded ultimately on the oneness of God. As a consequence, unity and well-
being in society, whether civil, ecclesiastical, or monastic, could be
guaranteed only with hierarchical subjection to legitimate authority, itself subject to the law of God. Being first and foremost a
monk, Theodore's perception of authority, law and obedience was
the perception of a man living within a monastic society that was
organized around evangelical principles and a monastic rule.

In what follows, the role of obedience within Stoudite society
and the nature of the laws to which a monk was subject will be
analysed. Having thus clarified Theodore's thinking on how a true
monastic society should function, his attitudes towards the wider
issues of the church of his day will then be examined, in particular
the Joseph affair which revolved around issues of authority and
order. This will lead on, in a subsequent section, to an examination
of the emperor's role in maintaining divine order.

2.2 MONASTIC OBEDIENCE

A datum of biblical theology and spirituality is that every disorder
in society and every disorder within an individual has as its radical
cause the disobedience of Adam who, transgressing the precept of
God, introduced sin into the world, and with it the fatal disorders
that are the effect of sin (Gen. 3: 12; Rom. 5: 19). Monasticism was
a way for the fervent Christian to learn to undo the act of Adam
by uniting to and imitating Christ who 'humbled himself and
became obedient unto death, even death on a cross' (Phil. 2: 8),
thus becoming 'slaves to righteousness' and not 'slaves to sin', nor
'sons of disobedience' (Rom. 6: 17–18; Eph. 5: 6. Cf. Heb. 3: 18, 4:
6).[4] This was done by submitting to an authority—ultimately
God's authority as mediated by a spiritual guide or/and the commands of a superior and the rules of the monastery. Self-will and

PG 31. 656C: 'Good order with its attendant harmony is characteristic of those who look to
one source of authority and are subject to one king . . . universal disorder and disharmony
are a sign that leadership is wanting.' For a good general introduction to the thought of St
Basil, see P. Rousseau, *Basil of Caesarea* (Oxford, 1994).

[4] *PC* 34. 97; *PC* 111. 281. On the notion of monastic obedience, see e.g. F. Valentine,
Religious Obedience (London, 1951); H. Mogenet, 'L'Obéissance religieuse, vertu évangelique
et humaine', *Revue d'ascétique et de mystique*, 27 (1951), 75–95; T. Špidlik, 'Obedience in Eastern
Church Tradition', *Centrum Ignatianum Spiritualitatis*, 10/2 (1979), 69–74.

the reliance on one's own judgement—considered to be the true obstacles to spiritual freedom and growth—were thereby chastened.[5] In Basilian coenobitic monasticism obedience (ὑκακοή) was of major importance.[6] Differing to some degree from Pachomian spirituality, Basilian spirituality stressed obedience to God's commandments rather than to a rule.[7] The difficulties of living in strict obedience to the commandments—μέχρι θανάτου— rendered the monk a true cross-bearer (σταυροφόρος).[8]

Theodore the Stoudite belonged to this same tradition, although he was still more emphatic than his predecessors about the central importance of obedience. He was 'le grand Docteur de l'obéissance monastique'.[9] A monk of a *koinobion* lived his obedience through subjection or subordination (ὑποταγή)[10] and a coenobite was defined as ὑποτακτίτης, ὑποτακτικός,[11] or ὑποτασσόμενος[12]—terminology not present in Basil's *Asceticon*,

[5] On the importance of a spiritual guide, and submission to his or her judgement, see I. Hausherr, *Direction Spirituelle en Orient Autrefois*, OCA 144 (Rome, 1955); Basil the Great, *Regulae Fusius Tractatae (RF)* 24, 25, 26, 27, 30, 35, 43, 45, 50, 54; *Regulae Brevius Tractatae (RB)* 98, 99, 104, 113, 152, 291 (*PG* 31, *passim*); Dorotheos, Letter 2, *Dorothée de Gaza: Œuvres Spirituelles*, SC 92 (Paris, 1963), 498–505; *Life of Saint Dositheos*, ibid. 122–45; John Klimakos, *The Ladder of Divine Ascent*, Step 4 'On Obedience', in *PG* 88, 677–764 (*The Classics of Western Spirituality* (New York, 1982), 91 ff.).

[6] Basil the Great, *RF* 28.2: *PG* 31. 989B; *RB* 116: *PG* 31. 1081C–1084A. Cf *RB* 1, 60, 74, 119, 137, 138, 152. Cf. Pseudo-Basil, *Constitutiones Monasticae*, ch. 22: *PG* 31. 1402C–1410D. See also D. Amand, *L'Ascèse monastique de Saint Basile de Césarée: Essai Historique* (Maredsous, 1948), 326–31; J. Gribomont, 'Obéissance et Évangile selon saint Basile le Grand', in *Supplément de la Vie Spirituelle*, 5 (1952), 192–215; idem, 'Commandements du Seigneur et libération évangélique: saint Basil', *Studia Anselmiana*, 70 (1977), 81–105.

[7] Amand, *L'Ascèse monastique*, 326. Cf. idem, 'Le Système cénobitique basilien comparé au système cénobitique pachômien', *Revue de l'Histoire des Religions* (1957), 31–80. For the Rule of Pachomios, see Th. Lefort, *Œuvres de saint Pakhôme et des ses disciples*, CSCO (1956), 159–60; A. Boon, *Pachomiana latina* (Louvain, 1932). For further details on Pachomios, see P. Rousseau, *Pachomius: The Making of a Community in Fourth-Century Egypt* (Berkeley, 1985).

[8] Basil, *RF* 28. 2: *PG* 31. 989B; *Introduction to the Ascetical Life*, ibid. 925D: τῷ σταυροφόρῳ βίῳ τῶν μοναχῶν. Cf. Phil. 2: 5–12.

[9] L. Regnault and J. de Préville, SC 92 (Paris, 1963), Introduction, 69.

[10] Although both ὑποταγή and ὑπακοή can be rendered in English as 'obedience' (often the case in this text), the former has the particular nuance of submission, subjection, or subordination ('being under a commander or ruler [ταγός]'), the latter having a more general meaning (from ἀκούω, to listen, give ear to, hear oneself called). Theodore most frequently uses the terms in their distinctive meanings (e.g, in *PC* 95. 239 he speaks of the difficulties of living ὑποταγήν τε καὶ ὑπακοήν—see also *PC* 49. 137, *PC* 131. 336; TC I. 74. 642, PK 2. 11, PK 16. 108, PK 69. 481, etc.). At other times no distinction is discernible.

[11] A term which today refers to novices.

[12] TC I. 9. 480, TC I. 11. 485; *MC* 107. 137; PK 5. 31, PK 11. 74, PK 49. 353, PK 54. 387, PK 91. 650, PK 95. 677, PK 100. 726, PK 109. 805, PK 113. 837; *PC* 17. 54, *PC* 38. 108, *PC* 79. 204, etc.

although found in the New Testament.[13] In becoming a monk one is admitted πρὸς τὴν ὑποταγήν.[14] One makes a profession (ἐπάγγελμα) of obedience.[15] This obedience was truly Christ-imitating,[16] being an interior disposition that went far beyond submission to an exterior command of a superior. It required total commitment, a response of the whole self, with all its interior faculties, μέχρις αἵματος,[17] expressed by placing oneself at the disposition of others and by fulfilling one's duties or διακονία within the community exactly (ἀκριβῶς) according to the rule.[18] Where there is obedience, Theodore states, there is the service of God, there is the illumination of light, there is peace, Satan is absent, and the passions are kept far off.[19] Apart from individual spiritual benefit, living with this submissive attitude led to the smooth and effective running of the monastery. Theodore applies the words of the Apostle Paul (1 Cor. 14: 40): 'All things should be done decently and in order (κατὰ τάξιν)' to those who have different functions within the monastery, urging them to do what is appropriate to their position and calling.[20] The same call to order is given to those slack in obeying the details of the Stoudite rule.[21] On one occasion Theodore complains about the way psalms are sung:

Ever since yesterday I have been annoyed at you on account of the psalmody; I ask and beseech you to sing the psalms in an orderly manner and according to the rules, and not simply haphazardly and confusedly. For this grieves not me, who am a sinner, but the Holy Spirit. He Himself ordained: 'Sing psalms intelligently (Ψάλατε συνετῶς [Ps. 46: 7 LXX]).' Intelligent singing is not served when, in organizing the choir, one does

[13] 2 Cor. 9: 13; Gal. 2: 5; 1 Tim. 2: 11, 3: 4; Eph. 5: 21. Cf. J. Leroy, 'L'Influence de saint Basile sur la réforme studite d'après les catéchèses', *Irénikon*, 52 (1979), 505 n. 42. Leroy notes that many of Theodore's technical terms are taken from Palestinian monasticism, not from Basil.

[14] *PC* 46. 128.   [15] *PC* 125. 318.

[16] MC 7, 18; MC 9, 25 (ὁ δὲ τὴν ὑπακοὴν ἔχων, χριστομίητος); MC 68, 191; PK 15, 98 (τῆς θεομιμήτου ὑπακοῆς); PK 27, 187 (=MC 32, 88) (Christ was obedient ἀνθρωπίνως to his parents for thirty years τυπῶν ἡμῖν τὸ ὑποτακτικόν); PK 47, 341 (=MC 29, 81); PK 113, 836 (=MC 11, 32).

[17] MC 12, 35. Cf. PC 125, 318: Μέχρι θανάτου τὴν ὑπακοὴν ἐπηγγείλω.

[18] TC I. 4. 466; TC I. 28. 524; *PC* 118. 300, *PC* 125, etc.

[19] PK 60. 427.

[20] PK 31. 230 (= *Oratio I, De Delectu Ciborum, PG* 99. 692A), PK 89. 635, PK 112. 826 (monks to keep order while Theodore is away), PK 120. 899. The notion of 'order', based on this same scriptural text, was also important for Basil the Great. See e.g. the passages in his *De Baptismo, PG* 31. 1516A, 1517A, 1520C, 1608C; *RF* I; *PG* 31. 905B–908B.

[21] *PC* 61. 163, *PC* 118. 300; PK 44. 398 (order at table), PK 120. 899. Cf. *MC* 17. 46.

not avoid beginning a verse before the preceding one has finished, or if
the psalmody is too loud or too quiet, or if the rhythm of the verse is
slower [than it should be] or faster. For this often results in slackness and
boredom. Let [each verse] answer the other, and let good order ($\epsilon\dot{\upsilon}\tau\alpha\xi\dot{\iota}\alpha$)
be conserved as much as possible.[22]

Good order is a sign of virtue,[23] lack of order ($\dot{\alpha}\tau\alpha\xi\dot{\iota}\alpha$) and what
is out of place or inordinate ($\tau\dot{\alpha}$ $\ddot{\epsilon}\kappa\tau\sigma\pi\alpha$) being contrary to piety
and associated with the devil.[24] The call to good order is also made
to those individuals who were trying to abandon the coenobitic
vocation God had given them.[25] The very foundation of coenobitic monasticism is shaken if, due to a lack of obedience, there is
disorder.[26]

Theodore explains the value of obedience to his monks by indicating how Christ achieved the economy of salvation through it,
whereas sin and death resulted from its absence in Adam. Then by
referring to various anecdotes from Byzantine hagiography he
shows how dramatic the consequences of one or the other can
be.[27] By obedience one can be enabled to swim safely across a rag-
ing torrent,[28] or from one's grave to converse with another.[29]
Conversely, through disobedience one can end up as lion's food or
find oneself being possessed by a demon. Theodore would often

---

[22] *PC* 99. 252.

[23] PK 47. 343, PK 91. 651, PK 93. 665; TC III. 21. 43; ep. 69. 38, ep. 71. 5, ep. 208. 17;
PC 58. 158, *PC* 61. 163, *PC* 75. 196, *PC* 79. 204, *PC* 112. 285, *PC* 117. 297, *PC* 118. 300 (also see
PK 89, 96, 120; *PC* 61).

[24] Cf. PK 56. 398, PK 75. 513, PK 78. 544, PK 82. 573, PK 102. 742, PK 118. 882. 884;
PC 7. 27, *PC* 8. 29, *PC* 12. 42.

[25] To those in exile who, despite being coenobitic monks, were content to live alone
rather than trying to seek out companions who would help them live virtuously: *PC* 2. 14,
PC 9. 33–4 (quoting Eccl. 4: 10: 'Woe to him who is alone when he falls'), *PC* 13. 44, *PC* 71.
186. Cf. also PK 9 (= *MC* 87); *PC* 31, 87, 101, 117, 130.

[26] Cf. PK 77. 536: 'See, brothers, how our number is increasing, with the need that
everything occur with order; when even a little thing is out of order our whole system of the
brotherhood is moved and confounded, ruining our world of virtues'; PK 112. 826 (monks
to keep order while Theodore is away). For a further and fuller discussion of the value of
order in Theodore's thinking, see Hatlie, 'Abbot Theodore', 46–61 and *passim*.

[27] Byzantines were fascinated by stories of the unusual and their imaginations were fed
by the lives of the saints, especially the Desert Fathers. Stories from the *Gerontikon*, from
Cyril of Scythopolis, the work of Dorotheos of Gaza, the *Ladder* of John Klimakos, and the
(often bizarre) accounts in *The Spiritual Meadow* of John Moschos are prime sources for
Theodore's own anecdotes.

[28] An anecdote taken from Dorotheos of Gaza, *Instructions* I. 22: SC 92 (1963), 179–80.

[29] The story of Akakios speaking from his tomb (also alluded to in *MC* 79. 13)—a sign of
his sanctity for heroism in obedience—is found in Step 4 of *The Ladder*. Theodore refers
explicitly to John Klimakos' doctrine on obedience in PK 73. 505.

present to his monks, as models of obedience, the examples of the saints (especially the Palestinian saints) whose lives contained numerous accounts of their outstanding obedience.[30] They were to be imitated 'as far as possible' and suitably (προσηκόντως), in a manner fitting to one's own proper vocation.[31] Their images are to be reproduced within ourselves.[32] Among those who excelled in obedience whom Theodore put up as role models were some of the recent deceased of his own community, such as the Abbas Gregory, Arsenios, and the Scythian ex-slave martyr Thaddeos.[33] The conclusion Theodore draws is that, in the spirit of the holy Fathers and especially of Saint Basil, even if an order were to be given which was likely to lead to death, this order had to be followed.[34] And the same applied even if the order were given by a superior who was insane.[35] For, so Theodore fully believes, 'By your obedience you will gain your souls.'[36]

[30] A favourite is Dositheos, the disciple of Dorotheos (TC I. 33. 535, TC I. 53. 585; *MC* 69. 194, *MC* 75. 212, *MC* 79. 12; PK 5. 31, PK 110. 815, etc). Other Palestinian saints include Euthymios and Sabas (cf. *Cyril of Scythopolis: The Lives of the Monks of Palestine*, trans. R. M. Price (Kalamazoo, 1991), 1–219), Domitianos, Hilarion, Silvanos, Zacharias. On these, see Chitty, *The Desert a City*, 13–14, 71–4, 82–103, and *passim*. Theodore's Egyptian models are Anthony the Great, Arsenios, and those associated with the beginnings of coenobitic monasticism and the rule of obedience: especially Pachomios, Theodoros, Petronios, and Horsisios. Lists of these saints in TC I. 33. 535; *MC* 75. 212, *MC* 79. 12–13, *MC* 95. 79, *MC* 107. 135; for Anthony alone: PK 5. 31; *PC* 43. 121, *PC* 49. 137, *PC* 102. 259, *PC* 126. 322; for Arsenios: *PC* 4. 19; *Laudatio S. Arsenii Anchoretae*, *PG* 99. 849B–881D (a compilation based mainly on the alphabetical apophthegmata: Chitty, *The Desert a City*, 62 n. 55).

[31] PC 38, 108: καὶ μιμεῖσθαι αὐτούς, καθ' ὅσον οἶόν τε, καὶ μιμεῖσθαι προσηκόντως· τούτέστιν, ὑποτακτίτης ὑποτακτίτην, ἡσυχαστὴς ἡσυχαστήν, ἐρημίτης ἐρημίτην, καθηγούμενος καθηγούμενον. Cf. John Klimakos, Step 1: imitate the saints, but not materially.

[32] *MC* 1. 3: 'Let us love the deeds done well of those whose images we are making within ourselves.' Cf. *MC* 36. 101 (on the saints as painters of the divine image); *MC* 95. 78 (on remembering the deeds of the pious Fathers, and with them as an example, making with the various colours [of virtue] an image of piety). These examples are an interesting testimony to the fact that in his own doctrine Theodore did not dispute the 'ethical' theory of images presented by the iconoclasts, but only their rejection of material images for veneration. On the ethical theory, cf. M. V. Anastos, 'The Ethical Theory of Images', *DOP* 78 (1954), 151–60.

[33] *PC* 133. 341. Cf. *PC* 95. 241.

[34] *PC* 125. 318–20. The possibility of physical trials, danger, and, with less likelihood, even death through obedience, was still real in the ongoing iconoclast crisis under Michael II. On the uncertainties of the emperor's policy cf. *PC* 114 and *PC* 116. For St Basil, see *RF* 28: *PG* 31. 989BC.

[35] *MC* 33. 93. What if the superior is a heretic? The question is never asked by Theodore, but it is certain that in this case there would be no obligation to obey.

[36] PK 2, 11. Cf. Lk 21, 19 where the text reads ἐν τῇ ὑπομονῇ ὑμῶν in place of Theodore's ἐν τῇ ὑποταγῇ ὑμῶν.

'The only true sacrifice that the Lord requires from us',
Theodore tells his monks, 'is the blessed and martyr-like cutting off
of self-will.'[37] The subjective aspect of monastic obedience was
clearly the most challenging and most difficult part of monastic
life. Renouncing the world was a matter of a single act of will made
at the time of taking the monastic habit. Embracing the state of virginity was likewise included in this single formal act that defined
the status of the monk.[38] Living the interior dimension of monasticism, namely the life of virtue, required a constant and persevering immolation of the will.[39] Abandoning one's will in favour of
that of authority opened one to receive God's gifts: the gifts that
enable one to live according to the Gospel, to live the spiritual
dimension of virginity, to combat the invisible evil forces that
attacked the soul. Obedience encapsulated every aspect of the
monastic struggle and the monastic life, for the coenobitic rule
itself left no room for acting according to one's own will: its purpose was to break it.[40] Living obedience well, according to
Theodore, was to live Christian life well.[41] Renunciation
(ἀποταγή) of the world, by which the world is crucified to the
monk, and obedience, by which the monk is crucified to himself,
were the hall-marks of the coenobite.[42] The monk's sole lot was to
carry the cross of Christ.[43] In one of his later catechetical instructions Theodore meditates on the difficulties of the internal act of
obedience:

[Do you find] the yoke of obedience heavy? Again, it is written: 'It is good
for one to bear the yoke since youth' (cf. Lam. 3: 27). Applying this to one
sole thing, it will serve the Lord. And also: 'My yoke is easy and my burden light' (Matt. 11: 30). Would one say that obedience produces nothing?
Here is the apostolic reply: 'Lo, we have left everything and followed you.
What then shall we have?' (Matt. 19: 27). And how awesome is the
promise and [how] full of glory! In like manner, have you not abandoned
everything to follow the Lord? Has not one left his parents, another his

---

[37] MC 7, 19. Cf. TC I, 26; MC 44, 125; PK 1, 5 (the renunciation of self-will is like being
the martyr Stephan); PK 15, 98; PC 28, 83: ἡ μαρτυρικὴ κοπὴ τοῦ θελήματος.

[38] PK 112, 830; PC 31, 91; ep. 489, 12–13: τὸ τῶν μοναχῶν σχῆμα παρθενίας ἐστὶν
ἐπάγγελμα καὶ μυστήριόν ἐστι μοναχικῆς τελειώσεως.

[39] Cf. MC 78. 8; PK 16. 104, PK 17. 119, PK 20. 138.   [40] Cf. PC 61. 163.

[41] The nature of the monastic vocation in relation to the more general Christian calling
will be examined below, Ch. 6.

[42] PC 126. 321.

[43] Ibid., cf. ep. 387. 10–11; PC 120. 305: 'you have no other treasure than the cross'.

brothers, another his wife and children, another his properties, another his fields, and everyone—which is more important than all the rest—his inclinations of will (τὰ θελήματα)?

With men it is this that is hardest to live with. If we are dealing with observing the prescribed fasts, of depriving oneself of sleep, of sleeping on the floor, of not washing, of living alone and all the other divine actions, all this can be done with the free will (αὐτεξουσίῳ θελήματι) of the one who performs these things. Whatever one does through free will, even if it is unpleasant by nature, can be done easily thanks to the will. But if this is done with renunciation of will (ἐν ἐκκοπῇ τοῦ θελήματος), even what seems easy is done with difficulty. It is this that our holy fathers have defined as the effusion of blood; and this feat only belongs to the one who is truly submissive (τοῦ ἀληθινῶς ὑποταττομένου), to the one who can say with the Apostle: 'It is no longer I that live, but Christ who lives in me' (Gal. 2: 20). As long as he is not living according to his own will (τῷ ἰδίῳ θελήματι), through the intermediary of the will of the *hegoumenos* he is living according to God. Furthermore, he imitates him who said: 'I have come down from heaven, not to do my own will, but the will of him who sent me' (John 6: 38). Look at the loftiness of this manner of life! Is it not an imitation of Christ (χριστομίμητον)? Is it not apostolic (ἀποστολικόν)?[44]

The themes of the cross and suffering ('the effusion of blood'), which are integral to the spirituality of obedience, are never very far from the mind of Theodore. The circumstances of persecution and exile in which Theodore found himself for so many years (796–7, 806–11, 816–20, and onwards), gave him first-hand experience of the meaning of the cross. He suffered most, physically and morally, during the iconoclast persecutions: physically, because he barely survived his harsh treatment under Leo V, and morally, because he witnessed numerous defections from his own confraternity and from the church at large.[45] On the one hand he could glory in the fact that it was his own monks who bore the brunt of the repressive measures of Leo V and who were the most disfavoured during the reign of Michael II,[46] on the other hand he recognized that this external imposition of an unsought cross was not of itself sufficient guarantee of a heroic Christian life from

[44] *PC* 128. 326–7.
[45] Details of several individuals who defected are found in the letters of this period and in the Small Catecheses. In the earlier Catecheses other occasional defections, not connected with the persecutions, are also recorded.
[46] Cf. *PC* 36, 49, 51, 86, 92, 97, 107, 114.

among his monks. A life of exile could just as well lead to spiritual
ruin as to spiritual gain. Living alone, frequenting the company of
women, and entering into commerce and enjoying the material
gains were the particular temptations that Theodore warned his
monks about.[47] The real cross that made a monk pleasing to God
was the cross of accepting in *obedience* the will of God in all things
and of continuing to adhere as far as was possible to the Stoudite
rule and to the instructions of the *hegoumenos*. During the period of
the renewal of iconoclasm the themes of suffering, the cross, and
the last things appear frequently in Theodore's writings, but this
spirituality is to be found in the earlier writings too, notably in the
Great Catecheses.[48] In this later period monks were to be ready to
be confessors or martyrs of the faith in the fullest sense. The spirituality of obedience was already a spirituality of individual heroism, confession of faith, and martyrdom. Now, in the current
circumstances, an obedient monk was to be ready, if circumstances
warranted it, to profess his faith by example and word in the public forum and to be ready to suffer physically for it, even unto
death.[49]

2.3 OBEDIENCE AND HEROISM

The heroes of any cause or of any belief are the martyrs. They have
literally 'witnessed' to the Truth, as they have perceived it, to the
point of the heroic giving of their lives to that cause. In the
Christian church the first witness to the truth of God's sovereignty,
paternity, and salvific will was Jesus Christ. He is the prototypic
martyr. In the Early Church the first cult to the deceased was the
cult to the martyrs who, by their final heroic deeds, allowed Christ
to suffer and conquer death in them, thereby witnessing to the
power of the resurrection. With time, and especially with the devel-

---

[47] Cf. *PC* 13, 31, 78, 87, 101, 103.

[48] These themes, of course, were traditional to all forms of monasticism.

[49] PK 116. 862 (= *MC* 8. 23): the monk was to be ready for death in confessing the truth
of doctrine: καὶ μέχρι θανάτου κατατολμᾶν ὑπὲρ τοῦ λόγου τῆς ἀληθείας. Theodore
himself was in exile διὰ τὸν λόγον τοῦ Θεοῦ: *PC* 19. 59. Cf. *PC* 72. 188, *PC* 74. 193. In his
later Catecheses Theodore associates the open confession of faith more and more with the
life of obedience: cf. *PC* 32, 42, 49, 73, etc. On this, see Hatlie, 'The Politics of Salvation:
Theodore of Stoudios on Martyrdom (*Martyrion*) and Speaking Out (*Parresia*)', *DOP* 50
(1996), 263–87.

opment of the ascetic and subsequently monastic movements, the
concept of martyrdom developed to include other forms of exemplary Christian witness. Methodios of Olympos, for example, considered a virgin who had preserved her chastity with effort and
patience, to be worthy of the martyr's crown.[50] One who died in
the exercise of charitable service could also be considered to be
worthy of the same honour as a martyr.[51] The concept of a 'daily
martyrdom of conscience' is found in Origen, for those who willingly carried the cross following their Saviour.[52] This 'white' martyrdom did not require the shedding of blood, and in ages when
there were no political persecutions it became a substitute for the
ultimate Christian achievement, and was accepted as such in
monastic culture.[53]

Theodore was very conscious of the difficulties of living the
ascetical life, ὁ ἀγών τῆς ἀσκήσεως.[54] The Lord himself had said
that 'the gate is narrow and the way is hard, that leads to life, and
those who find it are few' (Matt. 7: 14; cf. Luke 13: 24), a passage
Theodore frequently alludes to.[55] To think that the attainment of
God and his divine rewards was an easy matter was 'an illusion'

---

[50] *Symp.* 7. 3, ed. H. Musurillo, SC 95 (1963), 184–6.

[51] Dionysios of Alexandria considered this to be the case for a person who had died tend-
ing the sick during a pestilence: Eusebius, *Hist. eccl.* 7. 22.

[52] *Hom. in Numeros* X. 2: PG 12. 639A; *Exhortatio ad martyrium* 21: PG 11. 589B. Cf. 2 Cor.
3: 10: 'Indeed, this is our boast, the testimony of our conscience: we have behaved in the
world with frankness and godly sincerity, not by earthly wisdom but by the grace of God.'
The 'testimony of conscience' (τὸ μαρτύριον τῆς συνειδήσεως) is given an expanded
meaning by Origen, and it was this that entered monastic tradition.

[53] On the concept of monastic martyrdom in the Early Church, see E. Malone, 'The
Monk and the Martyr', *Studia Anselmiana*, 38 (1956), 201–28; A. E. D. van Loveren, 'Once
Again: "The Monk and the Martyr." St Anthony and St Macrina', *Studia Patristica*, 17 (1979
conference; publ. 1982), 528–38; D. Balfour, 'Extended Notions of Martyrdom in the
Byzantine Ascetical Tradition', *Sobornost*, 5 (1983), 20–35; Bishop Kallistos of Diokleia,
'What is a Martyr?', ibid. 7–18 (repr. as *The Seed of the Church: The Universal Vocation of
Martyrdom* (Witney, 1995)). For martyrdom as such in the Early Church, see e.g. W. H. C.
Frend, *Martyrdom and Persecution in the Early Church: A Study of a Conflict from Maccabees to Donatus*
(Oxford, 1965).

[54] PC 131, 334. Cf. PK 8, 49: τὸν ἀγῶνα καὶ ἱδρῶτα τῆς εὐσεβείας; PK 123, 919:
τὸν πολύθλιπνον καὶ πολύϊδρον ἡμῶν βίον; MC 63. 179, MC 74. 201 (salvation is hard
work), MC 82. 24, MC 109. 140; PK 85. 601 (the ascetical life is the 'art of arts' requiring
much labour); TC I. 4. 464 (salvation is difficult work), TC I. 59. 603 (the life of a monk is
full of hardships, effort, perseverance—in association with Gen. 3: 19), TC I. 73. 639 (the
lives of Isaiah, Jeremiah, Daniel, Zacharias, John the Baptist, and James are recalled to
show the efforts needed in monastic life); PC 95. 241 (Theodore quotes 1 Pet. 4: 18: 'If the
righteous man is scarcely saved, where will the impious and the sinner appear?')

[55] E.g. in MC 76. 214 (also, the kingdom of God taken by violence: Matt. 11: 12; Luke 16:
16); PK 8. 50, PK 30. 212, PK 85. 601 (= MC 98. 97), PK 111. 821; PC 94. 237.

and the 'height of stupidity'.[56] He taught his monks that of itself it
is an unequal struggle. First, the monk had to fight against his own
constitutional weakness—his nature being such that he was always
inclined to slide into sin.[57] Secondly, he had also to contend with
the evil spirits.[58] They were for ever on the look out, especially by
means of their *logismoi* (λογισμοί),[59] to penetrate and to destroy
the fortress of virtue built around his soul.[60] The monk was an
embattled soldier of Christ,[61] longing for the day when he could
lay aside his spiritual weapons and armour—of faith and humility,
service to others, obedience, prayer, compunction, tears, confession, and penance—to enjoy unceasing peace, joy, and eternal
happiness.[62] While on this earth, however, his life had to be lived
in spiritual tension. It was a life of trial. His strength, however,
came from Christ and his Spirit. It was the strength of the new life
won by Christ through his death on the cross. The source of life,

---

[56] *PC* 134. 343.

[57] Cf. TC III. 19. 39, TC III. 40. 81; PK 73. 501–2; *PC* 36. 104: ὀλίγορος ἡ φύσις καὶ
εὐόλισθος, *PC* 82. 210, etc.

[58] Cf. Eph. 6: 12: 'For we are not contending against flesh and blood, but against the
principalities, against the powers, against the world rulers of this present darkness, against
the spiritual hosts of wickedness in the heavenly places.' Quoted in e.g. *PC* 5. 23, *PC* 11. 39,
PC 91. 230; ep. 439. 11, ep. 465. 34, etc.

[59] Theodore frequently adds an adjective, and speaks of 'evil,' 'displaced,' 'demonic' and
'destructive' logismoi. Cf. *PC* 1, 12 (πονηροὶ λογισμοί bite like serpents); *PC* 3, 18; *PC* 4,
19; *PC* 129, 329; *PC* 113, 286 (τῶν ἐκτόπων λογισμῶν); *PC* 122 311; *PC* 128, 326; *PC* 129,
329; *PC* 130, 331 (demonic logismoi); *PC* 133, 340, etc. He speaks also of ταῖς πονηραῖς
ἐννοίαις: PK 105, 770, MC 39, 110; ἀτόποις ἐννοίαις: MC 43, 120. These, he says, are the
'origin and root of sins in us.' They are banished from the soul by spiritual exercises, especially by the regular practice of a sincere confession (ἐξαγόρευσις), which he calls τὸ μέγα
καὶ σωτήριον κατόρθωμα: PC 133, 340.

[60] *MC* 53. 147 (on virtue as a tower); PK 103. 755 (on the city of virtue built by the Lord).
For a useful summary account of the doctrine of *logismoi* and evil spirits in spiritual authorities prior to Theodore (including Dorotheos of Gaza and John of Damascus), see
T. Špidlík, *La Spiritualité de l'orient chrétien: Manuel Systematique*, OCA 206 (Rome, 1978),
225–36. See also R. Greenfield, *Traditions of Belief in Late Byzantine Demonology* (Amsterdam,
1988), 89–118.

[61] 2 Tim. 2: 3; Eph. 6: 13–17. Theodore often uses military imagery in his Catecheses,
e.g. in TC I. 29. 525, TC I. 87. 666; *MC* 24. 66, *MC* 51. 142, *MC* 69. 193 (monks are God's
chosen army); PK 5. 31 (ὁπλῖται Χριστοῦ), PK 13. 85 (= *MC* 37. 103), PK 41. 296 (= *MC*
110. 146), PK 94. 673 (στρατιῶται τοῦ παμβασιλείας Χριστοῦ), PK 96. 686–7 (= *MC*
91. 61–2), PK 117. 870, PK 123. 721; *PC* 51. 140, *PC* 91. 230, *PC* 116. 294, *PC* 129. 328–9, etc.

[62] *PC* 35. 101; PK 117. 870, PK 13. 85 (= *MC* 37. 103) (sword of obedience, the shield of
humility), PK 18. 126 (= *MC* 44. 123) (spear of obedience); On the doctrine of *Penthos* and
the gift of tears in oriental monastic tradition, see I. Hausherr, *Penthos: La Doctrine de la componction dans l'orient chrétien*, OCA 132 (Rome, 1944) (for Theodore, see pp. 51–2, 58, 80, 99,
145–6 and *passim*); M. Lot-Borodine, 'Le Mystère des larmes', *Vie spirituelle*, 48 (1936),
65–110. Theodore's doctrine is the same as that of Barsanouphios.

therefore, was in crucifixion and death: death to the 'old man', death to the passions that lead to sin, death to the world that ignores and is hostile to God, death to whatever makes access to God more difficult.[63] Martyrdom eloquently symbolized these Christian truths, and it formed part of Theodore's spiritual vocabulary.

Not only did Theodore present the martyrs as heroes of the faith,[64] but he also frequently compared the spiritual struggle of the monk to martyrdom, using the latter's different shades of meaning in patristic writings.[65] Anyone who succeeded in the Christian struggle, Theodore explains—whether bishops, priests, monks, or laity—would receive their reward for their 'martyrdom of conscience' (μαρτύριον τῆς συνειδήσεως).[66] In particular, this type of martyrdom defined the life of the ascetic.[67] Martyrs were not just those who spilled their blood, Theodore explains, but those who lived their lives in holiness and patience. They lived a godly life, witnessing, as did the martyrs of old, that 'Jesus is the Christ, the son of God and that in him is life eternal' (cf. John 20: 31).[68] This is 'what the Fathers taught',[69] and so with good reason Theodore could call his monks 'excellent martyrs' (καλλιμάρτυρες).[70] Approximating even more closely to the martyrs of blood were those who underwent physical suffering in openly confessing the faith. Confessors (ὁμολογηταί) were also martyrs.[71] Irene the patrician was a 'martyr of Christ' because, as a 'confessor of the Truth' during the time of Leo V, she was

---

[63] Cf. Rom. 6: 5–12. The purpose of the Catecheses was continually to remind the brethren of these essential truths of the ascetical life. Aware that 'it is of human nature to remember for a time and then to forget' (PK 108. 789–90), Theodore conceived his ministry as *hegoumenos* to be essentially that of encouraging, exhorting, threatening, and reprimanding his monks so that their lives always conformed to these truths. Cf. PC 122; PK 108, 118, 121, etc. where Theodore explains the need for constant repetition of the same teaching. For Theodore's spiritual doctrine in the Small Catecheses, see especially PC 1, 4, 5, 10, 56, 90, 91, 99 (on the nature of and reasons for the ascetical struggle); PC 25, 26, 28, 67, 84, 124 (on the struggle against the passions and *logismoi*).

[64] Cf. PK 95. 684

[65] On the different meanings and usages of μαρτυρέω, μαρτυρία, μαρτύριον, μάρτυς, see G. W. H. Lampe, *A Patristic Greek Lexicon* (Oxford, 1961), 828–33.

[66] PK 99. 716. Another expression Theodore sometimes uses is 'athlete of conscience' (cf. PK 94. 673).

[67] MC 66. 184; PK 2. 11, PK 15. 101 (= MC 54. 150); PK 95. 684; PC 98. 249. Cf. John Klimakos, *Scala Paradisi*, bk. 4, scholion 3: PG 88. 733C; John of Damascus, *De fide orthodoxa* 4, 15: PG 94. 1168B.

[68] PC 10. 36. Cf. TC I. 11. 485; PK 94. 673.   [69] TC I. 33. 536.

[70] PK 94. 673.   [71] Cf. Gregory of Nazianzus, *Oratio* 43. 5: PG 36. 500C.

'persecuted, homeless, without a city, detained and forever subjected to danger'.[72] But it was enough to persevere in the burdens and difficulties of the ascetic struggle to become worthy of the martyr's crown.[73] Carrying the cross, being crucified with Christ, dying to oneself, were descriptions of the martyr. In a letter to his sick mother, Theoktista, Theodore exclaims,

Hail, mother, living and having died. You are not dead because you are living, because by choice you have been dead to [secular] life, because you have fought the good fight, because you have been deprived of the things of earth in order that you might inherit the things of heaven; because you have engaged in the bloodless contests of martyrdom (τοῖς τοῦ μαρτυρίου ἄθλοις ἀναιμωτί).[74]

Writing to the Galatians, the Apostle Paul had told his readers: 'And those who belong to Christ Jesus have crucified the flesh with its passions and desires' (Gal. 5: 24). 'When did you come down from the cross? When did you remove the nails from your flesh?' Theodore asks an embarrassed monk, who had rather forgotten St Paul's admonition and had got himself into a fist fight with a lay novice.[75] A monk had to die each day to his passions by his daily ascetic struggle. Each day he was to experience a 'voluntary death in the Lord'.[76] This life of carrying of the cross (σταυροφόρος βίος) 'in everyone's estimation' constituted martyrdom.[77] It was not a one-off martyrdom but something to be endured daily (1 Cor. 15: 31) and 'uninterruptedly'.[78]

The ascetical struggle of a coenobite, however, lay above all in the difficulties of obedience or subordination, which meant repressing one's own will. 'Blessed is he who, in the work of God, forces himself each day, who puts up with the difficulties of obedience (τῆς ὑποταγῆς), for obedience is one of the greatest strug-

---

[72] Ep. 156. 14ff. In his eulogy of Plato, *PG* 99. 832AB, Theodore calls his uncle an 'athlete of Christ' and 'confessor of Christ' on account of his sufferings in the moechian controversy and the Joseph affair. He does not, however, call him a 'martyr', reserving the title in this case to the martyrdom of blood.

[73] Cf. TC I. 31. 532; PK 11. 74, PK 20. 140. 141, PK 32. 235, PK 96. 690, PK 113. 835 (= *MC* 11. 32), etc.

[74] Ep. 6. 34–7.

[75] *PC* 45. 125. On being crucified to the world, see also *MC* 59; PK 95; *PC* 10, 45, 100, 111, etc.

[76] *PC* 84. 135.   [77] *PC* 32. 94.

[78] *PC* 63. 188; cf. *MC* 99. 99; *PC* 84. 216; ep. 439. 22, etc. Also, cf. Athanasios, *Vita Antonii* 46–7, *PG* 26. 909B–912C (an ascetic is a daily martyr).

gles'.[79] The monk experienced a 'martyrdom of obedience' (μαρτύριον τῆς ὑποταγῆς or ὑπακοῆς)—an expression even more common with Theodore than 'martyrdom of conscience'[80]—and a concept that he attributes to Basil the Great.[81] It constituted a true martyrdom of will.[82]

Theodore's doctrine of the will (τὸ θέλημα) belongs to the same tradition as John Klimakos, Dorotheos, and the Palestinian monastic school, and, more generally, the school of desert spirituality: the will was not so much a faculty for free and virtuous action as an impassioned inclination that places an obstacle between the soul and God.[83] In Dorotheos 'will', taken in the singular, is but one of the 'wills' (τὰ θελήματα), namely desires or inclinations, that are produced spontaneously in the soul, usually the fruit of *logismoi*. To be rid of 'wills' is to be rid of self-will.[84] Dorotheos writes,

If therefore we wish to be perfectly free and liberated, let us learn to uproot our inclinations of will (μάθωμεν κόπτειν τὰ θελήματα ἡμῶν), and thus progressing little by little with the help of God we will arrive at detachment (εἰς τὴν ἀπροσπάθειαν). For there is nothing more profitable

---

[79] *PC* 91. 231. Cf. *PC* 16, 19, 95, etc.

[80] TC I. 61. 610; *MC* 66. 184, *MC* 107. 134; PK 16. 108 (= *MC* 55. 153), PK 20. 138, PK 37. 271, PK 78. 546, 547, 548 (martyrdom of obedience is a spilling of invisible blood and having spiritually cut-up body members), PK 80. 564, PK 84. 590; *PC* 98. 249, etc. Theodore also often uses as equivalent expressions: 'athlete of obedience' or 'athletic obedience'. *MC* 99. 99 ('Are you not daily martyrs by your athletic obedience?'), *MC* 66. 184; PK 9. 57, PK 79. 538, PK 95. 682, PK 102. 739, PK 106, 773, etc.

[81] PK 78. 546 (I have been unable to identify any such explicit reference in Basil's authentic ascetical works).

[82] TC I. 65. 619; PK 11. 73 (= *MC* 23, 63), PK 16. 104 (= *MC* 55, 151); *PC* 93. 236, *PC* 128. 327. Cf. *PC* 53, 94.

[83] For an introduction to the theology of John Klimakos, see Bishop Kallistos Ware, Introduction to *John Climacus: The Ladder of Divine Ascent*, 1–70; I. Hausherr, 'La Théologie du monachisme chez saint Jean Climaque', in *Théologie de la vie monastique*, Théologie historique, 49 (Paris, 1961), 385–410; G. Couilleau, *DS* viii (Paris, 1972), 369–89. For Dorotheos' doctrine on will, see T. Špidlik, 'L'Obéissance et la conscience selon Dorothée de Gaza', *Studia Patristica*, 9 (= *TU* 108) (1972), 72–8; idem, *La Spiritualité de l'orient chrétien*, 255–6. For the Desert Fathers, cf. D. Burton-Christie, *The Word in the Desert: Scripture and the Quest for Holiness in Early Christian Monasticism* (Oxford, 1993), 219 and *passim*.

[84] Cf. J.-M. Szymusiak and J. Leroy, *DS* iii. 1659. The terminology of 'wills' is found in Basil the Great, e.g. in *RF* 1: *PG* 31. 1081C; *De Baptismo*, ibid. 1560B, 1568B, etc. Theodore also uses the plural form, e.g. in *PC* 128. 326, *PC* 43. 121 (τὰ θελήματα τῆς σαρκὸς καὶ τῶν διανοιῶν); PK 74, 507 (ἡ κοπὴ τῶν θελημάτων). However, it is extremely rare in the New Testament, the only example, with this sense, being Eph. 2: 3: τὰ θελήματα τῆς σαρκὸς . . . (in some MSS, Mark 3: 35 also).

to a man than to remove his self-will . . . From detachment, one comes, with God's help, to perfect freedom from passion (εἰς τελείαν ἀπάθειαν).[85]

Irénée Hausherr expresses the doctrine of Theodore and the Palestinians even more succinctly ' "Retrancher la volonté propre", en cette courte formule se résume . . . tout le secret de la perfection; car c'est couper la racine de toutes les passions, et faire fleurir toutes les vertus.'[86] Barsanouphios and the Prophet John were the doctors of this spirituality of excision of one's own will (ἔκκοπὴ τοῦ οἰκείου θελήματος). Through Dorotheos it was passed on to Theodore.[87] But it is through *obedience* that self-will is combatted, or conversely, as Theodore puts it: 'where there is excision of the will there is perfection of obedience' (οὗ κοπὴ θελήματος, ἐκεῖ ὑποταγῆς τελείωσις).[88] Since the need to abolish or mortify self-will was absolute for the spiritual life, so obedience needed to be absolute. Theodore, as has already been seen, is clear about this attribute. It is to be 'an obedience that does not reason' (ἀδιάκριτος ὑπακοή).[89] This insistence on the absolute nature of obedience is in fact common to the whole oriental monastic tradition.[90]

As with other themes, Theodore never attempts a systematic exposition of the nature of the will and obedience, and still less any speculation on the subject.[91] He is content to cite authorities, in particular Dorotheos.[92] His overriding interest, as always, was in the preaching and practice of the ideas that made up monastic culture, and not their cataloguing or analysis.

---

[85] Dorotheos of Gaza, *Instructions* I. 20: SC 92. 177 (= *PG* 88. 1636BC). Cf. 13. 142; 16. 168, etc. This passage is cited verbatim by Klimakos: *PG* 88. 660D.

[86] Hausherr, *Penthos*, 104.

[87] On Barsanouphios, see I. Hausherr, 'Barsanuphe', in *DS* i. 1255–62; Chitty, *The Desert as a City*, 132–40. Theodore may have read Barsanouphios directly since he was known for his devotion to him and was even condemned for it (there being another Barsanouphios who was a 'monophysite' heretic). Cf. ep. 34, 127, 136–8; *Testamentum*, 1816BC. On one of the altar cloths of the Great Church, Theodore mentions in this passage from his *Testament*, there are icons of Barsanouphios, Anthony, Ephrem, and others, whose doctrine is 'of great profit to the soul' (πολλὴν ψυχικὴν λυσιτέλειαν).

[88] *Laudatio S. Platonis PG* 99. 836B.

[89] PK 82. 578; *PC* 95. 241; *MC* 5. 14. Cf. Dorotheos of Gaza, *Instructions* I. 25 (= *PG* 88. 1640C). For a discussion of this concept, found also in Basil the Great, see Regnault and Préville, SC 92 (1963), 70–1.

[90] Hausherr, *Direction Spirituelle*, 189.   [91] Cf. Szymusiak and Leroy, *DS* iii. 1658.

[92] Cf. *MC* 42. 117 and, especially, PK 44. 321.

Having established both the absolute necessity of obedience and the necessity of absolute obedience in Theodore's monastic spirituality it is now time to look in more detail at the *object* and ultimate *end* of the assent of obedience. The object or term of obedience is the manifestation of will of a recognized authority to whom the monk is subject. The ultimate end or purpose of obedience is the end or purpose of the coenobitic monastic life as such. With clarification in these two areas we will be in a position to understand better Theodore's expectations with regard to the observance of and obedience to the dictates of higher authority—to law in its various expressions—in the Christian world outside the walls of the monastery.

2.4 MONASTICISM AND THE COMMANDMENTS

Theodore has a very simple formula that sums up completely the purpose of monastic life: being agreeable to or pleasing God (ἡ πρὸς Θεὸν εὐαρέστησις).[93] To be pleasing to God, by searching out his will as revealed by his Son, and obeying the divine precepts, was in fact a common theme in Basil the Great, and indeed of primitive monasticism and early Christian spirituality.[94] The Gospel *Kerygma* led to an ethical task, and both were the subject of the primitive Christian catechism.[95] Faith and good works were inseparable. 'God brought us into the world', Theodore states, 'in order that, by serving Him with good deeds, we might become inheritors of the heavenly Kingdom.'[96] Theodore sees the ethical task of the monk primarily in terms of obedience to or keeping the

---

[93] Cf. Heb. 11: 5; Rom. 12: 2. TC I. 3. 463, TC I. 8. 478, TC I. 33. 535, TC I. 60. 609; *MC* 85. 37, *MC* 102. 110; PK 58. 410, PK 59. 416, PK 77. 531; *PC* 1. 12, *PC* 5. 21, *PC* 31. 92, *PC* 38. 110, *PC* 64. 171, *PC* 89. 226, *PC* 108. 275, *PC* 117. 298, *PC* 117. 298 (περὶ εὐαρεστήσεως Θεοῦ); PC 118, 298; PC 131, 334; PC 133, 342 (εὐαρεστοῦντες ἐνώπιον τοῦ Θεοῦ); ep. 387, 12 etc.

[94] For Basil, cf. *Moralia* 31: *PG* 31. 844D; *RF* 5; *De Baptismo*, *PG* 31. 1516A, 1556B, 1589A, 1604B, 1608A; ep. 207. 2 (ἡ κατὰ τὸ εὐαγγέλιον πολίτευμα). See also J. Ducatillon, *Basile de Césarée: Sur le Baptême*, SC 357 (Paris, 1989), Introduction, 22; Leroy, 'L'influence de saint Basile', 500; Lampe, *A Patristic Greek Lexicon*, 560 (s.v. εὐαρέστησις).

[95] Cf. P. Carrington, *The Primitive Christian Catechism* (Cambridge, 1940); C. H. Dodd, *Gospel and Law: The Relation of Faith and Ethics in Early Christianity* (Cambridge, 1950).

[96] TC I. 2. 459.

commandments.[97] To live an upright life was by definition to live in God's commandments,[98] which was to travel along the 'royal road', deviating 'neither to the right nor to the left'.[99]

But what were these commandments? In no place in Theodore's writings do we find the Decalogue listed, nor any other fixed list of commands taken from the Scriptures. His terminology for what is to be obeyed is also varied.[100] For Theodore, as with primitive monasticism, the 'commandments of the Lord' were not just the clearly identifiable orders or precepts given by God, but the whole Word of God which inspires conduct. Whatever can be learnt from exhortation, example, and even threat is to be understood as precept.[101] Every word believed to have been uttered by the Lord, and interpreted correctly by the New Testament writers, as a commandment to which all Christians, and, *a fortiori*, all monks who were 'true Christians' and who 'truly' followed the Lord,[102] were bound. Modern scholars of monasticism recognize how important the sacred Word was to early monasticism.[103] Basil the Great, especially in his *Moralia*, set out the objectives and norms of the monastic life by simply composing a vast 'tissue' of scriptural texts.[104] Early monasticism was a movement that attracted those

[97] The formula ἡ φυλακὴ τῶν ἐντολῶν, or a verbal variant of the same, appears extremely frequently in Theodore's exhortations, e.g. in TC I. 28. 524, TC I. 23. 514, TC I. 33. 535, TC I. 36. 542, TC I. 38. 548, TC I. 41. 553, TC I. 54. 588, TC I. 58. 601, TC I. 84. 660, TC III. 20. 42, TC III. 40. 80; *MC* 64. 179 (the commandments of God to be lived 'with youthful vigour'); PK 30. 221, PK 58. 410, 414, PK 64. 447, PK 78. 548, PK 84. 583, 585, PK 89. 651, PK 106. 773, PK 108. 797 ('the fulfilment of the commandments is sweeter than honey') PK 109, 802; PK 111, 819; PK 120, 896; PK 123, 919; *PC* 31, 92; *PC* 46, 130; *PC* 119, 301.

[98] TC I. 3. 462.

[99] Also 'middle and royal way': *MC* 72. 203, *MC* 89. 52; PK 58. 410, PK 105. 768; *PC* 47. 133. This formula, based on Num. 20: 17, was used by St Basil (e.g. *PG* 30. 409C), Gregory Nazianzene (*PG* 30. 409C), Gregory of Nyssa (*PG* 44. 992A), and others, including Barsanouphios and Dorotheos (*Instructions*, 10. 106, *PG* 88. 1725D). On this, see F. Tailliez, 'Βασιλικὴ ὁδός', *OCP* 13 (1947), 299–354.

[100] ἐντολή, ἔνταλμα, ἔνταλσις, ὑποθήκη, πρόσταγμα, νόμος, τὰ ἐντεταλμένα, τὰ δικαιώματα, τὰ προστεταγμένα . . .

[101] Leroy, 'L'Influence de saint Basile', 504.

[102] PK 20. 140, 141, PK 37. 264; ep. 64. 64, ep. 513. 52, ep. 486. 46–7. The monk was essentially a lay Christian who took the Gospel seriously.

[103] Cf. Burton-Christie, *The Word in the Desert*, 15 and *passim*; A. Veilleux, 'Holy Scripture in the Pachomian Koinonia', *Monastic Studies*, 10 (1974), 143–54; N. F. Marcos, 'La Biblia y los origines del monaquismo', *Miscelánea Comillas*, 41 (1983), 383–96.

[104] On the use of the bible by Basil, see Amand, *L'Ascèse monastique*, 75–87; Sister M. G. Murphy, *St Basil and Monasticism* (Washington, 1930), 35–42; J. Gribomont, 'Les Règles morales de saint Basile et le Nouveau Testament', *Studia Patristica*, 2 (= TU 64) (Berlin, 1957), 416–26.

who desired to live the commandments of the Lord according to a strict observance of the Gospel or what we might call *integral* evangelism (πρὸς τὴν ἀκρίβειαν τοῦ Εὐαγγελίου).[105] This original understanding of monasticism does pose questions concerning the lay or non-monastic state.[106] For present purposes, however, it is sufficient to emphasize that Theodore too considered the sole task of the monk to lie solely in living the Gospel integrally.

Because the monk was subject to the whole of the Gospel, it logically followed that he had to obey all the 'commandments' without exception, since they were all interrelated. To be unfaithful or disobedient to one aspect of evangelical living was to be unfaithful or disobedient to the whole. 'I do hope that we are keeping all the commandments (τὰς ἐντολὰς),' Theodore states in an early Catechesis,

and that we will not be condemned nor be put away on account of just one. I must not show myself to be a transgressor of the law on the basis of a single commandment by not receiving an old man, by not welcoming a cripple. Keeping the commandments is all of a circle; it is round. One [commandment] maintains the other. If we leave aside one single commandment we will be told that we are the least in the Kingdom of heaven. The term 'the least', according to the great and divine Chrysostom, means nothing other than condemnation to punishment. Let us then welcome children, the elderly, and the crippled.[107]

The influence here of Saint Basil is quite certain,[108] although integral evangelism was also a characteristic of Pachomian spirituality.[109] In the Prologue to the Great Rules (*Regulae fusius tractatae*), Basil writes as follows:

How long shall we defer our obedience to Christ, who has called us to his heavenly Kingdom? Why will we not recall ourselves from our accustomed way of life to the strict observance of the Gospel (πρὸς τὴν

---

[105] Basil the Great, Prologue to the Great Rules, *PG* 31. 892B. Cf. Amand, *L'Ascèse monastique*, 12: 'Le moine est le chrétien authentique et généreux, le chrétien qui s'efforce de vivre en plénitude le christianisme, et de pratiquer avec plus de fidélité toutes les vertus de l'Évangile.'

[106] On this subject, see below, Ch. 6.

[107] TC I. 55. 592–3. Cf. TC I. 3. 463 (we will be eternally punished if we do good in many things but fail in some), TC III. 40. 80; PK 30.221, PK 109. 802 (on the commandments as a circle). The idea of the commandments being part of the same circle is found in Basil the Great, *RF* 1: *PG* 31. 905B.

[108] Cf. ep. 34. 92–4: 'Saint Basil says that all the commandments are mutually related, so that when one is destroyed all the rest of necessity collapse with it.'

[109] Leroy, 'L'influence de saint Basile', 178.

ἀκρίβειαν τοῦ Εὐαγγελίου)? . . . We say, indeed, that we desire the Kingdom of heaven, yet we are not solicitous for the means whereby it is attained . . . According to the Apostle, indeed, it is necessary not only to conquer but to strive according to the rules (2 Tim. 2: 5); that is, not to neglect a small part even of what has been enjoined, but to carry out each detail as we have been commanded . . . But, if we think that we have fulfilled some one of the commandments (I should not presume to say we actually have done so; for all the commandments form an interconnected whole, according to the valid sense of the Scripture, so that in breaking one commandment we necessarily violate the others also), we do not expect to be visited with wrath on the score of the commandments which we have transgressed, but we anticipate rewards for our alleged obser-vance . . . Unless all were necessary to attain the goal of salvation, all the commandments would not have been written down, nor would it have been declared that all must be kept. What do all other righteous actions avail me if I am to be liable to hell-fire because I called my brother 'fool' (Matt. 5: 22)? What profit is there in being free from many masters if I am held in bondage by one? 'Whosoever commits sin, is the servant of sin,' says the Scripture (John 8: 34).[110]

According to Basil, furthermore, omissions, failure to give good example, and even 'involuntary' faults were equally transgressions of the commandments, equally acts of disobedience to God, and equally liable to eternal punishment.[111] David Amand declares that it is with mathematical rigour and 'impitoyable logique' that Basil draws his conclusion that the neglect of any good deed, with-out repentance, leads to eternal damnation.[112] The Stoics, who had an obvious influence on Basil,[113] likewise held to the rigorist doctrine that small and large faults are equally damaging.[114]

---

[110] *PG* 31. 892B–893C. Cf. *Moralia* 7, 11, 12, 33: *PG* 31. 712BC, 720B–725D, 724A–D, 752AB; *RF* 16: *PG* 31. 960BC; *RB* 233; *PG* 31. 1237C–1240A; *De iudicio Dei, PG* 31. 653A–676C.

[111] *De iudicio Dei, PG* 31. 653A–665C; *RB* 233; *PG* 31. 1237C–40A, etc. On this, see Amand, *L'Ascèse monastique*, 152–75, 280–3. On 'involuntary' faults, see the Homily on the Book of Proverbs, 9: *PG* 31. 404A–C, and *Moralia* 23: *PG* 31. 741CD. The latter, drawing on Rom. 7: 14–20, states, 'That he who is drawn into sin against his will should understand that because he was voluntarily mastered by another sin committed previously, he is now, as a consequence of the first sin, led into another against his will.'

[112] Amand, *L'Ascèse monastique*, 283.

[113] Ibid. 12–15, 61–75, and *passim*; J. Ducatillon, *Basile de Césarée*, 58–64; U. Neri, *Basilio di Cesarea: Il battesimo. Testo, trad., introd. e commento*, Testi e ricerche di scienza religiosa (Brescia, 1976), 86–8.

[114] Zeno, the founder of the first Stoic school, is recorded as saying, 'to strangle a duck without need is no less criminal than to kill one's father'. *Stoicorum veterum fragmenta* (= *SVF*), ed. I. von Arnim, 3 vols. (Leipzig, 1903–5), i. fr. 225, p. 54, ll. 20–2. Cicero, in *Pro Murena* 61,

Scriptural authority, such as the letter of James,[115] none the less, was Basil's decisive authority.[116]

However Basil is to be understood,[117] he did bequeath a tradition of exacting moral standards.[118] Theodore was not the least of Basil's disciples, and he refers to him explicitly in his own rigorist doctrine: 'There is no big or small sin, as the holy Basil says, for each equally constitutes disobedience demanding vengeance.'[119] Put even more simply, 'Obedience is life, and disobedience is death.'[120] As with Basil, Scripture was Theodore's ultimate authority.[121]

The obedience Theodore expected of his monks had to be total because the object of that obedience was, ultimately, nothing less than the Gospel. It was the monk's way to salvation. Salvation, therefore, depended on the monk's living his profession of obedience

states, 'omnia peccata esse paria'. Chrysippus, *SVF* iii. fr. 527, p. 141, ll. 27–30, states, 'He who is a hundred measures from Canope and he who is but one measure find themselves in an equal position, for neither one nor the other is at Canope. Similarly, one who commits a grave fault and one who commits a light fault are both, one and the other, off the right track.' Basil also used the Sentences of Sextus (H. Chadwick, *The Sentences of Sextus* (Cambridge, 1959), 12), e.g. in *De Baptismo*, *PG* 31. 1612B: 'That which is almost accomplished is yet not accomplished.'

[115] Jas. 2: 10: 'For whoever keeps the whole law but fails in one point has become accountable for all of it.' Basil also interprets Peter's act of humility, in John 13: 8, as indicating the same: 'Peter said to him, "You will never wash my feet." Jesus answered, "Unless I wash you, you have no share with me." ' The parable of the wise and foolish virgins, Matt. 25: 1–13, is yet another text Basil uses for his purpose.

[116] Ducatillon, *Basile de Césarée*, 62.

[117] Authors vary in their assessment of the rigorism of Basil. T. Špidlík, 'L'Ideal du monachisme basilien', in P. J. Fedwick (ed.), *Basil of Caesarea: Christian, Humanist, Ascetic*, (Toronto, 1981), i. 360–74, argues that Basil, as a bishop and pastor, was also a realist. None the less, because of his close study of the Scriptures he did set out the highest standards of moral living. This was not (disagreeing with Amand) a rigorism that was fed by Basil's fascination with the Stoic moral system. Rather, it was because of his desire for all Christians to experience θεωρία. See also the comments of Neri, *Basilio di Cesarea*, 84–5, esp. n. 141. That the *Moralia* and some other ascetical works were written after Basil became a bishop has been shown by J. Gribomont, *Histoire du texte des Ascétiques de saint Basile*, Bibliothèque du Muséon, 32 (Louvain, 1953), 240, 255–6.

[118] John Chrysostom, through his homilies, did likewise. Cf. J.-M. Leroux, 'Monachisme et communauté chrétienne d'après saint Jean Chrysostome', in *Théologie de la vie monastique*, 143–90.

[119] PK 108. 794. Cf. ep. 34. 92–4; *MC* 42. 117.   [120] PK 106. 796.

[121] Ep. 34. 94–9: 'And Basil does not say this on his own authority, but on the authority of Christ who was speaking in him, and who had said, "Whoever then relaxes one of the least of these commandments shall be called least in the Kingdom of heaven" [cf. Matt. 5: 19]—that clearly means "shall be damned." And the blessed James says, "Whoever keeps the whole Law but fails in one point has become guilty of all of it" [Jas. 2: 10].' For the use of this citation from James, see also ep. 39. 27; PK 30. 222.

with perfection or *exactness* (ἀκρίβεια, ἀκριβολογία),[122] for only by fulfilling the commandments in this way did he fulfil them at all. This complete or strict adherence to the law of Christ meant, echoing the words of the evangelist John, that there 'is truth in us'.[123] Theodore conceived his role as *hegoumenos* as that of a pastor whose duty it was to instruct and teach his spiritual sheep, and to lead them to salvation.[124] He was to lead them to pasture in those 'places of peace of the holy commandments of Christ'.[125] This meant giving definition to, or explaining precisely, how the law of Christ was to be lived concretely in the setting of the monastic life.

The law of the Gospel is summarized in the Sermon on the Mount (Matt. 5), which is the principal body of ethical sayings in the Gospels.[126] Theodore denotes the whole as 'the precept of the beatitudes'.[127] St Paul's ethical exhortations and practical precepts (or those attributed to him), especially in the epistles to the Romans, Corinthians, Colossians, Galatians, and Ephesians, were understood by Theodore, as with all early authors, to be the further unravelling of the Gospel, constituting one single whole.[128] The whole of the Christian ethical system was therefore a precept, command, or law to be obeyed by the Christian seeking salvation. Added to this, besides, was the way of life the coenobitic monk had chosen. Since this, through God's compassion or φιλανθρωπία, had been made available to the monk to make his path to salvation more secure,[129] the laws or rules governing monastic life were seen as God-given and salvific, and therefore of one kind with the rest of the commandments of the Lord, requiring equal obedience.[130]

---

[122] PK 83. 587, PK 92. 654 (= *MC* 10. 26); *PC* 46. 128.

[123] PK 8. 50. Cf. 1 John 2: 4.

[124] Cf. *Testamentum*, *PG* 99. 1817BC; *MC* 63. 176; PK 68. 476–7, PK 109. 799, PK 112. 824, PK 117, 865–7, etc.

[125] PK 118, 877: ἐπὶ τοὺς τόπους τῆς ἀναπαύσεως τῶν ἁγιῶν ἐντολῶν τοῦ Χριστοῦ.

[126] On the 'sermon on the mount' as law, see C.H. Dodd, *Gospel and Law*, 62ff. For St. Basil this sermon expressed the καινότης ζωῆς of the baptised: NERI, 76.

[127] One seeks God, he tells his monks, in PC 119, 301, διὰ τῆς φυλακῆς τῶν ἐντολῶν, δηλονότι, κατὰ τὴν τῶν μακαρισμῶν ὑποθήκην.

[128] There is room for further study of the choice of texts Theodore makes in the Catecheses and Letters once a critical edition of the whole corpus of Catecheses is made. The trends or blocks of texts could then be compared to those in Theodore's main sources.

[129] TC I. 44. 560; PK 9. 59 (= *MC* 87. 45), PK 113. 836 (= *MC* 11. 32).

[130] Cf. TC I, 70, 632: τῆς θεοκανονίστου ὑμῶν πολιτείας καὶ θεσμοπατροπαραδότου καταστάσεως. The question of salvation by the monastic habit will be further developed below, in Ch. 6.

Whenever Theodore spoke to his monks about the need to keep
the commandments he would therefore have in mind at the same
time the *manner* by which they were to be lived, namely, by the rules
and traditional teachings of monastic living.[131] The reasoning followed strict logic, for monastic living was nothing more than following the traditions of and imitating the life of the holy Fathers,
who in turn were the best imitators of Christ and exact followers of
the Gospel.[132] The saints are like stars in heaven that illuminate
our journey to God.[133] They are to be imitated because the Gospel
itself is not outdated, the precepts have not changed; God, with his
commandments, does not change, and therefore neither do the
rules of monastic life.[134] What the Fathers taught was what the
apostles taught,[135] and the saints to be imitated even included the
'illustrious fathers and prophets before the time of the law and at
the time of the law' such as Abraham and Moses.[136]

Commandments of God and rules of the monastery therefore
formed a whole, the heavenly crown being promised to those who
kept 'the commandments and the canons'.[137] 'Keep my humble
commandment and my word,' Theodore exhorts his monks, 'and
you will be sealed by the seal of the Spirit.'[138] The rule had to be
learned by heart,[139] and each ordinance (κανών θεσμός) had to
be obeyed perfectly,[140] including all details (τὰ μικρά).[141] The rule
and canons were to be followed totally (ἐπὶ πᾶσι καὶ ἐν πᾶσι καὶ

---

[131] Cf. *PC* 53. 146: κατὰ τὴν διατυτωθεῖσαν ἐξ ἀρχῆς παράδοσιν; TC I. 70. 632 (as
above).

[132] Cf. *MC* 48. 133, *MC* 65. 182, *MC* 69. 193–4, *MC* 75. 211, *MC* 79. 11, *MC* 95. 78; PK 6.
38, PK 17. 14, PK 25. 173, PK 58. 410, PK 60. 427, PK 78. 545, PK 80. 564, PK 121. 903; *PC*
55. 152, *PC* 122. 312; *Testamentum*, no. 12: *PG* 99. 1820C, no. 21: *PG* 99. 1821B, no. 24: *PG* 99.
1821C, etc. According to Theodore (ep. 489. 29–30), 'all the most prominent Fathers were
monks, and they lived divinely in monastic life': πάντες οἱ ἔξοχοι τῶν θεοφόρων
πατέρων καὶ μονασταὶ γεγόνασι καὶ τὸν μοναδικὸν βίον ὡς ἀγγελικὸν
ἐκθειάζουσιν.

[133] *PC* 42. 118. Cf. *PC* 89. 226: 'Learn . . . the exploits of the holy Fathers, how great their
eagerness, how great the bubbling of their spirit, their struggles, and how for these reasons
our good God glorified them and presented them as divine by the signs and prodigies that
they accomplished.'

[134] *MC* 36. 102.   [135] *PC* 97. 250.   [136] *PC* 69. 180.

[137] *MC* 69. 195. Cf. TC I. 33. 535, TC I. 36. 542; *PC* 13. 43–4, *PC* 31. 92, *PC* 95. 240, *PC*
131. 334; PK 91. 651, PK 120. 896, etc.

[138] TC I, 66, 624: . . . καὶ σφραγισθείητε τῇ σφραγίδι τοῦ Πνεύματος.

[139] MC 2, 6: ἐκμανθάνετε τὸν κανόνα, διεκστηθίζετε τὰ ἐνταλθέντα.

[140] Theodore occasionally addresses his monks as κανονιζόμενοι, e.g. in PC 79, 204.

[141] PK 108, 794. One example is the wearing of the monastic belt, which according to
Theodore is 'the Lord's own commandment (cf. Mt 10, 9)': PK 20, 145.

κατὰ πάντα);[142] otherwise it would be as if the monk were not living monastic life at all.[143] His personal salvation would then be at
stake, for if the monastic law were to be abandoned by him in this
way, he would *ipso facto* be abandoning the Lord himself.[144] To act
against the rule by secretly hoarding in one's cell objects taken
from the work place (needles, writing tablets, wax tapers, etc.)—to
take an example that Theodore gives in one instruction, which was
contrary to the spirit of sharing all things in common—was itself
enough to warrant loss of the Kingdom of God.[145] So firm a
believer of the absoluteness and inviolability of monastic mores is
Theodore, that he states in an early Catechesis that 'even if Peter,
Paul, a bishop or the Emperor' exhorted him to do otherwise or
threatened him, he would still not permit his monks to act against
(his understanding of) God's law or the established law of the
monastery (τὸν κείμενον νόμον).[146]

Theodore's monastic system was thus thoroughly rigorist. He
did not distinguish between what was a man-made law or tradition, or the will of the superior, from the revealed law of God, making both aspects of the same divine will, and making salvation
depend on the exact fulfilment of this will. Theodore, none the less,
was still a realist and was fully aware of the weaknesses of human
nature and the (sometimes severe) shortcomings of the monks in
his charge. His Catecheses often do leave the impression that
instead of being a school of virtue, the monastery was more like an
English boarding school with quarrels, grumbling, and backbiting
being the daily reality. Once, coming back from a short trip away,
he found one of his monks beating another with a rod and throw-
ing stones.[147] And like a tough schoolmaster, he would remonstrate with, threaten, and punish his monks for their own good, not
excluding temporary incarceration.[148] The task of salvation was
truly a difficult task, he would frequently remind his monks,[149] and

[142] PK 93, 666. Cf. PK 108, 797, PK 109, 802, PK 120, 896; TC I, 4, 466: ἡ ἀκρίβεια
τοῦ μοναχοῦ ἐν ἄπασιν.
[143] PK 44, 318; TC I, 3, 463; TC I, 4, 466: ἡ ἀκρίβεια τοῦ μοναχοῦ ἐν ἄπασιν.
[144] PC 31. 91.
[145] PK 35. 259–60 (= MC 107. 136). Theodore bases himself on I Cor. 6: 9–10, where
the Apostle Paul lists thieves among those who will not inherit the Kingdom of God. Also
cf. PK 14. 95, a Lenten sermon, where Theodore says that stealing vegetables from the
monastery garden is 'nothing less than a satanic deed'.
[146] TC I. 15. 498.   [147] PC 45. 125, PC 46. 128.   [148] TC I. 80. 653.
[149] TC I. 4. 464, TC I. 8. 475; PC 95. 239, etc.

Theodore's divinely ordained task as *hegoumenos* was to make sure that when the angel of death visited them they would not be caught unprepared.[150]

An intriguing story is told by Theodore which demonstrates not only how a man-made law (as long as it was a church law) was still to be respected as if it were divine law, but also how this fusion of concepts was not confined just to those living the strict regime of coenobitic monasticism. A 'well-informed' source had reported to Theodore that the ruler of the Bulgarians had issued an edict that required the Christian population to eat meat during Lent.[151] If they refused to abide with this edict they would be slaughtered. Some fourteen men refused to violate 'the Christian law' (τὸν χριστιανικὸν νόμον), and were deaf to the pleading of those of their fellow Christians who had given in to the demands 'of necessity'. To set an example of the consequences of refusing the will of the ruler, one of the defiant group was immediately put to death, and his wife and children sold as slaves. This, however, did not break the resistance of the others. Their 'confession of faith' led to torture and then eventual execution. Theodore's comments and choice of words are revealing. The group of fourteen, he says, did not 'give in', did not 'obey' the 'word of the impious one'. The others, 'unfortunately', were 'conquered'. This was news 'worthy of pity'. The fourteen looked only to God and towards their reward of eternal happiness.

Theodore clearly regarded it as a duty for the whole Christian group to become (what we might call) 'martyrs for meat'. He considers the ecclesiastical precept of fasting during Lent—being a manner by which all Christians are helped to salvation—to be a rule that forms part of the whole complex of divine commandments, the fulfilment of which is necessary for salvation. To illustrate the point Theodore selects two uncompromising passages of the Gospel: Matt. 10: 37–8 ('Whoever loves his father or mother

[150] On the appearance of an angel at the moment of death to take the virtuous soul to God, see *MC* 46. 127, *MC* 70. 196; PK 59. 422, 423; TC I. 11. 484; *PC* 132. 339, etc. On the appearance of demons before a sinful soul: PK 59. 424, etc. The subject of death and vigilance was a theme traditional to all forms of monasticism, and is found interspersed throughout Theodore's monastic writings. From his last Catecheses, for example, the following have meditations on this theme: *PC* 12, 22, 31, 36, 60, 76, 126, 132.

[151] *PC* 63. 166–7. Theodore calls the population 'prisoners', but as they included families the scenario must have been that of a Christian village in occupied territory. On the dating and circumstances of this episode, see Pratsch, *Theodorus Studites*, 198 (esp. n. 70).

more than me is not worthy of me; and whoever loves his son or daughter or wife[152] more than me is not worthy of me; and whoever does not take up the cross and follow me is not worthy of me)', Matt. 10: 28 ('Do not fear those who kill the body but cannot kill the soul'). And then turning to the Old Testament, he compares the martyrdom of the fourteen with the martyrdom of the seven sons in 2 Maccabees 7, who preferred excruciatingly painful tortures and death to the transgression of the law of Moses, through the eating of pig-flesh—an unclean or prohibited food.

What is instructive in this latter comparison and parallel is that, by implication, the rule of lenten fasting is assimilated to the law of Moses, in other words, divine law. Just as the king in the Maccabees account had tried to get the seven to renounce the 'command of the law that was given to our ancestors through Moses' (2 Macc. 7: 30), so too the Bulgarian ruler tried to make these fourteen true Christians renounce the traditions of the church, these being equivalent to the law of Christ.

2.5 INTERACTION BETWEEN FAITH AND DISCIPLINE

Theodore's constant preoccupation was to show how Christian faith is to be translated into action, thus meriting the rewards promised, and avoiding the punishments threatened in the Gospels. Living according to the divine commandments was to live according to 'faith working through charity' (Gal. 5: 6), which alone can save man,[153] and which was the distinguishing characteristic of the Christian.[154] Not faith alone, nor good works alone were sufficient for salvation, but both taken together (cf. Jas. 2: 14–26).[155] The correct understanding of this interaction became of paramount importance to Theodore during the moechian controversy.

In the first stage of the controversy, after Patriarch Tarasios had failed—in Theodore's judgement—to do his duty in upholding the indissolubility of Emperor Constantine VI's first marriage,

---

[152] In the original text of Matthew 'wife' is not included. It is found in similar passages, e.g. in Luke 14: 25.

[153] *PC* 21. 64, *PC* 29. 86.   [154] Cf. Basil the Great, *Moralia* no. 80, col. 22.

[155] Ep. 5. 42, ep. 28. 79, ep. 64. 50. Cf. *PC* 29. 86.

Theodore questions the integrity of the patriarch's faith. He states, 'How and in what sense can one who acts in an evil manner also be Orthodox, since Saint James declares [Jas. 2: 20] that the faith itself is demonstrated from the works, and that for those who are lacking in the one, there is no profit in the other?'[156] The need for faith and action to mutually interact—in this case for the leader of the church to respond appropriately to an infringement of ecclesiastical discipline (the remarriage of one still bound to his previous wife) and to a transgression of Gospel and apostolic teaching[157]—was for Theodore at the heart of the issue. 'The salvation of the soul depends on two things'; he would state many years later. 'It is not faith by itself, nor [a good] life by itself that brings salvation; but they mutually preserve and reinforce themselves.'[158] Theodore's insinuation of the patriarch's lack of faith was a reaction to the criticism he himself had received from the imperial secretary Stephen: 'You said that it is impossible for the leader or chief shepherd, when either unknowingly or willingly he does something that is forbidden by the commandments of the Lord, to be reprimanded by anyone, because such reprimanding is permissible only in cases where the faith itself is involved.'[159] Theodore, by implication, also criticizes the secretary's lack of understanding of the inseparability of faith and Christian action (discipline or morals). Patrick Henry seems not to fully appreciate Theodore's biblical and monastic mentality when, commenting on this letter, he says: 'This refusal on Theodore's part to admit a clear distinction or even an unclear distinction between the sphere of faith and discipline will play a major role in the shaping of his actions and attitudes for the rest of his life, and chapter two of the Epistle of James thus becomes one of the most crucial in the Scriptures for him.'[160] Theodore certainly can make a clear distinction of the two spheres of faith and discipline, for example as he does during the iconoclastic period;[161] yet what is true is that he does refuse to admit of any separation of the two in practice. At this early stage of his first involvement in controversy the issue, for Theodore, was about the example, or rather lack of it, of those in prominent positions contravening the commandments of God. For Theodore it was a matter of the need to abide by 'the

[156] Ep. 5. 40–3.   [157] Matt. 5: 31–2, 19: 3–9; 1 Cor. 7: 10–11, 27, 39.
[158] PK 29. 86 (written after 816).   [159] Ep. 5. 13–16.
[160] Henry, 'Theodore of Studios: Byzantine Churchman', 103–4.
[161] Cf. *PC* 29; ep. 64.

Truth' and to show that one is 'a faithful keeper of the laws of the Lord'.[162] Christian life itself was all to do with keeping not some, or most, but all of the commandments of God, and keeping them strictly. To contravene even the smallest of the commandments was to subvert the whole Gospel.[163]

In the second stage of the controversy, the 'Joseph affair', the matter of church discipline and its relation to the Gospel becomes much more clearly defined in the writings of Theodore. In 806 a synod of bishops reinstated the disgraced priest Joseph, but, much more serious in its effects and implications, in 809 a new synod deposed Archbishop Joseph for his opposition to this earlier decision and anathematized all others who refused to accept the principle being invoked for the hierarchy's actions: the principle of *oikonomia* of the saints.[164] Theodore's polemic was directed at two major issues: the authority of a church synod that acts contrary to earlier church canons, and the meaning of the 'economy of the saints'.

In his letters of the year 808 Theodore still frequently uses the argument of keeping the commandments and divine law as reasons for opposing the reinstatement of Joseph.[165] But as a result of the synodal interventions, he also focuses on the argument from church canons. 'We do not waver from the commandment and from the canons of the Fathers,' he writes to the brethren at Sakkoudion.[166] And writing to the monk Basil in Rome: 'This is not a schism of the Church. It is a defence of the truth and vindication of the sacred laws. What Your Honour suggests would be a breaking of the truth and would paralyse the canons.'[167] Elsewhere he writes, 'Nothing keeps us from communion with the Patriarch except the case of the Steward, because he was deposed by the sacred canons.'[168] If indeed the sacred canons of the church did establish the unequivocal deposition of Joseph, as Theodore believed, then no synod had the authority to break this ruling:

---

[162] Ep. 1. 7, 10, 24, 57, 73, ep. 3. 25, 33, 43, ep. 4. 23–4; *Laudatio S. Platonis Hegumeni, PG* 99. 833A. In *PC* 74. 192, Emperor Michael II is cited as an example of a 'son of disobedience' (cf. Eph. 5: 6) on account of both his iconoclasm and his (illegal) marriage with Euphrosyne, daughter of Constantine VI from his first marriage. As Euphrosyne was a nun the wedding was prohibited according to the 'correct interpretation of the commandments' (τῆς ὀρθῆς κρίσεως τῶν ἐντεταλμένων).

[163] Cf. ep. 34. 89 ff.   [164] See above, Ch. 1.6.   [165] e.g. epp. 25, 26, 31.

[166] Ep. 31. 33–4.   [167] Ep. 28. 118–21.   [168] Ep. 32. 24–7.

[The Church of God] has not permitted anything to be done or said against the established decrees and laws, although many shepherds have in many ways railed against them [cf. Jer. 10: 25]. When they have called great and very numerous synods, and given themselves the name of the Church of God, they were careful to put on a show of concern for the canons, while in truth acting against them.

Sir, a synod does not consist simply in the gathering together of bishops and priests, no matter how many there are . . . A synod occurs when, in the Lord's name, the canons are thoroughly searched out and maintained. And a synod is not to bind and loose in some random way, but as seems proper to the truth and to the canon and to the rule of strictness.

And no authority whatever has been given to bishops for any transgression of a canon. They are to follow what has been decreed, and to adhere to those who have gone before.[169]

The actual canons Theodore refers to in order to demonstrate the illegality of Joseph's actions and of his guilt do not, in fact, provide Theodore with a particularly strong argument.[170] There was nothing in canonical tradition which dealt precisely with this sort of case and those canons which Theodore does refer to only provide him with a 'how much more, then' conclusion.[171] Furthermore, as Patrick Henry correctly observes, even this involved 'some straining of the text and disregard of the context'.[172] The canonical argument, none the less, became important to Theodore. By showing that the canons of the 809 synod and the decisions of the earlier one were contrary to previously established decrees he would clinch his argument of their invalidity.

[169] Ep. 24. 62–80. Theodore's canonical 'fundamentalism' was not peculiar to him, but reflected the mentality of the age. See below, on the Second Council of Nicaea.

[170] The main canon Theodore uses is canon 7 of Neocaesarea: 'A presbyter shall not be a guest at the nuptials of persons contracting a second marriage; for since the digamist is worthy of penance, what kind of a presbyter shall he be, who, by being present at the feast, sanctioned the marriage?': P.-P. Joannou, *Discipline générale antique*, (Grottaferrata, 1962), i. pt. 2. 78. The canon is referred to in epp. 21. 17, 22. 84, 28. 38, 50. 35, 525. 28, 535. 26. Other canons Theodore refers to, dealing more specifically with clerical deposition, include canons 46, 47, 79 of the Code of Canons of the African Church (epp. 21. 20, 22. 91, 24. 83).

[171] Cf. Henry, *Theodore of Studios*, 116. For a close study of the canons, see ibid., 110–17; J. A. Fuentes Alonso, *El divorcio de Constantino VI* (Pamplona, 1984); D. Gemmiti, *Teodoro Studita e la questione Moicheiana* (Naples, 1993), 98 ff. (heavily dependent on Fuentes Alonso).

[172] Henry, *Theodore of Studios*, 116. Theodore also used argument by analogy. An example of this, although in a very different context, is ep. 462. 31–3. Here Theodore argues for the permissibility of lay administration of baptism in the absence of an Orthodox priest on the grounds of an analogy with canon 58 of the sixth ecumenical council (i.e. the Quinisext or Trullan synod of 692). The canon reads: 'None of those who are in the order of laymen may distribute the Divine Mysteries to himself if a bishop, presbyter or deacon be present'.

His monastic mentality, as has been seen, led Theodore to consider all regulations or 'canons', even if man-made, as being
endowed with divine authority, the transgression of which would
lead to damnation. Ecclesiastical canons were therefore as binding
as the Gospel itself.[173] Christ himself deposed those guilty of transgressing the ecclesiastical canons;[174] the 'truth itself' had deposed
the steward Joseph 'as being guilty according to several canons'.[175]
There is no more telling passage of Theodore's understanding of
the relationship between Scripture and the canons than what he
writes to the Magister Theoktistos:

> Shall we say: 'Since it is lawful for an archbishop together with his asso-
> ciates to do as he pleases, let him be for the duration of his archbishopric
> a new Evangelist, another Apostle, a different Law-giver?' Certainly not.
> For we have an injunction from the Apostle himself: If anyone preaches
> a doctrine, or urges you to do something against what you have received,
> against what is prescribed by the canons of the catholic and local synods
> held at various times, he is not to be received, or to be reckoned among
> the number of the faithful. And I forbear even to mention the terrible
> judgement with which the Apostle concludes.[176]

Ecclesiastical canons, then, participate in the authority of
Scripture. They are equivalent to the 'good works' that must stand
alongside faith. To the Patriarch Theodore writes:

> Even if we are great sinners, we are Orthodox and children of the uni-
> versal Church, repudiating every heresy, and receiving every ecumenical
> and local synod that is approved; and not only that, but also the canoni-
> cal constitutions promulgated by them. For he who appears to have right
> faith but is not guided by the sacred canons is not fully, but only half-way
> Orthodox.[177]

Writing to the monk Basil of the monastery of Saint Sabas in
Rome concerning this controversy, Theodore asks, 'Do you not
know that Christianity consists of two things, faith and works, and
if one is lacking the other does not profit the person who has it?'[178]
He then asks him to learn from the blessed Sabas and to cleave to
strictness in both faith and the canons: ἀκρίβειαν οὐ μόνον κατὰ

---

[173] Cf. Henry, *Theodore of Studios*, 117–18, especially his discussion of ep. 27.
[174] Ep. 21. 16–17.   [175] Ep. 25. 43–4.
[176] Ep. 24. 94–101. Cf. Gal. 1: 8: 'But even if we or an angel from heaven should proclaim to you a gospel contrary to what we proclaimed to you, let that one be accursed!'
[177] Ep. 25. 31–5.   [178] Ep. 28. 78–80.

τὴν πίστιν, ἀλλὰ καὶ κατὰ τοὺς κανόνας ἀσπαζέσθω.[179]
Theodore is playing on the technical sense of 'canon'. For the
monk, a canon is a rule of monastic life having salvific significance.
The canons or rules of the church are given this same meaning.
This rather strong doctrine is not the result of Theodore's lack of
distinction between the realms of faith and discipline, as Henry
might think. Rather, it is the result of that mentality that obscures
the differences between divine and human positive law with their
respective obligations. Yet this mentality was actually the mentality of the official church of the time, as is well attested by the following text from the Second Council of Nicaea:

> For those to whom the priestly dignity is allotted, the guide-lines con-
> tained in the canonical regulations are testimonies and directives. We
> accept them gladly and sing out to the Lord God with David, the revealer
> of God: 'In the path of your testimonies I have taken delight, as with all
> manner of wealth' [Ps. 118; 14] . . . And if the prophetic voice orders us
> 'for all eternity to observe the messages of God and to live in them' [Ps.
> 118: 88], it is obvious that they remain unshakeable and immoveable;
> thus Moses, who looked on God, declares, 'To these there is no addition,
> and from these there is no subtraction' [Deut. 12: 32]. The divine apostle
> takes pride in them when he cries out, 'These things which the angels
> long to gaze upon' [1 Pet. 1: 12], and, 'If an angel brings you a gospel con-
> trary to what you have received, let him be accursed' [Gal. 1: 8; 9].

> Since these things really are such, and have been testified to us in these
> ways, we exult in them . . . We joyfully embrace the sacred canons and
> we maintain complete and unshaken their regulation, both those
> expounded by those trumpets of the Spirit, the apostles worthy of all
> praise, and those from the six holy universal synods and from the synods
> assembled locally for the promulgation of such decrees, and from our
> holy fathers. Indeed all of these, enlightened by one and the same Spirit,
> decreed what is expedient. In the case of those whom they sent away
> under an anathema, we also anathematize them; those whom they sus-
> pended, we also suspend; those whom they excommunicated, we also
> excommunicate; those whom they placed under penalties, we also deal
> with in the same way.[180]

In this synodal text no distinction is made between divine and
ecclesiastical positive law—a characteristic of the whole Early

---

[179] Ep. 28. 83–4.
[180] Second Council of Nicaea, canon 1: N. Tanner (ed.), *Decrees of the Ecumenical Councils*,
2 vols. (London, 1990) i. 138–9.

Church.[181] The sacred canons are perceived as a whole, inspired by one and the same Spirit, and in unity with the whole of Scripture. Discipline and faith are treated together: heresy, warranting an anathema, and canonical transgressions, warranting penalties, are treated in the same context. A similar mentality is expressed in the second canon of the Trullan Synod (692).[182]

Theodore's allusion to Galatians 1: 8–9 in the above quoted epistle 24 may well have been inspired by this text. His position, expressed in the same letter and elsewhere, that no synod has the authority to innovate on or to contradict previous canons, also has full support in the Nicene Council as well as in the Trullan Synod.[183] Henry's criticism of Theodore's static understanding of the role of a council is thus not well placed:

Theodore seems to grant to a council only a judicial function, the application to specific cases of rules laid down in the past. The body of canonical legislation functions on the one hand as a collection of statutes promulgated by God, and on the other hand as a set of precedents on which all subsequent decisions must be made. All the canons have the authority of divine legislation, so Theodore does not distinguish between the authority of ecumenical and local synods.[184]

[181] Cf. P. Raï, 'L'Économie dans le droit canonique byzantin des origines jusqu'au XIe siècle. Recherches historiques et canoniques', *Istina*, 18 (1973), 261. This author explains how the church inherited the mentality of both Judaism and the Romans towards the Law, namely a sense of its divine, absolute, and immutable value. The New Testament presents law as the direct or indirect expression of the will of Christ, and the church continues the work of Christ and interprets his will by its own regulations: 'La loi ecclésiastique était donc couverte par l'autorité divine et acquérait de ce fait une stabilité semblable à celle de lois proprement divines.'

[182] Joannou, *Discipline générale antique*, i. pt. 1, 120–5. It might be hypothesized that this mentality was the effect of the acceptance, at the Trullan Synod of 692 (canon 2), of the so-called apostolic canons as truly authentic. The identification of apostolic doctrine with church discipline would then have been easier to make.

[183] Canon 2 of Trullo states: 'It has also seemed good to this holy Council, that the eighty-five canons, received and ratified by the holy and blessed Fathers before us, and also handed down to us in the name of the holy and glorious Apostles should from this time forth remain firm and unshaken for the cure of souls and the healing of disorders . . . But we set our seal likewise upon all the other holy canons set forth by our holy and blessed Fathers [here follows a list of ecumenical and local synods and a list of Fathers who had written canonical letters: Dionysios and Peter of Alexandria, Gregory Thaumaturgos, Athanasios, Basil, Gregory of Nyssa, Gregory the Theologian, Amphilochios, Timothy, Theophilos and Cyril of Alexandria, Gennadios] . . . And that no one be allowed to transgress or disregard the aforesaid canons, or to receive others beside them . . . But should any one be convicted of innovating upon, or attempting to overturn, any of the afore-mentioned canons, he shall be subject to receive the penalty which that canon imposes', Joannou, ibid.; English text from H. R. Percival, *The Seven Ecumenical Councils*, The Nicene and Post-Nicene Fathers, 2/14 (Edinburgh; Michigan, 1988 repr.), 361.

[184] Henry, *Theodore of Studios*, 121.

Because, according to Theodore, the two synods were acting contrary to past ordinances, they were not in fact synods at all.[185] This was not to deny to a true synod a legislative function, as long as its regulations were in harmony with past rulings.[186]

2.6 THE ECONOMY OF THE SAINTS

Theodore was a rigorist in his uncompromising pursuit for perfection; but perfection for him was merely the moral obligation of every true Christian to live according to the Gospel. The commandments of God had to be fulfilled by all with exactness or strictness, and likewise the canons of the church, which were an aspect of this same one and undivided divine will. The alternative was eternal punishment. But was Theodore a rigorist in the sense of being inflexible and insensitive to the complexities of human living and the realities of human weakness, of being incapable of sensible compromises when the need arose? Certainly, he did not see himself as this. He would not compromise on what he considered to be essentials or principles, but he could give way on lesser matters if a greater good demanded this. At issue was what precisely constituted a lesser matter, and what precisely were the circumstances that warranted giving way. This was the problem of οἰκονομία or the 'economy of the saints'.

In the history of Byzantine law 'economy' has never received any adequate and univocal definition.[187] Working definitions of

---

[185] The 806 synod is termed by Theodore 'that little gathering—I scarcely know what to call it'. Ep. 25. 60–1: ἡ συνέλευσις ἐκείνη ἡ μικρὰ καὶ οὐκ οἶδ' ὁποία εἰπεῖν.

[186] As was the case with the 22 canons of the Second Council of Nicaea.

[187] The literature on *oikonomia* is extensive. Some of the more recent studies include J. H. Erickson, 'Oikonomia in Byzantine Canon Law', in K. Pennington and R. Somerville (eds.), *Law, Church and Society: Essays in Honor of Stephen Kuttner* (Philadelphia, 1977), 225–36; C. Cupane, 'Appunti per uno studio dell'oikonomia ecclesiastica', *JÖB* 38 (1988), 53–73; M. Azkoul, 'Oikonomia and the Orthodox Church', *Patristic and Byzantine Review*, 6 (1987), 65–79; P. Raï, 'L'Économie dans le droit canonique byzantin des origines jusqu'au XIe siècle', *Istina*, 18 (1973), 273–7 (also other studies in this volume); J. A. Fuentes Alonso, '"Oikonomia" en la iglesia bizantina ante el divorcio de Constantino VI', in *Hispania Christiana: Estudios en honor del J. Orlandis Rovira*, 24 (Pamplona, 1988), 239–55; P. L'Huillier, 'L'Économie dans la tradition de l'Église Orthodoxe', *Kanon*, 6, Yearbook of the Society for the Law of the Oriental Churches (Vienna, 1983), 19–38 (other studies in this volume, too); G. Dagron, 'Le Règle et l'exception: Analyse de la notion d'économie', in D. Simon (ed.), *Religiöse Devianz* (Frankfurt, 1990), 1–18. For the application of *oikonomia* in sacramental matters, see the study of F. J. Thompson, 'Economy', *JTS* NS 16 (1965), 368–420, and the

modern authors have included: 'a merciful mitigation of law', 'the liberal policy of compromise in matters not concerning the fundamentals of the faith', 'elasticity in the interest of the Christian community', 'the relaxing of disciplinary canons—regarding the performance of the sacraments but not dogma—for the benefit, possibly political, of the community'.[188] The concept, however, has taken various forms in its historical evolution, and the term itself has always had more than one meaning.[189] Etymologically οἰκονομία derives from οἰκονομέω, to manage or order the affairs of a household.[190] Its use in early Christian literature reflects this root meaning: good management, ordering, disposition, careful and prudent handling etc.[191] In the canonical literature of the first centuries its most frequent meaning is the administration of church affairs and discipline, or a concrete hierarchical decision regarding church matters.[192] The relaxing or mitigation of penitential rules, as a theomimetic or christomimetic act of mercy towards the weakness of man, was not usually called an act of economy, but an act of φιλανθρωπία, συμπεριφορά or συγκατάβασις.[193] Terminology, however, evolved, and in the Byzantine period economy also came to mean a justified exceptional derogation from the normal sense of a discipline.[194]

bibliography in Y. Congar, 'Propos en vue d'une théologie de l'économie' dans la tradition latine', *Irénikon*, 45 (1972), 155–206.

[188] A. Kazhdan, 'Some Observations on the Byzantine Concept of Law', in A. E. Laiou and D. Simon (eds.), *Law and Society in Byzantium, Ninth-Twelfth Centuries* (Washington, DC, 1994), 203; J. Erickson, 'Oikonomia in Byzantine Canon Law', 225. These definitions do not exclude benefit to the individual.

[189] See esp. G. L. Prestige, *God in Patristic Thought* (London, 1952), 57–67, 98–101. See also P. L'Huiller, 'L'Économie dans la tradition de l'Église Orthodoxe', 27 ff.

[190] H. G. Liddell and R. Scott, *Greek–English Lexicon*, 2nd edn. (Oxford, 1925), 1204.

[191] See Lampe, *A Patristic Greek Lexicon*, 940–3; J. Reumann, 'The Use of "oikonomia" and Related Terms in Greek Sources to about A.D. 100, as a Background for Patristic Applications', unpublished doctoral dissertation (University of Pennsylvania, 1957), esp. 587–608; idem, "*Οἰκονομία* as "Ethical Accommodation" in the Fathers and its Pagan Background', *Studia Patristica*, 3 (= *TU* 78) (1961), 370–9; Prestige, *God in Patristic Thought*, 57–67, 98–101.

[192] L'Huiller, *L'Économie*, 29. Cf. P.-P. Joannou, *Discipline générale antique*, Index, cols. 236–7, under *Oikonomos* and *Oikonomia*.

[193] L'Huiller, *L'Économie*, 28–29; Joannou, *Discipline générale antique*, 237, nos. 2 and 3, and cross-references.

[194] As late as the 11th cent., though, 'strictness' and 'economy' could be used together in the older sense of administration. Thus Niketas Stethatos, in SC 81 (Paris, 1961), 468, has κατὰ τὴν τῶν κανόνων οἰκονομοῦμεν ἀκρίβειαν.

Although terminology evolved, the sense of this mitigation (at least in the period being dealt with here) was never that of creating a precedent and itself having the force of law. Alongside the mitigation was a strong sense of the need to keep the integrity of the canons and not to create an excuse for breaking them. It was a mitigation of strictness, for individual cases in special circumstances, not *ad faciendum*, but *post factum*.[195] Economy, in other words, was exceptional and conservative. With the moechian controversy the issue was not simply that of '*οἰκονομία* against *ἀκρίβεια*', as P. J. Alexander seems to suggest, with the Stoudites opting for the latter.[196] Theodore did accept the use of economy but disagreed with the hierarchy's particular application of it.[197] The disagreement could, it is true, be expressed as if he were opposed to economy as such, as in this text:

> Listen to Basil when he declares that the commandments of the Gospel are immutable . . . For they are not corruptible either by the flow of the times or human circumstances, but they themselves endure . . . So when they called the adulterous union salvific economy, by contrast, what else were they promulgating except the overthrow of God's commandments? [And that] the commandments may be exceeded a little here and may be surpassed there, while still being in force without change; that they may be surpassed on certain occasions and with the advent of human circumstances, just as they said in respect to the rulers . . .?[198]

Theodore's concern is that the application of economy should leave the commandments of the Gospel intact. 'To economize is a

---

[195] L'Huillier, *L'Économie*, 36; Raï, *L'Économie dans le droit canoniques byzantin*', 324; Erickson, 'Oikonomia', 229. Erickson makes the point that in this *oikonomia* differs from the Latin canonical institution of *dispensation*, which effectively gives licence to do what is otherwise prohibited. The canonical institution of dispensation, according to Raï (p. 260), was unknown to the Early Church. On these issues, cf. I. Žužek, 'L'Économie dans les travaux de la Commission Pontificale pour la revision du Code de droit canonique oriental', *Kanon*, 6 (1983), 71 ff. The Latin translations of Theodore's texts invariably translate *oikonomia* inaccurately as *dispensatio*.

[196] Alexander, *The Patriarch Nicephorus of Constantinople*, 96.

[197] Theodore once uses the term *ἐπιείκεια* as a synonym for *οἰκονομία*, in *Laudatio Platonis* 844B. As this is an editor's correction and no critical text is available, no significance can be accorded this term. For Theodore's use of economy, see especially A. P. Dobroklonskij, *Prepodobnij Feodor* (Odessa, 1913), i. 362–71, 696–703; J. A. Fuentes Alonso, '"Oikonomia" en la iglesia bizantina', 239–55; Raï, 'L'Économie dans le droit canonique byzantin', 273–7; Henry, *Theodore of Studios*, 98–100, 117, 135–42, 154–7; Hatlie, 'Abbot Theodore', 108–9, 115, 138–42, 154–5, 163.

[198] Ep. 48. 167–8.

slackening of strictness, but is not the abandonment of truth.'[199] He accepts that there can be a legitimate economy opposed to strictness, and that in certain circumstances, as long as there is agreement on doctrine, it is even necessary. In such circumstances, he states, it is only the ignorant and the inexpert who hold to *akribeia*, since they risk losing everything by not being willing to sacrifice a little.[200] In the same letter as the above quoted text he announces his concern, in a somewhat sarcastic way, over the lack of defined limits to the use of economy:

Is there economy for all men, and in transgression of every commandment, or just in some and for some? What are the criteria for deciding that economy applies to this transgression and these people, but not to that transgression and those people? Who has the power to exercise economy and how many are there? Bishops only, or priests too? Synodically or each one individually? And if it applies to emperors only, is it exclusively in cases of adultery, or in any other transgression?[201]

What was Theodore's own understanding of economy? Given that he had been implicitly condemned by the 809 synod for not accepting 'the economy of the saints', it is hardly surprising that he should have defended himself on this account, including writing a treatise, περὶ τῆς καθόλου οἰκονομίας (which unfortunately has been lost).[202] He does however state that his own views are based on the thesis on economy of Patriarch Eulogios of Alexandria (581–607).[203] This tract, which in fact expressed the standard understanding of economy and its limits in Theodore's own time,[204] has been preserved only in résumé in Photios' *Bibliotheca*.[205] According to this, there is a triple distinction to be made in the church's notion of economy:

1. By *oikonomia* a temporary concession (πρόσκαιρος, πρὸς βραχύ) can be made in matters that do not affect the dogma of the

---

[199] Ep. 452. 12–13: οἰκονομίαν εἶναι καθ᾽ ὕφεσιν ἀκριβείας, αλλ᾽ οὐκ ἔκπτωσιν ἀληθείας τοῦτο. This is actually a statement of another monk—during the later iconoclast period—but with which Theodore does not take exception, indicating his agreement. Cf. ep. 30. 14–17.

[200] Ep. 49. 88–92.   [201] Ep. 48. 184–90.   [202] Ep. 49. 63–4.

[203] Ep. 49. 62 ff.

[204] Cf. Erickson, 'Oikonomia', 231; Raï, 'L'Économie dans le droit canoniques byzantin', 270–2 and *passim*.

[205] Cod. 227, *Photius Bibliothèque*, Collection Byzantine, 4, ed. R. Henry (Paris, 1965), 111–14. *PG* 103. 953–6.

true faith to avoid great harm to the church. Only the 'servants of Christ, the dispensers of the mysteries of God, and those to whom has been committed the authority of the episcopal sees' have the right to decide on its use.

2. By *oikonomia* differences of terminology, especially if there is no serious danger of scandal, can be tolerated indefinitely.

3. By *oikonomia* technical barriers to communion—an occasional heretic's name in the diptychs and other such vestiges of past error—can be ignored.

What is stressed above all by Eulogios is that the integrity of doctrine in no way may be compromised. In other words, *akribeia* in doctrine was the very condition for any type of *oikonomia* in disciplinary matters.

Theodore follows Eulogios in this fundamental matter: that the exercise of economy must leave doctrine intact. Further, apart from one exception, it is by nature a concession restricted in its duration (πρὸς καιρόν).[206] As with Eulogios, and to counter the charge that he was acting contrary to the example set by the Fathers, Theodore illustrates his doctrine by referring to precedents from the past.[207] St Paul had exercised economy by the fact that he had circumcised Timothy, his new companion, 'because of the Jews that were in those places' (Acts 16: 3).[208] Athanasios had provided an example of 'perpetual' economy during the Arian controversy, accepting that the 'Italians' could use the term πρόσωπα in place of ὑποστάσεις.[209] Basil the Great used similar economy with regard to the term 'Holy Spirit'.[210] And exemplifying Eulogios' third distinction, Cyril of Alexandria, Theodore states, permitted communion with those who still commemorated Theodore of Mopsuestia in the diptychs, despite the fact that he was a heretic, since they otherwise upheld the 'most upright and

---

[206] Ep. 24. 21–5, ep. 49. 74–5.   [207] In epp. 24 and 49.

[208] Ep. 24. 28, ep. 49. 70–1. Cf. Eulogios, cod. 227, *Photius Bibliothèque*, 112.

[209] Ep. 49. 68–70. Cf. Eulogios, ibid. 113. This precise example is from Gregory the Theologian's *In Laudem Athanasii, Oratio* 21. 35: SC 270 (Paris, 1980), 184–6 = *PG* 35. 1124C–1125A. In Photios' abstract there is no mention of the technical terms themselves. On the relative poverty of Latin technical terms in this period, see A. Puech, *Histoire de la littérature grecque chrétienne* . . . , Collection d'Études anciennes, 3 (Paris, 1930), 358–9.

[210] Ep. 49. 71, ep. 24. 29. Cf. Basil the Great, ep. 236. 6: *PG* 32. 884B = *Saint Basile: Lettres* ed. Y. Courtonne (Paris, 1966), iii. 53–4. Eulogios, cod. 227, *Photius Bibliothèque*, 113 quotes Gregory of Nazianzus, Oratio 41. 7, *In Pentecosten*, *PG* 36. 437C, to the same effect. It is quite possible that the example of Basil was also in the original text.

most important dogmas of piety'.[211] The more important letters of
Cyril on economy, however, which existed in various collections,
are not given any mention by Theodore, presumably because
Eulogios had also neglected them.[212]

The exercise of economy, according to Theodore, must be such
that no harm is done to the church, that the circumstances are
serious enough to warrant its use, and that the end is truly a legitimate one, and is, in principle, for the public good of the
church.[213] It could be administered by priests in their own area
of competence, as well as bishops.[214] Rather than being a 'dispensation' from the law, economy was a measure of prudence
which, in permitting temporary departure from the full rigour of
the application of law, helped its eventual exact fulfilment. If the
latter were not the true purpose, then to economize would be to
sin in a twofold manner: one would do evil to achieve a good, and
the result would also be an evil under the cover of a good.[215] The
true dispenser of economy was like a doctor who applies an
appropriate remedy at short intervals, but whose interest lies in
eradicating the root cause of illness. The economizer was also like
a horse trainer trying to discipline a spirited horse in the fields.[216]
Such economy *ad tempus* was not 'reprehensible, absurd or illicit',
but only slightly remiss.[217] He gives as examples his own acts of
economy, thereby arguing that he was not as intransigent as made
out to be. Thus, in writing to the patriarch in the heat of the crisis, he says that his willingness to return to communion with

---

[211] Ep. 49. 58–61: ὀρθότατα καὶ καιριώτατα τὰ τῆς εὐσεβείας δόγματα (l. 60). Cf.
Cyril of Alexandria, ep. 72 (*PG* 77. 344C ff.). In Photios' abstract of Eulogios' work, it is said
that 'with such economy did Cyril not break communion with Theodore of Mopsuestia
who had been inflicted (with an) anathema in the East' (cod. 227, *Photius Bibliothèque*, 113).
On this see R. Devreesse, *Essai sur Théodore de Mopsueste* (Paris, 1948), 229–58. Eulogios, in
giving this example, seems to have missed the significance of the later condemnation of
Theodore by the Second Council of Constantinople (553), canon 12. 'If anyone defends the
heretical Theodore of Mopsuestia . . . and if anyone fails to anathematize him . . . as well
as all those who offer acceptance or defence to him . . . let him be anathema', Tanner,
Decrees of the Ecumenical Councils, i. 119–20.

[212] The letters in question are ep. 56, to Maximus, deacon of Antioch, and ep. 57, to
Gennadios, a presbyter of Jerusalem (in Joannou, *Discipline générale antique*, ii. 284–7). The letters were read during the first session of the Second Council of Nicaea and were canonized
in the Tarasian Recension of the *Syntagma in Fourteen Titles*. For details, see Erickson,
'Oikonomia', 231–2.

[213] Ep. 24 and ep. 49 *passim*.   [214] Ep. 27. 51–60.   [215] Cf. ep. 267. 20–3.
[216] Ep. 49. 75 ff.   [217] Ep. 49. 72–4.

Nikephoros, if Joseph were deprived of the active exercise of the priesthood, and his willingness to return to communion with his predecessor Tarasios at the end of the first crisis, were equally acts of economy. This returning to communion, he holds, is not the sort of action characteristic of those who adhere always to strictness (οὐ τῶν ἀκριβευομένων ἐστίν).²¹⁸ For 'nothing is more dear to God than concord and unity', as long as there is no breach of true faith, divine law, or the canons.²¹⁹ In the simoniac affair the then *hegoumenos* of Stoudios, Sabas, and his followers broke communion with Patriarch Tarasios.²²⁰ Theodore, on the contrary, although not criticizing Sabas, did not follow him on this. Tarasios was recognised by all as being Orthodox in faith, and although his handling of the simoniac bishops had not been convincingly regular, 'We yearned so for harmony . . . deciding that, as the Theologian says somewhere, in an ambiguous matter we ought to incline toward the more humanitarian side (ἐπὶ τὸ φιλανθρωπότερον), which is peace.'²²¹ This type of economy (although the term is not used in this last case) is that type which characterized the *penitential oikonomia* of the Fathers, where recognition of guilt and transgression was made by the penitent seeking reconciliation. It called for a less strict application of canonical punishments so that the latter could be seen as corrective or medicinal rather than vindictive.²²² The Trullan Synod called this the rule 'of humanity and consideration' (τῆς φιλανθρωπίας καὶ συμπαθείας).²²³ The renewed communion between Theodore and Patriarch Tarasios after the first phase of the moechian crisis depended on the patriarch's recognition of his

---

²¹⁸ Ep. 30. 16–17. According to Basil, canon 51 (Joannou, *Discipline générale antique*, ii. 142), any member of the hierarchy who has committed a serious fault should be suspended from his functions.

²¹⁹ *Laudatio Platonis* 833D, 844B.

²²⁰ Cf. M.-F. Auzépy, 'La Place des moines à Nicée II (787)', 19–21.

²²¹ Ep. 38. 80–3. Cf. Gregory of Nazianzus, *Oratio* 21. 15: *PG* 35. 1097B.

²²² Thus Gregory of Nyssa, canon 5, establishes: 'For those who have proved the more zealous in their conversion [from heresy or schism] and who show by their manner of life their return to the good, he who manages things profitably by means of ecclesiastical *oikonomia* can shorten the length of time required for a 'hearer' and make him more quickly to become a 'stander' and then shorten the length of time again, restoring him more quickly to communion . . . depending, again, on the state of the person being treated', Joannou, *Discipline générale antique*, ii. 219.

²²³ Canon 3: Joannou, ibid. i. pt. 1. 126.

having committed error.[224] Some of Theodore's later penitential prescriptions would involve this same sense of economy.[225]

Another use of economy was that of dissimulation, or silence over a transgression.[226] Theodore's initial silence after the 806 synod was ἐξ οἰκονομικῆς συγκαταβάσεως, an 'economic condescension'.[227] Some of the brethren of Sakkoudion had thought their leader had been too slack in the initial stages of the Joseph affair. He defends himself by claiming he had been using the economy of the holy Fathers:

As long as the time was one for the employing of economy and for keeping secret the matter of our not being in communion with Joseph the Steward, we acted thus, not out of fear, even though we are sinners, but rather from economical condescension. Thus in a way we imitated our holy Fathers, in so far as they used economy at the opportune time and thereby delivered themselves from temptations. On the one hand they spared those who were weaker and in distress; on the other hand they gave way a little in the manner of a steersman of a ship, in order that they might a little later achieve the desired success. But since it has now pleased our good God that the matter should come clearly into the open, we now write.[228]

The Magister Theoktistos had blamed Theodore, on the other hand, for not having compromised more. Theodore's response is, what more can be expected from him after having exercised econ-

---

[224] Ep. 30. 25–7: 'Would that my hands had been cut off so that I might not crown the adulterer; for did I not really crown him?' (αἱ χεῖρές μου κεκομμέναι ἂν ὑπῆρχον εἰς τὸ μοιχικὸν στεφάνωμα ἢ ἐγὼ ὅλως ἐστεφάνουν).

[225] During the iconoclast period Theodore was presented with a number of cases of conscience that resulted from the difficulties of withdrawing completely from the society of heretics. One question put to him was whether a person, cleric or lay, could approach communion from an Orthodox priest after having taken part in the singing of psalms with heretics. He responds that, applying economy, priests may do so but they must also do penance (οἰκονομικῶς μετὰ ἐπιτιμίου). A lay person may do so without any penance. A lector who has abstained from 'heretical communion' for two years but is guilty in other ways is granted the same permission. 'These things', Theodore adds, 'are said economically as a result of the weakness of men' (οἰκονομικῶς δὲ ταῦτα εἴρηται διὰ τὴν ἀσθένειαν τῶν ἀνθρώπων). Ep. 552. 58–68.

[226] A much later case of licit dissimulation—during the iconoclast persecution—was that of avoiding open disclosure of one's identity. In ep. 396 (*ann.* 818) Theodore tells his female correspondent that she is permitted, on account of the difficulties of the time, to shed her monastic clothes and dress as a secular. It would be better, he tells her, to be a secret nun than to give in to heretical *koinonia* under physical torture.

[227] Ep. 31. 5. This expression was more usually associated with penitential discipline. Cf. Erickson, 'Oikonomia', 227–8. Theodore is not using it in this sense here.

[228] Ep. 30. 1–11. Cf. ep. 21. 34–45; ep. 22. 118–33.

omy in keeping the matter hidden for two years? There was a time
for speaking and a time for prudent silence (cf. Eccl. 3: 7). Yet if
forced to—if Joseph remained undeposed—he was still willing to
continue to exercise this economy, in complete withdrawal from
the patriarch, 'leaving the judgement of the matter to the Lord'.[229]

Yet another type of legitimate economy mentioned by
Theodore concerned dealings with confirmed heretics. *Akribeia*
dictated total severance of communion or *koinonia* from all heretics,
as according to the well-established rules of the church.[230] 'It is
not just the unbelievers and heretics, the debauched and adulterers and those who commit similar sacrilege, who are placed under
the sword of the Dragon,' Theodore states in one of his late
Catecheses, 'but all who have indifferent and social relations with
them.'[231] After the 809 synod, when Theodore began to refer to
those in communion with Joseph and the 'moechian' hierarchy as
heretics, he insisted that there could be no relation of any sort with
them.[232] Several problems of morality and of propriety arose from
living in proximity with such people, one of which was that of the
acceptable limits of social intercourse. St Paul and the church
canons prohibited all forms of fraternalizing.[233] But could economy be applied? Theodore wanted strict separation, after all St
Paul had forbidden even eating with such sinners (1 Cor. 5: 11).[234]
Theodore inferred from this that even eating with anyone who had
transgressed this precept was forbidden.[235] None the less he could
foresee some circumstances which necessitated the relaxing of this
rule. A prisoner, such as he himself was, for example, had to receive
food from his heretical prison guard. Accepting this, rather than
starving, was an instance of *oikonomia*.[236]

---

[229] Ep. 24. 8–21.

[230] On shared cult, cf. apostolic canons 45 (44), 65; Synod of Laodicea, canons 6, 9, 32,
33, 34, 37; Athanasios, apol. 49; letter to Antiochus, canon 4; Timothy of Alexandria,
canons 9, 25; Theophilos of Alexandria, canon 2. On greeting or sharing a meal with
heretics, cf. Basil the Great, canon 96.

[231] PC 129, 329; Οὐδὲ γὰρ ἀπίστους μόνον καὶ αἱρετικούς, οὐδὲ πόρνους τε καὶ
μοιχούς, καὶ τοὺς τὰ ὅμοια ἐνεργοῦντας ἀνοσιουργήματα ὑπὸ τὴν ρομφαίαν αὐτοῦ
τίθησιν ὁ δράκων, ἀλλὰ καὶ τοὺς ἀδιαφόρως καὶ κοινωνικῶς πρὸς αὐτοὺς
ἔχοντας. Cf. 1 Cor 5, 9–11.

[232] The whole discussion of economy in ep. 49 is in answer to the question posed by
Naukratios as to why there could be no communion with the patriarch and all those who
celebrate with Joseph.

[233] 1 Cor. 5: 9–11; 2 Thess. 3: 6; Basil, canon 96: Joannou, *Discipline générale antique*, ii.
198–9 = Y. Courtonne, *Saint Basile: Letters* (Paris, 1957), i. 208–9.

[234] Cf. ep. 49. 131.	[235] Ep. 49. 128–30.	[236] Ep. 49. 141.

The Joseph affair, following on the 809 synod, created a disturbance which was fairly confined in its effects, involving only a lim-
ited number of groups and individuals.[237] The iconoclastic synod
of 815, on the other hand, had far more widespread repercussions.
It affected the church throughout the empire.[238] The question of
the limits of communion and social intercourse with the iconoclast
heretics became a concern for a much greater number of people
than in the Joseph affair. Theodore's basic attitudes, however, did
not change. In principle, rules were to be followed with strictness.
In one letter Theodore cites the Psalmist: 'Never let the oil of the
wicked anoint my head' (Ps. 140: 5) and holds that when
Athanasios prohibited *koinonia* with heretics, and those who were in
communion with heretics, this included eating with them.[239]
Elsewhere he says that, according to 'Chrysostom, and indeed
every saint', one becomes guilty of holding communion with
heretics if one enjoys their friendship and eats and drinks with
them.[240] A lay person was required to avoid receiving a blessing
from a heretical monk, singing psalms with him, and sharing bread
with him.[241] Yet Theodore recognised that avoiding close association with heretics, for example, if one were in the army, could lead
to dangerous situations.[242] Nevertheless, indifferent association
with heretics, even when it was done through fear, still merited
penance: fifteen genuflections (γονυκλισίας) and repetition of a
short penitential prayer fifty or a hundred times.[243] Those who in
some way represented the official Orthodox Church—a presbyter,
deacon, monk, or nun—were always expected to hold to *akribeia*,
'unless perhaps by way of economizing, but this rarely'.[244] Indeed,
Theodore himself on more than one occasion had to resort to this
practice, 'for economy is needed in compelling circumstances'

---

[237] In ep. 40. 88–9, however, Theodore states that there is hardly a presbyter who has
not been sullied by heresy.

[238] Cf. Alexander, *The Patriarch Nicephorus*, 137–47.

[239] Ep. 466. 16–22. Cf. Athanasios, apol. 49, *Contra Arianos* (*PG* 25. 336B ff.).

[240] Ep. 340. 26–7. Cf. *PC* 127. 325, where Theodore says heretics are 'beasts in human
form' and, quoting Ignatios of Antioch (*Letter to the Smyrnaeans*, 4. 1), says 'one should try not
only not to receive them, but even to meet them'.

[241] Ep. 500. 57–60. Cf. apostolic canon 65 (against laymen praying with heretics);
Laodicea, canon 33.

[242] Ep. 507. 22ff.

[243] Ep. 552. 51–7. This may be considered 'penitential' economy.

[244] Ibid., 48–50. οὐκ οἶδα εἰ μή τι οἰκονομίας τρόπῳ, καὶ τοῦτο σπανιώτερον (1.
50).

(ἐπεὶ γὰρ δεῖ οἰκονομίᾳ κεχρῆσθαι ἐν τοῖς ἀναγκαίοις). But even then Theodore's conscience would not allow him to accept more than a drink.[245]

In summarizing Theodore's attitude in the matter of association with heretics, it can be said that he adhered to *akribeia*, but not to the exclusion of some practice of *oikonomia*. As he would state in a Catechesis, 'In the past, in the measure when times demanded it, and rightly so, we have used economy.'[246] In this he was less rigorist than other iconophiles.[247] As long as there was no contradiction of the spirit of the law, and right faith was upheld, changes could be made to that law.[248]

It has been argued by some scholars that Theodore's attitude became less intransigent with time, notable differences being detectable between his perspective during the moechian and Joseph conflicts and that in later life, during the iconoclast conflict.[249] As Henry puts it, 'He began to adopt as a central principle of his thought . . . that knowing what is in people's hearts is God's business; and further, that the Lord is in control of events. A growing conviction of God's providence made Theodore less of a rigorist.'[250] But Henry also affirms that, 'his more moderate stand in the later struggle [according to the results of his lengthy analysis], while a retreat, was not a radical break from his earlier position; rather it was a re-arrangement of theological priorities'.[251]

As the above analysis has shown, Theodore always accepted the principles of economy. But it should also be stated that there is no

[245] Ep. 407. 36 ff., to Naukratios. Theodore took drink when in conversation with the heretical bishop of Chonae and with the exarch of five themes of Asia Minor. When with the latter he first blessed the cup three times with the sign of the cross before drinking.

[246] PC 97, 247: ᾠκονομήσαμεν ἐν τοῖς προλαβοῦσιν ἐφ' ὅσον ὁ καιρὸς ἀπῄτει καὶ εἰκότως.

[247] Cf. P. J. Alexander, 'Religious Persecution and Resistance', 250, who cites, in particular, the more rigorist attitude of St Peter of Atroa. See also ep. 477 on Theodore's less rigorist attitude towards penitents (analysis at Ch. 4. 8, below).

[248] Cf. ep. 462. 24–5: ἐπειδὴ ἐξ ἀνάγκης καὶ νόμου μετάθεσις. In this letter Theodore argues that the times permit laymen to administer baptism in the absence of an Orthodox priest, even though this is contrary to the letter of the law (more on this below, Ch. 5.1). Economy could also be used with monastic law, such as when there is a need—for the spiritual good of the monk or nun—to transfer to another monastery: ep. 530. 16 ff.; to receiving priests ordained 'without acclamations': ep. 549. 12–23; to allowing priests undergoing canonical penance to perform certain sacred acts (but not the eucharist): ep. 215. 20–2, ep. 536. 15–18, ep. 549. 111–19.

[249] Henry, in particular, argues this very cogently in *Theodore of Studios*, 259–65 and *passim*. Hatlie, in 'Abbot Theodore', *passim*, argues for the same.

[250] Henry, *Theodore of Studios*, 261.   [251] Ibid. 259.

evidence to suggest that the church hierarchy of the time understood economy to be an action contrary to the canons (as
Theodore asserts), or in any way different from the principles enu-
merated by Eulogios.[252] In other words, the hierarchy also
believed economy to be compatible with strictness, and its use to
be in harmony with the principles of the Gospel.[253] Thus the clash
between Theodore and the hierarchy was not over the *principles* of
economy as such, but over its actual or *concrete* application. Why,
then, was Theodore so intransigent in the Joseph case? The usual
explanation is that he could not, or would not, distinguish between
doctrine or faith (the condemnation of adultery in the Gospel) and
discipline (the treatment of the priest who blessed the illegal
marriage).[254] But, as has been argued above, this is an oversim-
plification. Theodore was aware of the difference, but at the same
time he believed that a gross infringement of divinely sanctioned
discipline was a statement on the faith of the one acting in this way.
Because Joseph's reinstatement was, according to Theodore, such
an infringement, this revealed a certain defective attitude of faith.
By blessing the emperor's marriage, Joseph had sanctioned adultery. In accepting Joseph back, the hierarchy had effectively done
the same. At least this was Theodore's interpretation after the 809
Synod had effectively accused *him* of being a heretic by not accepting their decisions.[255] Thereafter the controversy became one of
faith. Had the Synod not issued its condemnation, the idea of a
moechian heresy would probably not have arisen. What, then, was
the reason for Theodore's initial intransigence? He explains him-

[252] It is quite possible that the synod had Eulogios in mind when speaking of economy.
There is no support for the claim, made by Bury, *Eastern Roman Empire*, 34, that the hierar-
chy had declared the marriage of Constantine and Theodote valid. On this, see Henry,
Theodore of Studios, 59 n. 2; idem, 'The Moechian Controversy', 509–18.

[253] This was the meaning of the 'economy of the saints'. The writings of the Fathers on
economy—which combined economy with strictness—were studied during the first session
of the Second Council of Nicaea (Mansi, *Sacrorum Conciliorum*, xii. 1019 ff.). Even though this
occurred twenty years before the 809 Synod, it is hardly conceivable that within this time
there could have been an appreciable shift in the official interpretation of these same
sources. L. Saltet, in *Les Réordinations: Étude sur le sacrament de l'ordre* (Paris, 1907), 106–8, does
point out, however, that the patristic dossier chosen to study the reintegration of clerics
coming from heresy was selective in the latter's favour. This reflected a shift from the rigorism of earlier centuries.

[254] Cf. Raï, 276; 277; Henry, *Theodore of Studios*, 103.

[255] If it is true that Theodore overreacted to the decisions of the Synod, as undoubtedly
was the case (and as his own brother, Archbishop Joseph seemed to think: ep. 43), the same
might be said of the hierarchy in their somewhat injudicious use of an anathema.

self to the monk Symeon: Joseph's crime was serious and merited nothing less than deposition, otherwise 'divine matters would be playthings, and the canons pointless'.[256] Furthermore, Joseph had not shown the proper signs of penance and remorse, by failing to follow the established church procedure. This required that an excommunicated cleric plead his case within a year of his sentence, otherwise he can have no voice. Joseph, on the other hand, had not attempted to do so for nine years.[257] The very least condition for any application of economy towards transgressors of church order was repentance. A recent precedent was the reception, using *oikonomia*, of the iconoclast bishops at the Second Council of Nicaea.[258]

Together with this absence of due repentance, Theodore objected to Joseph being permitted active priestly ministry, even if he were, by economy, to be allowed an official clerical function: 'Let him be the Oikonomos; why does he have to exercise priesthood unworthily? Let him stop being a presbyter.'[259] The fact that Joseph's reinstatement was instigated by the emperor, a serious circumstance the hierarchy had to take into account, was not sufficient cause, in Theodore's mind, for such an application of economy.[260] But perhaps the most important reason for Theodore's opposition and intransigence, the one with the most

---

[256] Ep. 22, 91–92: εἰ δὲ τοῦτο ἀνεκδίκητον, παίγνια τὰ θεῖα καὶ ἔωλοι οἱ κανόνες.

[257] Ep. 22. 90–5. Cf. ep. 30. 30–2. The ruling referred to is canon 79 of the *Codex Africanus* of the Synod of Carthage (419): Joannou, *Discipline générale antique*, i. pt. i. 2. 320.

[258] The iconoclast bishops at the time of the Second Council of Nicaea were received through *oikonomia* because they had *repented* of their errors: 'We have sinned in the sight of God, and in the sight of the whole church and of this holy synod; we fell through ignorance, and we have no argument in our defence.' On the other hand, the Synod also declared 'no head or fabricator of a heresy may be admitted to the priesthood', Mansi, *Sacrorum Conciliorum*, xii. 1018, 1034. On the significance of this, see P. Henry, 'Images of the Church in the Second Nicene Council and in the *Libri Carolini*', in K. Pennington and R. Somerville (eds.), *Law, Church and Society: Essays in Honor of Stephen Kuttner* (Philadelphia, 1977), 237–52; Erickson, 'Oikonomia', 232–3.

[259] Ep. 21, 40–1: ἔστω οἰκονόμος, τί καὶ ἀναξίως ἱερουργεῖ; ἐξέλιπεν πρεσβύτερος. In ep. 24. 42, Theodore argues that this is already an example of economy by recalling an episode from the life of John Chrysostom. The latter reconciled six deposed simoniac bishops, allowing them to receive communion at the altar but not any exercise of the priesthood: Palladius, *Dialogus de Vita J. Chrysostomi*, ch. 15: XV, A.-M. Malingrey (ed.), *Dialogue sur la vie de Jean Chrysostome*, i. SC 341 (Paris, 1988), 290–4.

[260] Even at the Second Council of Nicaea the medicinal or penitential aspect of *oikonomia* took precedence over considerations of benefits to church and state, or what Erickson calls 'making a deal' ('Oikonomia in Byzantine Canon Law', 232). On the emperor's role, see below.

compelling psychological force, was the power and effect of *example*. The example of the saints was at the very foundation of monastic life, for it showed how Christian life should or could be lived. It gave a powerful incentive to continue persevering with the trials of asceticism. Bad example had a parallel and inversely detrimental influence. For Joseph to be allowed to function as a priest in Hagia Sophia, the central church of the empire, would have been to send a signal to all priests that his crowning of the adulterer was not an action that merited serious punishment, to the detriment of priestly discipline, church order, and faith.[261] Once the Synod of 809 issued its condemnation Theodore became convinced that the very foundations of the church were being attacked: its authority, its tradition, and the Gospel itself.[262] If the commandments of God were shaken, the very reason for imitating the Fathers and for living the monastic life was removed. Theodore was willing to suffer exile and punishment in defence of these values—the values for which he had already devoted his whole life, as a monk and superior, in upholding.

Of great importance during this affair was Theodore's inference, from the inappropriate application of economy, that the emperor's traditional status within the church was being redefined by the hierarchy.[263] This, alongside the subsequent reintroduction of iconoclasm by Leo V using ecclesiastical mechanisms, led Theodore to openly oppose the emperor's intervention in church affairs. This fact has led many commentators to place Theodore alongside other notable church Fathers in their fight against caesaropapism, making of Theodore an ardent advocate of church autonomy *vis-à-vis* the secular authorities. But did Theodore really advocate separation of church and state in ecclesiastical affairs? It will be argued in the next section that Theodore's position was not so different from that of the traditional Byzantine understanding of the relationship between church and state or church and emperor as is commonly supposed.

---

[261] Cf. Henry, *Theodore of Studios*, 130–4; Hatlie, 'Abbot Theodore', 165.
[262] This has been extensively treated by Henry, *Theodore of Studios*, 109–24. Cf. Hatlie, 'Abbot Theodore', 161 ff.
[263] Hatlie, 'Abbot Theodore', 166.

3

Church and Emperor

3.1 CHRISTIAN POLITICAL HELLENISM

> There is something sublime in the idea that the Emperor
> should be the image of God, imitating his generosity and
> clemency, and that the Emperor's foremost duty was to lead
> his subjects to God.[1]

Despite the fact that Theodore's life was dominated by conflicts
with occupants of the imperial throne (Constantine VI,
Nikephoros, and Michael II) his understanding and appreciation
of the role of the emperor and Empire *vis-à-vis* the church
remained very much traditional. Since the time of Eusebius, the
biographer of Constantine the Great and the first exponent of the
theory of the Christian monarch, the emperor had been regarded
by Christian writers as a special agent of God, appointed by him
to represent him in ruling all Christian peoples in a single
Christian Empire and leading them to true knowledge of God.
Hellenistic political theory had considered the king to be a benefactor of the human race, a guardian, good shepherd, physician,
and saviour.[2] Being a benefactor was the trait that was considered,
for example by Dion Chrysostom, to approach most nearly the
divine nature (of Zeus). Hence benevolence ($\phi\iota\lambda\alpha\nu\theta\rho\omega\pi\iota\alpha$) was
the virtue most recommended to a ruler.[3] In a real, though
undefined, sense he was divine. He was a sacred person, as was his
palace and anything else associated with him or his activity.
Earthly kingship was necessarily to be a copy of divine kingship,
the king being a true bridge between God and his subjects. He was

---

[1] F. Dvornik, 'Emperors, Popes, and General Councils', *DOP* 6 (1951), 22. The term
'Christian political Hellenism' is meant to convey Hellenistic imperial and political ideology
adapted to Christian usage. Dvornik uses the term 'Christian Hellenism', but this also has
a quite different theological meaning.

[2] Dvornik, *Early Christian and Byzantine Political Philosophy: Origins and Background*,
Dumbarton Oaks Studies, 9 (Washington, 1966), 506 ff.

[3] Ibid. 536.

thus thought of as a priest–king whose piety (εὐσέβεια) was a guarantee of the well-being of his kingdom.

This manner of thinking found a natural resonance amongst Christian philosophers,[4] and Hellenistic epithets continued to be applied to Christian emperors.[5] Rulers, according to Gregory of Nazianzus, were 'most divine' and 'most beloved of Christ'. They were the image of God and were called to imitate God in His benevolence and mercy. Their main virtues were to include nobleness and goodness (καλοκἀγαθία), benevolence (φιλανθρωπία), and Roman *humanitas*.[6] Similar beliefs are to found in the writings of Gregory of Nyssa, Basil the Great, and John Chrysostom.[7] 'God gave you to us. God will preserve you. You are ever-victorious, for you honour Christ' ran fifth-century acclamations of army and people.[8] Art and architecture also reflected the same imperial ideology.[9] The Golden Chamber throne-room in the imperial palace, for example, which witnessed many imperial ceremonies, had an image of Christ above the emperor's throne. Spectators could be reminded in a visual way that the enthroned emperor was a living embodiment on earth of Christ in heaven, the true *imago Christi*.[10] Another way of communicating imperial propaganda

---

[4] Dvornik, *Early Christian and Byzantine Political Philosophy: Origins and Background*, Dumbarton Oaks Studies, 9 (Washington, 1966), 616: 'Eusebius . . . gave Christian sanction to the pagan principle, so dear to Hellenistic political theorists, that a ruler should be a copy of God's perfection. As he understood it, this copy is not perfect until the ruler has given the world the twin benefits of peace and faith in God. This will enable him to achieve so faithful an imitation of divine monarchy that he will become the monarch of the whole universe, the representative of God on earth, the symbol of the one human race, of the one God.' Cf. Eusebius, *De Laudibus Const.* 2: *PG* 20. 1325.

[5] Cf. Dvornik, *Early Christian and Byzantine Political Philosophy*, ch. 10, 'Christian Hellenism', 611–58.

[6] Gregory of Nazianzus, *Or.* 4. 34: *PG* 35. 560, 685; *Or.* 17. 8, 9: ibid. 976. In *Or.* 36. 11 (*PG* 35. 277), he writes, 'Emperors, respect your people . . . Know how much has been committed to your conscience and what a mysterious thing your basileia is. The whole world is in your hands, however small the crown and weak the body. What is above you belongs to God alone; what is below you belongs to you also. If I may speak thus, be as gods to your subjects. The King's heart is in God's hand, as it is said [Prov. 21:1] and is believed. There should lie your strength, not in gold or in armies.'

[7] Dvornik, *Early Christian and Byzantine Political Philosophy*, 689 ff.

[8] Constantine Porphyrogenitos, *De cerimoniis aulae Byzantinae*, ed. J. J. Reike (Bonn, 1829), i. 411.

[9] See A. Grabar, *L'Empereur dans l'art byzantin* (Paris, 1936). Cf. A. Cameron, 'Images of Authority: Elites and Icons in Late Sixth-Century Byzantium', *Past and Present: A Journal of Historical Studies*, 84 (1979), 3–35 (repr. in A. Cameron, *Continuity and Change in Sixth-Century Byzantium* (London, 1981)).

[10] Cameron, 'Images of Authority', 17

was through coinage. Justinian II (d. 711) was the first to introduce the effigy of Christ on a Byzantine coin. On the obverse side of the solidus, with the figure of Christ, were the words *Rex regnantium*. On the reverse, with the emperor holding a cross, were the words *D. Justinianus Servus Christi*. The emperor was therefore Christ's deputy and the upholder of Orthodoxy.[11] He was not, of course, considered to be divine, as in pre-Christian political Hellenism, but the emperor still stood in unique relation to God. At times this relationship was expressed using a modified understanding of the pagan priest–king motif: it could be scripturalized and made to express a legitimate succession to the Old Testament kings and to their priesthood.[12] Even bishops of Rome occasionally described the imperial office in priestly terms.[13] Pope Gregory II (715–31) would write to the iconoclast Leo the Isaurian, who had said of himself, 'I am king and priest' (Βασιλεὺς καὶ ἱερεύς εἰμί), explaining that true imperial priesthood involved preserving the traditions of the Fathers: 'Hi sunt sacerdotes et imperatores qui id opere demonstrarunt.'[14] His letter is replete with the terminology and concepts of what can be termed 'Christian' political Hellenism.[15]

At the beginning of each session of the Second Council of Nicaea (787) the following formula would always be used: 'In the

[11] C. Head, *Justinian II of Byzantium* (Madison, 1972), 55–8.

[12] In the mosaics of San Vitale at Ravenna, Melchizedek, the mysterious priest-king of Jerusalem, wears the same vestments used by the emperor. Likewise, in the illuminations of a Paris MS David appears in similar robes to those habitually worn by the Basileus. Cf. Grabar, *L'Empereur*, 95 ff. On the history of the emperor as priest-king, see the excellent study by G. Dagron: *Empereur et prêtre: Étude sur le 'césaropapisme' byzantine* (Paris, 1996).

[13] Dvornik, *Early Christian and Byzantine Political Philosophy*, 644, 772, 781, and *passim*. Cf. 'Emperors, Popes, and Councils', 16–18, 21. This did not mean that the emperor was thought to have any priestly sacramental powers. Cf. Maximos the Confessor, *Acta: PG* 90. 117AB.

[14] *Ep. II ad Leonem Isaurum Imperatorem*, Mansi, *Sacrorum Conciliorum*, xii. 975D, 977A. See the discussion on this phrase by Gilbert Dagron, *Empereur et prêtre*, 169 ff.

[15] The emperor is κεφαλὴ τῶν χριστιανῶν, φιλόχριστος καὶ εὐσεβής, whose Empire is ἐκ Θεοῦ. Mansi, *Sacrorum Conciliorum*, xii. 959A, 970B, 979A, 959C. On this letter, see F. Dvornik, 'Constantinople and Rome', in J. M. Hussey (ed.), *The Cambridge Medieval History* (Cambridge, 1966), iv. 431–72, at 443–4. Leo III had also expressed himself in a similar Hellenic form in the preface to his *Ekloga* (*c*.726). This law book, which was in force during the lifetime of Theodore, was formulated totally in the Greek language (unlike the Justinian Corpus) and was thus more accessible to the Byzantine than previous legal texts. In the preface the emperor compares his imperial charge to shepherd the Christian flock to the charge given to St Peter. An excellent commentary on this preface is found in Gero, *Byzantine Iconoclasm during the reign of Leo III*, 48–58, where the author points out that this passage should not be interpreted as caesaropapist (pp. 51–2 n. 14).

name of the Lord and Master Jesus Christ our true God, during the rule of our most pious and Christ-loving lords Constantine and his mother Irene . . .'[16] The emperors were expected to take an active role in promoting the Orthodox Christian faith throughout the world (οἰκουμένη), a role which was an unquestioned duty.[17] Thus, in the *Oratio Tarasii* the new Orthodox patriarch describes the 'most pious' Emperor Constantine VI and his mother Irene as custodians of Christian faith and as zealots for the glory of God.[18]

3.2 CHURCH AND STATE IN BYZANTIUM

Ever since the time of Constantine the relationship of the state to the church had remained undefined and somewhat ambiguous.[19] God had founded the church, but he had also founded Rome and the Roman Empire. As God's vicegerent the emperor had care over the church as part of his overall care for his Christian subjects, a situation which was potentially threatening if, as did occasionally happen, the Emperor intervened unilaterally in doctrinal disputes.[20] His accepted role was to defend doctrinal orthodoxy,

[16] Mansi, *Sacrorum Conciliorum*, xii. 991E, 1051B, 1114A, etc.: Ἐν ὀνόματι τοῦ κυρίου καὶ δεσπότου Ἰησοῦ Χριστοῦ τοῦ ἀληθινοῦ Θεοῦ ἡμῶν βασιλείας τῶν εὐσεβεστάτων καὶ φιλοχρίστων ἡμῶν δεσποτῶν Κωνσταντίνου καὶ Εἰρίνης τῆς αὐτοῦ μητρός.

[17] In the *Epistula Imperatoris ad sacram synodum* the emperor's role is described in these words: 'ad concordiam et pacem universum Romanum imperium erigere contendens, praecipue tamen sanctarum Dei nostri ecclesiarum statum qua possumus cura et consilia conservare intendimus. Sacerdotumque concordiam per omnia firmam et stabilem esse desideramus': Mansi, *Sacrorum Conciliorum*, xiii. 504C.

[18] Ibid. xii. 986E. In the closing Letter of Tarasios and the Synod to the emperors, the latter are called 'leaders of the whole Christian people into piety (πρὸς εὐσέβειαν)'. They confirm the orthodox faith of the church, ensuring, by their assistance, stability in ecclesiastical affairs, and church unity. God's Spirit dwells in them. Ibid. *xiii.* 401A–B, E. '[Christ] the Saviour co-reigns with them': ὁ δὲ πάντων ἡμῶν σωτὴρ καὶ συμβασιλευῶν ὑμῖν. Ibid. 408C (Pope Hadrian I had to defend the use of this Hellenic idea before Charlemagne: 'De eo quod Constantinus et Irene in suis scriptis ajunt: Per eum qui corregnat nobis Deus', *Hadriani I Epistula ad Carolum Regem*, ibid. xiii. 804D).

[19] Cf. Dagron, 'Le Règle et l'exception', 141–68 and *passim*. See also S. Runciman, *Byzantine Theocracy* (Cambridge, 1977); Y. Congar, *L'Ecclésiologie du haut Moyen Age: De Saint Grégoire le Grand à la désunion entre Byzance et Rome* (Paris, 1968), 347 ff.

[20] Examples are the interventions of Constantius in the Arian dispute, the issuing of the *Henotikon* by Emperor Zeno (482), the condemnation of the *Three Chapters* by Justinian (543), Emperor Herakleios' *Ekthesis* (638), and the *Typos* of Constans II (648). These imperial acts were always self-limiting and incapable of full realization and implementation. Maximos the Confessor, for example, states (*Acta, PG* 90. 117), 'None of the emperors was able,

including through convoking church councils, but not to decide on issues that were the sole competence of the body of bishops. Yet, even in these situations, the concept of church and state as rival societies in partnership would be meaningless to a Byzantine. As one scholar has put it,

[The Byzantine] was not conscious of belonging to more than one society—the people of God, a flock which had indeed shepherds of different kinds, priests and Emperors, but was nevertheless one flock, one people, in every aspect of its life the *respublica Christiana*. To talk of 'did State rule Church or Church the State?' is to talk in the light of subsequent Western European history.[21]

The *ecclesia* and the *imperium* interpenetrated in such a way that they were inseparable, but Byzantine theory did provide for a distinction between the offices of the *sacerdotium* and those of the *imperium*.[22] No legislation, church or civil, ever defined the

through compromising measures, to induce the Fathers, who were theologians, to conform to the heretical teachings of their time. But in strong and compelling voices appropriate to the dogma in question, they declared quite clearly that it is the function of the clergy to discuss and define the saving dogmas of the universal church.'

[21] T. M. Parker, *Christianity and the State in the Light of History*, Bampton Lectures (London, 1955), 78. Compare the statement of Yves Congar, *Ecclésiologie du haut Moyen Age*, 349: 'L'empereur est loin de présider au seul ordre temporel, sous l'autorité spirituelle des prêtres; la vie de l'Église et la vie civile appartiennent au même ordre, celui de l'Empire'.

[22] The classical formulation of this distinction is that given by Justinian in the preface to his *Novella* VI: 'The greatest blessings of mankind are the gifts of God which have been granted us by the mercy on high: the priesthood and the imperial authority. The priesthood ministers to things divine; the imperial authority is set over, and shows diligence in, things human; both proceed from one and the same source, and both adorn the life of man ('Maxima quidem in omnibus sunt dona Dei, a superna collata clementia, sacerdotium et imperium: illud quidem divinis ministrans, hoc autem humanis praesidens, ac diligentiam exhibens; ex uno eodemque principio utraque procedentia humanam exornant vitam'). Nothing, therefore, will be a greater matter of concern to the emperor than the dignity and honour of the clergy; the more as they offer prayers to God without ceasing on his behalf. For if the priesthood be in all respects without blame, and full of faith before God, and if the imperial authority rightly and duly adorn the commonwealth committed to its charge, there will ensure a happy concord which will bring forth all good things for mankind ('erit consonantia quaedam bona omne quicquid utile est humano conferens generi'). We therefore have the greatest concern for true doctrines of the Godhead and the dignity and honour of the clergy; and we believe that if they maintain that dignity and honour we shall gain thereby the greatest of gifts, holding fast what we already have and laying hold of what is yet to come . . . We believe that this will come to pass if observance be paid to the holy rules which have been handed down by the Apostles—those righteous guardians and ministers of the Word of God, who are ever to be praised and adored—and have since been preserved and interpreted by the holy Fathers', Justinian, *Novellae*, 6, in R. Schoell (ed.), *Corpus Iuris Civilis*, iii. *Novellae* (Berlin, 1912), 35–6.

respective boundaries of these two powers,[23] for Christian political
Hellenistic theory did not provide for the possibility of a heterodox
ruler acting contrary to the canons and doctrinal traditions of the
church. Only when the reality proved greater than the theory did
individual churchmen speak out in defence of the constitution of
the church. Even in these cases the intention was not to deny outright the Hellenistic role of the *imperium* (namely, its rights to intervene in ecclesiastical affairs) but to ensure its proper functioning.
Its function was to aid and assist the *sacerdotium* in a relationship of
concord.

   With this background we now have the context within which the
language, the concerns, and the conflicts of Theodore Stoudite
with the emperor can be better understood.

3.3 THEODORE AND CHRISTIAN POLITICAL HELLENISM

Three and a half years after his return from exile in Thessalonica
(August 797) Theodore wrote a congratulatory letter to the
Empress Irene on the occasion of her tax reform for which she
received popular support.[24] The language is replete with
Hellenistic allusions. Irene's *basileia* is 'God-given' ($\theta\epsilon\acute{o}\sigma\delta\sigma\tau\sigma$),[25]
and he rejoices at the news coming from the 'sacred palace'.[26] The
'sacred' Irene is concerned for both the physical and spiritual wel-
fare of her Christian subjects.[27] She is beloved of Christ ($E\grave{\iota}\rho\acute{\eta}\nu\eta$

---

[23] However, some limitations to the intervention of the temporal power were enshrined
in canon law. One example is the restriction on the election of bishops, reaffirmed at the
Second Council of Nicaea (canon 3): Rulers ought not to elect the bishop ($\H{O}\tau\iota$ $\sigma\grave{\upsilon}$ $\delta\epsilon\hat{\iota}$
$\H{a}\rho\chi\sigma\nu\tau\alpha\varsigma$ $\psi\eta\phi\acute{\iota}\zeta\epsilon\sigma\theta\alpha\iota$ $\grave{\epsilon}\pi\acute{\iota}\sigma\kappa\sigma\pi\sigma\nu$), 'Any election of a bishop, priest or deacon brought
about by the rulers is to be null and void in accordance with the canon that says: "If any
bishop, through the influence of secular rulers, acquires responsibility for a church because
of them, let him be excommunicated" [Apostolic canon 30].' Tanner, *Decrees of the
Ecumenical Councils*, i. 140*. In practice the canon was often interpreted widely, allowing the
emperor a large say in the choice of candidate. Cf. below, p. 139.

[24] Ep. 7. Theophanes writes, 'In March of the ninth indiction the pious Irene forgave the
Byzantines the city taxes, and lightened the *commercia* [customs duties on imports and
exports] at Abydos and Hieron. These and many other benefactions earned her great
thanks' (*Chronographia*, AM 6293).

[25] Ep. 7. 73.   [26] Ep. 7. 5: $\grave{a}\nu\alpha\phi\alpha\nu\acute{\epsilon}\nu\tau\epsilon\varsigma$ $\H{a}\gamma\gamma\epsilon\lambda\sigma\iota$ $\tau\sigma\hat{\upsilon}$ $\grave{\iota}\epsilon\rho\sigma\hat{\upsilon}$ $\sigma\sigma\upsilon$ $\pi\alpha\lambda\alpha\tau\acute{\iota}\sigma\upsilon$.
[27] Ep. 7. 57, 15–16.

φίλη Χριστοῦ).²⁸ For Theodore, Irene's glory resides above all in her role as God's intermediary in restoring peace to the church. What he has particularly in mind is not just the affair of Constantine's marriage, for which he had been exiled, but Irene's role in restoring Orthodoxy at the Second Council of Nicaea.²⁹ It is through her that God has taken pity on his people, having inspired her to liberate her people from the equivalent of Egyptian slavery, namely the servitude of impious belief.³⁰ The piety of Irene is thus the glory of the church;³¹ it is the guarantee (σφραγίς) of Orthodoxy. She is the champion (ἔκδικος) of God and the defender of truth (τῆς ἀληθείας ὑπέρμαχος).³²

Theodore expresses the belief that the emperors are somehow appointed and elected directly by God, not being concerned with how they actually came to power.³³ For the emperor to have received the patriarch's coronation blessing was no doubt sufficient confirmation of this.³⁴ There is but one emperor as there is but one God.³⁵ The rulership is 'God-crowned' (θεόστεπτος) and—when the emperor is Orthodox—pious and Christ-loving (φιλόχριστος), being the image of God.³⁶ Such emperors are 'zealots' (ζηλωταί),³⁷ 'Christ-imitating' (χριστομίμητοι),³⁸ emulating things divine for the good of all.³⁹ For in true faith lies the salvation of the empire and all its subjects.⁴⁰

²⁸ Ep. 7. 74. Fatouros has noted (*Theodori Studitae Epistulae*, 26) that the whole sentence was taken almost *verbatim* from Gregory of Nazianzus, *Or*. 22. 1 (*PG* 35. 1132A). Εἰρήνη, of course, was not a proper noun in this case.
²⁹ Even though at this stage Theodore still did not consider the synod ecumenical.
³⁰ Ep. 7. 24–5, 18–19.
³¹ Lay and ecclesiastical personages are frequently called 'pious' in Theodore's letters, ἡ εὐσέβεια σου being a polite form of address. Already by the 4th cent. it was a convention to address ecclesiastics of whatever condition in this way: H. Zilliaeus, *Untersuchungen zu den abstrakten Anredeformen und Höflicheitstiteln im Griechischen* (Helsingfors, 1949), 68. On the use of this title by the Fathers in addressing the emperor, see Sister L. Dinneen, *Titles of Address in Christian Greek Epistolography to 527* (London, 1981), 29 ff.
³² Ibid. 85–7.
³³ Cf. ep. 16. 1–3, ep. 433. 15–16: τῶν θεοπροβλήτων ἡμῶν βασιλέων. Theodore must have been well aware, living so close to the palace and with his network of highly placed friends, of the intrigues of the imperial court before the coming to power of a new emperor. However, there is no comment, not even veiled reference, on any of this.
³⁴ Cf. ep. 31, 91–2, where Theodore asserts (in the context of the marriage ceremony) that 'according to Dionysios' God confirms and ratifies the blessing of the priest.
³⁵ TC 1. 45. 200. Cf. PK 3. 17.
³⁶ Ep. 429. 3–4, 33 (*ann*. 821, to Michael II), ep. 16. 8, ep. 56. 39–40; TC I. 45. 200.
³⁷ Ep. 25. 80.   ³⁸ Ep. 16. 37. Cf. ep. 424. 28, ep. 429. 11–12.
³⁹ Ep. 429. 36–7: ὡς ζηλοτυποῦσα τὰ θεῖα ἐπ' ὠφελείᾳ τοῦ παντός.
⁴⁰ Ep. 424. 31.

But what if an emperor acts contrary to the laws of God, is heterodox, and leads his people into error and impiety? Theodore had to face this question during the moechian and Joseph controversies and, more particularly, during the revival under Leo V of iconoclasm.

3.4 THE EMPEROR AND THE LAW

During the sole reign of Constantine VI Theodore was conscious that the emperor had broken the commandment of the Lord and the canons of the church, yet his reproaches were aimed primarily at Joseph the steward of Hagia Sophia and Patriarch Tarasios who had not opposed the 'adulterous' marriage forcibly enough. In these first letters Theodore avoids a direct confrontation with the emperor.[41] Writing to the *hegoumenos* Nikephoros, Theodore affirms: 'I hold the supreme and most devout Emperor in heartfelt love . . . I also commemorate the Emperor in the divine liturgy and pray for him both privately and publicly.'[42] These words, according to Patrick Henry, were written *after* he had broken communion with the emperor.[43] During the Joseph affair, but before the 809 Synod, he wrote to Patriarch Nikephoros apropos of the problems created by Emperor Nikephoros' favourable gesture towards Joseph. Even then he conceives the issue in purely ecclesiastical terms: 'Merely exclude one sheep, and that one only, from the priesthood and thus benefit the whole flock. Do not let the Church

---

[41] When he alludes to John the Forerunner reprimanding Herod (ep. 5. 36) Theodore seems to be justifying the rebuking of a patriarch by a priest, not an emperor. This is the analysis given by Henry, *Theodore of Studios*, 103 n. 1. Hatlie, 'Abbot Theodore', 126 n. 36, on the other hand, takes issue with Henry and thinks the context suggests a criticism of Constantine. However, he then adds, 'his comments are not only subtle, but isolated. The abbot's other contemporaneous writings do not repeat or further clarify the nature of Theodore's critique of the Emperor' (pp. 128–9).

[42] Ep. 4. 39–43: 39–43: ἀλλὰ καὶ τὸν αὐτοκράτορα καὶ εὐσεβέστατον βασιλέα ἐγκαρδιωμένον ἔχομεν τῇ ἀγάπῃ . . . καὶ μνημονεύομεν αὐτοῦ καὶ ἐν τῇ θείᾳ λειτουργίᾳ καὶ ἐπευχόμεθα ἰδίᾳ τε καὶ δημοσίᾳ.

[43] Henry, *Theodore of Studios*, 105–6: 'His overriding concern is to avoid the stigma of schism, and he must find some way to say he is still in communion with this [Patriarchal] Church. He does this through a liturgical finesse: he commemorates one with whom he would not share the liturgical celebrations.' Sirmond, to the contrary, in a note to the words εὐσεβέστατον βασιλέα (*PG* 99. 921D) writes: 'Scripta est haec epistula paulo ante primum exsilium, cum nondum se imperatoris communione sejunxisset.'

be infected by the disease of one—the Church which our Lord and God bought with his own blood.'[44]

There is no criticism of the emperor, nor any denunciation of the secular powers intruding into the affairs of the church.[45] This is also echoed in a letter written to the brethren of Sakkoudion in which is reported the interrogation of Archbishop Joseph, the brother of Theodore, by the logothete of the Course (τοῦ Δρόμου), where Archbishop Joseph states, 'I have nothing against our devout Emperors (τοὺς εὐσεβεῖς ἡμῶν βασιλεῖς) . . . but rather against the Steward who crowned the adulterer and as a result was deposed by the sacred canons.'[46]

Only after and as a result of the 'moechian' synod of 809 did Theodore begin openly to reflect on the role of the emperor in society and his relation to the church. One of the deductions Theodore makes from the decisions of the synod is that the hierarchy had retrospectively exempted Emperor Constantine VI from the law of God. 'If [this type of economy] applies to Emperors only,' Theodore asks provokingly, 'is it exclusively in cases of adultery, or in any other transgression?'[47] There is, in fact, no special gospel for emperors, he says in a letter written to Pope Leo III.[48] Elsewhere he argues in the form of a dilemma: if different laws apply to emperors and their subjects then the emperor is either God or there would be rebellion and sedition.[49] In the same letter Theodore alludes to Galatians 1: 8–9 where the Apostle Paul tells his readers not to listen even to an angel if the message were contrary to the Gospel, adding 'And is the Emperor greater than an angel?'[50]

By transgressing God's law and requiring that the church give sanction to his action, Constantine had rejected his true role of

[44] Ep. 25. 86–9. Cf. ep. 30. 52–5.

[45] Henry, *Theodore of Studios*, 126 n., writes, 'It is important to notice that the pollution, the disease, the profanation which Theodore sees is not conceived by him as an intrusion of the civil into the ecclesiastical sphere. The passage from Ezekiel goes on to speak of the sins of the rulers (Ezek. 22. 27: οἱ ἄρχοντες) but Theodore limits the citation to the priests. The problem is the specifically ecclesiastical one of a corrupt priesthood. This priest-monk makes his own not a priestly denunciation of secular rulers, but a prophetic denunciation of the priesthood.'

[46] Ep. 31. 17–20.   [47] Ep. 48. 189–90.

[48] Ep. 34. 79 (*ann.* 809): καὶ ποῦ τὸ τῶν βασιλέων εὐαγγέλιον;

[49] Ep. 36. 34–5 (*ann.* 809): . . . αὐτῶν δὲ ναί, δύο ταῦτα, ἢ θεὸς ὁ βασιλεὺς (μόνον γὰρ τὸ θεῖον οὐχ ὑπὸ νόμον) ἢ ἀναρχία καὶ στάσις.

[50] Ep. 36. 75: μὴ βασιλεὺς μείζων ἀγγέλου;

pious and Christ-loving emperor. In the encomium on his uncle
Plato, written after the latter's death in 814, Theodore calls the
emperor's rule 'adulterous' (ἡ μοιχικὴ βασιλεία). The emperor,
despite being honoured by the purple, had not wanted to act with
goodness nor to learn not to violate God's laws.[51] He had reneged
on his role as custodian of the true faith. Plato, in contrast, had
shown himself to be the true guardian of Orthodoxy.[52] Where the
emperor failed in his duty, drawing many others into error with
him, it was for Plato to stand up and witness to the truth. He took
the place of John the Forerunner, the 'great herald of truth' (ὁ
μέγας κῆρυξ τῆς ἀληθείας),[53] and challenged with evangelical
doctrine Constantine, whom Theodore openly compares to
Herod.[54] He laments over those who had co-operated with Caesar,
who had set his will before that of God,[55] accusing his adversaries
of proclaiming the will of the emperors as the will of God.[56]

The emperor, therefore, was not above the law. There was but a
single law, a single lawgiver (νομοθέτης), that is, God.[57] Law, for
Theodore, was an objective and absolute reality. It is created by
God and present in both nature and society, society's role being to
discover it in pre-existing justice. Thus, no one can be 'more law-
ful than the law'.[58] Hellenistic political theory, on the other hand,
had considered the king or emperor to be the embodiment of the
law, 'an animated law' (νόμος ἔμψυχος), the supposition being
that secular law, which was the absolute property of the king or
emperor as its creator and interpreter, was formulated according
to the principles of divine justice. Such an idea found currency
among some Byzantine emperors, in particular Justinian, who
enshrined it in his Novels.[59] For the most part Theodore does not

[51] *Laudatio Platonis* 833A.
[52] Ibid. Plato was ὁ πιστὸς τοῦ Κυρίου νομοφύλαξ.   [53] Ep. 5. 36.
[54] *Laudatio Platonis* 832AB. Cf. ep. 31. 66–7: τὸν δεύτερον Ἡρώδην; ep. 443, 29–32:
ἐνωτισάσθω οὖν πᾶς ἔχων νοῦν ὡς ἄρα δικαίως δεύτερος Ἡρώδης Κωνσταντῖνος,
ἐπὰν οὐκ ἄλλος ἔκτοτε μέχρι τοῦ δεῦρο πέπραχε τοιοῦτο, ὀνομάζοιτο, αὐτὸς
ἑαυτῷ προξενήσας πρακτικῶς τὸ ὄνομα.
[55] *Laudatio Platonis* 832CD.   [56] Ep. 34. 102.
[57] Ep. 36. 102; TC I. 45. 200. Cf. *MC* 35. 99, where Theodore says he fears no man,
prince or king, but God alone who is the Master, the Lord of all, the one King of Kings,
God of gods, the Emperor of all men.
[58] Ep. 43. 17–18. Cf. Kazhdan, 'Some Observations on the Byzantine Concept of Law',
200–1.
[59] Dvornik, *Early Christian and Byzantine Political Philosophy*, 597, 716, 723. Cf. Hatlie,
'Abbot Theodore', 90.

clearly distinguish between the realms of divine and secular law (much as he does not distinguish—at least in their binding obligation—between divine law and canons or ecclesiastical and monastic rules). This would suggest that he likewise rejected the theory of the νόμος ἔμψυχος, one reason being that the emperor was not in any sense equal to God.[60] And indeed there is no resonance of such a theory in Theodore.[61] None the less, he does on at least two occasions refer to formulated Roman law (τοὺς ῥωμαικοὺς νόμους) which he believes is worthy of respect,[62] and he does regard the emperor as the highest human authority as long as his commands do not contradict God's commands.[63] The emperor's role was thus to justly interpret, reform, and administer all laws that ultimately expressed the justice of God.

Emperor Constantine, in Theodore's estimation, had failed to uphold the law by entering into an illegal marriage with Theodote. He was no better than the heathens.[64] Michael, Theodore's biographer, similarly describes Constantine and Theodote as 'the lawless ones' (τοὺς ἀθέσμους), having rebelled against both divine and human laws (ἔξω θεσμῶν ἀποσκιρτήσας θείων καὶ ἀνθρωπίνων).[65] This serious failure to fulfil the true imperial role had serious consequences. The emperor's influence by example (ὑπόδειγμα) had been noxious. His bad example would be, and according to Theodore already had been, imitated by his subjects,[66] threatening church and civil order.[67] Theodore's interpretation that the 809 synod had exonerated Constantine led also to the evidently untenable conclusion that the emperor's place within civil and ecclesiastical society could be redefined.[68] Contrary to what he claims the synod affirms, the emperor does not stand outside the laws of Christian society, nor can exceptions for him be made.

---

[60] Few Byzantine political writers, in fact, were happy about this idea. See Dvornik, *Early Christian and Byzantine Political Philosophy*, 678–9; Hatlie, 'Abbot Theodore', 90 and n. 104.
[61] Kazhdan, 'Some Observations on the Byzantine Concept of Law', 203. Cf. Hatlie, 'Abbot Theodore', 90–1.
[62] Ep. 31. 57, ep. 455. 76.   [63] Ep. 470. 38–40.
[64] Cf. ep. 31. 95–7.   [65] *Vita B, PG* 99. 252D.
[66] Ep. 31. 92–4. Cf. Hatlie, 'Abbot Theodore', 143–7.
[67] Cf. ep. 227. 18–19, ep. 514. 14. (both to Maria, Constantine's first wife).
[68] Cf. Hatlie, 'Abbot Theodore', 166–7.

3.5 THEODORE AND CHURCH–STATE RELATIONS

The official imperial policy of relations between church and state at the time of the Second Council of Nicaea was that of harmony between two distinct institutions, the two 'great gifts vouchsafed by God to humanity'.[69] In the *Divalis sacra* of the Emperors Constantine and Irene to Pope Hadrian, which was read out to the synod, the first words ran: 'Those who receive from our Lord Jesus Christ, true God, either the imperial dignity or the honour of supreme priesthood, have to think of and care for that which pleases Him and have to direct and govern the people entrusted to them by Him according to His will . . .'[70] Theodore makes the same distinction between *imperium* and *sacerdotium*, secular institutions and the church, and the two were to co-operate closely. In his estimation the empress Irene was an ideal ruler because she assisted the church, allowing the bishops to work out problems synodically, without interfering herself.[71] His view that emperors were to heed the words of Matthew 22: 21 and 'Render unto God the things of God',[72] did not mean that the emperor was necessarily excluded from the affairs of the church. In a letter to Emperor Nikephoros written before the rehabilitation of the steward Joseph (806), he indicates, almost as a matter of course, how closely the *imperium* and *sacerdotium* should co-operate. 'Our good God', he writes,

must have been looking out for the welfare of his Church. He has brought Your Devotedness forward to rule over the present generation of Christians, so that the secular government, which was in disarray, might be set in order, and so that the government of the Church, should it be

---

[69] Cf. above, p. 131 n. 22. Leo III's declarations on kingship and priesthood, and having authority over the Christian flock—without ever mentioning the patriarch or clergy—seem, now, to have given way to a greater emphasis on Justinian's more balanced definition of the two powers. This was possibly in view of the misuse of the emperor's authority in initiating iconoclasm. Cf. Dvornik, 'Constantinople and Rome', 446; G. Ladner, 'Origin and Significance of the Byzantine Iconoclastic Controversy', *Medieval Studies*, 2 (1940), 127–49, esp. 135, 140; Werner, *Die Krise im Verhältnis von Staat und Kirche in Byzanz*, 113 ff.

[70] Mansi, *Sacrorum Conciliorum*, xii. 984E: Qui a Domino nostro Jesu Christo vero Deo nostro suscipiunt sive imperii dignitatem, sive principalis sacerdotii honorem, debent quae illi placita sunt, et cogitare et curare, et creditos sibi ab illo populos secundum ejus voluntatem regere et gubernare . . .

[71] Ep. 175. 17–19.   [72] Ep. 417. 42–3.

lacking in anything, might be restored. There can be fresh dough in both spheres.[73]

Later in the same letter he says: 'God has given two gifts to the Christians: priesthood and empire. Through both of these earthly affairs are administered and ordered as in heaven. Therefore, if either functions improperly, the whole is necessarily endangered.'[74] It seems surprising, given his reputation as a defender of the independence of the church, that Theodore should envisage such a close working relationship between the two God-given gifts. But the context of these statements was the election of a new patriarch, a change in church government that affected the interests of both church and state. Concerning the electoral procedure of the patriarch, Theodore has this to say to the emperor:

> The following suggestion is made with respect and reverence, only as a kind of aid to your memory. It will certainly not have been overlooked by Your Most Expert and Divine Prudence that you are to receive nominations of bishops, abbots, stylites, recluses and clergy (since the matter is of common concern, the stylites should descend and the hermits come forth); from those advanced you are then to select the ones who are outstanding in prudence, intelligence and manner of life, and in consultation with this group you are to select and designate the most worthy candidate.[75]

Theodore clearly apportions to the emperor a major role and responsibility in the election of the new patriarch, notwithstanding the canon of the Second Council of Nicaea which sought to restrict rulers' influence.[76] This leads Henry to comment:

> The most striking aspect of this letter to Nicephorus is the extent to which Theodore concedes authority to the Emperor in the process of election of a Patriarch. Theodore has been praised so often as a valiant intrepid defender of the Church's independence, of its right to govern its own affairs without imperial interference, that his deference to imperial prerogative in the very important matter of a Patriarchal election comes as

---

[73] Ep. 16. 1–7.
[74] Ep. 16. 40–3: ἐπειδὴ δύο ταῦτα δέδωκεν ὁ θεὸς τοῖς Χριστιανοῖς δωρήματα, ἱερωσύνην καὶ βασιλείαν, δι᾽ ὧν θεραπεύεται, δι᾽ ὧν κοσμεῖται ὡς ἐν οὐρανῷ τὰ ἐπίγεια· ὁποτέρως οὖν ἀναξίως ἔχει, καὶ τό ὅλον ἀνάγκη συγκινδυνεύειν. Cf. Justinian's *Novella* 6.
[75] Ep. 16. 28–36. For a good discussion on this passage, with its clear allusion to excluding lay candidates, see Henry, *Theodore of Studios*, 52–4.
[76] Cf. above, p. 132 n. 23.

something of a surprise. He does say that the Emperor is to receive a good deal of clerical advice, but the final decision is still to be the Emperor's.[77]

When the election of Archbishop Joseph of Thessalonica was discussed the emperor's legitimate intervention was also acknowledged.[78]

After the rehabilitation of Joseph in 806 Theodore initially looked to the emperor, as defender and protector of the church, for a resolution of the crisis that was developing. He writes to the Sakkoudion monks:

The Lord, who is a helper of those who stand up for His commandment, will bend the hearts of our pious Emperors to vindicate His Church, just as He did in respect to the adulterer, so that likewise it will seem proper to eject this man (Joseph) from the priesthood with a view both to the advantage of the most holy Patriarch and the entire Catholic Church . . . So pray for our Emperors, for the Patriarch, for the ejection of Joseph from the altar, for the peace of the Church.[79]

To have the emperor's 'interference' in this matter was highly desirable. He writes to the monk Symeon:

We need Your Piety (since you practise the monastic life in an exact manner) to whisper such statements into the ears of our pious despots. For we believe that if they send this man (Joseph) away with the blessing of the most holy Patriarch, the angels will stand up to clap. All the saints will join in praise. And the entire Church will exult. Much added divine assistance will visit their power, both in the containment of enemies and adversaries and in their peaceful and long life.[80]

Theodore was to be disappointed by the emperor's refusal to mediate, and he soon understood that it was in fact the patriarch who had acted according to the imperial will: he was under the emperor's thumb.[81] The 809 synod, which came as such a shock

[77] Henry, *Theodore of Studios*, 54. See also the commentary by Dagron, ibid. 231–3.
[78] Ep. 23. Commenting on this letter, written by Archbishop Joseph or Theodore in Joseph's name, Henry also writes (ibid. 60 n.), 'The unquestioned admission here of the imperial role in such an election should be added to the evidence from the Patriarchal election in modifying the generally-held view of Studite opposition on Church–State relations.'
[79] Ep. 33. 99–113.
[80] Ep. 22. 75–82. In epp. 21–2 Theodore writes of the devout rule and piety of the emperor: τῶν εὐσεβῶν ἡμῶν δεσποτῶν (ep. 21. 11, ep. 22. 76–7); ὅτε εὐσεβοῦσά ἡ βασιλεία (ep. 21. 36, ep. 22. 119–20); τοῖς εὐσεβέσιν ἡμῶν βασιλεῦσιν (ep. 22. 142–3). He emphasizes that his actions are not directed towards the emperor, for whom he has nothing but respect and reverence, but against Joseph: ep. 22. 3–7; cf. ep. 21. 11–13.
[81] Ep. 26. 25–6: ταμιευόμενον πάντα Καίσαρι.

to Theodore, was, he knew, the emperor's doing (ἔκ
προστάγματος βασιλικοῦ καθολικὴ σύνοδος), and was conducted with a view towards the emperor's interests
(δεδογματίκασιν οὖν ἐπὶ τῶν βασιλέων).[82] A good part of the
Joseph controversy thereafter became an imperial controversy,
with Nikephoros being seen increasingly as the real cause of the
problem.[83] Theodore's remarks in his letters after the synod had
taken place, about the will of the emperors being pitted against the
law of God and its dangerous consequences, can be read as referring equally to Constantine VI and to Nikephoros. The first had
committed adultery, the second, by orchestrating the synod's
anathema, had committed heresy.[84] This reaction to the Emperor
Nikephoros is all the more curious given that, according to
Theodore, Nikephoros himself had told him that he regarded
Theodote, the hapless wife of Constantine, an adulteress and her
progeny illegitimate and disinherited, as according to Roman
law.[85]

Despite the fact that the emperor's intervention in the Joseph
affair was construed implicitly in terms of promoting a heresy (a
'heresy by extension' one might say), Theodore's argument against
the *imperium* was focused around the issue of law. Writing to Pope
Leo, he states that the moechian synod—'a public synod in which
civil officials have also participated'—has determined 'that the
divine laws do not apply to Emperors' and that 'God's laws are not
established with equal force for everyone, and when it is a question
of Emperors, the laws cease to function and can be refashioned.'[86]
The emperor's primary duty within the church, on the contrary,
was to protect and preserve its law. If the emperor put himself
above the law, by making particular exceptions, this would eventually lead to the erosion of the whole body of church law with all
the ensuing harm that this brings. Also, just as with Constantine,

[82] Ep. 555. 53–4, 61.
[83] Ep. 556. 42. Theodore's biographer is much more explicit in implicating the emperor:
Vita B, 265CD, 267C. Cf. Hatlie, 'Abbot Theodore', 172–80.
[84] Cf. ep. 36. 34–9: 'There are two things here: either the Emperor is God—for only
divinity does not come under the law—or there is anarchy and sedition. For when the law
is not the same, how can there be peace? How can there be peace when the Emperor wants
nothing other than to commit adultery or commit heresy, and when those under his law
want no part either of the adultery or of the heresy because by doing so they would trespass
what was handed down by Christ and the Apostles?'
[85] Ep. 31. 55–8.   [86] Ep. 33. 31–2, ep. 34. 24–5, 76–9.

the emperor's example was of paramount importance: 'When the Emperor does something illegal, does it not both make and urge his people to comply? . . . For just as the emperor is, so are the people, since they seek only what he wants and says should come about.'[87]

Strictly speaking, therefore, the Joseph affair was not about a struggle to defend the church's autonomy from imperial interference, even though Theodore was aware of, and regretted, this interference. For Theodore it was primarily about the correct relationship of the emperor to God and to the church. A correct order would ensure beneficial, and not harmful, intervention.

In the light of this discussion it can be seen that J. B. Bury's thesis that, 'Nicephorus proceeded to procure a definite affirmation of the superiority of the Emperor to canonical laws' and that 'The significance of Theodore's position is that in contending for the validity of canonical law as independent of the State and the Emperor, he was vindicating the independence of the Church,' needs correcting.[88]

Despite Theodore's disappointment at Nikephoros' reign, his understanding of the emperor's position *vis-à-vis* the church still expressed itself in terms of co-operation. When Michael I, in 811, ascended the throne he arranged for a reconciliation between the patriarch and the Stoudites, made possible by the renewed deposition of the steward Joseph. The emperor's key role in this change of affairs, an example of beneficial intervention, is expressed by Theodore in a letter to the monk Antony, one of the many who still hesitated to restore communion with the patriarch:

But as I wrote to you before, since the one on account of whom there was all this dissension in our church has now, through the good pleasure of our supremely good God, been put out of the way, peace has won the victory, through the command and influence and favour—and I may add, the appeal—of our triumphant and Christ-loving Emperor—and through the co-operation and self-defence of our Most Holy Patriarch— for it is necessary from now on to call him that.[89]

[87] Ep. 36. 41–6.
[88] Bury, *A History of the Eastern Roman Empire*, 34, 36. Cf. Barker, *Social and Political Theory*, 88. On Nikephoros' motives, see Alexander, *The Patriarch Nicephorus*, 85–7.
[89] Ep. 56. 36–41. In the *Vita B*, 272D–273A, the biographer Michael explains how the emperor also appealed to the pope of Rome to effect this reunion. Following the example of Christ, the emperor was a mediator between those separated: καὶ γίνεται πρέσβυς χριστομίμητος καὶ μεσίτης τῶν διεστώτων.

This close co-operation between the authorities of the church and empire could also work in the reverse way, with decisions of state being influenced by churchmen. One example of this, in which Theodore's advice to the emperor was decisive, was the affair regarding the treatment to be meted out to Paulician and Athinganoi heretics.[90] The patriarch and his synod recommended capital punishment, on which the emperor initially intended to act. But through Theodore's intervention he suspended his edict of execution.[91] At first Theodore's view, that there was always a chance of conversion and that no priest had the right to condemn heretics to death, met with a lot of opposition from his peers.[92] To the end of his life, however, doubtless helped by reflecting on his own unjust treatment, Theodore held to the firm belief that spiritual ailments should be treated by spiritual means, not by the secular arm.[93] For this conviction he claimed support from the writings of the Fathers.[94]

---

[90] The vast literature on the Paulicians has been surveyed by P. Lemerle, 'L'Histoire des Pauliciens d'Asie Mineure d'après les sources grecques', *TM* 5 (1973), 1–144. See also, N. G. Garsoïan, *The Paulician Heresy: A Study of the Origins and Development of Paulicianism in Armenia and the Eastern Provinces of the Byzantine Empire* (The Hague, 1967); 'Byzantine Heresy. A Reinterpretation', *DOP* 25 (1971), 85–114. For further bibliography, see Haldon, *Byzantium in the Seventh Century*, 344 n. 63. On the Athinganoi see J. Starr, 'An Eastern Christian sect: the Athinganoi', *Harvard Theological Review*, 29 (1936), 93–106.

[91] See Alexander, *The Patriarch Nicephorus*, 99; W. Treadgold, *The Byzantine Revival*, 179–80 and endnote; V. Grumel, *Regestes*, nos. 383–4.

[92] Theophanes readily expresses his own disagreement (*Chronographia* AM 6304): 'Out of great zeal for God the most pious Emperor moved against the Manichaeans (now known as Paulicians) and Athinganoi in Phrygia and Lykaonia. At the behest of the holy Patriarch Nikephoros and other pious men, he decreed them liable to capital punishment. However, thanks to other, malignant, advisors (κακότροποι σύμβουλοι) he let the pretext of repentance mitigate this—those captured by this heresy cannot repent. These men ignorantly declared that their opinion was that the priests were not allowed to use capital punishment in their opposition to the impious. In this matter they opposed the holy scriptures in every respect'.

[93] Ep. 455. 79–81: σωμάτων γὰρ ἄρχοντες τοὺς ἐν τοῖς σωματικοῖς ἁλόντας ἐξὸν αὐτοῖς κολάζειν, οὐχὶ τοὺς ἐν τοῖς κατὰ ψυχήν· τῶν γὰρ ψυχῶν ἀρχόντων τοῦτο, ὧν τὰ κολαστήρια ἀφορισμοὶ καὶ αἱ λοιπαὶ ἐπιτιμίαι. It is in this letter that Theodore recalls having changed the mind of Patriarch Nikephoros, saying to him, 'The Church does not vindicate itself by the sword', and of remonstrating with the emperor ('God is not pleased by such an execution'): 82–6. Cf. ep. 94.

[94] Some patristic authorities, including John Chrysostom (*Hom. in Matth. 46. 1, 2*) are quoted in ep. 455. It is true, however, that the Fathers were never unanimous on this issue, leading to repressive anti-pagan laws. Cf. Dvornik *Early Christian and Byzantine Political Philosophy*, 697.

Theodore's reputation as an intrepid defender of the autonomy of the church belongs properly to the iconoclast period,[95] and it was during this period that Theodore becomes more outspoken towards the emperor: 'It has often been said that the distinguishing characteristic of this second period of Iconoclasm was the emergence of the Church–State conflict clearly into the open. . . . The Emperor was the prince of impiety (ἀσεβάρχης) and many people were ready to do his will.'[96] Up until this period he had always defended the canons and traditions of the church, and the equality of all, emperors included, before the laws of God. The veneration of images was an immemorial tradition of the church, as had been affirmed most recently by the Synod in Nicaea; any attempt to reverse, alter, or deny this teaching was considered by Theodore to be a gross transgression of the truth and an intolerable interference in the divinely established teaching office of the church.

Writing in exile to the patriarch of Jerusalem, Theodore describes the effects of the 815 iconoclastic synod in apocalyptic terms:

Persecution has overtaken us, O Most Blessed One, and of all persecutions it is most clearly like that of the pagans. For Satan has sensed that the blessed hope, the glorious appearance of our great God and Saviour Jesus Christ is at hand, so he has whipped up the flames of heresy even higher. This is the prelude to the appearance of Antichrist. What do I mean by this? The impiety that broke forth long ago under Leo [III] and Constantine [V], which raged for a long time but was then broken by divine judgement, has now been renewed by an Emperor [Leo V] who shares Leo's name and is his equal in wickedness.[97]

Theodore had played his part in trying to prevent this return to iconoclasm. At the Christmas Day meeting in 814 with the emperor in his palace Theodore was outspoken in his direct challenge.[98] The monk Michael reports his intervention:

---

[95] Cf. G. Ladner and H. E. Symonds, *The Church Universal and the See of Rome: A Study of the Relations between the Episcopate and the Papacy up to the Schism between East and West* (London, 1939), 223 ff.

[96] Henry, *Theodore of Studios*, 198. During the first period of iconoclasm it was John Damascene, living under Islam, who brought the conflict out into the open: B. Kotter (ed.), *Die Schriften des Johannes von Damaskos, Contra imaginum calumniatores orationes tres*, Oratio 2, cols. 11–13, 15, Patristiche Texte und Studien, 17 (Berlin, 1975), 101. 1–104. 4; 107. 1–108. 30. Cf. Barker, *Social and Political Theory*, 86–7.

[97] Ep. 276. 34–42.   [98] See above, pp. 55–6.

Pay attention, O Emperor [said Theodore], to what St Paul says to you through us on the subject of ecclesiastical order. Be informed that an Emperor is not permitted to obtrude himself as judge and decider in matters such as these (οὐκ ἔξεστιν βασιλέα ἑαυτὸν κριτήν τε καὶ δικαστὴν ἐν τοῖς τοιούτοις παρεισφέρειν). If you admit to being devout, then you must follow the apostolic canons. Now this is what is said: 'God has appointed in the Church first apostles, second prophets, third teachers (1 Cor. 12: 28).' See, it is these, not the Emperor who set forth matters having to do with faith (οἱ τὰ περὶ πίστεως) and who search out the things that are pleasing to God. The holy Apostles nowhere wrote that an Emperor manages ecclesiastical affairs (τὰ τῆς Ἐκκλησίας). . . . If you are willing to be a son of the Church . . . simply follow in all respects your spiritual Father [the Patriarch].[99]

The 'ecclesiastical affairs' are those matters to do with faith and dogma. It is in apposition to these divine realities that the emperor can be said to be confined to the administration of external or secular matters.[100] The emperor 'has no authority over our souls'.[101] One should not read into these texts a rejection of the Byzantine theory of the emperor or a change in Theodore's earlier views, but merely greater definition of respective competence. Never had the church accepted that the imperial powers could impose their views in matters of dogma.

This is borne out some years later in a letter written in 823 to Leo Sakellarios, who attempted to act as an agent for Michael II in arranging a meeting of the iconoclasts with Theodore. Theodore reflects, in the letter, how Leo V had also tried unsuccessfully to get him to discuss the theology of icons with iconoclasts, and he then proceeds:

[99] *Vita B*, 284AB.
[100] *Vita A* reports Theodore as saying, 'Ecclesiastical affairs (τὰ τῶν Ἐκκλησιῶν) pertain to priests and to teachers; the administration of external concerns (ἡ τῶν ἔξω πραγμάτων διοίκησις) is proper to the Emperor. For the Apostle says, "God has appointed in the Church first apostles, second prophets, third teachers"; he nowhere mentions Emperors. It is the former who legislate on matters to do with dogmas and the faith (τὰ περὶ δογμάτων καὶ πίστεως νομοθετεῖν). You are to follow them and in no way usurp their office': 181D–184A. *Vita C* (p. 281) is closer to *Vita B* in this section. After quoting St Paul, Theodore says, 'It is these who search out matters of the Church and who regulate the dogmas of the faith. Let the Emperor be the judge of civil [or of citizens] and external affairs: οὗτοί εἰσιν οἱ τὰ τῆς ἐκκλησίας διερευνᾶν ὀφείλοντες καὶ τὰ δόγματα θεσμοθετεῖν τῆς πίστεως. βασιλεύς δὲ τῶν πολιτικῶν ἔστω κριτὴς καὶ τῶν ἔξω πραγμάτων διαιτητής.
[101] TC I. 58. 601.

the question is not about secular and simply human matters, over which the Emperor and the secular tribunal have the power of judgement. On the contrary, it is about divine and heavenly dogmas, which are the responsibility of none other than those to whom God the Word himself said, 'Whatever you bind upon earth will be bound in heaven, and whatever you loose on earth will be loosed in heaven (Matt. 18: 18). But who are those to whom this authority is given? The Apostles and their successors. . . . Judgement concerning the divine dogmas belongs to them. It is the duty of Emperors and governors to offer assistance, to approve the things that are decreed and to reconcile differences arising out of secular concerns. But God has given them no power whatever over the divine dogmas, and anything they do in this realm will not last.

Therefore, Sir, it is impossible for the divine tribunal to be put alongside the secular tribunal.[102]

The point being made is that *judgement* (κριτήριον) does not belong to emperors. On the other hand, assistance, approbation of ecclesiastical decisions, and reconciliation did belong traditionally to the *officium* of the Christian emperor.

Similarly, in one of his last Catecheses Theodore explains how he had been 'mandated by the rulers to enter into dialogue with those responsible for impiety'. He explains at length why he chose to refuse to meet with the iconoclasts, during which he says the following:

The secular authority punishes whoever does evil in the same way that it assists those who do good. But it is to the holy apostles that has been given that authority coming from the Holy Spirit over divine dogmas, binding and loosing. The Lord, in fact, had said to them: 'Receive the Holy Spirit. If you forgive the sins of any, they are forgiven; if you retain the sins of any, they are retained' (John 20: 22–3). And also: 'Whatever you bind on earth shall be bound in heaven, and whatever you loose on earth shall be loosed in heaven' (Matt. 18: 18). It is clear that just as it was said to them, it was transmitted down the ages to their successors until our own day. Thus, in making themselves judges in such domains the rulers are despoiling the apostles of the power coming from the Spirit given them. How can these judges reach to the heights of the truth of dogmas when they have not been formed to the perfection of life (μὴ ἐν τελειότητι βίου κατηρτισμένοι)?[103]

---

[102] Ep. 478. 56–69, 78–9: οὐδὲ γὰρ περὶ βιωτικῶν καὶ σαρκικῶν ὁ λόγος, ὧν βασιλεὺς τὸ κράτος ἔχει τοῦ κρίνειν καὶ τὸ βιωτικὸν κριτήριον, ἀλλὰ περὶ θείων καὶ οὐρανίων δογμάτων. . . .
[103] PC 127. 324.

Taken in isolation certain expressions Theodore uses might lead
to the impression that his defence of the autonomy of the church
appears to be at the expense of the emperor's traditional role of
intervention in ecclesiastical affairs.[104] Theodore's intervention in
the Christmas Day meeting of 814 as reported in the *Vita Nicetae* by
Theosteriktos is another clear example of a text that needs to be
read in the full context of Theodore's thought:[105]

Theodore, the zealous teacher of the Church, abbot of Stoudios,
answered: 'Do not undo the constitution of the Church (ἐκκλησιαστικήν
κατάστασιν), for the Apostle spoke thus: 'And he gave some apostles, and
some prophets, and some evangelists, and some pastors and teachers, for
the perfecting of the saints' (Eph. 4: 11), but he did not speak of emperors.
To you, Emperor, has been entrusted the political system and the army
(ἡ πολιτικὴ κατάστασις καὶ τὸ στρατόπεδον). Take care of them, and
leave the Church to its shepherds and teachers (ποιμέσι καὶ διδασκάλοις)
according to the Apostle. If you do not agree to this—even if an angel
from Heaven should give us a message about a deviation from our faith
we shall not listen to him, and certainly not to you.'[106]

J. M. Hussey seems to draw her conclusions from this text alone
when she writes (and giving it a rather loose rendering):

It is unlikely that many East Romans would have wished to admit as a
working principle the early ninth-century Theodore the Studite's passionate reproach, 'Emperor, do not destroy the independence of the
Church. You are concerned with politics and war, that is your proper
business, so leave the affairs of the Church to clergy and monks.'[107]

In the same account, besides, others also remonstrate with the
emperor on account of his obtrusive actions.[108] The Patriarch

[104] J. M. Hussey, for example, has written, 'An occasional fierce monastic voice might
exhort the Emperor to confine himself to purely secular affairs. Such was the view of the
redoubtable Theodore Studites, but his understandable outburst was evoked in the heat of
the iconoclast controversy when imperial policy was attacking orthodoxy and in general his
views were not shared', *The Orthodox Church in the Byzantine Empire*, 303.

[105] Niketas was an abbot of the monastery of Medikion, in the region of Olympos. He
was known to Theodore the Stoudite, became a confessor of the faith during Leo V's reign
and died on 3 April 824. His life was written in 829–40.

[106] *AA.SS. Aprilis I*, (Antwerp, 1675), appendix, 35. p. xxx.

[107] Hussey, *The Byzantine World*, 3rd edn. (London, 1967), 86.

[108] Aemilianos, bishop of Cyzicus, e.g. had said, 'If as you said this is a church inquiry,
O Emperor, let it be inquired into in the Church as is the custom, for from old and from
the beginning church inquiries are inquired into in Church, and not in the Imperial Palace.'
Michael bishop of Synnada had said, 'If you are a mediator (μεσίτης), why do you not do
the job of a mediator? [I say this] because the one side you shelter in the Palace and even

Nikephoros, according to another account, is the one who tells the
emperor that he must give way to and embrace the decisions of the
church which are built on the foundation of the prophets, apostles,
and teachers, and not to attack them.[109] And this is said following
the emperor's declaration that he feels a pastoral obligation
towards the 'flock'.[110]

3.6 CONCLUSION

To conclude this section, therefore, it can be said that Theodore's
opposition to the emperor was an opposition to what might be
called caesaropapism or abusive imperial intervention in ecclesiastical affairs. It finds only faint expression in the Joseph affair—the
final stage of the moechian controversy—but is fully present during the period of iconoclasm. Yet it would be a mistake to think or
conclude that Theodore sought complete autonomy for the church
in the sense of seeking severance of all imperial influence on ecclesiastical government. If some of his reported statements in this
later period are not typically Byzantine, recalling to his modern
readers the writings of an Athanasios, a John Chrysostom, or a
John of Damascus,[111] it is because, like them, he was writing or
speaking in troubled times. Taken in full context, Theodore's
thoughts on the nature of the relationship of the emperor to the
church were still the thoughts of a traditional Byzantine, albeit a
worried Byzantine.

The order that Theodore saw in society, both monastic and civil,
the principles of which were laid done by the laws of God, required
effort, sometimes heroic effort, to maintain. Living life according

assemble and encourage, even giving them permission to teach their impious doctrines;
whereas the other side does not dare to utter a sound even on the streets and crouches down
everywhere before your decrees', *Vita Nicetae*, 34. p. xxix.

[109] *Vita Nicephori*, in *Nicephori Opuscula Historica*, 187 (= *PG* 100. 113BC).

[110] Ibid.: 'You, like all others, are well aware that God has appointed us to watch over
the interests of this illustrious and reasonable flock (τὴν μεγαλώνυμον καὶ λογικὴν
ποίμνην); and that we are eager and solicitous to smooth away and remove every thorn that
grows in the Church.'

[111] Cf. Damascene's statement, 'It appertains not to kings to make laws for the Church.
Kings have not preached the word to you, but apostles and prophets, pastors and doctors.
Political welfare is the concern of kings: the ecclesiastical system is a matter for pastors and
doctors; and this [the action of the Iconoclasts], brethren, is an act of brigandage', *Oratio II,
Contra imaginum calumniatores*, Kotter, *Die Schriften des Johannes von Damaskos*, col. 12. 102–4.

to Christian precepts was both the expression of the divine order and the indispensable means to achieve and uphold it. For Theodore 'holiness' and Christian life were one and the same thing. The official church provided tangible means by way of its sacred rites for its faithful first to enter into this life and then to continue progressing in it. Added to this, the monastic life was, for Theodore, the preferential way to secure the end goal—eternal salvation. In the chapters to follow we will examine both rites of sanctification and Theodore's theology of holiness. However, the main reason for the discussion on rites is to reveal a gross misunderstanding of a text that has led to a spurious development in Byzantine theology concerning the sacraments.

PART III

Principles of Holiness

4

Rites of Sanctification

4.1 INTRODUCTION

In only one of Theodore's extant writings, letter 489 to the monk Gregory written during the reign of Emperor Michael II (sometime between 821 and 826), do we have any clear statement on those rites of sanctification that might also be termed sacraments (Orthodox Christians refer to them as mysteries)—rites that reveal and effect God's saving power. Disappointingly for our purposes, the context of this statement is not even one of catechesis or instruction on the sacraments as such. Other references to the sacramental supports provided by the church are scattered throughout his writings and require gathering together, explanation, and interpretation, assisted often by contemporary or near-contemporary sources. The picture built up from this exercise helps us to understand better how the ninth-century institutional church experienced by Theodore lived its life, and how its faithful were expected to relate to it.

The letter to Gregory provides a useful starting point around which to build subsequent discussions on sanctifying rites, also allowing the structure of exposition that follows. Of much more importance, however, is the influence that this letter has had on subsequent generations, but based, this author believes, on a gross misunderstanding.

4.2 THE LETTER TO MONK GREGORY: ON THE MYSTERIES

From letter 389 we learn that during the second period of iconoclasm theoretical questions were being asked about the origins and credentials of monasticism.[1] In bringing back the theoretical

---

[1] Ep. 489 (ann. 821–6, to the monk Gregory).

154   *Principles of Holiness*

arguments against icons from the reign of Constantine V, the 815
Synod had perhaps inadvertently resurrected the ideological propaganda of that time against monasticism.[2] In the course of his
apologia in defence of the monastic institution Theodore gives a list
of six mysteries (μυστήρια):

And as certain people ask where the tradition of renouncing the world and
becoming a monk came from, nothing else needs saying except, where did the
tradition by which one becomes a Christian come from? He who first legislated
through apostolic tradition, subsequently made this known, instituting six mysteries (ἓξ μυστήρια ἐκτεθεικώς). First, concerning illumination (περὶ
φωτίσματος). Second, concerning the synaxis or communion (περὶ συνάξεως
εἴτουν κοινωνίας). Third, concerning the rite of myron (περὶ τελετῆς μύρου).
Fourth, concerning clerical consecrations (περὶ ἱερατικῶν τελειώσεων).
Fifth, concerning monastic consecration (περὶ μοναχικῆς τελειώσεως). Sixth,
concerning those who fell asleep in a sacred manner (περὶ τῶν ἱερῶς
κεκοιμημένων).
What is one to say about all this? If there is a doubt about one of the above
mentioned, one certainly then doubts about the divine tradition of all the others.
Take one away and the others are necessarily removed. And neither illumination,
nor the synaxis, nor the divine myron (θεῖον μύρον), nor clerical consecration
(ἱερατικὴ τελείωσις), nor the service for those who fell asleep in a sacred manner would exist if there were no monastic consecration (ἡ μοναχικὴ τελείωσις).
And we would be as the gentiles, atheists in the world, without hope (καί ἐσμεν
ἐθνόφρονες, ἄθεοι ὄντες ἐν τῷ κόσμῳ καὶ ἐλπίδα μὴ ἔχοντες). And it is such
a person who introduced the question of from where it is that a man should live
as a monk (μονάζειν ἄνθρωπον).[3]

Theodore thus establishes, in the course of his polemic, that there
are six μυστήρια of apostolic institution: baptism, the eucharist,
the myron (consecrated oil), orders, the monastic profession, and
funeral rites.

Theodore's list is directly dependent on the *Ecclesiastical Hierarchy*
of (Pseudo-)Dionysios the Areopagite, whom he names immediately preceding and following the quoted text.[4] The six rites
named and described by Dionysios are each denoted as μυστήριον

[2] Nikephoros, *Antirrheticus 3. Adv. Constantinum Copronymum*, PG 100. 516D–517A; George
Hamartolos, *Chronicon*, ed. de Boor, 338. Cf. above, p. 14.
[3] Ep. 489. 14–29 (24–5 missing in Migne, PG 99. 1524B).
[4] Ibid. 14. 33. In ep. 455. 56–7, Theodore refers to Letter 8 of Dionysios, to the monk
Demophilos, and uses a Dionysian expression that denotes Christ as the celebrant of the
sacred rites: ὁ θειότατος ἡμῶν ἱεροθέτης. G. Heil and A. Ritter (ed.), *Corpus Dionysiacum
II*, Patristiche Texte und Studien, 36, (Berlin, 1991), ep. 8. 186. 14. All references to the letters, the *Celestial Hierarchy* (*CH*) and the *Ecclesiastical Hierarchy* (*EH*) of Dionysios will follow
this edition. References to the *Divine Names* (*DN*) will follow B.R. Suchla, *Corpus Dionysiacum
I, De Divinis Nominibus*, Patristiche Texte und Studien, 33 (Berlin, 1990).

by an early editor in the subtitles of the work.[5] In the Dionysian corpus itself the term μυστήριον in the singular is never in fact applied to any specific rite as a whole. It is used once to mean a specific feature of a rite,[6] but otherwise its use is confined to referring to the Incarnation.[7] In the plural it can have various shades of meaning: ineffable conceptions or doctrines regarding divine things in general, certain sacred ceremonies, and the eucharistic elements.[8] The latter he calls 'the consecrating mysteries' (τὰ τελεστικὰ μυστήρια), 'the divine and sanctifying mysteries' (τὰ θεαρχικὰ καὶ τελειωτικὰ μυστήρια) 'the rite of rites,' (τελετῶν τελετή).[9]

Was Theodore's understanding of μυστήριον, in its singular and plural forms, any different from that of Dionysios? And if it was, did this imply that he accepted the Dionysian six mysteries as six 'sacraments' having a common status as modern authors seem to assume?[10] Theodore, in fact, was heir not only to Dionysian terminology, but also to that of the Septuagint, the New Testament, and the wider patristic tradition.

The primary sense of μυστήριον, as found in classical Greek authors, was that of 'knowledge difficult of access',[11] τὰ μυστήρια being the religious rites (or by transference, the implements of these rites) by which one was initiated into such knowledge.[12] The New

---

[5] P. Rorem, *Pseudo-Dionysius: The Complete Works*, Classics of Western Spirituality (New York, 1987), 195; idem, *Pseudo-Dionysius: A Commentary on the Texts and an Introduction to their Influence* (Oxford, 1993), 97. The titles are the following: μυστήριον φωτίσματος, μυστήριον συνάξεως εἴτ'οὖν κοινωνίας, μυστήριον τελετῆς μύρου, μυστήριον ἱερατικῶν τελειώσεων, μυστήριον μοναχικῆς τελειώσεως, μυστήριον ἐπὶ τῶν ἱερῶς κεκοιμημένων: *EH* 70. 1, 80. 7, 95. 8, 110. 9, 117. 1, 122. 22.

[6] *EH* 5.5. 112. 1.

[7] *Celestial Hierarchy (CH)* 4. 22. 23 (τὸ θεῖον τῆς Ἰησοῦ φιλανθρωπίας μυστήριον); *Divine Names (DN)* II. 126, 1–2; ep. 3. 159. 9. Cf. P. Rorem, *Biblical and Liturgical Symbols Within the Pseudo-Dionysian Synthesis*, Studies and Texts, 71 (Toronto, 1984), 41; idem, *Pseudo-Dionysius. A Commentary*, 97.

[8] Rorem, *Pseudo-Dionysius: Complete Works*.   [9] *EH* 79. 3; 17; 21.

[10] John Meyendorff, for example, although stating that *mysterion* was used 'concurrently with such terms as "rites" or "sanctifications"', then goes on to say 'Theodore the Studite in the ninth century gives a list of six sacraments: the holy "illumination" (baptism), the "synaxis" (Eucharist), the holy chrism, ordination, monastic tonsure, and the service of burial', *Byzantine Theology: Historical Trends and Doctrinal Themes*, 2nd edn. (New York, 1983), 191. See also, R. Taft, A. Kazhdan, and I. Kalavrezou, 'Sacraments', in *ODB* iii. 1825.

[11] L. Bouyer, 'Mysterion', in *Mystery and Mysticism* (New York, 1956), 20. This author argues that *mysterion* did not mean secrecy of *doctrine* but secrecy of *rites*. But cf. G. Bornkamm, *TWNT* iv, s.v. μυστήριον, p. 810 (= *TDNT* (Amsterdam, 1967) iv. 802).

[12] Cf. Liddell and Scott, *Greek–English Lexicon*, ii. 1156.

156   *Principles of Holiness*

Testament uses μυστήριον in a similar generic sense, while adding
other nuances from semitic usage.[13] Thus it can mean the revealed
secrets or plan of God in relation to man's salvation in Christ,[14] the
hidden sense (symbolical or typological) of an institution,[15] or the
unknown element of an action.[16] It did not, however, mean an
ecclesiastical rite, still less the secret of a closely guarded rite.[17]

The first faint traces of the application of the pagan term
μυστήρια to the sanctifying rites and religious practices of the
church is found in Clement of Alexandria.[18] Thereafter the term,
in its singular or plural form, could have in the same author the
sense of an ecclesiastical rite as well as the other senses of biblical
and common usage.[19] Another Hellenic term Christianized by the
Fathers, likewise taken from the pagan mystery religions, was
τελετή (from the verb τελέω and cognate τελέωσις) meaning
'rite'. By a rite of initiation entrance into the mystery religion was
accomplished or perfected. After the age of Clement τελεταί and
μυστήρια were often used interchangeably by the Greek Fathers
to refer to Christian rites.[20]

In the Latin world *sacramentum*, from which the English word
'sacrament' derives, likewise had no univocal meaning.

---

[13] A. E. Harvey, 'The Use of Mystery Language in the Bible', *JTS* NS 31 (1980), 320–36;
A. A. Michel, 'Sacrements', in *DTC* xiv. 1. 486. Cf. Bouyer, 'Mysterion', 21–3; *TDNT* iv.
817–24.

[14] Rom. 16: 25: . . . κατὰ ἀποκάλυψιν μυστηρίου χρόνοις αἰωνίοις σεσιγημένου
. . . Cf. 1 Cor. 4: 1; Eph. 1: 9; Col. 2: 2; Rev. 10: 7 (the mystery of God and of His Will); Matt.
13: 11; Mark 4: 11; Luke 8: 10 (the mystery of the Kingdom of Heaven); Eph. 3: 4; Col. 4: 3
(the mystery of Christ); Eph. 6: 19 (the mystery of the Gospel); 1 Tim. 3: 9, 16 (the mystery
of faith and of piety).

[15] Eph. 5: 32: τὸ μυστήριον τοῦτο μέγα ἐστίν, ἐγὼ δὲ λέγω εἰς Χριστὸν καὶ εἰς
τὴν ἐκκλησίαν.

[16] 2 Thess. 2: 7 (the mystery of iniquity): τὸ γὰρ μυστήριον ἤδη ἐνεργεῖται τῆς
ἀνομίας·

[17] Cf. Michel, *DTC* xiv. 486–7; Bouyer, 'Mysterion', 21.

[18] e.g. *Protrepticus* 12: *Clemens Alexandrinus*, GCS 1 (Berlin, 1972), 84. 6; *Stromateis* 4. 1:
Clemens Alexandrinus, GCS 2 (Berlin, 1985), 249. 8. For a discussion on Clement, see H. G.
Marsh, 'The Use of μυστήριον in the writings of Clement of Alexandria with special ref-
erence to his sacramental doctrine', *JTS* 37 (1936), 64–80.

[19] Cf. Lampe, *Patristic Greek Lexicon*, 891–3; *TDNT* iv, 824–6 s.v. μυστήριον. Cyril of
Jerusalem is, it seems (Bouyer, 'Mysterion', 32), the first author to apply without
qualification the language of the pagan mysteries to Christian rites. Even so, he also keeps
to New Testament usage.

[20] See Lampe, *Patristic Greek Lexicon*, s.v. τελετή, τελέω, 1385–7. Cf. P. Battifol, *Études
d'histoire et de théologie positive*, 2nd edn. (Paris, 1928), 37 ff.; H. Echle, 'The Terminology of the
Sacrament of Regeneration According to Clement of Alexandria', Ph.D. dissertation
(Washington DC, 1947), ch. 5, 'τελείωσις'.

Etymologically it denoted a consecrated thing or person, for example, a military oath of allegiance taken before the gods (*sacramentum
militiae*) which subsequently might be attested to by some form of
sign (*fidei signaculum*).[21] Inspired by the Pauline idea of *militia Christi*,
Tertullian adapted this classical concept of sacrament to the
Christian profession of allegiance made at baptism, making it comparable to Christian *devotio*. This opened the way for *sacramentum*,
as oath and initiation, to evolve to mean the object or content of
the baptismal promise: the creed or *regula fidei*. Pagan worship was
termed *non sacramenta*.[22] With time *sacramentum* came to be synony-
mous with *signaculum*, the sacred sign associated with a solemn
ecclesiastical rite.[23] Contact with the Greek language also gave to
the evolving term a content indicating *res occulta, res mysteriosa et
sacra*.[24] In the Old Latin (pre-Vulgate) version of the Bible
μυστήριον was habitually translated as *sacramentum*. The Vulgate,
however, tends to adhere to *mysterium*, although the epistles to the
Ephesians and Colossians employ *sacramentum* or *mysterium* indiffer-
ently.[25] In Ambrose both terms are used together, *sacramentum*
sometimes being used to denote the external aspect of a rite, *mysterium* its inner aspect, or both terms may be fused together, such as
in the expressions *sacramenta mysteriorum* and *mysteria sacramento-
rum*.[26] Although *mysterium* is used at times to denote a sacramental
rite, it can also be used, for example, to designate prayer.[27] Leo the
Great, likewise, has no difficulty in engaging both terms.[28] In
Hilary of Poitiers's vocabulary, *sacramentum* is applied to the mystery of the divine unity,[29] to the Lord's divinity,[30] and to the
Incarnation.[31]

From this analysis it can be seen that the term 'sacrament' may
be used to denote μυστήριον, as found in the literature of the

---

[21] Cf. P. G. W. Glare (ed.), *Oxford Latin Dictionary* (Oxford 1976), v. 1674–5. Other meanings are: an oath sworn by both parties to an action in vindication of their claims; the sum
of money staked by them in support of those claims and forfeited in the case of the losing
party to the gods (i.e. state); any solemn engagement or obligation. For a bibliography on
the semantic evolution of the word, see Michel, *DTC* xiv. 488.

[22] A. Hamman, 'Sacramentum', in *EEC* ii. 751; Michel, *DTC* xiv. 489.

[23] Michel, ibid.   [24] Ibid.   [25] A. Nocent, 'Sacraments', in *EEC* ii. 750.

[26] *Apologia David* 12. 58: CSEL 32/2. 339.   [27] Nocent, *EEC* ii. 750.

[28] *Serm.* 16. 1, 23. 4: CCL 138, 61; 106; *Serm.* 51. 7: CCL 138A. 302. Cf. Nocent, *EEC* ii.
750.

[29] *De trin.* 7. 23, 9. 19.   [30] Ibid. 10. 48.

[31] Ibid. 9. 25 ff.

period being dealt with here, as long as it is always borne in mind that it has a corresponding variety of possible nuances.[32]

The flexibility of patristic language is reflected in Theodore the Stoudite's own use of the term μυστήριον. In the letter to Gregory, certainly, it refers in some manner to ecclesiastical rites. Furthermore, as sanctioned by long tradition, in the plural form the eucharist is *par excellence* 'the mysteries',[33] 'the divine mysteries', 'the mysteries of the truth'.[34] Yet the term is more usually employed with biblical connotations: the 'mystery of the economy' (τὸ τῆς οἰκονομίας μυστήριον)[35] or 'mystery of salvation' (τὸ τῆς σωτηρίας μυστήριον),[36] or more specifically to the Incarnation, (τὸ τῆς σωματώσεως μυστήριον),[37] which Theodore also refers to as 'the great mystery of piety' (τὸ μέγα τῆς εὐσεβείας μυστήριον).[38]

The life of Christ and all its events, from his birth to his ascension to heaven, are mysteries to be commemorated liturgically, each feast constituting a μυστήριον.[39] Commemoration, besides, is not restricted to the celebration of the eucharist, but occurs through other symbolic customs too.[40] The eucharist recapitulates the whole of the divine economy, 'doing this figuratively by its most important part'.[41]

The mysteries, also, are things to be revealed,[42] and things which remain hidden even though revealed: the mystery of the

---

[32] On the question of terminology, see also, R. Hotz, *Sakramente—im Wechselspiel zwischen Ost und West* (Cologne, 1979), *passim*, but esp. 48–52.

[33] e.g. *PC* 24. 72, *PC* 107. 271. Cf. *Antirrheticus* 1, *PG* 99. 340CD.

[34] e.g. *Refutatio poem. iconomach.* 447C; ep. 393. 93; *Responsiones ad interrogata quaedam*, ad. 1. 1732A; *Antirrheticus 1, PG* 99. 340B: τὰ τῆς ἀληθείας μυστήρια. Cf. the language of the 9th cent. Divine Liturgy, which Theodore celebrated daily (see below), in F. E. Brightman, *Liturgies Eastern and Western. Being the Texts Original or Translated of the Principal Liturgies of the Church* (Oxford, 1896), i. 310, 319, etc.

[35] Ep. 491. 26. Cf. PK 23. 163; ep. 305. 18: 'the mystery of the economy of salvation' (τὸ τῆς σωτηρίου οἰκονομίας μυστήριον). The writer of Eph. 3: 9 has: ἡ οἰκονομία τοῦ μυστηρίου.

[36] Ep. 439. 23; cf. ep. 501. 24.   [37] Ep. 381. 57.

[38] Ep. 393. 52; ep. 469. 46. Cf. 1 Titus 3: 16.

[39] *PC* 20. 60, *PC* 26. 76, *PC* 64. 169, *PC* 73. 190 (the Lord's passion 'is a great and ineffable mystery'), *PC* 7. 26; TC I. 54. 528 (Easter); *MC* 28. 77 (the Nativity).

[40] *Antirrheticus* 1, *PG* 99. 340CD. Theodore mentions the carrying of branches, for the entry into Jerusalem, exchanging a kiss, to commemorate the resurrection, and fasting, to commemorate Christ's forty days in the desert. The written word and icons, he goes on to argue (*PG* 99. 340D–341A), are also ways of commemorating the mysteries.

[41] *PG* 99. 340C.

[42] *Oratio VI, In Sanctos Angelos* 742B. The Angel Gabriel is called the 'mystical revealer towards men of the hidden mysteries of God': ἐκφάντωρ θεομύστης τῶν ἀπορρήτων

divinity,[43] 'these Christian mysteries concerning the resurrection of the dead and life eternal',[44] the mystery of the Mother of God[45] and her coming back to life,[46] the mystery of John the Forerunner's birth,[47] and the exultation in the womb.[48] Theodore likewise uses the term to describe God's favour in the extraordinary vocation given to his own family.[49] Christian death, too, is described as mystery.[50] A darkly kept secret is also given this name.[51] Finally, Theodore uses the term μυστήριον in relation to the reality of the marriage blessing, and to the blessing that is associated with the remission of sins.[52]

Having now established that 'mystery' has a variety of meanings in Theodore, the questions to be asked once more are, first, does the expression 'six mysteries' in the letter to Gregory express the true thought of Dionysios? Secondly, does Theodore accept that these six ecclesiastical rites have a common status? Finally, does Theodore consider these 'sacraments' alone to have been instituted by Christ? To answer these questions it is first necessary to look more closely at the significance that Dionysios himself gave to these rites.

It is in fact known that the Areopagite uses a whole variety of terms for liturgical or sacred ceremonies, whereas the term τελετή is reserved exclusively for baptism, the eucharist, and the consecration of the myron. These three alone are the 'Dionysian sacraments', the rites of ordination, monastic tonsure, and funerals

τοῦ Θεοῦ πρὸς ἀνθρώπους μυστηρίων. Cf. ibid. 744D. τὰ μυστύριον τῆς βασιλείας τῶν οὐρανῶν are revealed sometimes to all the disciples, sometimes to just a few: *PC* 116. 270.

[43] Ibid. 736C: τὸ τῆς θεότητος μυστήριον.

[44] *Oratio IV, In Sanctum Pascha* 720A: καὶ ταῦτα Χριστιανῶν τὰ μυστήρια περὶ ἀναστάσεως νεκρῶν καὶ ζωῆς ἰωνίου πανηγυρίζομεν.

[45] *Oratio V, In Dormitionem Deiparae* 721D; cf. 728CD.

[46] Ibid. 728CD: τὸ τῆς παλινζωΐας oου μυστήριον.

[47] *Oratio VII, In S. Joannis Bapt. Nativitatem* 748D: ἴδωμεν τὸ ξενοπρεπὲς μυστήριον.

[48] *Oratio VIII, In Decollationem S. Joannis Bapt.* 756D: μέγα ... τὸ τελούμενον μυστήριον.

[49] *Oratio XIII, Laudatio Funebris in Matrem Suam* 892A: τοῦ μυστηρίου τὸ μέγεθος.

[50] *MC* 93. 70: τὸ τοῦ θανατοῦ ... μυστήριον; PK 95. 677; *PC* 12. 41, *PC* 121. 307, *PC* 126. 321.

[51] *MC* 56. 155 (regarding a forbidden relationship). In the rubrics of the Divine Liturgy certain prayers of the anaphora are said privately or 'secretly', μυστικῶς, by the priest: Brightman, *Liturgies*, 324, 328, 329, 330.

[52] Ep. 530. 41–2: πιστὸς ὁ λόγος τοῦ μυστηρίου ἐπί τε ἀφέσει τῶν ἡμαρτημένων ἐπί τε δεσμῷ ἀλύτῳ τῆς συναφείας.

being 'non-sacramental ceremonies'.[53] The editorial use of the term μυστήριον was an attempt at 'a literary symmetry', and was not, besides, an alternative for τελετή. It was a term used for the common purpose of describing the *content* of each rite, and nothing more. Rorem's conclusion is that this term 'wrongly implies a common status for the six rites, since ordinations, tonsure and funerals are not Dionysian sacraments'.[54] In fact, Dionysios' three τελεταί form the three members of the first of the three triple hierarchical triads that make up the *Ecclesiastical Hierarchy*. Their function is to bring about 'purification, illumination and perfection'. The other two triads are the clergy (divided into hierarchs, priests, and deacons) and the laity (monks, communicants, and those being purified—catechumens, penitents, the possessed). The conclusion to the discussion is an interpretation of the Christian funeral rite which strictly is an appendage to the main work and stands outside the hierarchical triad.[55] Why, then, does Dionysios restrict the term τελετή to baptism, the eucharist, and the consecration of the myron? The key lies in the very purpose of Dionysios' hierarchy,[56] which is to enable likeness to and union with God.[57] Baptism,

---

[53] Rorem, *Biblical and Liturgical Symbols*, 39–44; *Pseudo-Dionysius: A Commentary*, 97. For an even more detailed examination of Dionysios' terminology, see P. Scazzoso, 'La terminologia misterica nel corpus Pseudo-Areopagiticum. Provenienza indiretta e diretta dei termini misterici nel corpus', *Aevum*, 37 (1963), 406–29.

[54] Rorem, *Pseudo-Dionysius: A Commentary*, 97 Cf. idem, *Biblical and Liturgical Symbols*, 41.

[55] Rorem, *Pseudo-Dionysius: A Commentary*, 20–1, 95–6, 117. The structure of the hierarchy is summarized by Dionysios himself (*EH* 119. 8–15): 'The holy sacraments bring about purification, illumination, and perfection. The deacons form the order which purifies. The priests constitute the order which gives illumination. And the hierarchs, living in conformity with God, make up the order which perfects. As for those who are being purified, so long as they are still at as this stage of purification they do not partake of the sacred vision or communion. The sacred people are the contemplative [also called illuminative] order. The order of those made perfect is that of the monks who live a single-minded life.'

[56] The concept of hierarchy is central to Dionysios' thought. It is the manner by which authority and revelation is transmitted through a vertical structure beginning with God or 'the One', through a heavenly hierarchy of celestial beings and then to an ecclesiastical ('our') hierarchy and finally, to the lower legal hierarchy. It is an 'order which God himself has established' (ep. 8. 14 ff.). For an introduction to Dionysios, and his dependency on the philosophy of Neoplatonism, see e.g. R. Roques, *L'Univers dionysien: Structure hiérarchique du monde selon le Pseudo-Denys* (Paris, 1954); I. P. Sheldon-Williams, *The Cambridge History of Later Greek and Early Medieval Philosophy*, ed. A. H. Armstrong (Cambridge, 1967), 457–72; G. Gould, *Ecclesiastical Hierarchy in the Thought of Pseudo-Dionysius*, Studies in Church History, 26 (Oxford, 1989), 29–42; A. Louth, *Denys the Areopagite* (London, 1989); idem, *The Origins of the Christian Mystical Tradition: From Plato to Denys* (Oxford, 1981), 159–78. For further bibliography on Dionysios, see P. Rorem, *Pseudo-Dionysius: A Commentary*, 250–67.

[57] *EH* 69. 7 ff. Cf. *Pseudo-Dionysius: A Commentary*, 97.

Dionysios' preferential term for which is 'divine birth' (Θεογενεσία), is the start of the process.[58] The synaxis, meaning 'gathering', like the name *communion* grants 'communion and union with the One'.[59] It is also the culmination of several other rites, such as baptism and ordination, and completes or perfects them.[60] The consecration of the myron, 'which is another rite of perfection belonging to the same order' as the synaxis,[61] is a divine act that 'is the source of all perfection and consecration',[62] the holy ointment being used to perfect baptism[63] and to consecrate the altar for the rite of synaxis, as well as being used in other sanctifying ceremonies.[64] Each of these rites is a 'perfecter' to different degrees and each stands at the head of the other rites Dionysios describes. Each of these three rites is a 'sacredly initiating operation that draws our fragmented lives into a unifying divinization. [Each] forges a divine unity out of the divisions within us . . . [granting] us communion and union with the One.'[65] On these three rites all others depend and so, in Dionysios' conceptual scheme, they alone are given the name τελετή.[66]

Theodore, on the other hand, does not restrict himself to this terminology. The word τελετή is used in conjunction with the sacrament of myron,[67] but it can mean the celebration of any mystery,[68] including liturgical feasts, such as that of the Transfiguration,[69] the Nativity, or Epiphany.[70] In his letter to Gregory, Theodore also uses the expressions 'clerical consecration' and 'monastic consecration'.[71] In the *Ecclesiastical Hierarchy* the term

[58] Cf. R. Roques, 'Le Sens du baptême selon le Pseudo-Denys', *Irénikon*, 31 (1958), 427–49.

[59] *EH* 79. 12.   [60] *EH* 79. 13–14.   [61] *EH* 95. 1 ff.   [62] *EH* 103. 14.

[63] Cf. *EH*, 78. 14–15C: ἡ δε ποιεῖ τοῦ μύρου τελειωτικὴ χρῖσις εὐώδη τὸν τετελεσμένον.

[64] Cf. *EH* 95. 15–17: 'A consecrating prayer is offered over the ointment and this is then used in the holy sacraments of sanctification for almost all of the hierarchy's rites of consecration.'

[65] *EH* 79. 7–12.

[66] Cf. *EH*, 114. 10–13: 'Now, as often said before, it is through the three holy sacraments and powers that the three ranks of holy initiators preside over the three orders of those being initiated and work out their saving approach under the divine yokes.'

[67] *Ep.* 489. 19: περὶ τελετῆς μύρου.

[68] *Antirrheticus* 1 *PG* 99. 340C: Ἀλλὰ μὴν οὐδὲ ἀπεῖρξεν ἡμᾶς τῆς τῶν ἄλλων μυστηρίων τελετῆς.

[69] *PC* 20. 60: ἡ δὲ τῆς μεταμορφώσεως τελετή.

[70] *Antirrheticus* 1, *PG* 99. 340C.

[71] *Ep.* 489. 19–20, 25: ἱερατικῶν τελειώσεων, ἱερατικὴ τελείωσις, ἡ μοναχικὴ τελείωσις.

τελείωσις, as applied to clerical ordinations, depends upon and is derived from the wider concept of perfection in the Dionysian corpus: the divine perfection is the cause of all derived perfection, whether of the angels or of any other hierarchy.[72] Death, as the culmination of earthly life, is also called 'the blessed perfection in Christ'.[73] Clerics, who are purified and illuminated as lay people, achieve the culmination of the spiritual process in the ceremony called 'perfections', namely ordination by a hierarch.[74] Monks, according to Dionysios, are the 'perfected lay order',[75] yet the ceremony of religious profession is called τελείωσις only in one chapter's subtitle, and never in the body of the text.[76] Theodore, on the other hand, uses the term frequently in relation to the habit, although he is aware of its more general meaning in the Dionysian corpus.[77] The monastic schema, says Theodore, 'is the mystery of monastic perfection, as the divine and most wise Dionysios says'.[78]

Theodore, therefore, took from the *Ecclesiastical Hierarchy* only what suited his immediate purpose, without engaging in the finer points of Dionysian thought or terminology. His purpose was to associate the monastic habit with the authority of Dionysios, who was believed to have been the Areopagite converted by St Paul and mentioned in Acts 17: 34.[79] Thus to challenge the credentials of monasticism would be to challenge apostolic tradition itself.[80] It is with the language and logic of the preacher that Theodore then accuses the detractors of monasticism of being Gentiles, atheists, and those 'without hope'.[81] On the other hand, there is no evi-

---

[72] Rorem, *Biblical and Liturgical Symbols*, 42.

[73] *EH* 123. 9: τὴν ἐν Χριστῷ μακαρίαν τελείωσιν. This usage was in fact common from Origen onwards, and is found in Eusebius, *Historia Ecclesiastica*—a possible source for Dionysios.

[74] Rorem, ibid. For the application of the term τελείωσις: *EH* 110. 8, *EH* 115. 2. Cf. 107. 9, *EH* 111. 26, *EH* 113. 6, 16–17, etc. The rite is called ἀφιέρωσις in *EH* 119. 1, a term meaning 'sanctification' in general in *EH* 103. 5 and 114. 24.

[75] *EH* 119. 8–9. Cf. *EH* 116. 6 ff.

[76] *EH* 117. 1: Μυστήριον μοναχικῆς τελειώσεως.

[77] Cf. *PC* 127. 324, where Theodore refers to the successors of the apostles (the hierarchs) as having 'the perfection of life'.

[78] *Ep.* 489. 12–14: Τὸ τῶν μοναχῶν σχῆμα . . . μυστήριόν ἐστι μοναχικῆς τελειώσεως κατὰ τὴν φωνὴν τοῦ θείου καὶ πανσόφου Διονυσίου. Cf. *PK* 43. 310: τὸ μυστήριον τῆς τελειώσεως ἡμῶν.

[79] Cf. Rorem, *Pseudo-Dionysius: A Commentary*, 3, 14–15, and *passim*.

[80] A similar defence is made by George Hamartolos, *Chronicon*, ed. C. de Boor, 339, who, about fifteen years later, also lists Dionysios (among numerous other authorities) to prove this point.

[81] *Ep.* 489, 27–9.

dence to indicate that Theodore actually departed (apart from a freer use of terminology) from the thought or meaning of Dionysios. It is true that the expression ἓξ μυστήρια does give some kind of common status to the six sanctifying rites performed by the hierarchs or their delegates. But what kind of status is this? If it is accepted that the subtitles in the *Ecclesiastical Hierarchy* with the word μυστήριον were not intended to replace Dionysios' terminology or to distort his thought, but merely referred to the mysterious meaning or content of each rite, then it does not follow that the rites themselves have to have any other common denominator. The funeral service can be as much a mystery as baptism (or even the Incarnation) even though these mysteries belong to different orders. Theodore's use of the term μυστήριον in the rest of the corpus of his writings does not lend any support to the idea that his listing of the μυστήρια denotes anything more than the editorial titles of the *Ecclesiastical Hierarchy* intended. It is surely not without some significance that, with the exception of monasticism, in the letter to Gregory he uses the preposition περί, rather than a simple genitive, when mentioning the rites.[82] Thus he too, like Dionysios, would seem to be referring to the mystery *about* the rite of ordinations or funerals and not to the mystery *of* ordinations or funerals. And even when he does make one exception and uses the genitive with monasticism: μυστήριον ἐστι μοναχικῆς τελειώσεως,[83] which is likewise taken from Dionysios' editor,[84] this is not to necessarily imply that he is thinking of anything else other than the mysterious reality of monasticism.[85] Following on this, to say that all the six mysteries in this letter are therefore 'sacraments' is, at the very least, misleading. From the text the most that can be said is that Theodore believed there to have been six rites, one of which was monastic profession, of dominical institution (because referred to by a supposed witness from apostolic times). This was the common denominator which united the otherwise very diverse rites. Each of these rites, besides, had a hidden meaning or μυστήριον.

[82] In this he even departs from the subtitles of *Ecclesiastical Hierarchy*, perhaps making the editor's intentions even clearer. Cf. above p. 155 n. 5.

[83] Ep. 489. 12.   [84] *EH* 117. 1.

[85] Cf. ep. 69. 13, 16–17, where Dionysian language is applied to the monk: . . . πεφευγότος κόσμον διὰ τῆς μοναχικῆς τελειώσεως . . . ἀποκαρθέντος τῷ τῆς ἑνιαίας ζωῆς ἰδιώματι καὶ τελειωθέντος τῷ θείῳ μυσταγωγήματι. Cf. *EH* 117. 2–10, *EH* 118. 1–119. 15.

By way of negative argument, two other reasons can be put for-ward to show how unlikely it is that Theodore could have intended to identify each rite as a μυστήριον, giving them, in the process, equal status. First, had he done so he would have been unique in the first eight hundred years of the history of the Eastern church.[86] Theodore was not a creative theologian and all his thought seems to have parallels or precedents either in Scripture or in the work of others who preceded him. He was by nature a traditionalist and for him to create a premeditated 'new listing' of sacraments would be quite out of character. Secondly, nowhere does he repeat this idea or its language. Baptism he does term a mystery[87]—as according to patristic usage[88]— and likewise (in the plural) the eucharist—as according to the Euchologion, the principal prayer book of the Byzantine church.[89] As for the other rites of sanctification, no par-ticular significance can be given to any particular term. The rites themselves will now be the subject of attention. Baptism and Eucharist will receive separate treatment in Ch. 5.

4.3 THE MYRON

The rite of the consecration of myron is only mentioned once in the whole of the Theodorian corpus, in letter 489 alone. The rite was performed once a year during the Divine Liturgy of the Thursday of Holy Week, immediately after the consecration of the eucharist.[90] The prayer of consecration of the myron does indeed

[86] Cf. Lampe, *Patristic Greek Lexicon*, s.v. μυστήριον, 892–3.
[87] *Oratio III, In Vigiliam Luminum* 702B; *Oratio IV, In Sanctum Pascha* 716C: τὸ μυστήριον τοῦ βαπτίσματος.
[88] e.g. Eusebius, in *PG* 24. 837A; Athanasios, in *PG* 26. 236C; Basil the Great, in *PG* 32. 188B; Gregory of Nyssa, in *PG* 45. 85B; Cyril of Jerusalem, in *Cat.* 18. 32, etc.
[89] See above, p. 158 and M. Arranz 'Les Sacraments de l'ancien Euchologe constanti-nopolitain' (1) 285. In the earliest (8th-cent.) texts of the Euchologion, baptism is only once referred to as a mystery: τοῦ προκειμένου σου μυστηρίου τοῦ μεγάλου καὶ ἐπουρανίου. J. Goar, Εὐχολόγιον sive Rituale Graecorum . . . , 2nd edn. (Venice, 1730), 288 (= F. C. Conybeare, *Rituale Armenorum, being the Administration of the Sacraments and the Breviary Rites of the Armenian Church, together with the Greek Rites of Baptism and Epiphany Edited from the Oldest MSS.* (Oxford, 1905), 399). In this same baptismal service (ἀκολουθία) the plural term 'mysteries' appears to refer to more than the eucharist, e.g. 'may he be made worthy of your immortal and heavenly mysteries', (Goar, Εὐχολόγιον, 276; Conybeare, *Rituale Armenorum*, 394); '. . . fruit of the oil for the complement of the ministration of your holy mysteries' (Goar, Εὐχολόγιον, 289; Conybeare, *Rituale Armenorum*, 402).
[90] Cf. J. Mateos, *Le Typicon de la Grande Église*, OCA 166 (Rome, 1963), ii. 76.

refer to this action as a mystery,[91] but not in quite the same language as Dionysios.[92] The mystery involved in this consecration may well have been associated in Theodore's mind with the sacramental *use* of the myron, in particular the post-baptismal anointing or chrismation, when he refers to it again simply as the 'divine myron' (θεῖον μύρον).[93] The Euchologion consecratory prayer is also directed primarily at the post-baptismal use of the myron.[94] However, there can be no question of attributing to Theodore any reference to a separate sacrament of chrismation, as it was not customary to consider this separately from baptism.[95] Early euchologia knew of no such division of rites.[96] Certainly, the only other time Theodore explicitly refers to the liturgical use of the myron is when he discusses the manner by which heretics were to be received back into the true church.[97] The Euchologion of Theodore's day had a special rite entitled 'From the Patriarchal Euchologion, on How to Receive those from Heresies into the

---

[91] Goar, *Εὐχολόγιον: Ακολουθία τοῦ ἁγίου μύρου*, 502: . . . παράσχου ἡμῖν τοῖς ἀναξίοις χάριν εἰς τὴν διακονίαν τοῦ μεγάλου τούτου καὶ ζωοποιοῦ μυστηρίου . . .

[92] Cf. Dionysius, *EH* 4. 95. 9–17, *EH* 98. 18–22. Dionysios calls the consecration the 'perfection', τελείωσις, of the myron (*EH* 108. 2), a 'perfection-working', τελεσιουργία (*EH* 78. 17, 95. 4, 97. 8–9), and a 'sacrament-working', τελετουργία (*EH* 97. 19–20, 98. 16, 103. 16, 104. 3).

[93] Ep. 489. 24–5. Cf. Auzépy, *Vie d'Étienne le Jeune*, 96. 3, where Patriarch Germanos baptizes the infant future saint, after which he administers the 'chrism of the divine myron': καὶ βαπτίζεται εἰς τὸ τῆς ζωαρχικῆς Τριάδος ὄνομα . . . μετὰ δε τὴν τοῦ θείου μύρου χρίσιν.

[94] Goar, *Εὐχολόγιον*. Critical edition of text in Arranz, 'La Consecration du saint myron (Les Sacraments de l'ancien Euchologe constantinopolitain), 10', *OCP* 55 (1989), 317–38, esp. p. 327.

[95] Dionysios mentions chrismation in association with baptism in *EH* 2. 73. 5, *EH* 78. 14, *EH* 4. 102.18. On the problem of the relation of chrismation or 'confirmation' to baptism, see G. W. H. Lampe, *The Seal of the Spirit: A Study in the Doctrine of Baptism and Confirmation in the New Testament and the Fathers* (London, 1951); A. Hamman, *Le Baptême et la confirmation* (Paris, 1969); L. Ligier, *La Confirmation*, Théologie Historique, 23 (Paris, 1973).

[96] Post-baptismal anointing with the holy chrism or myron did not have its separate office, but is found as a single rubric in the *Ακολουθία τοῦ ἁγίου Βαπτίσματος*: Goar, *Εὐχολόγιον*, 287–91. The ritual merely says: Καὶ χρίει ὁ ἱερεὺς τοὺς βαπτισθέντας τὸ ἅγιον μύρον, ποιῶν σταυροῦ τύπον ἐπὶ τοῦ μετώπου . . . λέγων· Σφραγίς δωρεᾶς πνεύματος ἁγίου (p. 291; Conybeare, *Rituale Armenorum*, 405). It was not considered to be a separate 'sacrament' before the 13th cent.—the effect of Latin influence, as its then designation of τὸ μυστήριον βεβαιώσεως amply bears out. On this, see Goar, *Εὐχολόγιον*, 275–8; M. Jugie, *Theologia dogmatica Christianorum orientalium* (Paris, 1930), iii. 16; J. Meyendorff, *Byzantine Theology: Historical Trends and Doctrinal Themes*, 2nd edn. (New York, 1987), 191–2.

[97] Ep. 40 (809–11). This letter will be examined in more detail below, in the section on heresy and baptism.

Holy and Apostolic Church of God'.[98] Preceded by this, in the
Goar edition of the Euchologion,[99] is a chapter entitled 'Canons of
the Holy Apostles and the Divine Fathers on Baptism', in which
church legislation is summarized.[100] Theodore divides heretics
into three types, as according to the Euchologion.[101] For the
nature of the heresies themselves, he refers his correspondent,
Naukratios, to Epiphanios' *Panarion*, which he also sends to him.[102]
One type of heretic is that who requires (re)baptism.[103] Five other
groups of historical heretics are to be 'chrismated with the holy
myron' (χρίονται δὲ τῷ ἁγίῳ μύρῳ),[104] whilst several others,

[98] 'Εκ τοῦ εὐχολογίου τοῦ πατριαρχικοῦ· ὅπως χρὴ δέχεσθαι τοὺς ἀπὸ
αἱρέσεων ἐν τῇ ἁγίᾳ τοῦ Θεοῦ καὶ ἀποστολικῇ ἐκκλησίᾳ. Critical edition of text
given in Arranz, 'Les Sacraments de l'ancien Euchologe constantinopolitain' (2), 53 ff. The
title is given ibid. n. 28.

[99] The dating of this text is uncertain and may be posterior to Theodore.

[100] Goar, Εὐχολόγιον, 273. The canons cited are Apostolic canons 47, 49, 50;
Carthage, canon 48 (50), canon III; Neocaesarea, canon 6; Timothy of Alexandria, canons
1, 2, 4, 6; Cyril of Alexandria, canonical letter 4, canon 5. The canons relating to chrismation are: canon 48 of Laodicea: Ὅτι δεῖ τοὺς φωτιζομένους μετὰ τὸ βάπτισμα
χρίεσθαι χρίσματι ἐπουρανίῳ . . . (Joannou, *Discipline générale antique*, i. pt. 2. 150), and
canon 7 of Constantinople (381), which lists two groups of heretics—those requiring (re)bap-
tism, and those requiring just chrismation: καὶ σφραγιζομένους, ἤτοι χριομένους,
πρῶτον τῷ ἁγίῳ μύρῳ τό τε μέτωπον . . . καὶ σφραγίζοντες αὐτοὺς λέγομεν.
Σφραγὶς δωρεᾶς πνεύματος ἁγίου (Tanner, *Decrees of the Ecumenical Councils*, i. 35). It is
curious that Trullo canon 95 is not mentioned, which gives norms also for the reception of
non-Chalcedonians (the simple renunciation of their heresy) and whose listing of the three
main types of heretics (no difference is made between heresy and schism) is accurately mir-
rored in the rubrics of the liturgical texts.

[101] Ep. 40. 26–7. Theodore does not in fact make any direct reference to the texts of the
Euchologion. There is a probable indirect reference in his concluding statement in this
same letter to Naukratios. There he states his threefold division is not based on Epiphanios,
but on 'the commentaries of a certain scholarly man from the past who researched and
investigated (the matter) from the books of the Church in Byzantium'. Ep. 40. 172–5: ὡς
εὗρον παρασημείωσίν τινος τῶν ἀρχαιοτέρων φιλοπόνου ἀνδρὸς καὶ ἐκ τῆς ἐν
Βυζαντίδι ἐκκλησίας τὴν ἐκ βιβλίων ἔρευναν καὶ εὕρεσιν ποιησαμένου. Presumably
the books in question were the collections of canons and the liturgical texts or euchologia
in use at Constantinople.

[102] Ep. 40. 22–5.   [103] Ibid. 27–9.

[104] Ibid. 29–31. In the Euchologion the priest prays God to make (the convert) 'worthy
of the seal of the divine myron' (καὶ καταξίωσον αὐτὸν τῆς σφραγῖδος τοῦ θείου
μύρου). The rubric then says 'And he anoints him with the myron as with the newly illumined' (καὶ χρίει αὐτὸν τῷ μύρῳ καθὼς καὶ τοὺς νεοφωτίστους), followed by a
prayer in which the priest prays, 'Lord our God who have deigned to make perfect your servant N. through orthodox faith in you and the seal of your holy myron . . . (καὶ τῆς
σφραγῖδος τοῦ ἁγίου σου μύρου). Arranz, 'Les Sacraments de l'ancien Euchologe constantinopolitain' (8), *OCP* 49 (1983), 55. Cf. the rite of anointing (used for the reconciliation
of apostates to Islam) in the *Diataxis* of Patriarch Methodios: idem, *OCP* 56 (1990), 311–13.
Ironically, the schismatic Stoudites at the time of Methodios were themselves reconciled
through anointing according to the *Testament* of Methodios as quoted by Niketas of

those who are to be neither baptized nor chrismated, who are mostly non-Chalcedonians, are merely to repudiate their and all other heresies.[105] This consideration of the myron, none the less, which is associated with the issue of valid baptism and of reconciliation, hardly coincides with the office of the episcopal blessing of the ointment alluded to in the letter to the monk Gregory.[106]

4.4 PRIESTHOOD

Despite its sacred reality, Theodore never once refers to the priesthood or ordination to the priesthood as a μυστήριον, apart from what might seem to be implied in the letter to Gregory. When a layman is called by Christ[107] to receive ordination (χειροτονία),[108] he enters the clerical order (κλήρων τάξις).[109] The priest (ἱερεύς, πρεσβύτερος)[110] engages in sacred acts,[111] and thus has sacred dignity (ἱερατικὸν ἀξίωμα).[112] He is the very icon of Christ,[113] an intermediary between God and man representing Christ in his sacred actions,[114] and a 'dispenser of the mysteries of God'.[115]

Herakleia: *On the Heresiarchs*, ed. J. Darrouzès, *Documents inédits d'ecclésiologie byzantin* (Paris, 1966), 294–5 (this was pointed out to me by Professor John Erickson in conversation).

[105] Ep. 40. 31–6. On this phrase, see J. Gouillard, in *Byzantion*, 31 (1961), 378 n. 2.

[106] Another allusion to the myron is made in ep. 549. 86–94, when Theodore is asked the question whether or not a priest who has eaten together with a heretic could be accepted back for common meals and psalmody χωρὶς σφραγῖδος ἢ μετὰ σφραγῖδος (l. 89). The answer is that he could be accepted without anointing (l. 94).

[107] Ep. 253. 8–9. [108] Cf. ep. 442. 9, ep. 549. 12. [109] *MC* 17. 49.

[110] Theodore has several words for the priest taken from Neoplatonic vocabulary: ἱερουργός, θεῖος μυσταγωγός, Θεοῦ λειτουργός, μυστηριοφύλαξ, θύτης, τελετής, μύστης, ἱερώμενος: ep. 38. 49; *De Praesanctificatis* 1688C; ep. 40. 11, ep. 225. 123, ep. 153. 34; *MC* 17. 50; ep. 442. 7. For a comparison with Dionysian language, see the relevant words in A. van den Daele, *Indices Pseudo-Dionysiani* (Louvain, 1941). A useful study is A. Louth, 'Pagan Theurgy and Christian Sacramentalism in Denys the Areopagite', *JTS* NS 37 (1986), 432–8. It should be noted, however, that apart from the term πρεσβύτερος, the context must decide which of the sacred orders—bishop, presbyter, or deacon—is being meant by these terms.

[111] Ep. 442. 4–5, ep. 536. 16, 17: ἱερουργεῖν, ἐνεργεῖν τοὺς ἱερεῖς τῆς ἱερωσύνης, ἁγιάζειν, θεουργεῖν.

[112] *Adversus Iconomachos* 4. 493D. Cf. *Laudatio Platonis* 821C; ep. 462. 47, ep. 477. 15, ep. 552. 77.

[113] *Adversus Iconomachos* 4. 493D: ὁ ἱερεὺς . . . εἰκὼν οὖν ὑπάρχων Χριστοῦ; εἰκὼν Χριστοῦ . . . τὸ ἱερατικὸν δηλαδὴ ἀξίωμα.

[114] *Adversus Iconomachos* 4. 493C: ὁ ἱερεὺς μέσος Θεοῦ καὶ ἀνθρώπων ἱστάμενος, ἐν ταῖς ἱερατικαῖς ἐπικλήσεσι, μίμημά ἐστι Χριστοῦ. Cf. 1 Tim. 2: 5.

[115] Ep. 49. 92. Cf. 1 Cor. 4: 1.

Whatever the priest says, liturgically, is confirmed by God Himself.[116] So great is his dignity that, if he were to show infidelity, he must be removed from the sacred ministry and from public service, even if repentant.

4.5 BURIAL OF THE DEAD

In one of his early letters Theodore writes to his monks about their duty, if called upon, to see to the decent burial of the dead.[117] Neglected corpses seemed to have been a feature of ninth-century life in and around the capital city. Pilgrims or foreigners died during their sojourn in the city, and relatives of inhabitants were sometimes too poor to afford burial fees.[118] The fact that man is made in the image of God, Theodore argues, means that the monk should imitate the goodness and providence of God by extending charity towards the unburied dead. Using the offerings received for this purpose each year, any cadaver seen by or pointed out to a Stoudite in transit is to be given the appropriate rites by him and then be buried in a designated (purchased) tomb.[119] Twice a year, on the first day of September and during the period between Easter and Pentecost these dead were remembered in a special ceremony, denoted by Theodore as a sacred rite ($\tau\grave{\eta}\nu$ $\acute{o}\sigma\acute{\iota}\alpha\nu$ $\tau\epsilon\lambda\epsilon\tau\acute{\eta}\nu$).[120] Divine Liturgy would be celebrated, together with a $\pi\alpha\nu\nu\nu\chi\acute{\iota}s$ or memorial service and perhaps other prayers.[121] During the Divine Liturgy the deceased were commemorated by a *prosphora* (blessed piece of bread) brought to the altar, their names being read out by a deacon from the diptychs during the anaphora prayer.[122] Following this liturgical commemoration there was

---

[116] Ep. 22. 34–5: ὅσα ὁ ἱερεὺς ὑποφαίνει, ταῦτα καὶ Θεὸς κυροῦν ἐπαγγέλλεται.

[117] Ep. 13 (803–6?), 'on the care of the unburied'. Elsewhere only the bare fact of burial is mentioned, e.g. ep. 549. 116: εὐχήν τε ποιεῖν ἐπὶ ἐκκομιδῆς; ep. 536. 15: ἐκκομίζειν νεκρόν.

[118] Ep. 13. 11–13.   [119] Ibid. 14–21.   [120] Ibid. 28.

[121] Ep. 552. 5. The παννυχίς was originally a vigil service celebrated before a major feast or during Great Lent (but, contrary to what the name suggests, not an all-night service). On this, see M. Arranz, *Pannychis* I, *OCP* 40 (1974), 414–43; *Pannychis* II, *OCP* 41 (1975), 119–39. Arranz believes that the παννυχίς as an office for the deceased may have been a Stoudite creation: *Pannychis* II, 129. (The name *Panahida* is still conserved by the Slavs.)

[122] Ep. 552. 5, 145–6; Brightman, *Liturgies*, 331. Cf. R. F. Taft, *The Diptychs: A History of the Liturgy of St John Chrysostom*, OCA 238 (Rome, 1991), iv. esp. pp. 1–10, 95–120.

refreshment and distribution of alms to the poor.[123] There is no mention of the word μυστήριον in this letter or in any other similar context, and neither is it found in the funeral prayers of the Euchologion.[124]

Up to this point rites mentioned in the list of the letter to the monk Gregory have been examined. No evidence has been found to encourage the view that this letter represents Theodore's way of categorizing the sanctifying rites of the church. Now it is time to look at other rites not mentioned in the list: marriage, anointing of the sick, and penance. What place did these have in Theodore's understanding of the sanctifying mission of the church? Were they sacraments neglected in Theodore's list?[125]

4.6 MARRIAGE

Marriage or crowning (στεφάνωμα), according to the Prayers (*akolouthia*) of Crowning of the Euchologion from which Theodore quotes,[126] is a divine act. Christ is 'the sacred celebrant of mystical and undefiled marriage' (ὁ τοῦ μυστικοῦ καὶ ἀχράντου γάμου ἱερουγός) who blesses the marriage through the ministry of the priest.[127] The priest's prayer is sacred, for it invokes divine grace through the action of the Holy Spirit.[128] The ceremony is a *mystagogia*.[129] Its sacredness is symbolized also by the presence of the priest at the post-wedding celebrations, together with the other concelebrants that might have been present, much as Christ was present

---

[123] Ep. 13. 23–31.

[124] Goar, *Εὐχολόγιον*, 432–3, 437. There seems to have been a general custom, not alluded to by Theodore, to commemorate the recent dead on the third, ninth, and fortieth day as well as on anniversaries (ibid. 434). As with the custom explained in ch. 7 of the *Ecclesiastical Hierarchy*, oil was poured onto the cadaver before burial (the oil of a lamp, ibid. 433, μύρον or ἔλαιον, ibid. 437). Ash from the thurible (λείφανον) was also deposited with the body (ibid. 433).

[125] Cf. J. A. Fuentes Alonso, *El divorcio de Constantino VI*, 143–6, who argues that marriage and the anointing of the sick should belong to Theodore's 'list' of sacraments.

[126] Ep. 23. 22–8, ep. 31. 79–85: Goar, *Εὐχολόγιον*, 317.

[127] Goar, *Εὐχολόγιον*, 316. The words of the priest are 'confirmed and ratified' by God: ep. 31. 91–2. God gives the partners to each other and joins them: ep. 508. 8–9, ep. 454. 31. They will be together at the resurrection: ep. 454. 31–2.

[128] Ep. 28. 42–3: τὴν ἐπὶ τῇ συναφείᾳ ἱερὰν προσευχὴν λέγοντα . . . καὶ προσκαλούμενον τὴν θείαν χάριν; ep. 31. 60–1 (on the Holy Spirit).

[129] Cf. ep. 35. 53: ταῖς στεφανικαῖς μυσταγωγίαις.

at the Cana wedding feast.[130] Theodore refers to the reality of marriage as a mystery,[131] a consideration reinforced, if not directly suggested, by the designated reading of Ephesians 5: 20–33 in the Euchologion.[132] None the less, Theodore's emphasis on the sacredness of marriage is in its liturgical celebration.[133] As with the Fathers and canonical tradition, however, Theodore does not recognise the same sacredness for a second marriage.[134] Although second marriage is 'licit and permitted by God',[135] God's original blessing on Adam and Eve (Gen. 1: 27) was for monogamy.[136] Adam was *monogamos*.[137] Even the marriage epiclesis prayer (στεφανικὴ ἐπίκλησις) of the Euchologion reflected this original divine disposition, making of second marriage an 'indulgence' (συγχώρησις).[138] Even though

---

[130] Ep. 50. 41–5. The Cana wedding feast features centrally in the marriage ceremony, as the Gospel reading (John 2: 1–11: Goar, Εὐχολόγιον, 318), and in the invocations and priestly prayers ('That the Lord bless these nuptials as in Cana of Galilee', p. 315; cf. the priestly prayers in pp. 318, 319, 320).

[131] On the indissolubility of earthly marriage: ep. 530. 41–2. πιστὸς ὁ λόγος τοῦ μυστηρίου . . . ἐπί τε δεσμῷ ἀλύτῳ τῆς συναφείας.

[132] Goar, Εὐχολόγιον, 318. Theodore does not actually quote the words of v. 32, τὸ μυστήριον τοῦτο μέγα ἐστίν, which refer to Christ's espousal of the church of which marriage is a reflection, but to other passages of this same reading, e.g. vv. 25–7: ep. 48. 194–9; v. 28: ep. 470. 16; v. 33: ibid. 18.

[133] I disagree with the interpretation of Fuentes Alonso, *El divorcio de Constantino VI*, 145–6, of ep. 28. 42–3 and esp. ep. 35. 49–50, in which he tries to show Theodore's belief that marriage is a *cause of grace*: 'nos encontramos distintos comentarios en los que el matrimonio se nos muestra como causa de la gracia'. He admits that the texts themselves refer to the liturgical act, but inexplicably (yet according to Roman Catholic sacramental theology) transfers the sense to the marriage itself as if the partners were the cause of sacramental grace. The texts referred to do not, however, allow this reading, esp. ep. 35. 49–50. This reads: ὅτι μηδεὶς ἅγιος τὴν μερίδα μετὰ μοιχοῦ ἔθετο, οὐχ ὅτι καὶ μοιχωμένους ἐστεφάνωσε καὶ δώρων τῶν θείων μεταδέδωκεν. Immediately preceding this passage is a reference to the 809 synod's misuse of the term 'economy of the saints'. The sense of the passage is: 'not one saint (i.e. who had used economy) had anything to do with adultery, nor had crowned adulterers, nor gave them the eucharist'. The expression 'divine gifts' (the Latin translation—from which Fuentes works—reads 'et divina eis dona tradidit': 1030D) seems to have been seriously misinterpreted to mean the transmission of (matrimonial) sacramental grace. D. Gemmiti, in *Teodoro Studita e la questione Moicheiana*, 175–6, has simply abbreviated and translated Fuentes' work (with no hint of acknowledgement), repeating the same error: 'abbiamo ancora eloquenti passi teodoriani, in cui il matrimonio viene ritenuto *causa della grazia*' (p. 175).

[134] On the canonical penances for digamists, see J. Dauvillier and C. de Clercq, *Le Marriage en droit canonique orientale* (Paris, 1936), 195–200.

[135] Ep. 22. 85–6.   [136] Ep. 50. 48–52.   [137] Ibid. 52.

[138] Ep. 50. 52–6, 69, 72. Cf. ibid. 17–19: Ἡ μὲν οὖν διγαμία παρακεχώρηται δῆλον ὅτι ὑπὸ τοῦ ἱεροῦ ἀποστόλου καὶ δι᾽ αὐτοῦ παρὰ Χριστοῦ, οὐ μὴν νόμος, ὥσπερ ὁ Θεολόγος Γρηγόριος, ἀλλὰ συγχώρησις. For Gregory of Nazianzus: *Oratio* 37. 8 (*PG* 36. 292B), who writes, 'A first marriage is in full conformity with the law; the second is tolerated by indulgence; the third is noxious. But he who exceeds this number is plainly a

the marriage was valid,[139] only after penance had been imposed and fulfilled by the couple could the eucharist be received, thereby giving the marriage itself its full Christian meaning.[140] Only then could a priestly blessing be given 'as if it were a crowning, but in a secondary fashion'.[141] For Theodore, the crown was a sign of victory, the victory of keeping virginity intact against the onslaughts of passion.[142] A similar idea is expressed in the Euchologion prayer on the eighth day after marriage.[143] Yet, the Euchologion *akolouthia*, which Theodore knew well, had a variety of symbolic explanations for the crown.[144] To suggest that only the monogamist was deserving of it, and that this was supported by tradition, was only Theodore's personal opinion.[145]

swine.' The Apostle Paul did not regard second marriage as sinful, but as a lesser good. Cf. 1 Cor. 7: 8–9, 39; Rom. 7: 3; 1 Tim. 5: 14.

[139] Ep. 50. 75–6. On the civil legislation of the time and its relation to the canons, see Fuentes Alonso, *El divorcio de Constantino VI*, 73–112.

[140] Ep. 50. 59–74, 92–102. Theodore alludes to the connection between marriage and eucharist, e.g., in ep. 50. 101–2: κεφάλαιον γὰρ καὶ τέλος τῆς ζεύξεως τὸ ἅγιον καὶ ἐνιαῖον σῶμα καὶ αἷμα Χριστοῦ. Cf. ep. 35. 50: οὐχ ὅτι καὶ μοιχωμένους ἐστεφάνωσε καὶ δώρων τῶν θείων μεταδέδωκεν.

[141] Ep. 50. 68–9: ἐντεῦθεν εὐλογουμένους αὐτοὺς οἱονεὶ ὡς ἐπὶ στεφανώματος, κατὰ δεύτερον λόγον μετὰ συγχώρησιν. Theodore does not say if there is an actual crowning, although this may be inferred from the fact that a marital blessing without crowning would make no sense to a Byzantine. The ritual for digamists in the Euchologion (pp. 328–31) contains two penitential prayers followed by the normal crowning rite. Although this ritual would seem to date from after the time of Emperor Leo VI (who made the priestly blessing obligatory for marriage validity: Novella 89) something similar may have been used in Theodore's time after the period of penance of two years (ep. 50. 60). Theodore admits the (abusive) use of a crowning rite for digamists who have not undergone penance, practised since the time of the third marriage of Constantine V (ep. 50. 10–11). He comments on the 'ridiculous and absurd' practice of crowning the digamist on the shoulder instead of on the head (as was the case with a virgin partner), and sarcastically asks whether a trigamist should be crowned on the hand or on the knee? (ep. 50. 87–91).

[142] Ep. 22. 88–9: τοὺς νικητικοὺς ἐπὶ τῇ παρθενίᾳ στεφάνους. Cf. ep. 525. 30–1.

[143] Goar, Εὐχολόγιον, 325: Εὐχὴ ἐπὶ λύσιν στεφάνων . . . The crown is a sort of 'reward' for continence and for having approached marriage in purity. John Chrysostom, *In Epist. I ad Timoth.*, II, 8 (*PG* 62. 546), also sees the crown as a symbol of victory over temptations of the flesh (although not in a context of second marriage).

[144] Unity (p. 317: στεφάνωσον αὐτοὺς εἰς σάρκα μίαν); matrimonial consent (ibid., the actual crowning formula: Στέφεται ὁ δοῦλος τοῦ Θεοῦ (ὁ δεῖνα) τὴν δούλην τοῦ Θεοῦ . . .); glory and honour (p. 318, the crowning blessing: Κύριε ὁ Θεὸς ἡμῶν, δόξῃ καὶ τιμῇ στεφάνωσον αὐτούς. Cf. Heb. 2: 7); martyrdom (p. 319, invocation to the martyrs); pledge of a (maritally) chaste life (p. 320, concluding priestly prayer: ἀνάλαβε τοὺς στεφάνους αὐτῶν ἐν τῇ βασιλείᾳ σου ἀσπίλους καὶ ἀμώμους); previous continence (p. 325, reward for previous life: μισθὸν . . . τῆς σωφροσύνης).

[145] Ep. 50. 6–35. Cf. E. Herman, 'Εὐχὴ ἐπὶ διγάμων', *OCP* 1 (1935), 467–89, who argues that there was no ancient legislation forbidding the ecclesiastical blessing of second marriage. Theodore admits that others have different views, but he himself deduced the

4.7 ANOINTING OF THE SICK

No details about the rite of the anointing of the sick with the
euchelaion,[146] are to be found in the writings of Theodore. What is
known is that within the monastery those in charge of the sick had
a special duty to look after the holy oils (τὰ ἔλαια),[147] and
Theodore himself received the anointing on his deathbed.[148]
Some ritual was associated with this anointing, but practically
nothing is known about its detail.[149] Nor is it clear what the difference was between an 'official' liturgical anointing by a priest and a
self-administered anointing with holy oil received by the sick person as a blessing (εὐλογία), which seems to have been a common
practice despite not being found in the Euchologion.[150] Theodore
also employs a term—ἀπομύρισμα—which, if rendered as 'the oil
of the sick', as is probably accurate, introduces us, in another place,

tradition of prohibition from canons that actually did *not* directly forbid crowning. His principal argument is from Neocaesarea canon 7: 'A priest should not take part in the wedding
feast of one who marries a second time. For when one who is twice married requests the
imposition of a penance, what can the priest say who has approved the marriage by participating in the festivities?' Joannou, *Discipline générale antique*, i. pt. 2. 78. Only one known
canon, which is attributed to Patriarch Nikephoros (but unknown to Theodore), expresses
Theodore's convictions exactly: 'Those who enter a second marriage are not crowned and
are not admitted to receive the most pure mysteries for two years; those who enter a third
marriage are excommunicated for five years:' *PG* 100. 855A, canon 2. On the canon's
doubtful authenticity, see Grumel, *Regestes*, 405–6.

    [146] Goar, Εὐχολόγιον, 335, 338, 346. The rite is called Ἀκολουθία τοῦ ἁγίου ἐλαίου
. . . , ibid. 332–46.
    [147] Cf. *Epitimia*, I. 68, 1741C. Oil was also blessed on the vigils of feast days, followed by
the anointing of all. Cf. PK 19. 131 (= *MC* 27. 75): ὀφείλομεν ἑκαστοτε ἐπιβάλλειν τὸ
τῆς χρίσεως ἔλαιον . . .
    [148] As reported by Naukratios: *Naucratii confessoris encyclica* 1845A: καὶ κατὰ εἰωθὸς
ἐπαλειψάμενος καὶ κατασφραγισάμενος. Cf. *Vita B*, 67. 325B.
    [149] All that is known is that Theodore's members were smeared with oil and that he
received a 'signing'. Only a few prayers—of blessing of oil and petitions for the sick—are
found in the early Euchologion. Cf. Goar, Εὐχολόγιον, 549–50 (and 679, from the 11th-
cent. Bessarion MS); A. Strittmatter, 'The Barberinium S. Marci of Jacques Goar', *EL* 47
(1933), nos. 223–7 (p. 358). The complex ritual in today's Euchologion (with ideally seven
priests present) appears first in MSS of the 11th cent.
    [150] Cf. John Damascene, *De his qui in fide dormierunt*, *PG* 95. 264BD, who states that who-
ever administers the ointment should first anoint himself. In *Vita B* importance is attached
to the sanctity and orthodoxy of the person who blesses this oil. The lapsed heretic Bardas
dies as a result of anointing himself with holy oil sent to him by the iconoclast bishop of
Smyrna (205 BC), whereas a sick girl is cured through being anointed by oil blessed by
Theodore (209B).

to his only reference to anointing.[151] In a letter which presents him with various questions about the course of action to be adopted in various circumstances created by the iconoclast heresy the verb ἀπομυρίζειν is introduced.[152] Two questions are asked. First, is it legitimate for a monk to pray for, bless oil for, light candles for, and impart holy anointing (ἀπομυρίζειν ἅγια) to a heterodox believer who makes this request? Theodore replies in the negative.[153] Secondly, can a female religious (μονάστρια) anoint (ἀπομυρίζειν)? Only in urgent necessity, he replies, and when there is no priest or deacon or monk available.[154] If this is the true interpretation of this enigmatic verb, then we may deduce that it was a custom of the time for people, and not just those who were gravely ill, to come to church for anointing with the oil of the sick. Secondly, anointing of the sick could be ministered by the unordained, including by a female.[155] It must be pointed out, however, that in the past a very different interpretation has been given.[156]

4.8 PENANCE

Although Theodore once speaks of μυστήριον in connection with the forgiveness of sins,[157] he in no place speaks of an *ecclesiastical rite* of confession of sins, imposition of penance, or absolution. Indeed,

---

[151] Ep. 55. 19. Cf. Lampe, *Patristic Greek Lexicon*, 202, s.v. ἀπομύρισμα; Fatouros, *Theodori Studitae Epistulae*, II, 926. In his letter to the *patrikia* Irene, Theodore expresses his grave concern over the illness of the former's daughter, stating that he does not know how the prayers or the ἀπομύρισμα of such a sinner as himself can help her.

[152] Ep. 552. 79, 91, 92. The verb, like the noun, is one of Theodore's neologisms. In Lampe, *Patristic Greek Lexicon*, s.v. ἀπομυρίζω, a question mark is placed by the translation: 'anoint with holy oil'. Fatouros, *Theodori Studitae Epistulae*, 929, shows more certainty: 'oleo ungo'.

[153] Ep. 552. 78–81.   [154] Ibid. 91–3: ἐξ ἀπορίας πάσης ἱερωμένου ἢ μονάζοντος . . .

[155] This may correspond to what Arranz calls 'non-sacramental' anointing: 'Les Sacrements: La Consecration de saint myron' (7), 335 n. 24. It would seem to differ from the kind reported in the encyclical of Naukratios and the *Vita* (*PG* 99. 1845A, 325B).

[156] Cf. J. Pargoire, in *L'Église byzantine de 527 à 847* (Paris, 1905), 351. As an interesting aside, as pointed out to the author by Bishop Kallistos Ware, Leo Allatius in the 17th cent. takes ἀπομύρισμα to denote water used for wiping the holy table on Holy Thursday, which is then drunk by the faithful. However, it does not seem possible that Theodore can have this meaning in view.

[157] Ep. 530. 41–2: πιστὸς ὁ λόγος τοῦ μυστηρίου ἐπί τε ἀφέσει τῶν ἡμαρτημένων. Gregory of Nyssa, *De Vita Moysis*, *PG* 44. 413A, also uses the expression τὸ τῆς μετανοίας μυστύριον.

no Ἀκολουθία of penance is known from this time,[158] nor does Theodore ever state that the revealing of thoughts or confession (ἐξαγόρευσις) of the monk to his *hegoumenos* requires that the latter be a priest.[159] Although it was normal practice for a priest to listen to a penitent and to impose penance, in the absence of (an orthodox) priest it was not illicit, says Theodore, for a simple monk to take his place.[160] Absolution (λύσις), furthermore, could also be communicated by letter.[161]

It is significant, none the less, that the forgiveness of sins committed and confessed was not dependent on absolution, as would be the case in later practice.[162] The treatise περὶ ἐξαγορεύσεως

[158] That found in Goar, Εὐχολόγιον, 541, is from an Italo-Greek MS of the 16th cent. Cf. M. Arranz, 'Les Sacraments de l'ancien Euchologe constantinopolitain: Les Prières pénitentielles de la tradition byzantine' (8), 87–143 (esp. p. 91), 309–29; *OCP* 58 (1992), 23–82; 'Les Formulaires de confession dans la tradition byzantine', *OCP* 58 (1992), 423–59; *OCP* 59 (1993), 63–89, 357–86. Idem, *OCP* 57 (1991), 89–90, notes how only two penitential prayers exist in the oldest Euchologia for sins other than apostasy. One was for those 'in penitence' (τῶν μετανοούντων), used at the beginning of a term of canonical penalty (which included privation of the eucharist), the other was for 'those who confess' (τῶν ἐξομολογουμένων), recited before or following the confession of sins which was then followed by a period of penance.

[159] Nothing in legislation required the *hegoumenos* to be a priest, nor was it presupposed in the rite of profession in the texts of *Barberinus graecus* 336. Cf. canons 14, 19 of the Second Council of Nicaea: P. de Meester, *De monachico statu juxta disciplinam byzantinam*, Sacra Congregazione per la Chiesa Orientale. Codificazione Canonica Orientale, 2/10 (Vatican, 1942), 383; M. Wawryk, *Initiatio Monastica in Liturgia Byzantina*, OCA 180 (Rome, 1968), 26 n. 121. In practice, however, it seems that this was actually the case. Thus, Theodore directs the abbot to wear simple clothes, *excepting his liturgical vestments* (ἄνευ τοῦ ἱερατικοῦ): ep. 10. 70–1; *Testamentum* no. 19, 1821A.

[160] Ep. 549. 156–9: ἐπειδὴ δὲ ἐμφαίνει ἡ ἐρώτησις εἰ δεῖ καὶ τὸν μὴ ἔχοντα ἱερωσύνην διδόναι κατὰ ἀπορίαν πρεσβυτέρων καὶ πίστιν τοῦ προσιόντος, οὐκ ἔξω τοῦ εἰκότος καὶ τὸν ἁπλῶς μοναχὸν ἐπιτίμια διδόναι. The practice of confessing to simple monks was quite traditional since, being known or perceived as being holy, they could be approached as intercessors before God to secure forgiveness. As a text ascribed to Anastasios of Sinai says (*PG* 89. 372A): 'If you find a spiritual man, experienced and capable of curing you, confess before him without shame and full of faith, as if before God and not a human being.' On this whole question, see R. Barringer, 'Ecclesiastical Penance in the Church of Constantinople: A Study of the Hagiographical Evidence to 983 A.D.', D.Phil. dissertation (Oxford, 1979); idem, 'The Pseudo-Amphilochian Life of St Basil: Ecclesiastical Penance and Byzantine Hagiography', ΘΕΟΛΟΓΙΑ, 51 (1980), 49–61; idem, 'Penance and Byzantine Hagiography. Le Répondant du péché', *Studia Patristica*, 17/2 (1979, publ. 1982), 552–7; K. Ware, 'Prayer and the Sacraments in the *Synagoge*', in M. Mullett and A. Kirby (eds.), *The Theotokos Evergetis and Eleventh-Century Monasticism* (Belfast, 1994), 341–4.

[161] Cf. ep. 394.

[162] Cf. A. Almazov, *Tajnaja ispoved' v pravoslavnoj vostočnoj cerkvi* (Odessa, 1894); M. Jugie, *Theologia Dogmatica Christianorum Orientalium* (Paris, 1930), iii. 331–89; R. Taft, 'Penance in Contemporary Scholarship', *Studia Liturgica*, 18 (1988), 2–21; G. Wagner, 'Bussdisziplin in

(*De confessione*), with its twenty-seven canons on vices and sins, and the (110 plus 65) *Epitimia*, both attributed to Theodore, make no mention of absolution nor, still less, a rite of absolution.[163] Certain faults are punished by a minor excommunication—i.e. abstention from the eucharist or communion for a certain period of time—with full reintegration within the monastic community being accomplished by the fact of once again receiving communion. Only once, in the *Questions and Answers on Penance*, also attributed to Theodore, is there mention of the imposition of hands of a confessor (ἀνάδοχος), believed to represent the forgiving action of Christ, and which guarantees the full remission of sins after penance has been completed.[164] The context, however, is that of a monk who has committed several carnal sins and has scruples about whether God has truly forgiven him. The imposition of hands, therefore, is a guarantee of God's mercy, not the instrument by which it is transmitted. The very term ἀνάδοχος, which means 'sponsor', especially baptismal sponsor,[165] suggests that the confessor is but the guarantor of God's forgiveness.[166]

Theodore's understanding of the workings of penance can be illustrated by reference to his correspondence with a certain monk Loukianos. This monk had committed a grave fault (communion with heretics) that had harmed the whole community.[167] Theodore's first words to him are words from the book of Genesis (3: 9): 'Adam, where are you?'[168] God's words, he explains, are directed not just to Adam but to all who have transgressed his commandments.[169] For God understands fully the weakness of man, and in his love for mankind he has established the institution of

der Tradition des Ostens', in *Liturgie et remission des péchés* (Rome, 1975), 251–64; J. H. Erickson, 'Penitential Discipline in the Orthodox Canonical Tradition', *SVThQ* 21 (1977), 191–206.

[163] *PG* 99. 1721–9, 1733–57.   [164] *PG* 99. 1732CD.

[165] Ep. 17. 5, 32. Cf. the Euchologion: Goar, Εὐχολόγιον, 277; Conybeare, *Rituale Armenorum*, 395. The term was also used in a transferred baptismal sense to mean the sponsor at monastic profession: ep. 333. 26: ὁ τοῦ σχήματος ἀνάδοχος.

[166] Barringer has shown, e.g. in 'Penance and Byzantine Hagiography', that the function of the ἀνάδοχος was to take upon his own shoulders the burden of the struggles of the penitent. It was 'an emergency technique of Byzantine *cura pastoralis*' that helped the spiritually inexperienced not to give in to the delusion of the impossibility of salvation. Barringer, however, seems to have completely missed this particular text which offers interesting evidence for his thesis.

[167] Ep. 258. 9: τὴν τῆς ἀσεβείας κοινωνίαν. This fault was the equivalent of having abandoned the monastic way of life: ep. 394. 16.

[168] Ep. 258. 12; cf. ep. 394. 15.   [169] Ep. 258. 2–4.

repentance or penance/penitence (τὴν μετάνοιαν) by which he
recalls man from his fall and restores him to his former state of
spiritual health.[170] He is the God of penitents (Θεὸς τῶν
μετανοούντων), of those who accept the 'first and last medicine of
penitence' (τοῦτο πρῶτον καὶ τελευταῖον φάρμακον
μετανοίας).[171] What is this monk to do? First, he must confess his
fault (ἀνομία) to all the brethren in order that the Lord may forgive him. Then in a spirit of true and tearful compunction he is to
live the period of penance (τὸν τῆς μετανοίας καιρόν) given to
him by the superior. It is the monk himself, however, who requests
absolution (λύσις) from Theodore, who at this time is in exile.
Theodore readily complies, and tells the monk, in the name of the
Lord, to arise, to be whole, and not to lapse henceforth from the
faith.[172]

The absolution that Theodore offers is a sign that the monk
Loukianos has now been formally reconciled to his community as
well as to God. The fact that the monk himself requested it may
indicate that, because Theodore himself had expressed such concern for him, it was also a form of personal reconciliation with the
head of the monastery. However, it was the 'medicine' of penitence
that effected the forgiveness of sin, and not the absolution.[173]
Theodore himself, in this correspondence, quotes the psalmist (Ps.
34: 18), 'The Lord is near to the brokenhearted, and saves the
crushed in spirit.'[174] There is no indication elsewhere in his writings to suggest that Theodore believes it to be anything other than
the accomplishment itself of penance, together with hope in God,
that leads to God's forgiveness. Thus, it was not the mediation or
intercession of a priest or confessor that was the direct cause of
healing grace. Penance and the forgiveness of sin was not a 'sacrament' so much as a part of God's philanthropic economy.[175]

It was the special prerogative of the *hegoumenos* to lay down
epitimia for faults committed or confessed (not excluding incarcer-

---

[170] Ep. 394. 2–6.   [171] Ep. 258. 7–8.   [172] Ep. 394. 10, 18.
[173] Cf. ep. 550. 4–5: ἐπὶ παντὸς ἁμαρτήματος ἡ ἀξιόλογος μετάνοια τὴν
συγχώρησιν ἔχει.
[174] Ep. 258. 12–13.
[175] Cf. Arranz, 'Les Sacraments: Les Prières pénitentielles' (8), 90–2. The prayers of the
early Euchologia show that the role of the priest, or even of the non-ordained δεχόμενος,
was to solicit the pardon of God, the remission of sin, and the absolution of canonical penalties.

ation in the monastery detention centre),[176] and also to remit or
shorten them once he had judged that there had been genuine
conversion of heart.[177] In the latter case, he could then declare
authoritatively that God had forgiven the sinner.[178] Without true
repentance it was impossible for any human being to declare God's
forgiveness.[179] On the other hand, neither could the ministry of
reconciliation, or more exactly the ministry of penance, be denied
to repentant sinners. During the iconoclast crisis of Michael II's
reign there were monks who took a much more severe attitude
than Theodore to those who had lapsed and had subsequently
repented. One of these monks, another Theodore, had taken it
upon himself to compose and issue a circular letter (ἐγκύκλιος
ἐπιστολή) in which the sincerity of conversions was ques-
tioned and an intransigent refusal to administer the *pharmaka* of
penance advocated.[180] Iconoclasts, so this letter maintained, were
true Manichaeans and as such could not be reconciled with the
true church.[181] Although Theodore the Stoudite had himself
applied this epithet to iconoclasts,[182] as was commonly done by
iconophiles,[183] he does point out, with some measure of common
sense, that iconoclasts were Manichaeans only by similitude of
name or improperly speaking, and not in truth or properly

[176] Cf. TC I. 80. 653, where a monk who had 'deviated' was locked up for a period 'for
his salvation and the good of the brethren', until the *hegoumenos* (Theodore) 'examines him'
before releasing him.

[177] This is implied in the power to 'loose and bind' (Matt. 16: 19). Cf. TC I. 70. 633;
Testamentum no. 22, 1821B: ἔστω σοι κλείς, ἡ μεγίστη τῶν ψυχῶν φροντίς, τοῦ λύειν
καὶ δεσμεῖν, κατὰ τὰ Λόγια.

[178] A certain Hypatos, probably one of Theodore's monks, had committed a fault meriting exclusion from reception of the eucharist. Theodore writes to him to absolve him from
his ἐπιτίμιον after only a short time of penance. He declares that the ἐπιτίμιον has
effected its cure and that God has forgiven him: Ὁ Θεὸς συγχωρήσει σοι, ἀδελφέ, τὰ
ἁμαρτήματα (ep. 99. 8–9).

[179] Cf. ep. 302. 27–32.

[180] Ep. 477. Members of the clergy, it was also claimed, tried to attract as many *lapsi* as
possible and refused to recognize the penance administered by their colleagues. Theodore
Stoudite denounces this letter on the account of both its content (misguided norms and
instructions) and its presumption of arrogating to itself an authority which was proper only
to the episcopate.

[181] Ep. 477. 202–3.   [182] e.g. in ep. 425. 41; *Antirrheticus* 3. 15. 397A.

[183] Cf. S. Gero, 'Notes on Byzantine Iconoclasm in the Eighth Century', *Byzantion*, 44
(1974), 35–6: '"Manichean", like "Jew" and "pagan", was simply a standard and indis-
criminate term of abuse . . . "docetic iconoclasm" . . . is an invention of iconophile polemi-
cists.' Cf. K. Parry, 'Theodore Studites and the Patriarch Nicephoros on Image-Making as
a Christian Imperative', *Byzantion*, 59 (1989), 174–5.

speaking.[184] To refuse penance to the lapsed would be 'Pharisaical' and 'Novatianist'.[185] The Lord himself was the model for the exercise of οἰκονομία towards those who show true μετάνοια.[186] He did not judge sinners according to the full rigour of the law, for repentance (μετάνοια) was itself a detraction from the strictness of law (παρατροπὴ τῆς τοῦ δικαίου ἀκριβείας).[187] The Lord himself had preached repentance; repentance constituted τὰ φάρμακα of the soul, and it led to emendation of life (ἐπανόρθωσις). Penances (αἱ ἐπιτιμίαι) were therapeutic and remedial (ἰατρεῖαι). They were part of the divine economy.[188]

Theodore never conceived of penance as anything other than medicinal, restoring health and beauty of soul to the one who, through sin, is spiritually sick.[189] Even the spiritually dead are brought back to life through penance.[190] The medicines of penance, such as exclusion for a time from participation in the eucharist, were not vindictive—the punishment that satisfies the demands of justice—but the means by which the cure is effected.[191] In this life God is not a judge but a merciful doctor.[192] He pardons and 'ignores'[193] the sins of those penitents who turn to

---

[184] Ep. 477. 202–13: . . . ἀλλὰ τοσοῦτον ἔχοντα τὸ πρὸς ἄλληλα ταὐτόν, ὅσον τὸ κατὰ τοὔνομα κοινὸν τοῖς ἄλλοις ἐξαλλάσσοντα. καὶ τὰ μὲν κυρίως ὠνόμασται, τὰ δὲ οὐ κυρίως, καὶ τὰ μὲν κατὰ κατάχρησιν λέλεκται, τὰ δὲ κατὰ ἀλήθειαν. Theodore is applying, in this instance, the terminology and concepts of the *Categories* of Aristotle. When he spoke as a preacher, however, in this same period (821–6) he would not make this distinction, e.g. in *PC* 6. 25: ἀλλ' οἱ μὲν εἰκονομάχοι ἴσα τῶν μανιχαίων φρονοῦντες . . . .

[185] Ep. 477. 133–5: ἢ δῆλον ὅτι Φαρισαικῆς διανοίας ἡ ἐπίπληξις καὶ Ναυατιανικῆς μισανθρωπίας ἡ ἀπαγόρευσις.

[186] Cf. Ep. 477. 70–82, 116–32.   [187] Ibid. 109–10.   [188] Ibid. 67, 72, 78–9, 84–9.

[189] Cf. *PC* 8. 29, *PC* 20. 61–2, *PC* 82. 210, *PC* 93. 235–56, *PC* 129. 329: πάλιν ὑγιαστέον διὰ μετανοίας; PK 103. 735 (= *MC* 24. 67): ἰατρεία δὲ ἡ δι' ἐξαγορεύσεως ἐπιτιμία; PK 113. 839 (= *MC* 11. 33); ep. 60. 15: τὸ τῆς ὑγείας φάρμακον; ep. 258. 7–8, ep. 394. 2–6, ep. 448. 32–5, ep. 550. 11–12, etc.

[190] Ep. 199. 9; cf. ep. 154. 11–12, ep. 444. 49–51. The context of this 'death' is the embracing of heresy and the abandonment of monastic life.

[191] Cf. epp. 60, 432, 450.

[192] Ep. 444. 47–8: ἴδε Θεὸς ἀγαθός, ἴδε ἰατρὸς ἐλεήμων.

[193] In the oldest Euchologion MSS for the Εὐχὴ ἐπὶ ἐξομολογουμένων, God is asked to 'ignore' (ὡς ἀγαθὸς πάριδε, from παρορῶ: ignore, overlook, neglect, not to regard) rather than 'forgive' (συγχώρησον) the sins of the penitent: Arranz, 'Les Sacraments: Les Prières pénitentielles' (8), 100–1. Cf. Εὐχὴ ἐπὶ μετανοούντων: καὶ πάρεδεὼς πολυέλεος τὰ πταίσματα αὐτῶν ἅπαντα (Goar, Εὐχολόγιον, 537); παρορῶν τὰ αὐτῷ πλημμεληθέντα (Arranz, ibid. 97). Cf. ep. 99. 3: ἐν τῷ ἐλέει τοῦ Θεοῦ τοῦ παρορῶντος πᾶν ἁμάρτημα. The Euchologion also uses the same verb παρορῶ in a prayer for forgiveness during the baptismal service: Goar, Εὐχολόγιον, 288; Conybeare, *Rituale Armenorum*, 398–9.

Him with sincere hearts.[194] The giving of penances on the part of the *hegoumenos* was thus an act of charity.[195] They were also to be administered sparingly.[196]

Compunction or grief for sin (πένθος) was an integral component of penitence, tears being traditionally likened to the purifying waters of baptism.[197] In the eighth century prayers of the Euchologion, the repentance of kings David and Manasseh,[198] and the tears of Peter and the adulteress[199] feature as the precedents and models of those who received God's forgiveness.[200] Theodore also frequently alludes to these same examples (possibly indicating his use of these prayers?), although in place of the adulteress he alludes to the popular story of Mary of Egypt.[201]

Repentance or penitence (μετάνοια) traditionally had an absolutely central place in the spirituality of monastic life.[202] Indeed, the monastic vocation itself was conceived to be a vocation of penance or continual conversion to the Lord,[203] being an

---

[194] *PC* 54. 147: ὁ ἀγαθὸς ἡμῶν Θεὸς . . . συγχωρεῖ δὲ τὰ παραπτώματα ἡμῶν, εἴπερ ἐξ εἰλικρινοῦς καρδίας σὺν φόβῳ τε καὶ τρόμῳ προσπέσωμεν καὶ προσκλαύσωμεν αὐτῷ τὴν πρὸς τὸ ἐξῆς βελτίωσιν ἐπαγγελλόμενοι; ep. 99. 3–4.

[195] Ep. 60. 19–20, ep. 61. 19: ὁ ἀγαπῶν ἐπιμελῶς παιδεύει (cf. Prov. 3: 12; Heb. 12: 56); ep. 453. 21–2.

[196] Cf. ep. 444. 52–4 (where Theodore says he is being as lenient as possible towards the monk Euarestos who had apostatized and returned); ep. 453. 21–2.

[197] Cf. Hausherr, *Penthos*, 135–51.

[198] On David's sin, the rebuke by the prophet Nathan, David's repentance, and the return of the gift of prophecy, see 2 Sam. 11–12 and Ps. 51. Manasseh was the blackest of all the kings of Judah, credited with the worship of foreign gods, superstitions of various kinds, oppression, and murder. He was the occasion of the decision of Yahweh to destroy Judah (2 Kgs. 21: 1–17; 2 Chr. 33: 1–10). His conversion is recounted in 2 Chr. 33: 11–20.

[199] Peter's denial of Jesus and tears of repentance: Matt. 26: 69–75 and parallels; the adulteress: Luke 7: 36–50 (the story in John 8: 1–11 seems to be a late interpolation and was unknown to the Greek Fathers and commentators before the 12th cent.).

[200] Arranz, 'Les Sacraments: Les Prières pénitentielles' (8), 97, 99; cf. Goar, Εὐχολόγιον, 536, 537.

[201] Cf. *PC* 20. 62 (David, Manasseh, Peter, Mary of Egypt), *PC* 93. 235–6 (David, Manasseh, Mary of Egypt, and David the Robber turned monk, cf. John Moschos, *Pratum Spirituale*, ch. 143); ep. 477. 73–6 (the good thief, cf. Luke 23: 40–3, Peter, David). One version of the story of Mary of Egypt, a converted prostitute, is told by Moschos, *Pratum Spirituale*, ch. 31 (*PG* 87. 3049). Her chronology cannot be established, although she may have been from the 5th cent. For sources and bibliography, see A. Kazhdan and N. Ševčenko, 'Mary of Egypt', *ODB* ii. 1310.

[202] As it has in Christian life.

[203] Cf. the words of the catechesis given by the priest at monastic profession, comparing the monk to the prodigal son, Goar, Εὐχολόγιον, 408: καὶ αὐτοὺς Χριστὸς ὁ Θεὸς ἡμῶν συγχαίρει μετὰ τῶν ἁγίων αὐτοῦ ἀγγέλων ἐπὶ τῇ σῇ μετανοίᾳ. For a commentary, see Symeon of Thessalonica, *PG* 155. 490 ff.

institutionalized God-given opportunity to repent of the sins committed since baptism.[204] The first part of the rite of profession,
with the monk waiting in the narthex of the church, ready to be led
to the royal doors, was taken from the ancient rite of public penitence.[205] It symbolized the penitential nature of the monastic
life.[206] An integral part of the perpetual 'healing' process of
monasticism was frequent ἐξαγόρευσις.[207]

'Numerous are the struggles of asceticism . . . but none like
ἐξαγόρευσις, together with obedience.'[208] Without it, great harm
is done to the life of the monk, for it is the principal, and even sole
means against the snares of the devil.[209] It has the power of extin-
guishing the flames of hell.[210] Conversely, it was the best way to
preserve the integrity of the soul and growth in the spiritual life.[211]
Theodore frequently alludes to the importance of ἐξαγόρευσις,
one of his remaining catecheses being devoted entirely to it.[212] The
difficulties of ἐξαγόρευσις lay in its very nature. It was, in itself, a
disagreeable exercise where one exposed to one's *hegoumenos* or
spiritual father shameful thoughts and temptations.[213] The benefit
of this exercise lay in the effect of the examination of such spiritual
burdens—they would be dissipated, allowing further progress on

---

[204] This opportunity was likened to a second baptism. Thus, in Goar, Εὐχολόγιον, 408:
Δεύτερον Βάπτισμα λαμβάνεις σήμερον, ἀδελφέ, τῇ περιουσίᾳ τῶν τοῦ
φιλανθρώπου Θεοῦ δωρεῶν, καὶ τῶν ἁμαρτιῶν σου καθαίρῃ. Cf. PK 9. 59 (= MC 87.
45), PK 113. 836 (= MC 11. 32). More on this below, pp. 235–8.

[205] Even after Theodore's time penitent monks excluded from communion were
expected to remain with the catechumens in the narthex of the church during Divine
Liturgy: *Epitimia* no. 11, 1733D.

[206] P. Raffin, *Les Rituels orientaux de la profession monastique*, Spiritualité Orientale, 4 (Maine-
et-Loire, 1992), 52.

[207] Also referred to, but less frequently, as ἐξαγγελία or ἐξάγγελσις, e.g. in MC 15. 42;
PK 25. 177; MC 18. 52, MC 68. 191, MC 49. 135; *Hypotyposis* no. 22, 1712B; *Epitimia*, I. 25–6,
1736C; ibid. II. 2, 1749A; PK 11. 74 (ἐξαγγελτικός), PK 68. 476. On the place of *exagoreusis*
in the life of the monk, see I. Hausherr, *Direction Spirituelle en Orient Autrefois*, OCA 144 (Rome,
1955), esp. 152–77.

[208] *Laudatio Platonis* 812CD.   [209] Cf. PK 77. 533, PK 82. 579, PK 87. 623–4.

[210] Περὶ ἐξαγορεύσεως, 1721B.

[211] Cf. TC I. 29, TC I. 36, TC I. 57, TC I. 80; PK 25. 174–6, PK 92. 600, PK 103. 753,
etc.

[212] *PC* 133, entitled Περὶ τῆς σωτηριώδους ἐξαγορεύσεως . . . Cf. J. Leroy, 'La Vie
quotidienne', 33 n. 4; Hausherr, *Saint Théodore Studite*, 34–6; idem, *Direction Spirituelle*, 171–2.

[213] On the importance of the spiritual father, see (among many possible studies)
K. Ware, 'The Spiritual Father in Orthodox Spirituality', *Cross Currents*, 24 (1974), 296–313.
On the spiritual father in Theodore: T. Špidlik, 'Superiore-padre: l'ideale di san Teodoro
Studita', *Studia Missionalia*, 36 (1987), 109–26 (an article I was not able to consult).

the road of virtue.[214] Even if one thought that one's confidant was
not spiritual enough, or even if one thought of him as ignorant,
God would still always reward the exercise. The counsel was to be
received as if coming from the mouth of God.[215] It did not necessarily imply the confession or admission of moral faults or sins,[216]
although it often did include it, in which case the *hegoumenos* or spiritual father would impose a penance.[217] By exposing all the movements of the soul (ἐξαγγελτικὸν κατὰ πᾶσαν κίνησιν τῆς
ψυχῆς),[218] one is rendered totally pure.[219] A monk was expected
to reveal his thoughts and any sins at the very least once a week to
the *hegoumenos*,[220] who made himself available every morning during Orthros.[221] In a large monastery such as the Stoudios the
hegoumenos would also have delegated assistants.[222] Neither would
the *hegoumenos* himself be deprived of the benefits of this spiritual
help.[223]

---

[214] Cf. Περὶ ἐξαγορεύσεως 1721A: ἐξαγόρευσίς ἐστι λόγων καὶ ἐνθυμήσεων
αἰσχρῶν ἀνήδονος ὑπόμνησις· διάλυσις δὲ ἡ τούτων διάκρισις, ἐπὶ ἀγαθὴν ὁδὸν
ὁδηγοῦσα τοὺς προσερχομένους.

[215] Ibid. 1721B; *MC* 39. 110.

[216] Theodore scarcely ever uses the term ἐξομολόγησις, as does the Euchologion
(Goar, Εὐχολόγιον, 537), for the confession of sin. The sole example that I have noticed,
though not without ambiguity in its possible sense, is ep. 453. 7 (a monk who had defected
returns to his monastery and makes an *exomologesis*, promising future stability). It is used as
an exact equivalent of ἐξαγόρευσις in its wider sense in Περὶ ἐξαγορεύσεως 1721A, but
otherwise it means confession of faith in the Lord (e.g. PK 42. 302 (from Ps. 99: 4); *In
Dormitionem Deiparae* 729A). The term ὁμολογία is also occasionally used for confession of
sin (e.g. in ep. 549. 62), but generally it is used to mean confession of faith or monastic
profession. Theodore does not have a specific term for personal admission of sin.

[217] Cf. PK 103. 753. In PK 117. 872, Theodore tells his monks to reveal 'everything' to
the spiritual father—thoughts and sins. For he is as 'above a natural father as the soul is to
the body'.

[218] *MC* 68. 191.

[219] *MC* 33. 93, *MC* 9. 225: ὁ ἐξαγορεύων καθαρὸς ὡς ὁ ἥλιος . . ..

[220] *Epitimia* II. 2, 1749A. A monk was not allowed to eat before confessing if he had not
been to the *hegoumenos* for a week. In the first part of this same collection of penances (I. 26,
1736C) a punishment of separation was inflicted if the period exceeded two weeks. The fact
that there are two different disciplines on this same matter argues for the different origins
of the respective parts of this collection.

[221] He would leave the choir during the fourth ode and sit in a quiet corner of the
church: *Hypotyposis* no. 22, 1712B.

[222] TC I. 57; cf. *Epitimia*, I. 25, 1736C.

[223] He would have his own spiritual father to whom to open his soul: ep. 10. 55;
Testamentum no. 24, 1821C. Theodore's spiritual father was Plato, until the latter's death. In
the *Testamentum* (1818A) he mentions that the semi-recluse Enklistos is his spiritual guide.

4.9 CONCLUSION

The sanctifying rites of the church examined in this section, namely the myron, priesthood, burial of the dead, marriage, anointing of the sick, and penance, were understood to provide, each in their own way, a sacred moment in which God's presence could be encountered and felt. Yet the rites differ hugely among themselves. In the case of the rite of burial of the dead, for example, the active participants of the rite rather than the one for whom it is performed are placed within this privileged moment of sanctifying grace. If we turn to the letter of Gregory, from where the discussion of this section began, we might have supposed that elsewhere Theodore would have revealed more of his understanding of how the sacred rites of the church worked and how they were related to each other. Theodore actually shows a disappointing lack of interest in such matters. What he says of matrimony, for example, is found within the context not of the theology of holiness but of God's commandment not to commit adultery through an illicit marriage (the moechian dispute). Besides, matrimony does not feature in the 'list' of sacraments. Likewise, the discussion of what Theodore says on penance was a discussion that reflects modern-day interests in the sacramentality of penance. There is actually no allusion to this in the list. One clear conclusion from this discussion is that the notion of a sacrament of confession in the modern sense whereby the priest imparts a sacramental absolution by virtue of his special power to forgive sins is quite absent.

The main conclusion of this section concerns the meaning of the list of six rites or *mysteria* of the church as expressed in the letter to the monk Gregory. It can be stated quite categorically that the list had no special significance for Theodore as a list of sacraments in the modern sense. The letter was actually, this author believes, solely an attempt to strengthen the credentials of monasticism by giving the monastic profession both an apostolic and a quasi-sacramental nature. This will be explained more fully in the body and conclusions of Part III when looking at the nature of monasticism. Before reaching this point there are some interesting matters to be raised concerning the sacraments of baptism and eucharist, the subjects of our next discussion.

5

Baptism, Eucharist, and Heresy

5.1 THE RITE OF BAPTISM

In the ninth century, according to the Euchologia, baptism was administered at the patriarchal church of Saint Sophia five times a year: twice on Holy Saturday (morning and evening), on the day of Epiphany, on Lazarus Saturday, and on Pentecost.[1] Adult pagan converts from barbarian lands were among those baptized on these occasions.[2] Although the texts were composed for adults, most baptizands were children. They tended to be baptized at the age of reason, although infant baptism, especially in case of emergencies, was also practised.[3] In this particular period the function of the baptismal sponsor seems to have been more formal than of any practical importance. Wealthy parents, who could see to the proper Christian education of their offspring, would sometimes elect to have a heavenly sponsor represented by an icon present at the ceremony. Theodore the Stoudite agrees with and praises the piety of the Spatharios John, who provided his child with an icon of St Demetrios to act in place of an ἀνάδοχος:

We have heard that your Lordship had done a divine deed and we have marvelled at your truly great faith, O man of God. For my informer tells me that in performing the baptism (τὸ φώτισμα) of your God-guarded child, you had recourse to a holy image of the great martyr Demetrios

[1] M. Arranz, 'Les Sacraments de l'ancien Euchologe constantionopolitain' (6), 104–6.
[2] The ἀνάδοχος was expected to reply to the baptismal interrogations if the baptizands did not know Greek. Cf. the Euchologion text in Conybeare, *Rituale Armenorum*, 395; Goar, *Εὐχολόγιον*, 277. Theodore the Stoudite writes to one prominent Bulgarian convert in ep. 479.
[3] A newly born infant would be brought to church by the wet-nurse on the eighth day to receive its name, and then by its mother on the fortieth day. From this time, until the age of reason (around the age of 7?), the child would be considered an 'unbaptized Christian', and would be subject to what Arranz calls an extended 'first catechumenate'. See, Arranz, 'Les Sacraments de l'ancien Euchologe constantionopolitain' (2), 47–9, 63–4, 71, 284, 294 n., 290–3, 302; *OCP* 50 (1984), 44. For evidence from Theodore on the practice of baptizing children, and infants in danger of death, cf. ep. 462. 19, 49–50; ep. 17. See also, C. Pujol, 'Baptismus infantium in ecclesiis orientalibus', *Periodica*, 72 (1983), 203–37, 563–91.

instead of a godfather (ἀντὶ ἀναδόχου τινός). How great is your confidence! 'I have not found so great faith, no, not in Israel' [Matt. 8: 10]—this I believe Christ to have said not only at that time to the centurion, but even now to you who are of equal faith. The centurion found what he sought; you, too, have won what you trusted in. In the Gospel the divine command took the place of bodily presence, while here the bodily image took the place of its model (ἀντὶ τοῦ πρωτοτύπου); there the great Logos was present in His word and invisibly wrought the incredible miracle through His divinity, while here the great martyr was spiritually present in his own image and so received the infant (τὸ βρέφος δεχόμενος). These things, being incredible, are unacceptable to profane ears and unbelieving souls, and especially to the iconoclasts; but to your piety clear signs and tokens have been revealed.[4]

This kind of practice, however, was considered by others to be gravely abusive.[5]

Baptism took place at the baptismal κολυμβήθρα[6] or φωτιστήριον.[7] The texts of the Euchologion use the term φώτισμα, or 'illumination', to refer to the full reality and rites of baptism, which includes more than the concrete actions of washing (λουτρόν) or immersion (βάπτισμα, βάπτησις).[8] Theodore

---

[4] Ep. 17. 2–17. Translation taken from C. Mango, *The Art of the Byzantine Empire 312–1453* (Toronto, 1972), 174–5. The analogy with the faith of the centurion may indicate that this infant was ill. For a discussion of Theodore's theology of 'animated' matter, see K. Parry, 'Theodore Studites and the Patriarch Nicephoros on Image-Making', 164–83.

[5] Cf. *Letter of the Emperors Michael II and Theophilos to Louis the Pious (824)*, Mansi, *Sacrorum Conciliorum*, xiv. 420BC. 'Many clerics and laymen . . . have become originators of evil practices . . . Many people wrapped clothes round them [the images] and made them the baptismal godfathers of their children (*et filiorum suorum de baptismatis fontibus susceptrices faciebant*).' The ἀνάδοχος of the monastic postulant (who received the cut hair of tonsure) was also often replaced, according to this letter, by an icon.

[6] *In Vigiliam Luminum* 708B: τὴν τῆς υἱοθεσίας μητρόμοιον κολυμβήθραν; ep. 479. 64–5: ἀποτεχθέντες ἀμφότεροι ἐκ μητρὸς τῆς υἱοθετικῆς κολυμβήθρας τοῦ βαπτίσματος). Dionysios, in *EH* 2. 72. 12–13, calls the font τὴν μητέρα τῆς υἱοθεσίας; cf. Cyril of Jerusalem, *Mystagogia Catechesis* 2. 4: καὶ τὸ σωτήριον ἐκεῖνο ὕδωρ καὶ τάφος ὑμῖν ἐγίνετο καὶ μήτηρ. On the patristic notion of the baptismal font as mother, see J. Daniélou, *Bible et Liturgie* (Paris, 1951), 67–9. In one place Theodore calls baptism itself the 'mother of adoption': ep. 317. 22.

[7] Cf. Auzépy, *Vie d'Étienne le Jeune*, 96.3. The two baptisteries of Hagia Sophia were called by this term, although the larger of the two was also called κολυμβήθρα: Arranz, 'L'Office de l'Asmatikos Hesperinos ("vépres chantées") de l'ancien Euchologe byzantin', *OCP* 44 (1978), 127 n. 55; idem, 'Les Sacraments de l'ancien Euchologe constantionopolitain' (4), 67–8 n. 16; idem, *Évolution des rites d'incorporation et de réadmission dans l'Église selon l'Euchologe byzantin* (Rome, 1978), 38 n. 22.

[8] On this terminology, see Arranz, 'Les Sacraments de l'ancien Euchologe constantionopolitain' (4), 60–3.

Baptism, Eucharist, and Heresy 185

also refers to it as a *mystagogia*.[9] The spiritual illumination conferred with baptism was a major theme with the Fathers, especially the Cappadocians.[10] Indeed, the feast of the baptism of Christ in the River Jordan (τὰ Ἐπιφάνια, or Θεοφάνια) was already in the fourth century called τὰ φῶτα, being associated with a rite of the blessing of the waters.[11] 'The holy day of lights', states Gregory of Nazianzus in his homily given on the vigil of the feast, 'takes its origin from the baptism of my Christ, the true light that gives light to everyone [John 1: 9].'[12] In the fourth century baptism was also conferred on this day, as well as on Pascha and Pentecost.[13] Theodore preaches on baptism on this occasion of the feast of lights.[14] The essence of the rite of baptism was the triple immersion in water with the triple invocation of the Trinity.[15] Theodore also indicates the formula to be used, which corresponds exactly to the formula found in some of the earliest Euchologia manuscripts: 'N. is baptized in the name of the Father, and of the Son and of the Holy Ghost' (βαπτίζεται ὁ δεῖνα εἰς τὸ ὄνομα τοῦ πατρὸς καὶ τοῦ υἱοῦ καὶ τοῦ Ἁγίου Πνεύματος).[16] Could this rite ever be celebrated in a church held by (iconoclast) heretics? Theodore is

---

[9] *In Sanctum Pascha* 716D.

[10] Cf. C. Moreschini, 'Luce e purificazione nella doctrina di Gregorio Nazianzo', *Augustinianum*, 13 (1973), 535–49.

[11] Cf. John Chrysostom, *PG* 49. 365 ff.; Gregory Nazianzene, *Oratio* 39.

[12] *Oratio* 39, *PG* 36. 336A.

[13] Cf. *Oratio* 40, *PG* 36. 392B.

[14] *In Vigiliam Luminum* (Ἐὶς τὴν παραμονὴν τῶν Φώτων) 700C–708D.

[15] Ibid. 708B. Theodore uses the expression 'the triple hypostasis of the divine blessedness'. The language in this passage is remarkably similar to that used by Dionysios and suggests Theodore's dependence on the latter. Theodore states that the triple pouring of water on the burnt offering, as commanded by the prophet Elijah on Mount Carmel (1 Kgs. 18: 34–9), could be interpreted in two ways: Οἶμαι δηλοῦν ἢ τὴν τρισσὴν τῆς θείας μακαριότητος ἐν τῷ βαπτιζομένῳ ἐπιβοωμένην ὑπόστασιν, ἢ τὴν τρισσὴν αὐτοῦ τοῦ τελουμένου κατάδυσιν. Dionysios, *EH* 72. 21–73. 2, in describing the actions of the hierarch, writes: . . . τρὶς μὲν αὐτὸν ὁ ἱεράρχης βαπτίζει, ταῖς τρισὶ τοῦ τελουμένου καταδύσεσι καὶ ἀναδύσεσι τὴν τρισσὴν τῆς θείας μακαριότητος ἐπιβοήσας ὑπόστασιν.

[16] Ep. 308. 30–1. This formula seems have been widely used from at least the early 6th cent. It is recorded in Theodore Lector. *Historia Ecclesiastica* 2. 25; *PG* 86. 196B–197A; cf. the slightly later John Moschos, *Pratum Spirituale*, ch. 176: *PG* 87. 3. 3045A, where an 'Amen' is added after each name is invoked. For the Euchologion, see Goar, Εὐχολόγιον, 294. Other ancient MSS add νῦν καὶ ἀεὶ . . . to this formula, without completing the phrase (Goar, ibid. 290 completes it, adding εἰς τοὺς αἰῶνας τῶν αἰώνων, Ἀμήν). Cf. Arranz, 'Les Sacraments de l'ancien Euchologe constantinopolitain' (6), 71–2. Arranz expresses some indecision over whether or not the formula of Goar, Εὐχολόγιον, 294, presupposed the further ending. The evidence from Theodore suggests that it did not.

emphatic that no one should even enter such a church, let alone have services in it. Rather, a baptism can be celebrated in the 'purest place' of a private home, on the altar or table where the eucharist is celebrated.[17] This provision was a provision of *oikonomia*.[18] Another was that of the minister of the sacrament. Baptism belonged to the things of the priesthood (τὰ τῆς ἱερωσύνης),[19] and according to the canons its administration was restricted to a bishop or presbyter.[20] Yet Theodore believed that in the absence of an Orthodox priest or bishop an unordained monk or even a layman could baptize in case of necessity. It would still be a true baptism.[21] Thus he refused pointedly to criticize one particular monk, the Stoudite Erastos, who had gone ahead and baptized the children of those iconophiles who had approached him. In defending the actions of this unordained monk, Theodore claims not to be speaking as one who had not done his study, nor to be in contempt of the divine constitutions.[22] Prescriptive law, he argues, is not necessarily absolute, and in times of necessity exceptions had to be made: ἐξ ἀνάγκης καὶ νόμου μετάθεσις.[23] He was probably reminded by his correspondent that the canons did not permit baptism by an unordained minister,[24] and the best Theodore

---

[17] Ep. 552. 114–18. The sponsors and parents of the children to be baptized had, of course, to be of irreproachable faith (ll. 119–20).

[18] In normal circumstances it was forbidden to celebrate the eucharist or to baptize in the oratory of a private home. Trullo, canon 59, establishes: 'Baptism is by no means to be administered in an oratory which is within a house (ἐν εὐκτηρίῳ οἴκῳ ἔνδον οἰκίας), but they who have been judged worthy of the immaculate illumination are to present themselves at the public churches where they are to receive this gift': Joannou, *Discipline générale antique*, i. pt. 1. 195). Trullo, canon 31, prohibits eucharistic celebration without special permission from the bishop (Greek commentaries add baptism to this prohibition, although it is omitted in many of the main manuscripts: Joannou, ibid. i. pt. 1. 162, ad. 6). Cf. the first-second synod, Πρωτοδευτέρα (AB) σύνοδος, (861), canon 12, which refers to this same canon of Trullo: Joannou, ibid. 469, ad. 7.

[19] Ep. 462. 19.

[20] Cf. Apostolic canon 47; Laodicea, canon 46; Basil, canon 1 (Joannou, *Discipline générale antique*, ii. 97 = Y. Courtonne, *Saint Basile: Lettres* (Paris, 1961), ii. 123, ep. 188, canonical letter to Amphilochios). In *MC* 32. 89 (= PK 27. 190), because John the Baptist baptized Christ, Theodore considers him to be a priest above other priests because ordained by God Himself: ὦ ἱερέως θεοχειροτονήτου καὶ πάντων ἱερέων ὑψηλοτέρου . . . .

[21] Ep. 308. 28–9, 31–2: Συμφέρει τὸν ἀβάπτιστον, εἰ μὴ εὑρίσκοιτο ὀρθόδοξος ὁ βαπτίσων, ὑπὸ μοναχοῦ, ἢ καὶ τούτου μὴ ὄντος, ὑπὸ λαϊκοῦ βαπτισθῆναι . . . ἢ ἀφώτιστον ἐκδημῆσαι. καὶ ἀληθῶς ἐβαπτίσθη.

[22] Ep. 462. 17, (*ann.* 823): . . . οὐ μὴν οὕτως ἀμαθεῖς, ἢ τῶν θείων διαταγῶν καταφρονηταί.

[23] Ibid. 24–5 (the same expression is used in ep. 308. 32).

[24] St Basil, canon 1, was quite emphatic that a lay person had neither the spiritual gift nor the authority to baptize.

could do for a canonical counter-argument was to draw on the authority of the Trullan Synod ('the sixth synod, in the divine canons') in an analogous but different case, declaring that it did permit lay people to give themselves holy communion in the absence of a priest.[25] And no one, he adds, could argue or reprehend what was divinely expressed by the Fathers.[26] But this was not so much an argument of authority as it was an argument by analogy. If a lay person could have physical contact with holy things, and even administer them, in one instance, then it could be permitted in another. Theodore must have been aware of the difference between administration of an already confected sacrament (giving of communion) and being the very instrument of a sacrament (baptizing). It was no light matter to deviate so radically from the rules governing the minister of the sacrament. Indeed, Theodore could argue for a relaxation of the rules in the opposite direction. In times of great need even a suspended priest, who had been in communion with the heretics proper, could administer baptism.[27] But to allow an unordained minister to confer baptism required well-established precedent, and preferably a concrete sign from God. This Theodore was able to find in 'facts' from the past (ἐν τοῖς πάλαι χρόνοις γιγνόμενα).[28] The facts were actually part of the hagiographical tradition and were found in two rather odd, but entertaining, stories.[29] The first comes from *The Spiritual Meadow* of John Moschos.[30] In this story there was a baptism using sand in place of water when a person was in danger of dying in the desert. Theodore states that there was both a rite of baptism and, as a result, a baptized person.[31]

De la Beaune, the author of the *Praefatio Posthumae Sirmondianae Editioni Praemissa*, normally has only praise to lavish on

---

[25] Ibid. 31–4. Cf. ep. 552. 35–9. The canon referred to is canon 58.

[26] Ep. 462. 35–6: οὐ τολμῶμεν παρὰ θειωδῶς τοῖς πατράσιν ἐκπεφασμένα εἰπεῖν τι ἢ ἐπιτιμῆσαι.

[27] Ep. 536. 15; ep. 549. 111–19. This, states Theodore, was the policy of the confessor bishops and *hegoumenoi*.

[28] Ep. 462. 25–6. Cf. ep. 308, 32–3: ἐξ ἀνάγκης γὰρ καὶ νόμου μετάθεσις, ὡς γέγονε πάλαι καὶ ἀποδέδεκται.

[29] Both these stories are also found in the 14th-cent. Nikephoros Kallistos, *Historia Ecclesiastica* III. ch. 37: PG 145. 973–6. The heading is: περὶ τῶν δύο Ἑβραίων τῶν ὑπὸ ἄμμου καὶ ὑπὸ παίδων ὑπερφυῶς βαπτισθέντων.

[30] *PG* 87. 3, ch. 176, 3044D–3045C.

[31] Ep. 462. 26–7: καὶ ὃν μὲν ἀμμώδει ἐπιχύσει κατ' ἐρημίαν, ἐπειδὴ θάνατος παρῆν, βαπτίσαντα καὶ βαπτισθέντα, καὶ ἄλλον ἄλλως.

Theodore.[32] In this particular instance, however, he fails to share Theodore's respect for the 'facts' of history. He writes: 'sed si ita sensit, fatendum est omnino erravisse'.[33] As he correctly points out, the story in the *Spiritual Meadow* ends with the decision of the local bishop to have the adolescent baptized again with water.[34] Theodore omits this detail, which would have undermined his whole argument. For him the more important part of the story would have been the fact that the 'baptism with sand' had been accompanied by a miraculous healing.[35] As was usually the case in hagiography, the miraculous confirmed the integrity of a person or his action. Thus the credentials of this unusual baptism were likewise authenticated. After all, was not the crucified good thief truly baptized by the Lord hanging on the cross? God was able to effect salvation even outside the ordinary boundaries of his Providence.[36]

The second of Theodore's 'historical facts' was derived from the anonymous *Life of Athanasios*,[37] although it was also recorded in the

---

[32] *PG* 99. 57A–92B.

[33] *Praefatio* 73A.

[34] Ibid. 72D. Cf. Carthage, canon 72 (on rebaptism of the doubtfully baptized); also Trullo canon 84.

[35] The whole account is as follows. A story from a certain Abbas Andreas was related to John Moschos and his companion Sophronios. He and nine others had fled to Palestine at a time of 'war and confusion'. There was a Hebrew adolescent in the group who fell dangerously ill through hunger and exhaustion. He was left to die in the desert, but he begged to be baptized. However, there was no water and none of them were members of the clergy. Guided by a divine inspiration, one of the group suggested the boy be baptized with sand, using the appropriate formula. He was stripped and sand was poured over his head three times, as the invocation to the Trinity was made. Whereupon the boy was miraculously restored to health and strength. After this, the ecstatic group, after arriving at the town of Ascalon, went to the local bishop, named Dionysios, and explained the whole affair to him. The bishop was not unimpressed. He in turn convoked his clergy to discuss the issue of whether the 'baptism' was to be considered a real one or not. The clergy were divided over the matter because of the miracle that had accompanied the act. Finally 'it seemed good to the blessed Dionysios to send the brother to the holy Jordan and for him to be baptized there'. Cf. Wortley, *The Spiritual Meadow*, 144–6.

[36] Cf. Luke 23: 43; *In Sanctum Pascha* 716CD: 'O what a great Mystery! The thief came to his senses. It was necessary that there be water for him to be baptized; he hung from the cross, but there was no other place of baptism, no spring, no lake, no rain. There was no one to perform the liturgical rite (τὴν μυσταγωγίαν). All the disciples had fled for fear of the Jews. But Jesus did not lack the flowing waters, for although he hung from the cross he was still the creator of the waters. And since it was impossible for the thief to enter the kingdom without baptism, the Saviour let blood and water flow from his wounded side in order to free the thief from the impending evils, and demonstrate to those who place their hope in him that his precious blood is the price of redemption.'

[37] *PG* 25. 212A ff. The *Vita* is summarized in Photios' *Bibliotheca*, and was thus presumably also available to Theodore had he wished to consult it.

Spiritual Meadow.[38] Theodore reminds his correspondent of this
story, which must have been well known in religious circles. Briefly,
the story (which Theodore gives only in summary form) concerns
Athanasios, the future champion of Orthodoxy. Once, as a child,
Athanasios had been playing at the seaside pretending to be a
bishop. Other children played the roles of priests, deacons, and
catechumens. During their acting out of a baptismal ceremony,
Bishop Alexander from the city of Alexandria happened to be
passing by. He was greatly perturbed by what he saw. The clergy
that were with him were sent to call up the children. As, on interrogation, it transpired that the whole baptismal rite had been performed exactly according to the stipulations of the church, the
bishop declared authoritatively that the baptism was to be considered a true one and therefore could never be repeated.[39] The
childish action, writes Theodore, was taken by Alexander to represent a truly divine act; Athanasios acted like a priest, and the
child he had baptized was considered truly regenerated. Thus, he
concludes, even a child can truly baptize.[40]

Not everyone would agree with Theodore's conclusions.[41]

5.2 HERETICAL BAPTISM

A question asked during the moechian conflict (following the
Synod of 809), was what is to be made of baptisms conferred by

[38] Moschos states that he derived his story from Rufinus, *The Ecclesiastical History*.

[39] *Pratum Spirituale*, ch. 197: 3084B–3085C; Rufinus, *Historia Ecclesiastica*, I. 14: *PL* 21.
486C–488A. The bishop, writes the latter, 'videt ab his geri quaedam etiam secretiora et
mystica'. He sought the advice of his clergy before pronouncing his judgement: 'conlocutus
cum concilio clericorum'.

[40] Ep. 462. 28–31: ὅπως ἡ παιδικὴ πρᾶξις ὁραθεῖσα πρὸς τοῦ μακαριωτάτου
Ἀλεξάνδρου ἐνεκρίθη ὡς θεοτελὴς καὶ ἐλογίσθη ὁ τελέσας ὡς ἱερεὺς καὶ ὁ
τελεσθεὶς ὡς ἀναγεννηθείς.

[41] Matthew Blastares, for example, in his commentary on apostolic canon 47 denies that
lay baptism can be valid: *PG* 144. 1108–9. Likewise, Nikodemos and Agapios of the Holy
Mountain, the editors of the *Pedalion* (the Greek collection and concordance of canons, first
published in 1800) deny outright that a lay person can baptize in any circumstance. One of
their authorities is precisely Bishop Dionysios, in the 'baptism with sand' story, who insisted
on the rebaptism of the boy (commentary on apostolic canon 49, *The Rudder (Pedalion) of the
Metaphorical Ship of the One Holy Catholic and Apostolic Church* . . . , translated by D. Cummings
(Chicago, 1957), 76 (cf. pp. 69, 72). On the other hand, Patriarch Photios did admit its validity, but only in real cases of necessity: *PG* 102. 773–6. The so-called canons of Nikephoros,
canons 13 and 16, respectively allow a monk or deacon to baptize in an emergency, or even
a layman, with the condition that he be a Christian: *PG* 100. 853; *Pedalion*, 970 (= canons 6–7).

heretics?[42] The issue seems to have arisen once Theodore had established in his own mind, and then in the minds of others, that those who held to the decisions of the synod were true heretics.[43] If this was to be taken at face value then, according to some early canons of the church, baptism administered by the adherents of the moechian heresy (ἡ μοιχειανικὴ αἵρεσις) were surely to be considered as non-existing.[44]

The question might appear somewhat unusual, as it was not the practice of the Greek church of that time to rebaptize heretics, unless there was manifest deficiency in the Orthodox faith concerning the Trinity, or defective form in the actual baptizing.[45] Naukratios, who had posed the question, should have been aware of the practice and legislation of his church. Understandably, he was unclear about how to relate the moechian heresy to the rest of the historical heresies. Theodore's keenness to identify his opponents as heretics was not particularly contagious. Not only were many unconvinced by his reasoning, his extreme position actually led to countercharges of heresy.[46] Among his own sympathizers he did his best to explain his understanding of heresy, and why it was that the adherents of the 809 synod qualified as heretics.

Heresy was doctrinal aberration or *innovation* (καινοτομία) that departed from the inheritance of the Fathers.[47] According to Theodore, if serious enough and left unchecked it would herald in the Antichrist.[48] In his letter to the monk Athanasios, which is an

---

[42] Ep. 40. 20–1.

[43] The first consistent applications of this term to the proceedings of the synod appear in ep. 33. 24 (to Pope Leo III, 809), 55, 57; ep. 34, 117 (idem), 135.

[44] Ep. 40. 37–9. Cf. ep. 39. 47.

[45] L. Saltet, *Les Réordinations: Étude sur le sacrament de l'ordre* (Paris, 1907), 94–6. In the Euchologion 'canons of the holy apostles . . .' (Goar, Εὐχολόγιον, 273), the discipline emphasized is that of not rebaptizing heretics, with the exception of those groups named in canon 7 (9) of Constantinople I (Eunomians, Montanists or Phrygians, Sabellians, 'and those similar') and those not baptized according to τοὺς θεσμοὺς τῆς ὀρθοδόξων ἐκκλησίας.

[46] Cf. ep. 40. 232 ff. In ep. 34. 126 ff., Theodore's opponents denounced him before Pope Leo in Rome for commemorating the monophysites Barsanouphios, Isaias, and Dorotheos. Theodore was particularly sensitive to this charge, and spared no expression in convincing the pope of his Orthodoxy. See also PK 80. 562 ('People say I'm stupid . . . but I'm no heretic').

[47] Ep. 48. 287–8. Cf. ep. 36. 80–1. 'Innovation' became a technical term for heresy in the 4th cent. Cf. Lampe, *Patristic Greek Lexicon*, 693 s.v. καινοτομ-έω; καινοτόμημα; καινοτομία.

[48] Ep. 34. 104–6. For references in Theodore's letters to the Antichrist, see Fatouros, *Theodori Studitae Epistulae*, ii. 864 s.v. ἀντίχριστος. Cf. Henry, 'Theodore of Studios', 164–6.

apologia for the charge of heresy against the 'moechians', Theodore
claims in a rather rhetorical fashion that ultimately the latter are
redefining the nature of God: 'What else are they saying, but that
the commandments of God are changeable . . . and what does this
amount to other than a declaration that God himself is changeable
($\tau\rho\epsilon\pi\tau\acute{o}s$) . . . and that the Gospel is indifferent for salvation and
damnation?'[49] Theodore explains how heresies come about. No
heresy contains the whole of impiety. Some are completely foreign
to the Gospel, whilst others 'clothe themselves in certain words of
the Gospel', and having missed the right sense of those words that
they considered ambiguous turn into heretics.[50] Being innovators,
heretics are alienated from God and his Gospel, the root of all
heresy being the devil.[51]

Heresies sprang up outside the Gospel from the time of Christ's incarnation. Then after the devil had been repulsed by the gradual advance of
grace, he imperceptibly appropriated material from the Gospel itself. He
has given birth to heresies all the way up to that of the Iconoclasts by covering the bait with the very words and text of Scripture.[52]

In the letter to Naukratios, Theodore answers the question of the
relationsip of baptism to heresy by resorting to 'the commentaries
of a certain scholarly man', probably the early seventh-century
Timothy of Constantinople, who lists classical heresies according to
the mode by which the adherents, once repentant, were received
back into the Orthodox church in earlier centuries.[53] There were

[49] Ep. 48. 174–5, 182–3.
[50] Ep. 36. 102–9. On Theodore's understanding of heresy in the moechian period, see
Henry, 'Theodore of Studios', 149–53, 161–70. With regard to the iconoclasts, Theodore
has this to say (*PC* 29. 85): 'How many men, on the outside of the Gospel ($\H{\epsilon}\xi\omega\ \tau o\hat{v}$
$\epsilon\dot{v}a\gamma\gamma\epsilon\lambda\acute{\iota}ov$), live in the error of unbelief ($\dot{a}\pi\iota\sigma\tau\acute{\iota}as$)? Others, on the inside of the Gospel
($\H{\epsilon}\nu\delta o\nu\ \tau o\hat{v}\ \epsilon\dot{v}a\gamma\gamma\epsilon\lambda\acute{\iota}ov$), have erred with regard to the faith and are shipwrecked, such as
the $\epsilon\dot{\iota}\kappa o\nu o\mu\acute{a}\chi o\iota$.'
[51] Ep. 36. 7, 80–1. The belief in the devil's involvement in the genesis of heresy was very
Byzantine, with roots in the early patristic era.
[52] Ep. 36. 112–17. Cf. *MC* 5. 15 (= PK 49. 356), on the devil as cause of irreligiosity, athe-
ism, and heresy.
[53] Ep. 40. 172–4. *De receptione haereticorum, PG* 86. 11 ff. Cf. Saltet, *Les Réordinations*, 56–7;
M. Jugie, *Theologia Dogmatica Christianorum Orientalium*, iii. 436 n. 2: 'Theodorum de
Timotheo loqui pro certo habemus.' This categorization is also found in canon 7 (9) of
Constantinople I (381) and Trullo, canon 95, as well as in the Euchologion (Goar,
$E\dot{v}\chi o\lambda\acute{o}\gamma\iota o\nu$, 273). Why did not Theodore invoke the authority of the sixth council? A possible explanation is that the canon itself as we now have it was a later interpolation (part of
the text we have is also corrupt: Percival, *The Seven Ecumenical Councils*, 405 nn. F. J.
Thompson, 'Economy', *JTS* NS 16 (1965), 415).

three modes: rebaptism, anointment with chrism, and formal renunciation of error. In the first category were the (pre-Trinitarian) heretics of the second and third centuries, including the Marcionists, Montanists, and Manicheans.[54]

Naukratios had quoted an ancient discipline: 'Those who have been baptized or ordained by such persons [heretics] cannot belong either to the clergy or to the faithful.'[55] Theodore interprets this by reference to another canon of the same collection of apostolic canons which required a proper Trinitarian formula for baptism.[56] He also quotes St Basil who had distinguished between heretics, schismatics, and the παρασυναγωγή.[57] Heretics, according to this division, were those who had broken totally with the church and professed a faith foreign to it, especially with regard to the Trinity; schismatics were those who had left the church because of ecclesiastical disagreements, but this could be remedied; illegal congregations or parasynagogues were composed of rebellious clergy who refused to subject themselves to penance. Schismatics and those belonging to illegal congregations, Theodore adds, can also be called heretics in an improper or 'participated' sense.[58] This is because there is a diabolical unity among them all:

Heresy in general thus appears to be a sort of chain woven by the devil, with each individual heresy connected to another, and as it were all attached to one head of impiety and opposition to God, even if they are distinguishable by differences of name, time, place, numbers, characteristics, power and activity. Similarly, one and the same body is not one single member, but many, and these members differ among themselves as to activities, powers, characteristics, places and honours.[59]

[54] Ep. 40. 27–9.

[55] Ep. 40. 37–9, corresponding to the second part of apostolic canon 68: Joannou, *Discipline générale antique*, i. pt. 2. 43.

[56] Ep. 40. 40–1. Apostolic canon 49: 'If any bishop or presbyter, contrary to the ordinance of the Lord, does not baptize into the Father, the Son and the Holy Spirit, but into three Fathers, or three Sons, or three Paracletes, let him be deposed': ibid, i. pt. 2. 32. Roman tradition insisted only on the correct trinitarian *form* for baptism. It is probable that the apostolic canons also presupposed correct faith, as was the case in all of Greek tradition. On this, see Saltet, *Les Réordinations*, 38, 40, and *passim*; Thompson, 'Economy', 411.

[57] Ep. 40. 42–7. Cf. Basil, canon 1: Joannou, *Discipline générale antique*, ii. 94 (= Courtonne, *Saint Basile: Lettres*, ii, ep. 188. 121, to Amphilochios). On these distinctions, see M. Girardi, 'Notizie di eresia, scisma e parasinagoga in Basilio di Cesarea', *Vetera Christianorum*, 17 (1980), 49–77.

[58] Ep. 40. 56–66.

[59] Ep. 40. 71–7. In ep. 532. 32–50, conversely, Theodore notes that all repudiation of heresy by the ecumenical councils is organically linked, as branches to a root or as a stream

Indeed, historically the notion and language of heresy and schism had always been fluid and ill-defined, the distinction being absent in key liturgical and canonical texts.[60] Theodore gives himself licence to use the term 'heresy' freely, sometimes in one sense, sometimes in another.[61]

Let us now turn our attention again to the moechians. According to Theodore, the resolutions of the 809 synod turned them from being an illegal congregation ($\pi\alpha\rho\alpha\sigma\upsilon\nu\alpha\gamma\omega\gamma\acute{\eta}$) into heretics.[62] Were their sacraments valid? Despite Theodore's invective, and his debating point that ultimately they had violated the whole Gospel and given God a mutable nature, the moechians were hardly heretics in the carefully defined sense of letter 40. After all, their fault primarily concerned matters of discipline. Indeed, it seems the whole point of the letter to Naukratios was to explain Theodore's use of language. Even though it is not made explicit, the moechians were in an improper sense ($\kappa\alpha\tau\grave{\alpha}$ $\kappa\alpha\tau\acute{\alpha}\chi\rho\eta\sigma\iota\nu$) heretics or, in the phrase of John Erickson, 'heretics by extension'.[63] This would mean baptism was perfectly valid when administered by a moechian priest. It is true that in the same letter to Naukratios Theodore states that priests ordained by a heretical (i.e. moechian) bishop are not to be considered 'true ministers of God'.[64] If this were to mean that the ordination itself was invalid (in the modern canonical sense), then, according to the authority of St Basil which Theodore respects, the baptisms administered by these priests would likewise be invalid.[65] But did Theodore really intend to say that newly ordained moechian

---

to a spring, to the 'divinely inspired symbol' of the first council, which has 'exploded every heresy'.

[60] Cf. S. L. Greenslade, *Schism in the Early Church* (London, 1953), 90–104, and *passim*.

[61] Take his statement, in ep. 556 (to the monk Gregory, ann. 810–11), 62–3, 'Schism, according to Chrysostom, is nothing less ($o\mathring{\upsilon}\delta\grave{\epsilon}\nu$ $\mathring{\epsilon}\lambda\alpha\tau\tau o\nu$) than heresy.' Cf. Chrysostom, *In Ep. ad Ephes.*, Hom. 11 5.

[62] Ep. 33. 22–6: 'These present transgressors became, in the divine Basil's terminology, an illegal congregation when, in their first meeting [806], they received the performer of adulterous marriage and joined him in priestly functions. But they did not stop there. As though to acquire for themselves a reputation for complete heresy, they held another public synod . . .'.

[63] J. Erickson, 'The Problem of Sacramental "Economy"', *The Challenge of Our Past* (Crestwood, 1991), ch. 8, p. 119 (ch. originally published in *SVThQ* 29 (1985), 115–32). See also 'Reception of Non-Orthodox into the Orthodox Church', *Diakonia*, 19 (1984–5), 68–86.

[64] Ep. 40. 138–40: $o\mathring{\upsilon}\chi$ $o\mathring{\iota}\acute{o}\nu$ $\tau\epsilon$ $o\mathring{\upsilon}s$ $\chi\epsilon\iota\rho o\tau o\nu\epsilon\hat{\iota}$ $\tau\hat{\eta}$ $\mathring{\alpha}\lambda\eta\theta\epsilon\acute{\iota}\alpha$ $\epsilon\mathring{\iota}\nu\alpha\iota$ $\lambda\epsilon\iota\tau o\upsilon\rho\gamma o\grave{\upsilon}s$ $\Theta\epsilon o\hat{\upsilon}$. Their ordination is 'heretical'. Ibid. 135: $\chi\epsilon\iota\rho o\tau o\nu\acute{\iota}\alpha\nu$ $\alpha\mathring{\iota}\rho\epsilon\tau\iota\kappa\acute{\eta}\nu$.

[65] Basil, canon 1: Joannou, *Discipline générale antique*, ii. 97.

priests would have to be reordained? The answer must surely be in the negative for the same reasons given above, namely his 'improper' use of the term heretic. Besides, Theodore must have been aware that reordination, as well as rebaptism, had long been abandoned by the church of Constantinople for non-trinitarian heretics. Even the rigorists at the Second Council of Nicaea accepted the sacraments of the iconoclasts.[66] This is not to say that the sacraments of non-trinitarian heretics might not be considered by the official church as being defective in some way. Heretical orders, for example, could be 'rectified' by an episcopal blessing (not consecration) with the laying on of hands (although this does not seem to have been required for iconoclast clergy).[67] Theodore obviously considered moechian orders to be defective in some undefined way, thus also making their baptisms irregular. It is very doubtful that he would have considered moechian sacraments completely null. With the iconoclasts, however, Theodore adopts a much more hardline position.

Unlike the moechian heresy, iconoclasm had been condemned by a solemn council of the church.[68] The Seventh Council had treated the veneration of images as a dogmatic matter, and condemned those who rejected this ecclesiastical tradition as heretics,

---

[66] Saltet, *Les Réordinations*, 106–8. The letter of Basil to Amphilochios (ep. 188) was also quoted during the discussions of the council: Mansi, *Sacrorum Conciliorum*, xii. 1023 ff. Was the rigorist concession to the iconoclasts one based on theological principle or on 'sacramental' economy? It is clear from one of Theodore's letters that he regarded heretical ordination as such as being totally null in principle (ep. 53. 50 ff.). In this same letter he states that if the credentials not only of a suspected heretical priest were to be investigated, but also those of his ordaining bishop, 'the gift of the priesthood, by virtue of which we have the right to be called Christians, would cease to such an extent that we should lapse back into pagan worship': ibid. 90–1. Ultimately this issue had to rest with God (ibid. 57–8). During the second period of iconoclasm there were many iconophiles who travelled West—to Rome, Naples, 'Longibardia', and Sicily—in order to be ordained by bishops free from the pollution of iconoclast heresy (presumably under the assumption that their orders would be invalid): ep. 549. 12–23. All this argues for a predominant view among 9th-cent. iconophiles that iconoclast sacraments are in principle invalid.

[67] This is the interpretation given to canon 8 of the First Council of Nicaea, by Patriarch Tarasios. The canon allows for the rehabilitation of Novatian or Cathar clergy by χειροθεσία, as opposed to χειροτονία. For a discussion of this canon, see Thompson, 'Economy', 403–6. For Tarasios at the Second Council of Nicaea: Mansi, *Sacrorum Conciliorum*, xii. 1022C.

[68] Theodore actually looked for his main support not in the Seventh Council, but in Trullo, canon 82 (a proof text in iconophile florilegia). See e.g. epp. 221. 124, 416. 30, 532. 204. For a discussion on the reasons for this, see Henry, 'Theodore of Studios', 183–6.

and their theological justification as heresy.[69] The problem of the
validity of sacraments was thus more pertinent, since more clearly
defined. And here Theodore is more explicit than during the
moechian controversy. His recommendation that a monk or even
a simple lay person baptize a child when there is no Orthodox
priest available does seem to imply that heretical baptism is invalid.
In letter 308 to the monk Ignatios (written in 818), for example,
Theodore states that it is better to have baptism from the hands of
an unordained Orthodox person than to 'leave this life unbaptized'.[70] This phrase is equivalent to 'being baptized by an iconoclast priest'. In the same letter, looking to his sources of early
heresies, he gives as an example of baptismal heterodoxy the belief
of the Sabellians, a third-century sect, who taught that the Trinity
was a single hypostasis under three names.[71] He implies from this
example that for the iconoclasts to simply perform the Orthodox
rite does not necessarily mean that they have correct faith in the
Trinity, the ceremony being, rather, a mockery of 'random talk'
and 'game-playing'.[72] Prior to this, Theodore affirmed that the
eucharist of the iconoclasts was invalid because of their (supposed)
denial of the incarnation. The words of the celebration of the
eucharist may have been orthodox, he states, but a different meaning was intended.[73] This thought is now carried over with regard
to baptism. Theodore no longer makes distinctions. All iconoclast
sacramental prayers are transformed into the 'demonical'.[74]

Is this letter truly representative of Theodore's theological views,
bearing in mind that it contradicted the policy of the church during last general council at Constantinople? Does he really consider
the iconoclasm to be a heresy on a par with trinitarian heresies
such as Sabellianism or with other heresies of the first category
on his historical list? Or has he adopted a rigorist view towards

---

[69] Anathemas 1 and 3 of the council read: 'If anyone does not confess that Christ our
God can be represented in his humanity, let him be anathema'; 'If anyone does not salute
such representations as standing for the Lord and his saints, let him be anathema.' But this
council also, for the first time in any general council, established that the acceptance of
ecclesiastical traditions was strictly related to Orthodox faith: 'If anyone rejects any written
or unwritten tradition of the church, let him be anathema' (Anathema 4). Tanner, *Decrees of
the Ecumenical Councils*, 137–8.
[70] Ep. 308. 31: ἢ ἀφώτιστον ἐκδημῆσαι. Cf. ep. 549. 119.
[71] Ibid. 21–3. Sabellians were traditionally included in the group requiring (re)baptism.
[72] Ibid. 24–6.   [73] Ibid. 16–20.
[74] Ibid. 27: ἐπεὶ καὶ γόητες καὶ ἐπαοιδοὶ χρῶνται θείαις ᾠδαῖς ἐν τοῖς
δαιμονιώδεσι.

iconoclast sacraments because of his intense personal aversion
to the iconoclasts? He considered them to be totally alienated
from Christ and spiritually dead,[75] and this attitude resulted
in him being accused of 'Cyprianizing'.[76] Would Theodore have
been accused of this had he not in fact taken an extreme view
towards those separated from the true Church, comparable to the
third-century Bishop Cyprian of Carthage under whose leadership
the African Church embroiled itself in controversy with Rome for
insisting on rebaptizing Novatian schismatics?[77] It would in fact be
hard to deny that, during the period 818–19 from when these
sources date, Theodore did subscribe to the view that iconoclast
baptism, together with the other sacraments, was invalid (and not
just defective).[78] Neither is there anything to suggest in his later
writings that he ever softened this view.[79] On what theological
grounds (bearing in mind the distinctions made during the
moechian period) could he deny iconoclast baptism?

The doctrines at stake that Theodore believed were being denied
were true veneration of Christ and the true nature of the incarnation. With this was associated the whole economy of salvation.[80]
The 'heresy' was therefore primarily Christological. His argument
would seem to run along these lines: incorrect belief in the nature
of Christ would make correct belief in the Trinity impossible, resulting in the impossibility of baptizing in a truly Christian manner. He

---

[75] Cf. ep. 407. 23–4: οὐκοῦν ἠλλοτρίωνται Χριστοῦ, ἄρα ἐνεκρώθησαν, ἄρα ἐν
σκότει διαπορεύονται.

[76] Ibid. 29–30: ἐγὼ δὲ κυπριανίζειν αὐτὸν ἐν τῷ πράγματι ᾠήθην.

[77] A summary of this baptismal controversy (which ended in the early 5th cent. under
Augustine of Carthage, affirming the Roman practice of not requiring rebaptism), is found
in R. J. De Simone, 'Baptismal Controversy', *EEC* i. 109; cf. Thompson, 'Economy', 401–2;
Saltet, *Les Réordinations*, 9–31 and *passim*.

[78] Patriarch Nikephoros seems also to have held that iconoclasts 'denied' their own ordination and subsequently had no status in the church: *Apologia minoris*, *PG* 100. 841B. In the
unedited *Refutatio et Eversio*, 203ʳ, Nikephoros again states that if the iconoclasts of the 815
synod denied the doctrine of the Second Council of Nicaea, then their own ordainers were
(iconophile) heretics, and so they themselves received orders that were 'null and void'.
Alexander, *The Patriarch Nicephorus*, 248.

[79] In a letter to the monk Jacob, ep. 466. 31–5 (*ann.* 823?), Theodore refers to Jacob's
question of whether or not iconoclast baptism of children is valid. Instead of replying,
Theodore mentions that he has just recently sent out a letter on this question, saying that
instead of repeating himself he will send Jacob a copy. Unfortunately this letter is lost.

[80] A fine essay that summarizes these issues is P. Henry, 'The Formulators of Icon
Doctrine', in Henry (ed.), *Schools of Thought in the Christian Tradition* (Philadelphia, 1984),
75–89. A more detailed but less incisive study is Martin, *A History of the Iconoclast Controversy*,
'The Theology of the Second Iconoclastic Period', ch. 10, 184–98.

could then search the lists of 'first category' heresies and recognise in the iconoclasts—the enemies of Christ (Χριστομάχοι)—those ancient heresies that were understood as having denied the reality of Christ's (circumscribable and depictable) flesh: Docetists, Manichaeans, Valentinians, and Marcionists, all of whose sacraments the church did not recognize.[81]

This reasoning, with its sacramental implications, would not be shared by later Orthodox authorities.[82]

To complete the discussion on Theodore and the rites of sanctification some attention will now be given to the eucharist and, together with this, the nature of the eucharist celebrated by a heretic.

5.3 THE EUCHARIST

Theodore had great personal devotion to the eucharist, and he would try to celebrate the Divine Liturgy and communicate every day,[83] whenever liturgical canons would not prohibit it.[84] This was

---

[81] Ep. 221. 31–8. In ep. 477. 202–13, written during the last period of his life (821–6), five to ten years after ep. 221, Theodore admits that the iconoclasts are only 'improperly speaking' Manichaeans (and by implication Valentinians and Marcionists). He still accused them, none the less, of (a new form of) docetism. In the three-part *Antirrhetici*, also written in the last stages of his life, Theodore continued to accuse them of adhering to the doctrines of the Docetists (*Antirrheticus* 1. 4. 333A), Acephaloi and Apollinarists (ibid. 3. 23. 401A), and even the Montanists (3. 24. 401A). These were also traditionally (re)baptized by the Orthodox.

[82] No account describing the official liquidation of iconoclasm in 843 (such as the *synodicon vetus* in its two different versions) gives any impression that iconoclasts were reconciled with anything other than repudiation of their heresy. Their sacraments were not considered invalid. Cf. J. Gouillard, 'Le Synodikon d'Orthodoxie', *TM* 2 (1967), 119 ff.; C. Mango, 'The Liquidation of Iconoclasm and the Patriarch Photios', in *Iconoclasm*, ed. Bryer and Herrin (Birmingham, 1977), 133–4.

[83] Ep. 30. 29–30 (on commemorating the patriarch each day); ep. 32. 43–4, ep. 554. 49–51; *PC* 59. 159. In the 9th cent. it was customary to celebrate the Liturgy of St John Chrysostom during weekdays, and that of St Basil on Sundays: P. de Meester, 'Les Origines et les développements du texte grec de la liturgie de S. Jean Chrysostome', *ΧΡΥΣΟΣΤΟΜΙΚΑ* (Rome, 1908), 264–8; R. Bornert, *Les Commentaires byzantins de la Divine Liturgie du VIIe au XVe siècle* (Paris, 1966), 163.

[84] Trullo, canon 52 (a development of Laodicea, canon 49) established that on all days of Lent, except Saturdays and on the feast of the Annunciation, the Liturgy of the Presanctified (ἡ τῶν προηγιασμένων ἱερὰ λειτουργία) be celebrated. Joannou, *Discipline générale antique*, i. Pt. 1. 189. The Typikon of St Sabas, adopted by the Stoudites, prescribed the Presanctified only on Wednesdays and Fridays of Lent, and on the first three days of Holy Week: M. Arranz, 'La Liturgie des Présanctifiés de l'ancien Euchologe byzantin', *OCP* 47 (1981), 332–88. The explanation of the Presanctified Liturgy attributed to Theodore

not typical of the practice of the day,[85] but something he would strongly encourage his monks to do, so long as they were properly disposed.[86] But his monks were accustomed to less frequent communion, and Theodore's exhortations represented his own ideal.[87] Yet it was an ideal that represented the best of Oriental tradition.[88] Even in exile he would try to celebrate daily if circumstances permitted, using a glass chalice when nothing better was available.[89] According to his biographer, Theodore also received the eucharist on his deathbed.[90]

Receiving the eucharist, Theodore tells his uncle Plato, gave him great consolation.[91] 'What gives greater joy and light to the soul than divine communion?' he asks.[92] Christ's body and blood is the 'tree of life' of the new Paradise.[93] It is with the language of the mystic that he speaks of the eucharist as an 'ineffable and infinite' gift. 'Not only did he die for us, but he gave himself to us as food. What more proper way is there to show the power of his love ? . . . [than giving us] the bread of life . . . the cup of immortality.'[94] His eucharistic Christocentric spirituality is given eloquent expression in another Catechesis:

He nourishes our spirit by the holy mysteries, full of a tenderness that is greater than that of a mother or wet-nurse, and he embraces us lovingly. A mother, in fact, nourishes her own infant with her milk only for a cer-

(1688B–1689C) is, in its present redaction, later in date: R. F. Taft, 'Presanctified, The Liturgy of', in *ODB* iii. 1715.

[85] Cf. E. Herman, 'Die häufige und tägliche Kommunion in den byzantinischen Klöstern', *Memorial L. Petit*, Archives de l'orient chrétien, 1 (Bucharest, 1948), 210–11; K. Ware, 'Prayer and the sacraments in the *Synagoge*', in M. Mullett and A. Kirby (eds.), *The Theotokos Evergetis and Eleventh-Century Monasticism* (Belfast, 1994), 338.

[86] *PC* 8. 29, *PC* 46. 129, *PC* 59. 159 ('do we not receive daily his pure body and blood?'), *PC* 107. 271–2.

[87] Cf. ep. 484. Theodore considers it negligent on the part of his monks only to communicate when they attend the Synaxis on Sundays. On other days, he says, they simply do not bother to show up (*PC* 107. 271–2).

[88] Ep. 554. 49–51: ἐξ ἀναγνώσεως καὶ ἐρωτήσεως τῶν Ἀνατολικῶν μαθὼν τὸ χρῆναι τοὺς ἡσυχάζοντας εἰ δυνατὸν καθ' ἑκάστην μεταλαμβάνειν τῆς θείας κοινωνίας. Cf. Basil, ep. 93: Courtonne, *Saint Basile: Lettres*, i. 203–4.

[89] Ep. 554. 55.   [90] *Vita B*, 325B; *Naucratii confessoris encyclica* 1846A.

[91] Ep. 554. 48.

[92] Ibid. 53–5: καὶ τί γὰρ μεῖζον εἰς ἀγαλλίασιν καὶ φωτισμὸν εἴη ἂν τῇ ψυχῇ πλέον τῆς θείας κοινωνίας.

[93] *PC* 12. 40: ἀνέῳξεν ἡμῖν πάλιν τὸν παράδεισον, ἀπολαύειν τοῦ ξύλου τῆς ζωῆς, ὅπερ ἐστὶ τὸ ζωοποιὸν αὐτοῦ σῶμα καὶ αἷμα. Cf. *MC* 43. 120; *PC* 46. 129: τὸ τῆς ἀθανάτου πηγῆς.

[94] *PC* 107. 272.

tain period; but our true master and father gives his own body and his own blood as food and drink all the time. O impenetrable goodness, O unsurpassable gift! How is it possible not to love him and not to cherish him? Not to attach ourselves to him without cease?[95]

When speaking of the spiritual life, Theodore could affirm that health and growth of the soul was assured by 'tears which have great force, along with compunction, and before all these means, and together with them, participation in the sacred mysteries'.[96] These mysteries are the 'mysteries of the truth' (τὰ τῆς ἀληθείας μυστήρια), and, he adds for the benefit of the iconoclasts, not just a *typos* or symbol for the body and blood of the Lord.[97] Theodore's engagement with the iconoclasts, whom he accuses of eucharistic disincarnationalism,[98] leads him to express himself with disconcerting realism. It is God whom we eat in the eucharist.[99] 'What did Christ say? "Whoever eats me will also draw life from me" [John 6: 57]. And he cannot be eaten unless in the flesh.'[100]

The eucharist also had another profound significance. All who received it became one body with one another.[101] It made the church the body of Christ, according to the words of the Apostle Paul: 'And as there is one loaf, so we, although there are many of us, are one single body, for we all share in the one loaf' (1 Cor. 10: 17–18).[102] This Pauline idea of the church as the undivided body of Christ is fundamental to Theodore's ecclesiology. The church was founded on unity: one Lord, one Faith, one God, one Church (εἷς κύριος, μία πίστις, εἷς Θεός, μία ἐκκλησία).[103] This may explain to a large degree his psychological tenacity in resisting whatever he considered to be the cause of disunity within the

[95] *PC* 24. 72.
[96] *PC* 107. 271: πολλὰ ἰσχύει τὰ δάκρυα, ἡ κατάνυξις, καὶ γε πρὸ πάντων καὶ μετὰ πάντων ἡ μετάληψις τῶν ἁγιασμάτων. On the eucharist as a key element of monastic life, cf. ep. 431. 19–21; TC I. 87. 666; PK 17. 122.
[97] *Antirrheticus* 1. 10. 340B. For iconoclast eucharistic doctrine, see S. Gero, 'The Eucharistic Doctrine of the Byzantine Iconoclasts and its Sources', *BZ* 68 (1975), 4–22.
[98] Cf. ep. 532. 98–9: οὐκ ἂν δὲ ὁ μὴ περιγραφόμενος εἴποιεν ἐσθίεσθαι, εἰ μή τί γε ἄρα φάντασμα εἶεν.
[99] Ep. 380. 111–12: ἐὰν δέ που ἀκούσειεν ὅτι καὶ ἐσθιόμενον ἔχομεν Θεόν.
[100] Ibid. 113–15: . . . οὐκ ἂν δὲ ἄλλως βρωθείη, εἰ μὴ ἐν σαρκί.
[101] Ep. 452. 38–47; *PC* 129. 330.
[102] Ibid.: ὅτι εἷς ἄρτος, ἓν σῶμα οἱ πολλοί ἐσμεν, οἱ γὰρ πάντες ἐκ τοῦ ἑνὸς ἄρτου μετέχομεν.
[103] Ep. 273. 31–2. Cf. Eph. 4: 5.

church, and his horror at being accused of initiating disunity by not following the lead of the head of the church.[104]

Theodore's theology of coenobitic monasticism was also founded on this idea of being one body. His conception of the *koinobion* as a microcosm of the church,[105] as a body with Christ as its head, represented by the *hegoumenos*,[106] was inspired by St Basil the Great,[107] the *Monastic Constitutions*[108] and Dorotheos of Gaza.[109] More directly, it was inspired by Scripture itself.[110] The theme runs throughout his monastic writings.[111] To abandon monastic life, therefore, was an 'apostasy' from the church as such.[112]

5.4 HERETICAL EUCHARIST

Heresy was the worst enemy of the unity of the church. It set man against man as well as man against God and his church. It

[104] Ep. 25. 29–32, to Patriarch Nikephoros: 'We are not schismatics (ἀποσχίσται), O holy head, from the Church of God; God forbid that should ever happen. I am a sinner in countless ways, but I am Orthodox and a child of the Catholic Church'. Cf. ep. 28. 25–9.

[105] Cf. *MC* 62. 173; ep. 397. 8–9: μία ἐκκλησία κοινοβιακή ἐσμεν, and references below, n. 111. On the monastery as church, see A. de Vogüe, 'Le Monastère, Église du Christ', *Studia Anselmiana*, 42 (1957), 25–46; A. F. Lascaris, 'The "Monastic" Ecclesiology of the Byzantine Church', *Communio*, Commentarii Internationales de Ecclesia et Theologia, 3 (Seville, 1970), 145–74, esp. pp. 168–70; J. Leroy, 'La Réforme studite', 199–200; idem, 'Saint Théodore Studite', 434.

[106] The *hegoumenos* is viewed as a pastor with a flock to tend: PK 10. 69, PK 30. 210, PK 56. 401, PK 68. 476–7, PK 77. 531 (the monks were Theodore's λογικὰ πρόβατα), PK 117. 865–6; *MC* 86. 42; TC I. 4. 464–5, TC I. 15. 497; *Testamentum* 1817BC, 1820C; ep. 10. 40–3, 54–5, ep. 14. 23–5, ep. 61, ep. 481 ff.; ep. 506. References to the monastic community as a 'flock' are numerous in the epistles: cf. Fatouros, *Theodori Studitae Epistulae*, ii. 885, s.v. ποίμνη; ποίμνιον.

[107] *RF* 7 (*PG* 31. 928C–932A), *RF* 24 (ibid. 981D–984C). Cf. J. Gribomont, 'Obéissance et Évangile selon Saint Basile le Grand', *Vie Spirituelle*, Suppl. 21 (15 May 1952), 192–215; idem, 'Saint Basile', in *Théologie de la vie monastique*, 99–111; P. Scazzoso, *Introduzione alla Ecclesiologia di San Basilio* (Milan, 1975), 188 ff.; D. Amand, *L'Ascèse monastique*, 134–8.

[108] Pseudo-Basil, *Constitutiones Monasticae*, ch. 18 (*PG* 31. 1381BC). Cf. ibid. ch. 21: *PG* 31. 1396B; ch. 27: *PG* 31. 1417B; ch. 32: *PG* 31. 1421B.

[109] *Instructions* VI. 77.

[110] Esp. 1 Cor. 10, 12; Rom. 12: 5; Acts 2: 46, 4: 32, 5: 12 (on living together with one heart and mind); 1 Pet. 3: 8 (unity of spirit, sympathy, love of brethren, tender heart, and humble mind).

[111] In TC I. 3, 5, 11, 13, 36, 45, 47, 57, 59; TC III. 20; *MC* 17, 31, 65, 82; *PC* 7, 8, 44, 48, 60, 62, 97, 114; PK 36, 46, 50, 55, 56, 73, 75, 77, 86, 93, 94, 102, 117, 122. Cf. ep. 61. 23–4, ep. 387. 18–19, ep. 397. 8–9, ep. 406. 55–6, ep. 460. 51–3, ep. 482. 72–4, ep. 547. 9.

[112] *MC* 62. 174; PK 73. 504.

destroyed the peace and unity of the monastic community which the eucharist built up.[113] Heretics were 'bastard' (νόθοι) disciples of Christ, who 'bore his holy name' but had a perverted faith.[114] 'Let those partaking in heresy be put to shame . . . Like creatures who feed by night (νυκτινόμα ζῶα), they flutter their wings in the night of heresy and preach with assurance, but when day breaks and the morning star of Orthodoxy shines, they hide in their own holes of filthy thoughts.'[115] Heretics were to be avoided at all costs, and being in communion with a heretic, even if done through fear, made one no different from the heretic himself. Even during the time of the moechian heresy Theodore would affirm that, according to Chrysostom, a person in communion with a heretic was just as much an enemy of God as the heretic himself.[116] Furthermore, Theodore later explains to the *hegoumenos* Niketas, communion (κοινωνία) with a heretic, and participation (μετάληψις) in heresy amounted to the same thing.[117] 'There exist two fornications: one concerns the faith and the other the body. He who has been taken by communion with heretics—he is the one who has fornicated with regard to God.'[118]

Communion with heretics could take different forms, with different degrees of seriousness, from accepting gifts from them,[119] living with them,[120] and—to what amounted to the ultimate capitulation and to formal heresy—to share in the eucharist with them. For a priest this would mean either concelebrating with a heretical priest,[121] or simply commemorating a heretical hierarch during the eucharistic liturgy.[122] For all others it meant accepting the eucharist from the hands of a heretic. If anyone did this he would himself canonically become a heretic, even though there might

---

[113] Cf. PK 77. 539 (on the eucharist as gift of peace and order). On the eucharist and its unitive function within the monastery, cf. C. Pujol, 'La eucharistia y la paz en la monaquismo bizantino segùn san Teodoro Estudita (759–826)', *Actos del XXV Congreso Intern. eucarístico* (Barcelona, 1952), ii. 617–22.

[114] *PC* 64. 170–1.   [115] *PC* 36. 103.   [116] Ep. 39. 68–9.

[117] Ep. 452. 31 ff.

[118] *PC* 3. 16: δύο τοίνυν εἰσὶ πορνεῖαι· μία μὲν ἡ ἐπὶ τῇ πίστει, ἑτέρα δὲ ἡ ἐπὶ τῷ σώματι. ὁ γοῦν ἁλοὺς τῇ αἱρετικῇ κοινωνίᾳ, οὗτός ἐστιν ὁ ἐκπορνεύσας εἰς Θεόν.

[119] Giving gifts to heretics was also prohibited (e.g. ep. 552. 32–3), as well as praying for them (e.g. ibid. 140–6; *PC* 129. 330).

[120] Cf. above, pp. 121–3.   [121] cf. ep. 21. 39.

[122] Cf. ep. 39. 53–4, ep. 40. 78–83, 103–108, 137–8 (ὄντος δὲ ἐν τῇ αἱρέσει διὰ τοῦ ἀναφέρειν αὐτὸν αἱρετικόν), ep. 553. 34–5: μὴ ἀναφέρειν τὸν αἱρεσιάρχην.

have been no professed apostasy from the true faith.[123] The prohibition of communicating with heretics was 'apostolic teaching'
and the teaching of the 'holy fathers'.[124] Saint Athanasios, according to Theodore, established that there could be no communion
with heretics or with those in communion with heretics.[125] The
iconoclasts, and those in communion with them, were the subjects
of the Apostle Paul's condemnation (2 Cor. 6: 14–16): 'What partnership have righteousness and iniquity? Or what fellowship has
light with darkness? What accord has Christ with Belial? Or what
has a believer in common with an unbeliever? What agreement
has the temple of God with idols?'[126] In his polemic Theodore
often makes use of these Pauline expressions.[127] It was also the language of the apostolic canon that totally rejected heretical sacraments.[128] This was, as has been seen, quite probably Theodore's
own sustained conviction concerning iconoclast sacraments.
Iconoclasts, he holds, might say the words of the Orthodox liturgy,
but they understand them differently from the author of the texts
(the church) and do not believe what the sounds signify. Every
liturgy shows that Christ truly became man, whereas the iconoclasts deny this by denying he can be depicted.[129] The conclusion
to be drawn is that their eucharist is thus non-existent.

To be in communion with heresy was to be alienated from God,
from Christ, and from the body of Christ.[130] It was to become a
denier of Christ (ἀρνησίχριστος),[131] and to join in with the persecution and crucifixion of Christ.[132] It associates one with the

---

[123] In *PC* 129. 330, after Theodore condemns those who have indifferent relations with
heretics, he quotes the words of Ecclus. 13: 1: 'Whoever touches pitch will be defiled, and
anyone who associates with the proud will come to be like them.'

[124] *PC* 97. 248.

[125] Ep. 466. 17–19. Cf. Athanasios, apol. 49, *Contra Arianos*, *PG* 25. 336B ff.

[126] *PC* 97. 246–7. 2 Cor. 6: 17 (= Isa. 52: 11) reads: 'Therefore come out from them, and
be separate from them, says the Lord, and touch nothing unclean' Cf. *PC* 84. 214; ep. 495.
26.

[127] Ep. 125. 12, ep. 225. 89, ep. 233. 11, ep. 257. 6, ep. 294. 23, ep. 396. 5, ep. 471. 41, ep.
495. 7, ep. 531. 25, ep. 534. 4, ep. 545. 33, ep. 549. 37, ep. 552. 81.

[128] Apostolic canon 46: 'We ordain that a bishop or presbyter who has admitted the baptism or sacrifice of heretics be deposed. For what accord has Christ with Belial, or what has
a believer in common with an unbeliever?'

[129] Ep. 308. 15–20.

[130] Ep. 141. 17–18, ep. 202 (τῆς Θεοχωρίστου συναφείας), ep. 233. 8 ff., ep. 396. 21
(κοινωνῆσαι τῇ ἀρνητικῇ αἱρέσει καὶ ἀποστῆναι Χριστοῦ), ep. 404. 29–30 (τῆς
ψυχοφθόρου αἱρέσεως, ἧς ἡ κοινωνία ἀλλοτρίωσις Χριστοῦ), Cf. ep. 407. 9–10, 23,
ep. 410. 36, ep. 416. 45, etc.

[131] Ep. 452. 69.   [132] Ep. 244. 10–14.

devil.[133] To abstain from heretical communion, on the contrary, was to show love towards and communion with God.[134]

In the period 809–11, Theodore had developed a view of heresy as an evil imitation of the church.[135] During the iconoclast period he founded this on eucharistic theology. The eucharist was the body of Christ. Heretics formed a body opposed to Christ, their eucharist being identified with this body. Participating in this eucharist built the heretical body. Theirs was not the true eucharist. Just as the Orthodox who partake of the divine bread (ὁ θεῖος ἄρτος) become one body (with Christ), so all who partake of the heretical bread (ὁ αἱρετικὸς ἄρτος) become bound together as a body opposed to Christ.[136] This heretical bread, most emphatically, was not the body of Christ.[137] It was *poison*, the bread of deceivers who only pretend to tell the truth and to be true guides.[138] It was a sacrifice unacceptable to God; the guardian angel of the church, on the authority of St Basil, being compelled to depart on account of the heretic's impiety.[139] Preoccupation with the eucharist as the formal sign of adhesion to the ecclesial body was such that, as Theodore reports, the heretics would even force open the jaws of iconophiles to make them receive their communion.[140] Theodore's own advice was to 'keep the deposit of the faith whole, give yourselves to death gladly, rather than participate in the leaven of the heterodox (ἢ τῆς ζύμης μετασχεῖν τῶν ἑτεροδόξων)'.[141] By participation, though, was meant *voluntary* participation.[142] This also applied, *mutatis mutandis*, to other aspects of *koinonia* which were non-eucharistic.[143] Those who did

---

[133] Ep. 553. 28–9: τὸ γὰρ κοινωνεῖν παρὰ αἱρετικοῦ . . . ἀλλοτριοῖ Θεοῦ καὶ προσοικειοῖ διαβόλῳ.

[134] Ep. 507. 19–22.   [135] Henry, 'Theodore of Studios', 197. Cf. above, pp. 191, 192.

[136] Ep. 452. 44–7. Cf. ep. 534. 5–8.

[137] Ep. 531. 21: αἱρετικὸς γὰρ ὁ ἄρτος ἐκεῖνος καὶ οὐ σῶμα Χριστοῦ.

[138] Ep. 308. 9–10: ἡ παρὰ τῶν αἱρετικῶν κοινωνία οὐ κοινὸς ἄρτος, ἀλλὰ φάρμακον, ep. 452. 68: ἰοβόλος ἄρτος; PC 51. 141; *Testamentum* 1816A. Cf. Rom. 3: 13 (= Pss. 5: 9, 140: 3): 'Their throat is an open grave, they use their tongues to deceive. The venom (ἰὸς) of asps is under their lips.' The work of the heresiologist Epiphanios, with which Theodore was familiar, was called Πανάριον, or 'medicine-chest', since it was the author's intention, as he describes it, to provide antidotes to the poisonous bite of the serpent of heresy. Theodore's 'poison' language may have well been influenced by Epiphanios.

[139] Ep. 424. 8–11, ep. 549. 36. Cf. Basil, ep. 238: Courtonne, *Saint Basile: Lettres*, iii. 58. 22 (= *PG* 32: 889B). See also John Moschos, *Pratum Spirituale*, ch. 4.

[140] Ep. 340. 27–31.   [141] Ep. 59. 11–12.   [142] Ep. 340. 27–31.

[143] Such as entering a church held by heretics, praying in their cemeteries, receiving gifts, singing psalms with them, and having impartial social intercourse.

participate, and who subsequently repented—the *lapsi*—were the subject of numerous precise regulations.[144] Thus, for example, those in priestly orders, not excluding bishops, were prohibited from celebrating the eucharist.[145] A priest could distribute communion in times of necessity if the eucharist had been celebrated by another priest of integral faith.[146] Where there was a shortage of priests it was preferable to ordain new priests than to readmit the *lapsi* to full priestly functions.[147]

5.6 CONCLUSION

The eucharist, in its celebration and reception, therefore, was the goal of unity, reconciliation, and peace, as well as being the sign and symbol of the achievement of these ends. It did not exist apart from or outside the faith of the church. It was an ecclesial sacrament before being a sacrament of individual benefit or private devotion.[148] Only priests of truly Orthodox faith could truly celebrate the eucharist and confect the body and blood of Christ. Heretics were cut off from Christ's body by reason of their heterodoxy, and could profit none from their own liturgical celebrations.

[144] See epp. 549 and 552, which are questions and answers. Theodore's authority in the last years of his life extended far beyond the Stoudite community. The deposed (legitimate) bishop of Constantinople, Nikephoros, was in exile and Theodore assumed leadership of the Orthodox iconophile party. When consulted on what was to be done with the *lapsi*, Theodore considered his answers to be provisional, although based on good authorities, pending the decisions of a future Orthodox church council. Cf. ep. 215, ep. 294. 14–18, ep. 446, ep. 545, ep. 536. 21–4.

[145] Cf. ep. 446. 22–4 and ep. 466.

[146] Ep. 536. 17–18. He was permitted in such circumstances to baptize, bury the dead, confer the monastic habit and bless the Theophany water and read the Gospel at Orthros. Ep. 536. 15–16. Cf. ep. 549. 111–19. From ep. 552. 40–3, Theodore stipulates that when even such a priest was unavailable, communion could be received by a monk or nun from the reserved sacrament by taking it in the hand and placing it on the book of the Gospels ('sacred book') covered by a pure linen or altar cloth (ἐπικαλυμματίς), reciting hymns, and consuming directly with the mouth. Following this is ablution of the mouth with wine.

[147] This measure was not so much Novationist, as caution on the part of Theodore in not exceeding his authority in reconciling apostates, which was an episcopal prerogative. See also ep. 545.

[148] Cf. PK 100. 723: one who falls and is under penance cannot have ἱερᾶς κοινωνίας τῶν θείων δώρων. Penance almost always presupposed abstention from eucharistic communion. Interior conversion was the precondition for reconciliation with the body of Christ, through communion, which had been harmed through the penitent's sin. The eucharist was never seen as a means of conversion (except perhaps obliquely by inciting spiritual growth).

These merely increased their separation from Christ. Theodore's eucharistic ecclesiology, *eucharistia facit ecclesiam—nulla eucharistia extra ecclesiam*, was not new.[149] Its application to the iconoclasts (and less unambiguously to the moechians) was. There was no blurring of the boundaries: the iconoclasts remained *extra ecclesiam*, where there was no eucharist, and where there was *nulla salus*.

Similar conclusions are to be drawn for the sacrament of baptism.

[149] Cf. Theodore's near contemporary John Damascene, *De fide Orth.* 4. 13: *PG* 94. 1153B; idem, *In 1 Cor 10, 17*: *PG* 95. 649.

6

Sanctification of Lay Person and Monk

6.1 INTRODUCTION

In Orthodox Christianity, the rites of sanctification, especially baptism and eucharist, are the means by which Christian life is made possible. It is by being a member of Christ's church that redemption and holiness is brought to the individual. Theodore's theology of sanctification is thoroughly, if narrowly, ecclesial. Outside the context of the true Orthodox Church there can be no authentic holiness; even charismatic holiness with the accompaniment of the miraculous is at best irrelevant.[1] Put very bluntly, an iconoclast could not be holy: his heterodoxy puts him outside the true church and outside the realm of operation of the Spirit. Holiness of life, besides, was sacrament-centred. Being ecclesial it was necessarily baptismal, and, as a constant remembrance of this, eucharistic. Yet, the true home of holiness was the society of the monk who had 'left the world'. Those who remained in the world, lay people or 'seculars,' had to make their way through life around the borders of the true paradise of the church: the monastic life. This was not because the lay person's Christian vocation was any different from that of the monk, but because life in the world exposed one to anxieties, trials, and temptations which easily led one away from one's Christian goal. Despite this division within church society, there was only one theology of holiness.

A study of Theodore's spiritual theology, with its anthropological and sacramental presuppositions, will be the subject of the final section of this work. The method of study adopted will be that of a descriptive exposition with annotations. The foundations will be laid to place Theodore's thought within the wider context of the development of Byzantine spirituality.

---

[1] Cf. *MC* 17. 50 (miracle-workers can also go to hell); *PC* 119. 303–4 (signs and prodigies performed by heretics are permitted by the providence of God).

6.2 THEODORE'S ANTHROPOLOGY: CREATION AND THE FALL

For Theodore, as with many earlier spiritual authors, the asceticism of Christian life was dictated by an anthropology developed around the protological and eschatological themes of Adam's creation, fall, and eventual restoration.[2] The eventual state of man at the *eschaton*, according to this spirituality, will correspond to the state of original beatitude.[3] How the pre-lapsarian Adam was is how the Christian ought to be.

Beauty of Creation

When God brought us into existence from non-being, Theodore tells his monks, he created us with an original beauty, and he created us for good works.[4] So man's purpose today is to 'serve a living and true God' (1 Thess. 1: 9), giving him glory by keeping his commandments.[5] The very act of creation was an act of beauty, God 'beautifying' man in honouring him with his image and likeness: καὶ γὰρ ἐκάλλυνεν ἡμᾶς ὁ Θεὸς κατ᾽ ἀρχὰς μὲν ἐν τῷ παραδείσῳ διὰ τοῦ κατ᾽ εἰκόνα καὶ καθ᾽ ὁμοίωσιν ἀξιώματος.[6] Theodore's preference for the verbal form ἐκάλλυνεν, in place of ἐποίησεν, as found in the Septuagint version

---

[2] As Gregory of Nyssa, the prime exponent of this anthropology, puts it, 'The succession of steps by which we were ejected from paradise, exiled with our first father, is that which we are actually able to reverse in order to return to our primordial beatitude', *De Virginitate* 12. 4. 15. Gregory's protological thought is given explicit approval by Theodore in ep. 471. 17–20. Cf. J. Daniélou, *Sacramentum Futuri: Études sur les origines de la typologie biblique* (Paris, 1950), 13 ff. For a recent and very stimulating study and critique of this type of theology, see J. Behr, *Asceticism and Anthropology in Irenaeus and Clement*, Oxford Early Christian Studies (Oxford, 2001).

[3] The term 'man' is to be taken in an inclusive sense of both male and female, unless otherwise dictated by the context. The return to the original state is expressed by Theodore, as with earlier authors, by the term *apokatastasis*. On this term, see e.g. H. Crouzel, 'Apokatastasis', *Sacramentum mundi* (Freiburg, 1967), i. cols. 231–4; T. Špidlik, *La Spiritualité de l'orient chrétien* (Rome, 1978), 39, 144–5.

[4] *PC* 29. 84. Cf. *PC* 103. 260 (creation *ex nihilo*).

[5] *PC* 14. 46; PK 78. 548, PK 83. 583.

[6] *PC* 100. 232 (= *MC* 26. 74). Cf. *MC* 93. 70, where man is said to have been constituted 'in divine honour' (ἐπὶ . . . θείας τιμῆς). When man is restored through Christ he 'is made beautiful according to the archetypal beauty' (εἰ δὲ καὶ ἀνακαινοῦται, δηλονότι καὶ ὡραΐζεται κατὰ τὸ ἀρχέτυπον κάλλος): *PC* 54. 148. Cf. ep. 518. 44.

of Genesis,[7] is but one indicator of a frequently expressed aesthetic sense towards God's creation. The reality and attraction or lovability of beauty—in God, nature, and the soul—are in fact constant themes of the Catecheses.[8] This theme of beauty has a perfect pedigree in the Greek Fathers, beginning with the Cappadocians, and is prominent in Basil the Great whom Theodore may well have been most influenced by.[9] Another Basilian theme—God's *philanthropia*—is also very common in Theodore.[10] God is thus totally and irresistably lovable: 'Let us love with love our lovable God.'[11]

One would expect, given this aesthetic vocabulary, and given Theodore's interests in defending icon worship, that occasional references to the beauty of art, especially iconic art, would feature in his talks to the monks. And yet, curiously, in vain does one search for any such instruction. Indeed, outside the iconoclast context of defending the theoretical rationale for icon worship, there are no 'internal' texts that survive that explain why and how icons should be used in daily worship!

Man's Constitution and Original Integrity

When God made man in His own image, he was glorified with incorruptibility and immortality (ἀθανασίᾳ καὶ ἀφθαρσίᾳ).[12] He

[7] Gen. 1: 26: καὶ εἶπεν ὁ Θεός Ποιήσωμεν ἄνθρωπον κατ' εἰκόνα ἡμετέραν καὶ καθ' ὁμοίωσιν; Gen. 1: 27: καὶ ἐποίησεν ὁ Θεὸς τὸν ἄνθρωπον κατ' εἰκόνα Θεοῦ ἐποίησεν αὐτόν.

[8] Thus, in the Small Catecheses: on the beauty of God/Christ/the Lord: *PC* 20. 61, *PC* 43. 121, *PC* 57. 154, 155, *PC* 108. 274 ('Do we love beauty? What is more lovable than the Lord by the beauty of whom everything is adorned?'). On the beauty of nature: *PC* 6. 24 (nature brought into beauty by the resurrection), *PC* 68. 177–8, *PC* 100. 253–4 (cf. *MC* 43. 120, on the immense beauty of God and his creation: the sun, stars, sea, living creatures, trees, stones, etc.). On the beauty of the soul: *PC* 20. 61, *PC* 43. 121, *PC* 57. 150. On the beauty of virtue: *PC* 20. 61 ('nothing is beautiful or lovable except virtue'), *PC* 55. 150, *PC* 100. 254, *PC* 77. 199 (the beauty of monastic obedience).

[9] e.g. from *In Hex. hom.* 7. 7: *PG* 29. 180C (on God adorning heaven and beautifying the earth); *RF* 1 (on the divine beauty). Cf. M. A. Orphanos, *Creation and Salvation according to St Basil of Caesarea* (Athens, 1975), 60–6; J. Callaham, 'Greek Philosophy and the Cappadocian Cosmology', *DOP* 12 (1958), 31–57. Cf. Plotinus, *Enneads*, 1. 6. Basil also took from Aristotle (*De partibus animalium* 1. 5. 645ᵃ ff.) the idea of beauty being found in achievement of ends, an idea that also influenced Theodore (see e.g. *PC* 20. 61).

[10] *PC* 20, 30, 40, 43, 86, 101, 115, etc. Cf. *De Baptismo, PG* 31. 1532C, 1540C, 1557D, 1564A etc. Also see the Anaphora of the Liturgy of St Basil.

[11] *PC* 78. 202: ἀγαπήσει ἀγαπῶμεν τὸν ἀγαπητὸν Θεὸν ἡμῶν. Cf. *PC* 94. 238, *PC* 131. 336: ἀγαπῶμεν καὶ ὑπεραγαπῶμεν τὸν ἀγαθὸν Θεὸν ἡμῶν.

[12] *PC* 6. 24. Cf. *PC* 4. 20, *PC* 117. 296 (Adam was immortal 'by the grace of God': κατὰ χάριν); ep. 471. 16–17.

was 'constituted in divine honour'.[13] With his fragrant virtues, man was like a blossoming meadow within paradise, and his was a sweet odour before God (εὐωδία ἦν Θεῷ).[14] He was 'kingly' in his exercise of virtue.[15] His soul bore the imprint of God,[16] the imprint of the Father.[17] Theodore uses the tripartite scheme traditional to the Greek Fathers in describing the human soul: rational (τὸ λογιστικόν/νοερόν/νοῦς/λογός), irascible or spirited (τὸ θυμικόν), appetitive or concupiscible (τὸ ἐπιθυμητικόν).[18] God has a purpose for each of these faculties. The rational, the highest faculty, had been given to us that we might believe in the Holy Trinity in a right way. The irascible is the faculty with which the soul is able to fight the devil courageously. With the appetite faculty we are enabled to cherish and love God our Creator.[19] Man is frequently defined by his highest faculty alone.[20] But he is also described using other schemes, e.g. the commonplace Aristotelian triple

---

[13] *MC* 93. 70.

[14] *PC* 6. 24. Cf. *PC* 41. 116 ('the good odour of the fruits of the Spirit in paradise'), *PC* 111, 282. For paradise as a symbol of virtue, see Daniélou, *Sacramentum Futuri* , 45–54.

[15] *Homilia II in Nativitatem B.V. Mariae*, *PG* 96. [680C–697A], 684A: ὁ ἄνθρωπος βασιλικῶς εἰς γυμνάσιον ἀρετῆς ἐν παραδείσῳ τίθεται. This homily was long attributed to John Damascene, and it is found, in Migne, among his works. Yet, for many years scholars have believed the true author to have been Theodore the Stoudite. Cf. C. van de Vorst, 'A propos d'un discours attribué à S. Jean Damascène', *BZ* 23 (1914), 128–32; J. E. Bifet, 'Culto y devoción mariana en San Teodoro Estudita', *Burgense, collectanea scientifica*, 13 (1972), 445–55; Fatouros, *Theodori Studitae Epistulae*, 28*–9*.

[16] Ep. 481. 9–10: ψυχῶν ἄρχειν τῶν κατ᾽ εἰκόνα Θεοῦ πεποιημένων.

[17] Ep. 380. 194–5: οὐκ αὐτὸς σὺ . . . εἰκὼν Θεοῦ καὶ κατὰ εἰδέαν πατρῷαν γεννηθείς.

[18] *PC* 30. 88: ἡ ψυχὴ ἡμῶν ἐκ τριῶν μερῶν συνέστηκεν· ἐκ λογιστικοῦ καὶ θυμικοῦ καὶ ἐπιθυμητικοῦ. Theodore translates this Platonism into evangelical doctrine when he writes: 'Love God with all your three faculties, as the commandment requires' (ἀγαπᾶτε τὸν Θεὸν ἐξ ὁλοκλήρου τῶν τριῶν δυνάμεων, καθὼς ἡ ἐντολὴ κελεύει). Ep. 64. 5152. Cf. Matt. 22: 37. The tripartite division first appears in Plato: *Timaeus* 69d, 90d; *Phaedrus* 426a; *Respublica* 4. 434d–441c. In the Fathers: Clement of Alexandria, cf. *Stromata* v. 80. 9; Gregory of Nazianzus, cf. Poems 2. 1. 47; Evagrius, cf. *Practicos* 89. For Gregory of Nyssa, cf. the references in G. B. Ladner, 'The philosophical anthropology of St Gregory of Nyssa', *DOP* 12 (1958), 59–94. For Basil the Great: Orphanos, *Creation and Salvation*, 67–77.

[19] *PC* 30. 88. On a similar function of the faculties in St Basil, see Orphanos, *Creation and Salvation*, 77.

[20] The image of God in man is τὸ νοερὸν τῆς ψυχῆς. *MC* 30. 84. Cf. *Oratio IX. Laudatio S. Joannis Evang.* 9. 781D: ὁ νοῦς, πρῶτος ὢν καὶ οὗτος τῶν τῆς ψυχῆς δυνάμεων. Reason and the image of God are at times used as a doublet: man has been adorned 'with reason and the image of God' (οἱ λόγῳ καὶ εἰκόνι Θεοῦ τετιμημένοι). *PC* 6. 24; man is λογικὸς καὶ θεοείκελος: *MC* 68. 190, unless he abandons God, when he becomes ἄλογος: PK 82. 575; *MC* 43. 120. Heretics are those 'lacking in intelligence' (τοῖς νοῦν ἔχουσιν): *PC* 36. 103.

distinction of σῶμα, ψυχή, and νοῦς,[21] and Aristotle's five powers or faculties of the soul (τῶν πέντε τῆς ψυχῆς δυνάμεων).[22] Theodore, unsurprisingly, does not neglect the language of Scripture, in particular of St. Paul,[23] an example being the distinction between the 'outer man' (τὸν ἔξω ἄνθρωπον) and the 'inner man' (τὸν ἔσω ἄνθρωπον).[24] Plato and Plotinus speak of ὁ ἐντὸς ἄνθρωπος,[25] which is an expression Theodore, like many of the Greek Fathers, also frequently uses.[26]

Part of man's inner being are his spiritual senses. Theodore tells his monks that he is always vigilant over them with his 'inner' eye.[27] He in fact belongs to the tradition, initiated by Origen, that gives metaphorical expression to the reality of grace in the domain of knowledge of God through use of the language of interior senses corresponding to the five exterior ones.[28] Operation of the spiritual senses presupposes purification of the soul and the state of ἀπάθεια.[29] To be under the influence of the Spirit is to have illumined the eye of the mind, intellect, or soul, and to keep the eye of

---

[21] e.g. in *MC* 34. 95.

[22] e.g. in ep. 380. 168–74 (cf. Aristotle, *De anima* 428ᵃ): mind (νοῦς), cogitation or reasoning (διάνοια), opinion (δόξα), imagination (φαντασία) and perception (αἴσθησις). With regard to the bodily senses, Theodore writes that by 'faith in the Trinity', the paralytic at the pool of Bethesda had his 'five senses' (τὰς πέντε αἰσθήσεις) miraculously cured: *Oratio VI. In Sanctos Angelos* 744B.

[23] In 1 Thess. 5: 23, for example, Paul distinguishes, but in a non-Hellenistic sense, πνεῦμα, ψυχή and σῶμα (cf. PK 86. 615). For him, πνεῦμα is not a physical element of the soul but a communication of God: H. Mehl-Koehlein, *L'Homme selon l'Apôtre Paul*, Cahiers Théologiques, 28 (Neuchâtel-Paris, 1950). From this developed the distinction of ὁ ἄνθρωπος ψυχικός—πνευματικός, although Theodore himself ignores it. He often employs the term λογικός as a synonym for πνευματικός, but his most favoured categorization when preaching is that of the enlightened or illuminated *v.* those still in darkness. See below.

[24] Rom. 7: 22; 2 Cor. 4: 16; Eph. 3: 16. TC III. 19. 39; PK 95. 684 (the 'obedience of the inner man'); *PC* 11. 38, *PC* 37. 106, *PC* 54. 147–8, *PC* 57. 154, *PC* 71.186, *PC* 129. 329; ep. 480. 39–40 (the inner man is the 'home of God'): ὁ οἶκος τοῦ Θεοῦ, ὅστις ἐστὶν ὁ ἔσω ἡμῶν ἄνθρωπος; ep. 508. 20, etc.

[25] *Resp.* 9. 589a; *Enneads* 1. 1. 10, 5. 1. 10.

[26] *PC* 11. 38; *PC* 71. 186, etc. From Origen onwards this terminology became common.

[27] *MC* 92. 67.

[28] K. Rahner, 'Le début d'une doctrine des cinq sens spirituels chez Origène', *Revue d'ascétique et de mystique*, 13 (1932), 113–45. For the development of this doctrine in later authors, see B. Fraigneau-Julien, *Les Sens spirituels et la vision de Dieu selon Syméon Le Nouveau Théologien*, Théologie Historique, 67 (Paris, 1985), esp. pt. I.

[29] Fraigneau-Julien, ibid. 41. On *apatheia*, see T. Špidlik, *La Spiritualité de l'orient chrétien*, 261–70 and bibliography on 378–9.

the heart on the commandments of God.[30] It is to give heed to the words of divine wisdom using the ear of the soul or heart.[31] Such a person is able to sense the good odour or perfume of the activity of the Spirit in the life of another, through his virtues.[32] An enlightened and virtuous Christian is one who gives out the good odour of the Spirit, 'like a beautiful plant in paradise, and like the unfading roses on the holy altar'.[33] The language of the senses by no means exhausts Theodore's use of allegory.[34]

From Thoughtlessness to Loss of Remembrance

It is within his graced nature, with its spiritual senses, for man to contemplate the beauty and wonder of God. Adam, 'our forefather' (προπάτωρ) and the 'first formed' (πρωτόπλαστος) had initially been solely occupied with 'heavenly contemplations'.[35] He lived in joy and happiness, in the 'paradise of delights',[36] and was 'filled with divine visions and initiations'.[37] It was a life lived in the state of virginity (as proved, Theodore contends, from the fact that

---

[30] τὸ ὄμμα τοῦ νοῦ: *Oratio IX. Laudatio S. Joannis Evang.* 782D; cf. *MC* 43. 120; *MC* 69. 194; ep. 414. 6–7; τὸ ὄμμα/τοὺς ὀφθαλμοὺς τῆς διανοίας: *Laudatio Platonis* 809B, 824D; *MC* 83. 27, *MC* 87. 43, *MC* 92. 67; *PC* 9. 56, *PC* 107. 271, *PC* 129. 329, ep. 510. 28, ep. 532. 147; τὸ ὄμμα/τοὺς ὀφθαλμοὺς τῆς ψυχῆς: TC I. 61. 610 (ψυχικοῖς ἀφθαλμοῖς); *PC* 66. 175; PK 30. 210; τὸ ὄμμα/τοὺς ὀφθαλμοὺς τῆς καρδίας: TC I. 3. 462; ep. 407. 8, ep. 447. 11, ep. 472. 14.

[31] ἡ ἀκοὴ τῆς καρδίας: ep. 510. 28–9; τὸ οὖς τῆς ψυχῆς: ep. 472. 15; cf. PK 117. 867.

[32] Cf. 2 Cor. 2: 14–15. The virtuous man exudes the good fragrance of God (*PC* 43. 120) as opposed to the fetid odour of the passions: ἡ δυσωδία τῶν παθῶν (*PC* 36. 104).

[33] PK 47. 344 (= *MC* 29. 82).

[34] Thus, on one occasion he tells his monks to 'wash the feet of your hearts' (τοὺς πόδας τῶν καρδιῶν ὑμῶν): *MC* 51. 143. Often he adds the adjective νοητός to the noun taken in allegory. Some examples are: prayers are like stones thrown against the 'intellectual Goliath' (τοῦ νοητοῦ Γολιάθ): PK 64. 451; the Lord frees us from the 'intellectual hand' of Pharaoh (ἐκ χειρὸς τοῦ νοητοῦ φαραώ): *MC* 58. 161; one has to fight the 'intellectual Amalek': *MC* 62. 173; the demons are 'intellectual wild beasts' (οἱ νοητοὶ θῆρες): PK 117. 867; these 'intellectual wolves' are ejected from the sheepfold: *MC* 66. 185; the devil eats stolen sheep νοητῶς: PK 82. 573; one must ascend to God via the 'intellectual ladder': *MC* 74. 209, and to offer oneself to him on the 'intellectual altar': *MC* 75. 211.

[35] *PC* 6. 24. Cf. PK 117. 868.

[36] PK 83. 586; *MC* 59. 165: ἐν τῷ παραδείσῳ τῆς τρυφῆς. Cf. Dorotheos of Gaza, *Dorothée de Gaza: Œuvres spirituelles*, ed. L. Regnault and J. de Préville, SC 92 (Paris, 1963), 146 = *PG* 88. 1617B (the very same ideas in this passage are found in Theodore almost verbatim).

[37] *PC* 49. 136: θείαις ἀμφάσεσι καὶ μυήσεσιν ἀποπληρούμενος (this language recalls the mystical language of Dionysios: cf. ep. 409. 46 ff.). For Basil, cf. *PG* 31. 532D, where Adam is said to have been filled with 'illumination' (ἔλλαμψις) and divine knowledge (γνῶσις)'.

Christ, the new Adam, was born of a virgin!).³⁸ He lived this way whilst the 'hearing' of his soul was kept healthy and he listened to the divine voice.³⁹ But he fell from this 'angelic' life through an act of disobedience (παράβασις).⁴⁰ He fell away from the 'command-ment of God', a commandment of abstinence from a forbidden fruit, that left him like a beast with no reason.⁴¹ Adam had been deceived by the serpent through his thoughtlessness (ἀβουλία),⁴² having been attracted to what seemed to be beautiful, but in real-ity was not.⁴³ 'It was beautiful to see and good to eat, the fruit that made me die,' Adam is made to say after his fall.⁴⁴ The devil is a master at disguising what is evil as good and beautiful. 'In the same way as he who is darkness disguises himself as an angel of light, so he also knows how to disguise evil as good, what is bitter as sweet, what is dark as luminous, shameful as honourable, deadly as life-giving.'⁴⁵ He is thus a 'polymorphous' serpent,⁴⁶ a 'multi-headed dragon'.⁴⁷ 'Don't let him take us by the neck with his teeth or hit our souls on all sides with his tail,' warns Theodore.⁴⁸ From the time of Adam up to our own time the devil is the sworn enemy of mankind—the thief of paradise, the deceiver of Adam, the inven-tor of sin, disseminator of evils, the adversary of God.⁴⁹

---

³⁸ *MC* 90. 57: ἐπειδὴ παρθενία ἦν ἐν τῷ παραδείσῳ πρὸ τῆς παραβάσεως, καθὼς Χριστὸς παρέδειξε γεννηθεὶς ἐκ παρθένου, ὁ δεύτερος Ἀδάμ. Cf. *PC* 46. 129; *PC* 110. 278; ep. 398. 37–8 (Christ honoured virginity by being born of a Virgin). Adam lived in the state of monogamous marriage after the fall.

³⁹ PK 117. 868.

⁴⁰ PK 3. 17, PK 58. 413. On paradise and angelic life in patristic literature, see G. M. Colombas, *Paradis et vie angélique* (Paris, 1961).

⁴¹ PK 117. 868; TC III. 16. 33; *PC* 4. 20, *PC* 49. 136. The idea of Adam having broken the divine rule of fasting is Basilian: *Hom. de Jejunio*, *PG* 31. 168AB.

⁴² PK 49. 356, PK 83. 584 (κατὰ τὴν διὰ τοῦ προπάτορος ἡμῶν ἀβουλίαν καὶ παρακοὴν καὶ φιληδονίαν); *MC* 49. 137, *MC* 94. 75. This thought, found in Basil, comes from the Platonic idea that there can be no unvirtuous act or sin committed in full know-ledge. Cf. Orphanos, *Creation and Salvation*, 88. In Basil, 'satiety' of soul (cf. Plato, *Phaedrus* 247c, 248c), leading to arrogance and pride, explains why Adam chose what appeared to the eyes as agreeable and charming in place of true spiritual beauty: Amand, *L'Ascèse monas-tique*, 147; Orphanos, *Creation and Salvation*, 88. Theodore also uses this concept in *MC* 22. 62: 'Blessed is that soul who knows no satiety (ὁ κόρος) in its love of God, desire of future goods and rejection of the perishable present.'

⁴³ *PC* 66. 175; TC III. 16. 33; *MC* 43. 120 (Eve was the one deceived by the beauty of the 'sinful fruit'). These same ideas are found in Basil the Great, *PG* 31. 344C–345A.

⁴⁴ *PC* 54. 158.   ⁴⁵ *PC* 54. 148. Cf. *PC* 66. 174–5; *PC* 71. 185.

⁴⁶ *PC* 54. 158; PK 9. 59: ὁ πολύμορφος ὄφις. Cf. *PC* 82. 211.

⁴⁷ PK 41. 295: τὸν πολυκέφαλον δράκοντα. Cf. Rev. 12: 3.   ⁴⁸ PK 45. 329.

⁴⁹ PK 49. 356 (= *MC* 110. 141). Cf. *MC* 56. 155. Other descriptions for Satan or Belial (*MC* 86. 41) include: 'the snatcher of souls' (PK 105. 768) who comes in the night, dark and

Sanctification of Lay Person and Monk

213

The result of Adam's transgression and falling prey to Satan was the immediate expulsion from paradise.[50] Man lost the integrity of his nature, being subject to passions and sin that disfigure the soul, obscuring its beauty and nobility.[51] From being incorruptible he became mortal and corruptible, subject to all the pains of corruptible life: to toil, heat, cold, hunger and thirst, and to death.[52] No longer was he in that state which was free from marriage, slavery, unhappiness, and grief.[53] His heart was hardened and his mind darkened.[54] Each of the faculties of soul received a new proclivity to sin. The devil's attacks are described by Theodore:

The devil has changed and perverted the faculties of the soul. Using the faculty of desire, he seduced our ancestor Adam with food; using the irascible faculty, he incited Cain to kill his brother Abel. Using the faculty of reason, he has precipitated human kind into idolatry. Such is the method of the enemy and his jealousy.[55]

Human nature has been made weak, lazy, and attracted to what is base.[56] It is negligent and unstable.[57] The proclivity to sin is well described in the lists of vices that Theodore warns his monks against, where 'small weaknesses' can lead to the 'death of sin'.[58] He enumerates, in one Catechesis, six 'spirits of malice' that affect the soul: lust, gluttony, avarice, despondency (ἀκηδία), dejection (λύπη), and pride.[59] The list is two short of the eight ἀκάρθαρτοι

---

black or like a lion (1 Pet. 5: 8) (PK 13. 88 = MC 37. 105), the 'archdevil' (MC 56. 155), 'wild beast, wolf, savage dragon, crooked serpent' (PK 44. 314; cf. TC I. 11. 486), 'the worker of lawlessness': ἐργατῆς τῆς ἀνομίας (PK 117. 869), 'the ruler of this world' who 'plans our destruction day and night' (PK 82. 576, 579). Other metaphors, such as the noetic Pharaoh, Goliath, Amalek, etc. are also used (see above, p. 211 n. 34). This language was common among later Byzantine authors: R. Greenfield, *Traditions of Belief in Late Byzantine Demonology* (Amsterdam, 1988), 14.

[50] Gen. 3: 23–4.
[51] Cf. PC 54. 147, PC 100. 254; MC 17. 47. For St Basil on this same theme, see PG 31. 332D–333A; Amand, *L'Ascèse monastique*, 146; Orphanos, *Creation and Salvation*, 84.
[52] PK 117. 868; PC 79. 203; TC I. 3. 461, etc.   [53] PC 110. 278.
[54] PK 3. 17.
[55] PC 30. 88. Cf. PC 40. 114, where Theodore describes what constitutes 'the old man'. ἡ παλαιότης consists in the corruption of the lower two faculties, namely the twin vices of pleasure (ἡδονή) and envy (φθόνος). The first is what led to the sin of Adam. The second is illustrated by the murder of Abel by Cain. From these two sins countless evils have arisen: ἐκ δυοῖν τούτων τῶν ἁμαρτημάτων τὰ μυρία κακὰ ἐπεπόλασε τῷ κόσμῳ.
[56] PC 85. 217, PC 90. 229, PC 105. 265.
[57] PC 36. 104: ὀλίγωρος ἡ φύσις καὶ εὐόλισθος.
[58] PK 73. 501–2.   [59] PC 4. 19.

λογισμοί in Evagrius.[60] He is of course familiar with the lists of vices in the New Testament,[61] but there is no particular pattern in his own.[62] Since he preached to his own coenobitic monks, however, he would constantly indicate the vices to which they were particularly prone.[63]

The devil would have no power over man, and would not be able to incite him to give in to his passions, if man were but to remember God:

We will render an account before the formidable tribunal of Christ of how we have lived in resisting the devil, who is the enemy of Christ, and who torments us and flogs us by the attack of incessant logismoi and mortal pleasures, doing this in such a way as to make us deny the existence of God. In truth, those who are of corrupt morals give in to and follow the adversary, saying by their very deeds that God does not exist, according to what was said by the holy David: 'The fool says in his heart, "There is no God" [Ps. 52: 1].' In effect, if the devil did not introduce forgetfulness (λήθη) and, as it were, the denial of God in the souls of men, then he would not be able to persuade the spirit to yield to the desires of the flesh, to the excesses of sin, to drunkenness, licentiousness, revelry, drinking-bouts, greediness, idolatry [cf. Rom. 13: 13; 1 Cor. 5: 12] and every other type of out-of-place behaviour (ἄλλο τῶν ἐκτόπων).[64]

---

[60] *Evagrii de octo vitiosis cogitationibus ad Anatolium* 1, PG 40. 1272A. The two other vices listed by Evagrius are anger (ὀργή) and vainglory (κενοδοξία). The order in Theodore also differs slightly from Evagrius in that the latter has lust before gluttony, and dejection before despondency. For a discussion of Evagrius' list in John Klimakos (on whom Theodore was probably dependent), see Ware, *John Climacus: The Ladder of Ascent*, Introduction, 62–6. In this same tract (1275B) Evagrius mentions the works that are effective in combatting the passions: prayer, recitation of the psalms, *lectio divina*, remembrance of death and the last judgement, and manual labour. Theodore frequently alludes to the same ideas, although not necessarily with word-for-word similarity (e.g. *MC* 28. 77: prayer, listening to θείων ἀναγνωσμάτων, psalmody).

[61] Esp. Rom. 1: 29, 13, 13; 1 Cor. 5: 11, 6: 9–10; Eph. 4: 31–2, 5: 3; Gal. 5: 19; 1 Tim. 1: 10; 1 John 2: 16; 1 Pet. 2: 1; cf. PK 103. 752; *PC* 34. 98, *PC* 39. 111–12, *PC* 40. 114, *PC* 46. 128, *PC* 133. 340, etc.

[62] Cf. *MC* 25. 71, *MC* 41. 114, *MC* 60. 169, *MC* 62. 175; PK 4. 24, PK 7. 41, PK 17. 117, PK 19. 136 (= *MC* 27. 77), PK 55. 391, PK 103. 752 (= *MC* 24. 68); *PC* 4. 19, *PC* 9. 33, *PC* 34. 98, *PC* 54. 148.

[63] e.g. sins of the tongue: grumbling (γογγυσμός), slandering (καταλαλία), arguing (ἀντιλογία), idle chatter (ἀργολογία), laughter (γέλως): *PC* 34. 98, *PC* 39. 112 (empty talking 'irritates the Holy Spirit'), *MC* 41. 114, *MC* 60. 169; PK 55. 391; cf. 1 Cor. 10: 10, 1 Pet. 2: 1. For sins of intellect and will: egoism (φιλαυτία), particular opinion (ἰδιογνωμοσύνη/ ἰδιογνωμία), self-determination (αὐτοδιάκρισις): *PC* 9. 33; TC I. 64. 618; self-sufficiency (αὐταρεσκεία), self-rule (ἰδιορρύθμια/αὐτορρύθμια), self-wilfulness (αὐτοθελησία), having a different will (ἑτεροθελία), vainglory (κενοδοξία), self-cultivation (ἰδιοπραγμοσύνη): *MC* 25. 71, *MC* 62. 175; PK 55. 391; *PC* 54. 148.

[64] *PC* 10. 36–7. On ἡ μνήμη τοῦ Θεοῦ in Dorotheos of Gaza, see *Instructions* XII, Regnault and Préville (eds.), SC 92 (1963), s. 124.

6.3 THE RESTORATION OF MANKIND
IN CHRIST

> I believe in the Father and the Son and the Holy Spirit, the
> holy, consubstantial and sovereign Trinity, in whose name I
> have been baptized, regenerated and perfected . . .
> Moreover, I confess one of the Trinity, our Lord Jesus Christ,
> who through his immeasurable love for mankind came in the
> flesh for the salvation of our generation. He assumed flesh
> without human seed from the holy and immaculate
> Theotokos.[65]

Christ came into the world to restore man to his former dignity. He
was 'imaged according to our likeness', being 'not other than what
we are',[66] even though he still retained his divinity, lordship, and
kingship.[67] Theodore had a particular devotion to the humanity of
the Lord, because it was this, he was convinced, that was being
denied by the iconoclasts: 'Christ is not Christ if he cannot be
depicted' (Χριστὸς οὐ Χριστὸς, εἰ μὴ ἐγγράφοιτο).[68] It was a
humanity that he could describe with graphic and surprising realism,[69] as well as relate to with great affection.[70] In order to free us
from our 'unjust' and 'diabolical' servitude, which was caused by
Adam's fall, he became sin for our sake.[71] He became 'sin for us'
because: 'He was wounded for us and accepted an undignified
death (τὸν ἀτιμώτατον θάνατον)', 'He took our infirmities
(ἀσθενείας) and bore our diseases (νόσους)', and, as Theodore
explains with a rather interesting phrase, 'by assuming a nature *corrupted* by sin' (τὴν ἐξ ἁμαρτίας φθαρεῖσαν ἡμῶν φύσιν
ὑπεδύσατο). Whether or not Theodore really meant to suggest

---

[65] *Testamentum*, 1814BC.

[66] Ep. 418. 21–2: ἐξεικονίζεται καθ' ὁμοίωσιν ἡμῶν, ἵνα μὴ ἄλλο τι εἴη παρ'
ἡμᾶς.

[67] Ep. 411. 48–53: Θειότης, Κυριότης, Βασιλεία.

[68] Ep. 381. 56. For a fuller discussion on the role of Christ's humanity in Theodore's
iconophile writings, see K. Parry, *Depicting the Word. Byzantine Iconophile Thought of the Eighth
and Ninth Centuries*, (Leiden, 1996), *passim*.

[69] See e.g. ep. 359.

[70] Christ is ὁ ἐνσώματος Θεὸς, ὁ φωστὴρ καὶ σωτὴρ τῶν ψυχῶν ἡμῶν, but he is
also 'ὁ Χριστός μου', (PK 27. 187, 188, 189 (= *MC* 32. 88, 89)), an expression of endear-
ment also used by Gregory Nazianzene (e.g. *Or.* 39: *PG* 36. 336A = *SC* 358 (1990), 150). Cf.,
above, on Theodore's eucharistic devotion.

[71] *PC* 101. 255–6 (τῆς τοῦ διαβόλου δουλείας), *PC* 40. 101, *In Sanctum Pascha* 713A (τῆς
ἀδίκου δουλείας); *PC* 30. 87 (cf. 2 Cor. 5: 21).

Christ assumed a wounded rather than perfect human nature—
thereby emphasizing his icon-depictable solidarity with us—can
only be a matter for speculation.[72]

By being 'our first born brother, our head, high priest, mediator
and conciliator before our Father and God', Christ was able to
'recall' us from the corruption and destruction that had been our
lot.[73] By his incarnation, and the life he offers us, we are made into
children of God (John 1: 12–13) and deified.[74] Life in Christ translates itself into a life of virtue, by which we are made into gods (cf.
Ps. 81: 6).[75] Theodore expresses his theology of redemption both
in terms of the incarnation alone, and in terms of the passion,
through which Christ 'adorned [men] with the archetypal beauty
of deification'.[76] The effects of Christ's saving work are also
described with Dionysian language. Beauty is restored by Christ,
the Sun of Justice (Mal. 4: 2) who illuminates all things with 'incorruptible sparkling beams' (μαρμαρυγαῖς ἀφθαρσίας);[77] after his
resurrection, Jesus ate with his apostles and 'initiated them into the
most mystic and secret realities'.[78] The πολυπαθὴς θάνατος introduced into the world through Adam has now been conquered,[79]
and with the restoration of all things (ἀποκατάστασις) God will no
longer be known in faith, but in knowledge, which is immediate
(αὐτοπτικῶς).[80] 'The Theophany will be seen in most pure contemplations, as the most wise Dionysios says, which will whirl
around us like flashing lights, just as the disciples experienced at
the divine Transfiguration. We will participate in God's intelligible
illumination with a mind free from matter and from passion.'[81]

---

[72] *PC* 30. 87. Cf. Matt. 8: 17. Unfortunately Theodore in no other place, to my knowledge, repeats, let alone develops, this most interesting theological idea of Christ's corrupt
human nature. In *MC* 59. 165 he gives the nearest equivalent: ὅτι δι'ἡμᾶς ἄνθρωπος
γέγονεν ὁμοιοπαθὴς ἡμῖν (an expression found also in Justin, *Dial.* 48. 3 and Eusebius,
HE 1. 2. 1).

[73] *MC* 49. 137; ep. 459. 21–3. Cf. ep. 62. 17–18; *PC* 40. 113.

[74] *PC* 29. 84, *PC* 8. 28; ep. 62. 16–18, ep. 459. 21–4.

[75] Ep. 62. 26–8: ἡ ἀρετὴ ἐκ Θεοῦ καὶ θεία, ἡ κακία ἐκ σατανᾶ καὶ σατανᾶς· οἱ
τὴν πρώτην ἑλόμενοι Θεοῦ καὶ θεοί, οἱ τὴν δευτέραν δαίμονες καὶ τοῦ σατανᾶ. Cf.
MC 45. 127; *PC* 79. 203, *PC* 118. 299.

[76] Ep. 518. 44: καὶ ὡραιοῖ τῷ ἀρχετύπῳ κάλλει τῆς θεώσεως.

[77] *Homilia II in Dormitionem B.V. Mariae* 696CD.

[78] *PC* 6. 25: μυῶν τε αὐτοὺς τὰ μυστικώτερα τε καὶ ἀπορρητότερα.

[79] PK 9.					[80] Ep. 23–6, ep. 409. 46.

[81] Ep. 409. 46–50. Cf. Dionysios, *DN* 1. 4: B. Suchla, *Corpus Dionysiacum*, i. 114. 7–115. 1.

The Feast of the Transfiguration puts before our eyes, Theodore explains, the 're-establishment' of the future world,[82] where, through the ineffable power of God, individuals will recognize each other after each soul finds its own body.[83] The body will be incorruptible like the bodies of our first parents (οἱ προπάτορες ἐν Παραδείσῳ), and 'a brother will recognize his brother, a father his child, a wife her husband, and a friend his friend. I would add that an ascetic will also recognize an ascetic, and a confessor of the faith a confessor of the faith, a martyr his companion of struggle, an apostle his fellow-apostle.'[84] The resurrection of the body—even if it had been devoured by 'a wild beast, bird or fish'—is postulated by the fact of the last judgement. A person's individuality, according to Theodore, is assured only by the presence of his or her body. Only recognizable individuals can be judged as such. To think otherwise is to be part of the impiety of the 'mythology of Origen' (καὶ τῆς Ὠριγένους μυθολογίας ἴσον ἐστὶ κατὰ τὴν ἀσέβειαν).[85]

Reasons for Asceticism

The end of life won for us by Christ—the vision of God and the resurrection of the incorruptible body—is therefore the return to the state of paradise. But paradise is already realizable in this life by anticipation and participation. The call to 'return to our anterior state' (πρὸς τὴν προτέραν ἡμῶν κατάστασιν) rings throughout Theodore's ascetical writings, whether in these words or implicitly.[86] To be a committed Christian was to 'serve God and to recover once more the pristine dignity of our first parent'.[87] This was likewise the doctrine of Dorotheos of Gaza.[88] 'Let us run to

---

[82] PC 20. 60: ἡ δὲ τῆς μεταμορφώσεως τελετὴ τὴν τοῦ μέλλοντος αἰῶνος ἀποκατάστασιν ὑπογράφει.

[83] PC 22. 67, PC 56. 153; TC I. 11. 484.   [84] PC 22. 68.

[85] Ibid. 67–8. (This argument was quite traditional, going back as early as Athenagoras' De Resurrectione.) Theodore also denounces Origen in ep. 471. 41–3. Cf. ep. 532. 42–3, where the condemnation of Origen is associated with the principal work of the fifth ecumenical council: εἶτα ἡ πέμπτη, τὴν πρὸ αὐτῆς ἐπισφραγίσασα, Ὠριγένην τε καὶ τοὺς ἀμφ' αὐτὸν προυπαρκτίτας ἀνεθεμάτισεν.

[86] The expression is used e.g. in PC 8. 29, PC 11. 38, PC 20. 61, PC 111. 281; MC 90. 55, MC 93. 70; PK 26. 181 (τὸ ἀρχαῖον πολίτευμα ἡμῶν), etc. Cf. Gregory Nazianzene, Or. 40. 8: PG 36. 368C: εἰς τὸ ἀρχαῖον ἀποκαταστάσεως.

[87] MC 90. 55.

[88] Regnault and Préville (eds.), SC 92 § 176. Cf. L. Regnault, 'Théologie de la vie monastique selon Barsanuphe et Dorothée (VIᵉ siècle)', in *Théologie de la vie monastique*, 318.

the light, to life, ineffable joy and that sweet and blessed paradise.'[89] Together with Dorotheos, implicit in Theodore's doctrine
is the notion that contemplation ($\theta\epsilon\omega\rho\acute{\iota}\alpha$) is the ultimate goal of the
Christian, because it is with the eyes of the human spirit that God
is to be enjoyed, as was the case in paradise.[90] The practical exer-
cises of Christian virtue, which Theodore denotes as $\pi\rho\hat{\alpha}\xi\iota\varsigma$, are
necessary for the purification of the soul. With a pure soul the spir-
itual senses can perceive God with lucidity in $\theta\epsilon\omega\rho\acute{\iota}\alpha$.[91] The
effects of purification of soul, in other words, are produced on the
intellect.[92] The intellect is then able to enjoy true *gnosis*,[93] a term
that Theodore, perhaps taking it from Dorotheos, often employs.[94]
It was the traditional doctrine of the Evagrian school that the
Kingdom of God realized itself in spiritual knowledge.[95]
Theodore's persistent concern for his monks was that they be pos-
sessed by or be 'enlightened' with $\phi\hat{\omega}\varsigma$ $\gamma\nu\acute{\omega}\sigma\epsilon\omega\varsigma$.[96] Preaching on
the feast of the Theophany, he tells his monks that when Christ was
baptized in the river Jordan a light shone from the waters 'intel-
lectually and sensibly' ($\nu o\epsilon\rho\hat{\omega}\varsigma$ $\kappa\alpha\grave{\iota}$ $\alpha\grave{\iota}\sigma\theta\eta\tau\hat{\omega}\varsigma$). On account of this,
he continues, we too are illumined by the 'light of knowledge'.[97]
God is the light that illumines every mind and soul; for this to happen the mind and intellect have to be purified.[98] But the mind or
intellect is not only the sanctuary of God; it is also the battlefield
for struggle with the devil who comes with his *logismoi*.[99]

[89] *MC* 43. 120.
[90] Cf. Regnault, 'Théologie de la vie monastique', 318. For the Fathers, contemplation
of divine realities was a foretaste of heaven and a return to paradise: cf. Gregory
Nazianzene, *Or.* 16. 9: *PG* 35. 945C; Maximos the Confessor, *Ambigua*: *PG* 91. 1088A; John
Damascene, *In Transfig.* 20: *PG* 96. 576A, 585; *In Transfig.* 10, 561B etc.
[91] *MC* 36. 101: by *praxis* we are purified, by *theoria* we are 'elevated'; PK 87. 622; *PC* 30. 89
($\tau\grave{o}$ $\pi\rho\alpha\kappa\tau\iota\kappa\grave{o}\nu$); *PC* 113. 286. The distinction of $\pi\rho\hat{\alpha}\xi\iota\varsigma$—$\theta\epsilon\omega\rho\acute{\iota}\alpha$ has a long history. Cf. A.
J. Festugière, *Contemplation et vie contemplative selon Platon* (Paris, 1936); R. Arnou, $\Pi\rho\hat{\alpha}\xi\iota\varsigma$ et
$\Theta\epsilon\omega\rho\acute{\iota}\alpha$. *Étude de détail sur le vocabulaire de la pensée des Ennéades de Plotin* (Paris, 1921). Origen sym-
bolized the two ideas in the figures of Martha and Mary: *In Joannem*, frag. 11, 18, GCS 10. 547.
[92] Cf. note in *SC* 92 (1963), 163.
[93] For the distinction of $\pi\rho\hat{\alpha}\xi\iota\varsigma$—$\gamma\nu\hat{\omega}\sigma\iota\varsigma$, and $\tau\grave{\alpha}$ $\pi\rho\alpha\kappa\tau\iota\kappa\grave{\alpha}$—$\tau\grave{\alpha}$ $\gamma\nu\omega\sigma\tau\iota\kappa\acute{\alpha}$ in
Evagrius, see his *Practicos*, Prol., *SC* 171, p. 493. Cf. Špidlik, 73. On the general usage of the
term *gnosis* in Christian literature, see P. Th. Camelot, 'Gnose chrétienne', *DS* (1967), vi.
509–23; Lampe, *Patristic Greek Lexicon*, 318–20, s.v. $\gamma\nu\hat{\omega}\sigma\iota\varsigma$.
[94] Cf. Regnault, 'Théologie de la vie monastique', 318.
[95] Found in another of Theodore's sources: Cassian, *Collat.* 1. 14: *SC* 42 (1955), 93.
[96] *MC* 28. 80, *MC* 35. 98, *MC* 99. 98.
[97] PK 27. 190 (= *MC* 32. 90): $\pi\rho\grave{o}\varsigma$ $\tau\alpha\hat{\upsilon}\tau\alpha$ $\phi\omega\tau\iota\sigma\theta\hat{\omega}\mu\epsilon\nu$ $\kappa\alpha\grave{\iota}$ $\dot{\eta}\mu\epsilon\hat{\iota}\varsigma$ $\phi\hat{\omega}\varsigma$ $\gamma\nu\acute{\omega}\sigma\epsilon\omega\varsigma$.
[98] Cf. *MC* 34. 95: $\dot{\alpha}\gamma\nu\acute{\iota}\sigma\alpha\tau\epsilon$ $\tau\grave{\alpha}\varsigma$ $\psi\nu\chi\acute{\alpha}\varsigma$ $\tau\epsilon$ $\kappa\alpha\grave{\iota}$ $\tau\grave{\alpha}$ $\sigma\acute{\omega}\mu\alpha\tau\alpha$, $\kappa\alpha\theta\acute{\alpha}\rho\alpha\tau\epsilon$ $\tau\grave{o}\nu$ $\nu o\hat{\upsilon}\nu$ $\kappa\alpha\grave{\iota}$
$\tau\grave{\eta}\nu$ $\delta\iota\acute{\alpha}\nu o\iota\alpha\nu$; *MC* 74. 208: $\kappa\alpha\theta\alpha\iota\rho\acute{\omega}\mu\epsilon\theta\alpha$ $\kappa\alpha\grave{\iota}$ $\phi\omega\tau\iota\zeta\acute{\omega}\mu\epsilon\theta\alpha$ . . .
[99] PK 88. 628 (the devil gets to the mind [$\delta\iota\acute{\alpha}\nu o\iota\alpha\nu$] through entering into dialogue).

Salvation, therefore, ultimately rests on the intellect, which moves from ignorance to the light of knowledge (ἐξ ἀγνωσίας εἰς γνῶσιν).[100] A soul labouring under vice is one that is 'without illumination and heavenly contemplation.'[101] A soul free from passion experiences the joy of keeping its thoughts on God and being able to enter ever deeper into the contemplations of the unspeakable greatness of God, even to the point of forgetting itself.[102] 'Let us put on the garment of intellectual light,' Theodore states; 'let us look up to heaven above and know the *logos* of creation.'[103]

An Enlightened Mind and a Quiet Heart

Theodore tells his monks that they are 'mental beings' (λογικοὶ ὄντες), who are concerned with 'things perceptible by the mind' (τὰ νοούμενα).[104] Contemplation of heavenly things is the normal work and the normal fruit of the ascetical life.[105] It belongs to the illuminated mind, to the 'intelligent' person.[106] Monks in fact come to the monastery to be illuminated—by listening to Theodore's Catecheses, by reading the Fathers, by living the monastic rule and the commandments of God.[107] They are to

---

[100] *PC* 48. 132. [101] *MC* 52. 144.

[102] *PC* 47. 131: ἐμφιλοχωροῦσα ταῖς περὶ Θεοῦ ἐννοίαις καὶ ἐμβαθύνουσα ταῖς θεωρίαις τῶν ἀπορρήτων αὐτοῦ μεγαλείων, ὡς καὶ ἑαυτῆς ἐπιλανθάνεσθαι. This last expression should also be compared to a mystical expression Theodore uses in *PC* 41. 115–16. By studying the lives of the saints, Theodore tells his monks, 'flying towards the divine love, the soul is pierced through with pain' (ἐντεῦθεν κατανύσσεται ψυχὴ ἀναπτερουμένη πρὸς θεῖον ἔρωτα). Cf. *Laudatio Platonis* 817A. Theodore was not just a dry moralist in his preaching!

[103] *PK* 107. 181: καὶ ἐνδιδυσκόμεθα φῶς νοερόν . . . βλέπομεν εἰς οὐρανὸν ἄνω καὶ γινώσκομεν λόγον κτίσεως. Cf. *MC* 35. 99: 'What is more beautiful and more delightful to the living God than the splendour of virtues and the purity of the soul, the illumination of the intellect and the elevation of the mind to things above (ἐκλάμψεως νοῦς καὶ ἐπάρσεως πρὸς τὰ ἄνω διανοίας)?'

[104] *PK* 72. 498.

[105] Cf. *MC* 15. 42, *MC* 80. 17 ('let us ascend the mountain of the Lord and contemplate with the eyes of the soul the joy of the promises of heaven'), *MC* 83. 27; *PK* 60. 427, *PK* 114. 844 (= *MC* 14. 40); *PC* 25. 75 (ταῖς ψυχικαῖς δυνάμεσιν ἀναθεωρῶμεν τὰ οὐράνια), *PC* 34. 99 (monks are to renew themselves with prayer, requests to God, tears and ταῖς ἀναθεωρήσεσι τῶν οὐρανίων θεαμάτων); *PC* 90. 229, *PC* 129. 329, *PC* 111. 282, etc.

[106] *TC* III. 19. 39 (intelligent men follow Theodore's advice), *TC* III. 34. 68 (those with minds/intelligence will act upon the reality of approaching death), *PC* 64. 169 (Theodore tells his monks to celebrate the feast of the day with intelligence: μετὰ κατανοήσεως) etc.

[107] *MC* 35. 97, *MC* 39. 109, *MC* 45. 127, *MC* 84. 30, *MC* 92. 67 (monks come to be illumined through the agency of Theodore); *MC* 79. 11; *PC* 41. 115 (the νοῦς of man illuminated by reading the Fathers); *MC* 69. 194 (the Fathers had their intellectual eyes illumined); *PK*

220   *Principles of Holiness*

grow from 'light to light, glory to glory',[108] 'splendour to splendour, contemplation to contemplation'.[109]

Control of the passions—ἀπάθεια—is central to this spirituality. 'He who is in control of his passions is truly blessed, above every nobility, more glorious than kings, above every power and authority, worth more than the whole world.'[110] By *apatheia* Theodore means the ridding of both bodily passion, through the mortification of the five senses, and of impassioned thoughts.[111] *Apatheia* is the result of a life of virtue[112] that allows one to gain the friendship of the angels,[113] becoming like unto them.[114] Its fruits are ἡσυχία, peace, and the ability to love without passionate attachment.[115] It is not only the goal of the monk,[116] but being the very reason for the Lord's incarnation it is therefore the goal of every Christian.[117]

The passions are wild beasts that require muzzling;[118] to be mastered by them is to be taken into Egyptian captivity.[119] Theodore's task as *hegoumenos* is to be like Moses and lead his monks through the difficult passage of the life of passion, through the Red Sea of sin, and settle them in the land of the perfection of *apatheia*.[120] Positing *apatheia* as the monastic ideal was not to subordinate it to a greater ideal of *theoria* reserved to hesychasts. With

---

58. 413, *PC* III. 282; *MC* 17. 47 (illumination through prayer, the psalms, etc.); *MC* 70. 195, *MC* 79. 14 (illuminated way of the commandments).

[108] PK 80. 563: φωτὶ φῶς προσλαμβανόμενοι καὶ ἐκ δόξης εἰς δόξαν μετερχόμενοι. Cf. *MC* 74. 208.

[109] *MC* 61. 171: ἐκ λαμπρότητος εἰς λαμπρότητα καὶ ἐκ θεωρίας εἰς θεωρίαν.

[110] TC III. 16. 34.

[111] *PC* 3. 18, *PC* 4. 19, *PC* 7. 27 (the soul wars with τῶν σαρκικῶν ἐπιθυμιῶν: 1 Pet. 2: 11); PK 105. 769, etc.

[112] Cf. *PC* 93. 236.   [113] *PC* 132. 339.

[114] PK 58. 411 (ἡ ἰσάγγελος ἀπάθεια); *PC* 38. 108.

[115] *MC* 34. 96 (καὶ εὐλαβηθῶμεν, καὶ ἡσυχάσωμεν), *MC* 82. 26; PK 39. 284 (every monk is to be a lover of *hesychia*), PK 60. 427, *PC* 2. 15 (ἡσυχάζοντες ἐν ταῖς ξενίαις ὑμῶν), *PC* 34. 97, *PC* 47. 131, *PC* 16. 52 (ἀγαπᾶν, ἀλλὰ μὴ προσπαθῶς), etc.

[116] Cf. *PC* 38. 108 (the Fathers are to be imitated, who 'lived in the flesh after the manner of the angels in the total absence of passion'); *MC* 6. 17 (monks are οἱ ἐν σαρκὶ καὶ ὑπὲρ τὸ σῶμα· οἱ ἐν κόσμῳ καὶ ἐκτὸς τοῦ κόσμου διὰ τῆς ἀπαθείας).

[117] *PC* 64. 169: The Son of God became man to free us from the law (Gal. 4: 5), 'so that we might no longer be slaves, but free; that we might no longer be exposed to the passions, but be free from them (μηκέτι ἐμπαθεῖς, ἀλλ' ἀπαθεῖς); that we might no longer be friends of the world, but friends of God; that we might no longer live according to the flesh, but according to the Spirit'. Cf. ep. 439. 23–4 (βλέπετε πῶς ἀναστρέφεσθε, μὴ ὡς ἐμπαθεῖς, ἀλλ' ὡς ἀπαθεῖς, μὴ ὡς φιλόσαρκοι, ἀλλ' ὡς φιλόθεοι).

[118] *PC* 28. 82.   [119] TC I. 87. 665.

[120] TC I. 60. 606: . . . πρὸς ἀπαθεῖς τελειότητα κληροδοτήσῃ (the expression τελεία ἀπάθεια is Evagrian: *Practicos*, ch. 60, *SC* 171 (1971), 640). Cf. *MC* 59. 164: from the Egypt of sin God led us into the region of *apatheia* (ἐπὶ τὴν γῆν τῆς ἀπαθείας), *MC*

Theodore, the two were inter-connected, expressing different
aspects of the same monastic perfection.[121]

That *apatheia* was the true Christian ideal was a traditional
thesis.[122] Theodore's allegory of the journey across the Red Sea to
the promised land of *apatheia* also had patristic precedent;[123]
Moses and the Exodus, with the crossing of the Red Sea, was
understood already in primitive Christianity as a *typos* or symbolic
anticipation of the sacrament of baptism.[124]

6.4 BAPTISM AND LAY HOLINESS

Life Restored Through Baptism

Life in Christ, however it was theorized and lived, was initiated
with baptism. 'If I am uninitiated, it is not possible that I, not

62. 176: through fire and water we enter into the peace of *apatheia* (εἰς τὴν τῆς ἀπαθείας
ἀνάπαυσιν).

[121] This conclusion follows from the analysis of Theodore's Christian anthropology.
Θεωρία is ultimately the common goal of every ἀσκητής, whether a coenobite, hesychast,
stylite, or other. In every case ἀπαθεία must have been attained. Theodore's attitude to
non-coenobites is rather interesting. In most of his texts where he mentions them he shows
profound respect, insisting that they are different callings from God which must be followed
faithfully (cf. 1 Cor. 7: 24, 15: 23: *PC* 38. 108). 'If you have been called to hesychasm, don't
try and be a subordinate (ὑποτακτίτην). If you are called to be a subordinate, don't try and
be a hesychast': *PC* 38. 109; cf. *PC* 17. 54; PK 89. 650. It is the devil who 'suggests inappropriate projects to deprive one of what is appropriate (to salvation)': *PC* 38. 108; cf. *PC* 101.
257. The only suggestion of a development of vocation that Theodore makes is that of a subordinate who has become perfect in subordination, such as Plato: 'If a person has not first
learnt submission (τὴν ὑποταγὴν), how can he subordinate his warring passions? How can
he ascend the mountain of hesychasm when he has not kept steadfast obedience?': *Laudatio
Platonis* 816D. It is probable that Theodore's later spiritual father Enklistos, who is referred
to as a recluse (ἔγκλειστος) living ἐν ἡσυχίᾳ, followed the same path as Plato: *Testamentum*
1817A. With both Plato and Enklistos the virtues of obedience had first been learnt. The life
of obedience was regarded by Theodore as a higher calling than that of the hesychast
because, on the one hand (following the thought of St Basil), it imitated more closely the life
of the Lord whose life was one of obedience, and not that of a hermit (*MC* 16. 44, *MC* 60.
169), and, on the other hand, hesychasm lacks the perfection of renunciation of self-will and
independence of action (cf. *PC* 28. 83).

[122] Cf. Gregory Nazianzene: a true Christian is ἐν πάθεσιν ἀπαθής (*Or.* 26. 13: *PG* 35.
1245B; *Or.* 36: *PG* 36. 277BC; *Or.* 40. 44: *PG* 36. 421B); Dorotheos of Gaza: cf. J.-M.
Szymusiak and J. Leroy, *DS* iii. 1659.

[123] Gregory of Nyssa, *Life of Moses*, *PG* 44. 361C: 'Do you not see that the Egyptian army,
and all its forces, horses, chariots and their riders, archers, slingers and foot soldiers—all
these are the various passions of the soul to which man yields? All these powers cast themselves into the water after the Hebrews whom they pursue.'

[124] Cf. J. Daniélou, *Sacramentum Futuri*, 131–201.

having been baptized, be saved.'[125] In a sermon delivered on the Feast of the Resurrection, Theodore meditates on how water and blood gushed forth from the side of Christ in order to wipe out 'the record of sin written against us' (τὸ καθ' ἡμῶν χειρόγραφον τῆς ἁμαρτίας) so that we might be purified and receive back paradise.[126] This flow of blood and water announced the redemptive effects of 'the washing of regeneration and renewal in the Holy Spirit' (Titus 3: 5) which brought us back to our origins (εἰς τὸ κατ' ἀρχάς).[127] By the illumination of baptism one became a 'son of God' (cf. John 1: 12–13; Rom. 8: 14; Gal. 3: 26), a 'son of light' (cf. Luke 16: 8; John 12: 36; Eph. 5: 8; 1 Thess. 5: 5). Those who remained unenlightened (ἀφώτιστοι), have absurd thoughts and engage in absurd activities. They live in darkness and without hope.[128] With holy baptism one is enriched with all knowledge of good.[129] And just as God had made man beautiful in the first creation, so in restoring him to his dignity through baptism he 'beautified' man.[130] The newly baptized is perfected in the spirit (ὁ τελεσθεὶς ἐν πνεύματι).[131] He now lives spiritually (πνευματικῶς), not bodily (σωματικῶς).[132] He is like a new shoot, fresh and vigorous, immaculate and free from the stigmas of his previous sins.[133] New birth brings with it new family relations. The idea of having been spiritually adopted by God through

---

[125] Ep. 383. 42–3: ἐάν εἰμι ἀμύητος, οὐκ ἐνδέχεται μὴ βαπτισθησόμενον σωθῆναί με. (The term ἀμύητος can be used, as here, to mean 'unbaptized' (cf. ep. 462. 49), or to mean 'uninstructed' (cf. ep. 486. 51).)

[126] *In Sanctum Pascha* 713A, 716C. Cf. Col. 2: 14.   [127] *PC* 122. 312.

[128] Ep. 308. 31; ep. 489. 37–8 (the unbaptized are bereft of their senses); ep. 479. 12–17: 'O marvellous calling!, O laudable redemption!; you have been taken out of the darkness into his wonderful light [cf. 2 Pet. 2: 9]. You have been stripped of the old man σὺν τοῖς ἀτόποις καὶ ἐθνικοῖς λογισμοῖς τε καὶ πράξεσιν [cf. Col. 3: 9]. You have put on Christ [cf. Col. 3: 9]. You bear the title of Christian instead of pagan, son of light and of day instead of son of darkness and night of impiety [cf. 1 Thess. 5: 5].'

[129] *PC* 133. 340.

[130] *PC* 100. 232: 'Once again [God] beautified us in grace (πάλιν ἐκάλλυνεν ἡμάς ἐν τῇ χάριτι) through the washing of regeneration and renewal of the Holy Spirit, whom He poured out abundantly on us through Jesus Christ our Saviour (Titus 3: 5–6).' Cf. Gregory of Nyssa, *In diem luminum*, where the vocabulary of beauty is found within the context of baptism: Ὑμεῖς δὲ πάντες, ὅσοι τῷ δώρῳ τῆς παλιγγενεσίας ἐνκαλλωπίζεσθε καὶ καύχημα φέρετε ἀνακαινισμὸν τὸν σωτήριον . . .; ὡς χιτῶμα . . . τὸν ἱερὸν καὶ κάλλιστον τὸν τῆς παλιγγενεσίας μετενδυόμεθα . . . W. Jaeger and H. Langerbeck (eds.), *Gregorii Nysseni Opera* (Leiden 1967), ix. 237. 23–4, 236. 9–11. (My thanks to Dr. John Behr for having pointed this out to me.)

[131] *In Vigiliam Luminum* 708C.   [132] *MC* 29. 81; *In Vigiliam Luminum* 708B.

[133] Cf. ibid. 708C.

Christ is a central truth that inspires a sense of dignity and
Christian confidence.[134] The waters of baptism are a 'spring of
adoption' (τὸ τῆς υἱοθεσίας νᾶμα), and the baptismal font the
'maternal font of adoption' (τὴν τῆς υἱοθεσίας μητρόμοιον
κολυμβήθραν).[135] 'Let us give thanks to Him,' exclaims
Theodore, 'because he has led us into sonship through holy baptism.' We are of one body (συσσώμους) and conformed
(συμμόρφους) to Christ. Ours is a 'divine generation' that 'belongs
to the interior man'. We bear the 'the signature of adoption'
(ὑπογραφῇ υἱοθεσίας).[136] 'Through the cleansing waters of
regeneration and renewal in the Holy Spirit', Theodore writes to
the Iconomachs, each of the faithful becomes 'conformed to the
image of Jesus, God'.[137] As children of God through Christ, we
have received new rights. We are 'heirs of eternal goods';[138] we
have the right to enter the Kingdom of Heaven.[139] As adopted
sons of God are related to each other in a new way by the Holy
Spirit.[140] We are brothers.[141] As a result of our new elevated status
we have been placed under God's special providence. As long as
we hold on to our baptismal grace, we are provided with angels to
serve and protect us.[142]

---

[134] Cf. Rom. 8: 14–17; Gal. 3: 26–8, 4: 6–7.   [135] *In Vigiliam Luminum* 708AB.
[136] *PC* 29. 84, *PC* 36. 104; ep. 459. 24–5. Cf. Eph. 3: 6; *Oratio adversus Iconomachos* 5. 496B;
Laudatio S. Joannis Evang. 776D.
[137] *Oratio Adversus Iconomachos* 5. 496A: ὅτι τῶν πιστῶν ἕκαστος διὰ λουτροῦ
παλιγγενεσίας, καὶ ἀνακαινίσεως Πνεύματος ἁγίου, σύμμορφός ἐστι τῆς εἰκόνος
τοῦ Ἰησοῦ τοῦ Θεοῦ.
[138] *PC* 36. 88: [Christ will say on the last day] ἐποίησα ὑμᾶς συγκληρονόμους τῶν
αἰωνίων ἀγαθῶν ...
[139] Cf. *In Sanctum Pascha* 716D.
[140] Ep. 479. 64: νῦν δὲ ἀπὸ τοῦ Ἁγίου Πνεύματος ἔχομεν ὡς σύγγονον.
[141] Ep. 459. 24.
[142] *In Sanctos Angelos* 744B. 'that you may believe, O faithful one, that a baptized man
who guards purity is provided with invisible angels to serve and protect him': ἀλλ' ὅπως
σὺ πιστωθῇς ὁ πιστός, ὅτι βαπτισθεὶς καὶ φυλάττων τὴν κάθαρσιν, ἀγγέλους
ἀοράτως πρὸς διακονίαν καὶ τήρησιν κομίζεται. Cf. PK 19. 134 (= *MC* 27. 76) (an angel
will lead you into the land of milk and honey); *PC* 88, 224; TC I, 41, 554: 'May our Lord
God give you an angel of peace, a faithful guide, a guardian of your souls [cf. Liturgy of St
John Chrysostom: Litany of the Precious Gifts and Litany of the Lord's Prayer], that he be
with you day and night, chase out evil demons and keep you in all prosperity'; *PC* 45, 125:
οὐκ ἠδέσθης τὸν φύλακα τῆς ζωῆς σου ἄγγελον; PK 103, 754 (= *MC* 24, 67): θεὸν
ἔχομεν βοηθόν, ἐπίκουρον τῆς ζωῆς ἡμῶν ἄγγελον.

Only One Call to Holiness

To live according to baptismal grace was to live according to the
commandments of the Lord. Every living soul is called to live in
this way.[143] It was to live according to the Gospel and to 'please the
Lord' in everything.[144] But God had called individuals to different
vocations, which were different ways of 'pleasing the Lord' and living according to his commandments, including belonging to the
'lay order' (ἐν τῷ λαικῷ τάγματι).[145] The laity,[146] who were of
the common life (τοῦ κοινωνικοῦ βίου),[147] and, from the perspective of the monk, outsiders (τῶν ἔξωθεν),[148] were bound
essentially to the same obligations of Christian living as monks
were. The following lengthy quotation expresses a complete theology of holiness for monks and laity alike:

Let us consider what we are, why and where we are and, along with this,
where we are heading. We are creatures of God, the work of his hands,
made in the image and likeness of the Creator, possessing the Kingdom
of everything that is under the sky. . . second to the angels, as were those
of [our] first nature (ἀγγέλων δεύτεροι, ὡς αὐτοὶ τῆς πρώτης
φύσεως). Why do we exist? We exist for the glory of his power, emulating the angels, through keeping his commandments in everything (διὰ
τῆς κατὰ πάντα φυλακῆς τῶν ἐντολῶν αὐτοῦ). . . .

Where are we, if not in a place of exile, in the darkest of places? This is
on account of the cowardice, the disobedience and the concupiscence of
our first father, passed on in us, his descendants. Thus we ought to weep
and enter into mourning, to grieve and to groan, in imitation of those

---

[143] PK 41. 294 (= *MC* 110. 143).

[144] During the rite of baptism the priest prays that the newly baptized might always act
so as to please the Lord: ἵνα ἐν παντὶ ἔργῳ καὶ λόγῳ εὐαρεστοῦντές σοι: Conybeare,
Rituale Armenorum, 404.

[145] *MC* 22. 62; TC I. 3. 426; PC 31. 91 (ὁμοταγῶν καὶ ἑτεροταγῶν), PC 38. 109–10
(. . . ἕκαστον ὡς κέκληκεν ὁ Κύριος, οὕτω περιπατείτω καὶ οὕτω πολιτευέσθω
καὶ οὕτως εὐαρεστείτω τῷ Κυρίῳ); ep. 507. 7, ep. 112. 31. On this same doctrine in St
Basil, cf. *De Baptismo*, PG 31. 1581BC, 1604A; *Moralia* nos. 70–9, ibid. 816D–860B.

[146] Theodore also uses the term μίγας (meaning 'mixed', therefore of the world) for a
lay person: *In Dormitionem Deiparae* 720C; ep. 410. 48, ep. 538. 33. Cf. Gregory Nazianzene,
Or. 43. 62: PG 36. 577A.

[147] PC 79. 203, PC 87. 222, PC 94. 237 (ἡ τῶν βιωτικῶν ζωή); PC 94. 238; TC I. 3. 426
(οἱ ἐν τῷ βίῳ); ep. 387. 6–7 (ἐν τῷ κοινῷ βίῳ), ep. 42. 35, etc.

[148] Ep. 410. 47; PC 120. 306 (τοῖς ἔξω); PK 83. 586 (πᾶς ἄνθρωπος ἐσωτικὸς καὶ
ἐξωτικὸς . . .). For St Basil, οἱ ἔξωθεν meant pagans outside the church rather than
Christian people outside the cloister: J. Gribomont, 'Le Renoncement au monde dans
l'idéal ascétique de saint Basile', *Irénikon*, 31 (1958), 303.

about to befall a sad fate by order of the emperors, considering what we have fallen away from, from what dignity of life, from what angelic rank, from what blessed happiness in paradise, and, also, considering the time when we will have to appear before the Master whom we have offended and render an account of our life and conduct during this exile.

Where are we heading? Into another world, to a society of angels, three times blessed, to the luminous choir, to life without end, towards the terrible universal judgement where the judge of all, God seated on the throne of glory, will judge all things in a flash, rendering to each according to his deeds, giving to those who have kept his commandments a place on the right, ineffable joy, the delight of eternal goods, the kingdom of heaven and what the spirit of man is unable to contemplate. Those who have disobeyed, who have through cowardice and love of pleasure and indifference committed evil, adultery, fornication, theft, envy, murder, intemperance, impurity, infidelity, apostasy, pride, vain-glory and the other types of vice, will merit eternal punishments . . . each according to his sins.

What sensible man, consequently, who has done violence to [his own] nature, will not generously put up with everything, even if it means dying for the good, in order to shine on that day like the sun, to take his place among the ranks of the saints, among the choirs of angels . . . to participate in the joy of the martyrs, the delights of the prophets and apostles? What a pity it would be if, on account of the immediate pleasures of the flesh, because of smallness of heart, love of the world (διὰ τὴν φιλόκοσμον ἕξιν), because of vile and valueless ephemeral things, we were to risk having the sad fate of being placed on the left and being led into tortures, into exile without return, into punishment without respite, bound by chains impossible to break . . . .

This, my children, is what everyone must meditate on—those who seem to be running well and those who hesitate, the courageous and the discouraged, the great and the small, the rich in virtue and the poor, in a word, every man, whether he belongs to us or is from outside, and every tribe and tongue (καὶ μὴν πᾶς ἄνθρωπος ἐσωτικὸς καὶ ἐξωτικὸς καὶ πᾶσα φυλὴ καὶ γλῶσσα).[149]

On another occasion Theodore defends the use of religious images for all Christians, against the opinion that they are useful only for the uninstructed, the 'more simple and less perfect' (τοῖς ἁπλουστέροις καὶ ἀτελεστέροις). In response he quotes Galatians 3: 28: 'There is neither Jew nor Greek, there is neither slave nor free person, there is neither male nor female; for you are

---

[149] PK 83. 583–7. For a comparison, see Basil, *Moralia* no. 80, ch. 1–11: *PG* 31. 860C ff.

226 *Principles of Holiness*

all one in Christ Jesus,' and Ephesians 4: 5: 'One Lord, one faith, one baptism'. 'What is this new division,' he asks, 'of the holy nation and royal priesthood (Exod. 19: 6; 1 Pet. 2: 9) into two unequal segments, the more perfect and the inferior?'[150]

Monk or Lay Person?

Christians, therefore, cannot be divided into groups of more and less perfect; the principle must also hold for the division between monks and laity. There was but one baptism, which made everyone a member of the holy nation and royal priesthood. And laity were by definition the baptized.[151] A 'true' Christian was whoever imitated Christ and bore his seal.[152] And Theodore knew and wrote to numerous lay people who were exemplary in their living of Christian virtue, even to the point of heroism.[153] The sole difference between lay people and monks was in the way or circumstances in which Christian life was lived, especially with regard to marriage. It was marriage, above all else, that separated the lay person from the monk.[154] An instructive text is a letter to the Spatharios Marian, 'our friend, a good man, a most praise-worthy leader, pupil of piety, disciple of orthodox doctrine, a man of God and a lover of monks (τῷ φιλητῇ τῶν μοναστῶν)'.[155] Theodore writes:

See, my Lord, how you should walk. This is what the Apostle cries out: not as the unwise, but as the wise (Eph. 5: 15), not as a lover of the flesh,

[150] Ep. 499. 18–24.

[151] Recalling Dionysios' triadic division of the non-clerical orders in the *Ecclesiastical Hierarchy* (Suchla, *Corpus Dionysiacum*, ii. 115. 1–17), Theodore states (ep. 489. 35–6), that among those who are not clerics there is a triple order: of the initiates or catechumens, of the baptized (τῶν πεφωτισμένων), and of monks. Dionysios calls the second group 'communicants': 'The intermediate order (ἡ μέση τάξις) is made up of those who enter upon the contemplation of certain sacred things and who, because they have been well purified, commune therein to the extent that is possible for them.'

[152] Ep. 470. 5–6: οὐδὲν οὖν ἄλλο ἐστιν ὁ ἀληθινὸς χριστιανὸς ἢ Χριστοῦ μίμημα καὶ ἀποσφράγισμα. He continues in this letter the thought that Christians are all branches of the same tree, members of the same body, glorifying the Lord in both soul and body. Cf. ep. 504, on keeping intact faith and right conduct, committed to the consul Demetrios by the Holy Spirit.

[153] Cf. PC 63. 166–7, ep. 156. 14 ff.; ep. 412. 8–9, 11, 17–18, ep. 538. 33, ep. 399. 2, 8–9, etc.

[154] Cf. PC 35. 99: εἰς δύο γὰρ διῃρημένου τοῦ ἀνθρωπίνου βίου εἴς τε γάμον καὶ ἀγαμίαν; ep. 500. 44–5: κοινὴ δὲ χρῆσίς ἐστιν ἡ τοῦ βίου ἐπιγαμία.

[155] Ep. 464. 6–8.

but as a lover of God (μὴ ὡς φιλόσαρκος, ἀλλ᾽ ὡς φιλόθεος), not as immortal, but as anxious about one's end. We have a common fate, an unsurpassable boundary. For it is said 'there is no man who lives who will not see death' (Ps. 88: 48). What, you ask, are the characteristics of both? I will explain them to you, my friend. Belonging to the first is dancing, jesting, games, obscene language, bouts of drunkenness, gluttony, self-exaltation, empty conceit, an accumulation of adornments, desire for riches and many other and graver things which due to reverence for your dignity I will omit. Those doing such things will not inherit the kingdom of God, as the Apostle says (Eph. 5: 4). I will now show you the things proper to the other. Poverty of spirit, tears of compunction, gentleness, peace, mercy, the mind's contemplation of God (νοῦ πρὸς Θεὸν θεωρία), contempt of money, hatred towards the world (μισοκοσμία), frugality, temperance over each power of the faculties; and simply to love the Lord more than wife, children, parents, brothers and all persons, for he made us and gave himself up to death for each of us.

These and similar things are of the true Christian (τοῦ ἀληθινοῦ Χριστιανοῦ). Do not think, my Lord, that what I have said only concerns the monk. Although it affects the monk more intensely (κᾶν ἐν τῷ μονάζοντι ἐπιτεταμένως) all these things equally (τὰ πάντα ἐφίσῃς) affect the lay person, with the exception of celibacy and poverty (πλὴν ἀγαμίας καὶ ἀκτημοσύνης), for which a secular (ὁ κοσμικὸς) is not to be condemned. And yet here too there are times for continence and rules for frugality (ὅμως κἀνταῦθα ἐγκρατείας καιροὶ καὶ αὐταρκείας θεσμοί). For he says, 'having food and clothing, with these we shall be content. But those who desire to be rich fall inevitably into the pit' (1 Tim. 6: 8; cf. ibid.: 9). And again, 'Let those who have wives live as though they had none' (1 Cor. 7: 29). Behold, my Lord, you have made me announce to you the just ordinance of God.[156]

According to this text, celibacy and poverty distinguish the lay person from the monk,[157] but otherwise the obligation to fulfil the commandments, to be a lover of God (φιλόθεος), to live virtuously (including μισοκοσμία) and to avoid vice, to strive for θεωρία (which presupposes ἀπάθεια), are exactly the same. The monk, however, is expected to strive for these things 'even more intensely'. Motivation or obligation of state, not goal, is the difference. Even with celibacy and poverty, a lay person, according to this 'Gospel'

---

[156] Ibid. 9–34. Cf. ep. 459, to Julianos the tailor, where Theodore gives a similar programme for lay Christian life.

[157] Also cf. ep. 200. 10, ep. 472. 38; *PC* 110. 278.

ethic, is obliged in due season to participate in these values.[158] For St Basil, it seems, poverty was not a counsel but a commandment: οὐ δεῖ πλουτεῖν, ἀλλὰ πτωχεύειν, κατὰ τὸν τοῦ κυρίου λόγον.[159] Although Theodore does not follow Basil in this, he places little emphasis on poverty (except in so far as it is an aspect of the renunciation of the world). It is otherwise with virginity.

Theodore's appreciation and understanding of human and marital love is clear: 'When a man loves a woman, he gives himself entirely to the beloved; he breathes her, he thinks only of her. If you mention the sun, he has no wish to see the sun, but only her whom he desires. If you propose a meal with him, he wants to have no part in it, but only in her.'[160] He knows the value of married life and knows how to express his high admiration for it.[161] The death of a spouse was like a sword cleaving a person in two;[162] spouses will be reunited at the resurrection.[163] Yet living in the state of virginity was definitely to be preferred.

[158] The time of Great Lent, for example, was a season for alms-giving, temperance with regard to food and sexual intimacy (full continence being the rule). The time of Lent, Theodore states in *PC* 54. 147, is like a sea port unbattered by waves; all men who come to this port enjoy spiritual calm. He says this οὐ γὰρ μόνον μοναχοῖς, ἀλλὰ καὶ λαικοῖς. Cf. *MC* 60. 168: fasting leads to humility—λόγος γὰρ ἐστι καὶ τῶν ἔξω. On the norms for lenten marital continence and continence 'in due season', cf. R. Cholij, *Clerical Celibacy in East and West* (Leominster, 1989), 144–56. In the *Catechesis Chronica* 1696D–1697A (although of doubtful authenticity), it is stated that everyone (ὁ δὲ σύμπας λαὸς τοῦ Χριστοῦ) is to observe the fast of the Feast of the Exaltation of the Cross (14 September), three days of fasting in the week before the Feast of the Nativity of the Lord (second, fourth and sixth days—abstaining from fish and oil). The same type of fasting is prescribed during the fasts 'of the holy apostles' and 'of the Mother of God (θεομήτορος)'.

[159] *Moralia* no. 48, *PG* 31. 2769A; cf. ibid. 2768C: a Christian is required κατ᾽ ἐντολὴν τοῦ κυρίου to distribute to the poor all that is beyond τοῦ ἐπιδεομένου τῶν πρὸς τὸ ζῆν ἀναγκαία, i.e. the minimum necessary of food and clothing. For a discussion of this and parallel texts, see Neri, *Basilio di Cesarea*, 78–81. Cf. also Gribomont, 'Le Renoncement', 286. For Dorotheos of Gaza virginity and poverty were both counsels and not commandments, being the two 'gifts' that the Fathers brought to God in their effort to 'come to virtue' away from the world. *Instructions*, SC 92 (1963), 164–7 (*PG* 88. 1629AB): δῶρά . . . εἰσι παρθενία καὶ ἀκτημοσύνη· ταῦτα οὔκ εἰσιν ἐντολαί, δῶρά εἰσιν . . . ἰδοὺ οὐκ εἶπε πώλησόν σου τὰ ὑπάρχοντα, ὡς ἐντελλόμενος, ἀλλ᾽ ὡς συμβουλεύων. Cf. John Klimakos, *John Climacus, The Ladder of Ascent*, Step 2, *PG* 88. 656B, and the comment by Neri, *Basilio di Cesarea*, 81: 'si nota ancora nel Climaco la professione monastica non appaia affatto assimilata a quella battesimale (unlike Basil), ma sia contrapposta ad essa come superiore'.

[160] *PC* 3. 17.

[161] One's married partner is given by God as one's life helper: ep. 304. 12, ep. 454. 10–11, ep. 505. 17–20, ep. 508. 8–9 (θεόδοτος σου σύζυγος); Cf. the picture of family life in ep. 497.

[162] Ep. 467. 4–5, ep. 497. 8–9.

[163] Ep. 454. 31–2: καὶ αὖθις διαζεύξας ἐνώσειν διὰ τῆς ἀναστάσεως. Theodore also recommends to his widow correspondent: φυλάττουσαν τὴν χηρείαν ἐν Κυρίῳ

6.5 MONASTIC HOLINESS AND
SECOND BAPTISM

Reasons for Living in Virginity

The profession of monasticism was also the profession of virginity—τὸ ἐπάγγελμα τῆς παρθενίας.[164] 'What is more excellent than virginity, the cares of which are how to please the Lord?'[165] Whoever puts on the tunic of virginity (τὸν τῆς παρθενίας χιτῶνα) espouses the incorruptible spouse, and this for eternity.[166] All other marriages, on the contrary, dissolve at death.[167] Yet, it was not the fact of being unmarried as such that made one a bride of Christ, but the virginity of soul, unsullied and beautiful, which virginity or continence of body helped to foster:

It is due to our beauty of soul that we have been espoused to Christ; this is what the blessed Paul affirms: 'I betrothed you to Christ to present you as a pure bride to her one husband. But I am afraid that as the serpent deceived Eve by his cunning, your thoughts will be led astray from a sincere and pure devotion to Christ' (2 Cor. 11: 2–3). Do you see the greatness of the gift: to be worthy of having Christ as your young spouse? . . . Our soul resembles a young maiden being brought to the nuptial bed. In the same way as she removes herself from the sight of other men, takes herself to the interior of the chamber, doing everything to keep herself pure until the time of the marriage comes, so too the soul must do all it can to keep itself pure from pernicious passions, the source of sin, until it leaves this life.[168]

(l. 36). (He does not speculate on the relationship of those married for a second time. But there will be no marriage as such in heaven; all will be like angels: ep. 470. 31. Cf. Matt. 22: 30.)

[164] PK 112. 830; PC 31. 91; ep. 444. 4, ep. 489. 12–13, ep. 548. 26 (παρθενικὸν ἐπάγγελμα), etc. Theodore also praises those who choose virginity but remain in the world: ep. 161. 11, ep. 200. 9–13 (is equivalent to having a monastic will: τοῦτο γὰρ τὸ θέλειν ὑμᾶς μονάσαι); ep. 436, ep. 489. 54–6, ep. 193. 9–10 (a widow, considered to be numbered among the 'virgins of the bridal chamber').

[165] Ep. 66. 7–8: τί γὰρ κρεῖττον παρθενίας, ἧς ἡ μέριμνα πῶς ἀρέσει τῷ Κυρίῳ . . . ; Cf. 1 Cor. 7: 32.

[166] PK 112. 830; MC 11. 32, MC 75. 211, MC 83. 28; PC 65. 171 (παρθενία ἐστὶν ἡ νύμφη καὶ μεριμνήτρια Χριστοῦ), PC 130. 333; ep. 62. 13–14, ep. 63. 20–1, ep. 228. 25, ep. 431. 16–17 (ὁ πνευματικῶς νοούμενος γάμος), ep. 458. 32–5, ep. 483. 4–5, 21–2 (μία γὰρ ἐπιθυμία καὶ εἷς ἔρως ἀληθινός, ὁ Κύριος ἡμῶν Ἰησοῦς Χριστός, ὁ καλὸς καὶ ὡραῖος νυμφίος), etc. Theodore applies this bridal imagery to both males and females.

[167] Cf. ep. 66. 23–4: οὐχὶ πᾶσαι συζυγίαι ἀποζεύγνυνται διὰ θανάτου.

[168] PC 57. 155. Cf. PC 53. 146 (protect the soul, the bride of Christ), PC 118. 299 (our only love is the 'young spouse that is Christ'), ep. 427. 8–9 (marriage garment must be ἔνδυμα

Without virginity of soul ascetics could easily end up living 'adulterously' with women.[169] Lived as it should be, virginity was 'the queen of virtues', having the first place in the Kingdom (Rev. 14: 4).[170] It attracts divine love in a similar way to that by which a shiny surface reflects light.[171]

Every virtue is great, and the supreme desire is to have acquired it. But assuredly, nothing is as great as the possession of virginity. Virginity, in effect, was resplendent first of all in paradise before our ancestors were deceived by the serpent. The mother of Christ (μήτηρ Χριστοῦ) is given her name from virginity [i.e. the Virgin]. Virginity transforms men into angels. If marriage is born of corruption and ends in corruption, virginity resurrects the world through incorruptibility.[172]

Despite its dignity, seen in terms of the beginning and end of salvation history marriage had to be considered a corruption of virginity, for it represented the cares and anxieties of the fallen world that prevented or corrupted the soul's pure contemplation of God and heavenly things. It represented love of the flesh and the human passions that soiled the pristine beauty of God's original creation. Monastic life was a return to this state.[173] It was to be lived in virginity because the virgin state represented the incorrupt, passion-free soul that could look on God with clarity of intellect. Not being subject to 'corruption', monks were like bodiless angels (ἄσαρκοι καὶ ἀσώματοι ἄγγελοι).[174] They were half-men, half-angels:

καθαρότητος (Matt. 22: 13)). In principle this doctrine was equally applicable to lay people. To the *patrikia* Irene Theodore says that even as a married woman she can be a 'spouse of Christ' as long as she keeps faith: νύμφη Χριστοῦ χρηματίζεις, κἂν ἀπὸ ἀνδρός, συμπολῖτις τῶν δικαίων καὶ ἁγίων, εἴπερ ἐμμενοῦμεν ταῖς θείαις ὁμολογίαις ἕως τέλους. Cf. Origen, *Schol. in Cant. Cant.* 7. 1, 8. 8: *PG* 17. 280C, 285C.

[169] Cf. *PC* 65. 172; ep. 444. 4–6.

[170] *PC* 65. 171–2: παρθενία ἐστὶν ἡ βασίλισσα τῶν ἀρετῶν. Cf. *PC* 35. 99: 'Very great is the exploit of virginity, which attains the very summit of heaven.'

[171] *Laudatio S. Joannis Evang.* 784C–785B (on Jesus' special love for the virgin disciple John).

[172] *PC* 46. 129.

[173] *MC* 90. 55: 'What do you seek . . . if not to serve God, and to recover once again the pristine dignity of our first parent . . . ?' PK 8. 51, PK 26. 181: 'Seek and search out the old way of living in the delights of paradise from where we were expelled. Let us recall to mind and recognize our old life. Let us withdraw from the deceiving world and go towards God'; ep. 444. 7, ep. 486. 70–2. Cf. also above, Ch. 6.3.

[174] *MC* 51. 141. This text also states that to live in virginity was to 'be in the flesh but be fleshless, to be in the body but be bodiless, to be in the fire without burning, to be impassible in passions (ἐν πάθεσιν ἀπαθεῖν)'. We can be angels on earth if we so wish (ἄγγελοι ἐσμὲν ἐπὶ γῆς εἰ θέλομεν).

Humankind is divided in effect into two categories: marriage and celibacy. Marriage unites those in the world below, celibacy fills the world above. The one is made to be submitted to corruption whilst the other has been judged worthy to shine with incorruptibility. And if one were to behold a man supported by wings, one would with good reason be astonished before the presence of this semi-man and semi-angel, so likewise the one living in virginity provides a sight remarkable to both men and angels. He is in the flesh and yet above the flesh, in the world and yet above the world (ἐν σαρκί ἐστι καὶ ὑπὲρ τὴν σάρκα, ἐν κόσμῳ καὶ ὑπὲρ τὸν κόσμον).[175]

Dangers of Worldliness

Living at the same time in and out of the flesh, in and out of the world, in this present life and yet above it,[176] means simply that the monk 'is he who looks only towards God, who covets God alone, who attaches himself to God, who chooses to serve God alone, living in peace with God and being the cause of peace for others'.[177] Thus, 'it is truly given to us (even if this is said boldly, it is not out of place) to know the mysteries of the heavenly Kingdom before those who are in the world'.[178] Why is this so? Because those in the world (τοὺς κατὰ κόσμον) see and yet do not see (cf. Matt. 13: 13). And he adds this piece of rhetoric:

What things do they do? They say riches and present glory are blessed; they rejoice in luxuries and pleasures; they exult in perfumes and drunkenness, luxurious clothes and horses, having many relatives, an abundance of possessions, beautiful homes, splendid precious stones and a variety of other vanities. They laugh, stamp their feet, leap around like kid-goats, they stuff themselves and grow fat like pigs ready for the slaughter. Nor will I speak of their many other passions.[179]

---

[175] PC 35. 99–100. Cf. MC 6. 17: οἱ ἐν σαρκὶ καὶ ὑπὲρ τὸ σῶμα· οἱ ἐν κόσμῳ καὶ ἐκτὸς τοῦ κόσμου διὰ τῆς ἀπαθείας. It is not virginity as such but the state of soul (*apatheia*) that it helps engender that places one on the level of the angels. This is the ideal of every Christian.

[176] Cf. PC 9. 32: ἐν σαρκὶ καὶ ὑπὲρ σάρκα . . . ἐν ζωῇ τῇ παρούσῃ καὶ ζῶν ὑπὲρ τὰ ὀρώρενα.

[177] PC 39. 110.

[178] PK 26. 179. Cf. PK 24. 170 (= MC 20. 57): καὶ ἀλλόζωος ὑπὲρ τοὺς φρονοῦντας τὰ ἐν κόσμῳ; ep. 69. 32–3: καὶ μάλιστα ἡμεῖς οἱ καὶ γνώσει καὶ βαθμῷ τῶν πολλῶν διαφέροντες.

[179] PK 26. 180.

Worldliness, in a word, is what keeps a Christian from truly knowing God, from being a 'true' Christian. In his letters to married
people (many of whom belonged to the Byzantine aristocracy),
Theodore is extremely careful to distinguish married life in itself
from worldliness.[180] He does not emphasize what he would feel
free to tell his monks, namely that it takes away from contemplation.[181] In his sermons to his monks, however, marriage with its
earthly worries is frequently associated with the world understood
as a spiritual world which refuses to live according to the commandments of God. Marriage therefore represents the full potential of worldliness.[182] It is the world the monk rejects, for it is
worthless.[183]

The rejection or renunciation (ἀποταγή) of this world, of this
'present age' and all associated with it—parents, friends, home,
city, possessions, and all things associated with the flesh and the
world (τὰ περὶ σάρκα καὶ κόσμον)[184]—was the formal exterior
element of monasticism, of whatever form it took, which distinguished the lifestyle of a monk from that of a lay person.[185]
Without this, Theodore taught, it is extremely difficult for the aver-
age Christian to attain perfection.[186] Rejection of the world
('hatred of the world': τὸ πρὸς τὸν κόσμον μῖσος) for the sake of
the Gospel (cf. Matt. 19: 29; Mark 10: 29; Luke 14: 26, 33; Luke 18:
29), which was an interior value for lay people, was exteriorized to

---

[180] Cf. J. Gouillard, 'La Femme de qualité dans les lettres de Théodore Stoudite', *JÖB*
32/2 (1982), 445–52.
[181] On the anxieties and cares of married life, cf. TC I. 3. 426; *MC* 30. 85 ('we are liberated from the uncertainties of life and safe from its tempests'); *PC* 110. 278, *PC* 131. 334, etc.
Renouncing these cares and anxieties in pursuit of pure contemplation was an ideal of the
Cynics. Cf. J. Gribomont, 'Le Renoncement', 461.
[182] This is how Basil the Great represents marriage in *RF* 5: *PG* 31. 920C–925A. Cf.
Gribomont, 'Le Renoncement', 299 and *passim*.
[183] Cf. TC I. 64. 617; TC I. 67. 627 (τῶν ἐν βίῳ τὰ ἐπίγεια, ὑμῶν τὰ ἐπουράνια·
ἐκείνων ὁ κόσμος, ὑμῶν δὲ ὁ οὐρανός), TC I. 80. 653: οἱ ἐξ εὐτελεστέρου βίου κατὰ
τὸν κόσμον; PK 72. 496, PK 74. 509, PK 102. 742, PK 119. 885, PK 121. 904, etc.
[184] *MC* 68. 190
[185] Cf. *PC* 49. 137, where monastic perfection (ἡ μοναχικὴ τελείωσις) is described as
ἡ ἄρνησις τοῦ κόσμου, ἡ ἀλλοτρίωσις τῆς πατρίδος, τοῦ γένους, τῶν φίλων, τῶν
ἰδίων, ἡ ὑποταγή, ἡ ὑπακοή, ἡ ὁμολογία. On this, see also M. Wawryk, *Initiatio
Monastica*, 4–9.
[186] Cf. *PC* 23. 69, *PC* 52. 143; ep. 395. 23–4. Because of the corruption of the world the
monastic vocation was the means of salvation for many. See below. Cf. St Basil, *RF* 6: *PG*
31. 925AC; *Exhortatio de renuntiatione saeculi et de perfectione spirituale*, *PG* 31. 625C–648C. In the
Moralia Christian life was *not* defined in terms of fleeing the world: Gribomont, 'Le
Renoncement', 292.

the point that a monk could no longer visit his own mother, father or family.[187] Heaven has now taken the place of earth, God the Father in place of parents, the brother monks in place of family, the angels in place of former friends. Jerusalem is one's new city.[188] Some monks even left their wives. This was the case of the monk Pachomios: 'up until his death no one knew that he had separated from his wife and children'.[189] 'What closer bond is there than marriage,' Theodore asks, 'since the two constitute one flesh, according to the Word of God? And yet they too, separated by the sword of the Gospel, are led here.'[190] Where he felt it was right, Theodore would encourage this separation even if the other partner were unwilling.[191]

Because of the difficulties of the Christian vocation in the world, the monastic life was for many the only way to salvation. Entering the monastery was to enter the 'harbour of salvation'.[192] The 'superiority' of the monastic vocation, therefore, with regard to the lay vocation, was that the one was a sure way that led to being a zealous or true Christian, the other was fraught with dangers.[193] Within this context it is a 'more divine life', having 'greater honour'.[194] And yet it was the very same life, based on the same Christian truths, the same way of salvation, the same baptism.

---

[187] Monks were by definition κόσμον μισήσαντες καὶ τὰ περὶ κόσμον (PK 74. 509). Cf. *PC* 131. 335: 'Who does not love and cherish his parents? And yet, leaving them for the love of God (ἐξ ἀγάπης Θεοῦ), the sons of men assemble here.' For lay people, cf. ep. 464.

[188] *MC* 68. 190, *MC* 66. 184, PK 54. 386.

[189] TC I. 59. 604. Cf. *MC* 108. 138; PK 94. 672 ('and some gave up wife and children': καὶ γὰρ τις καὶ γυναῖκα καὶ τέκνα ἐγκαταλέλοιπεν); ep. 323. 10–11 (a handsome young man left his wife to join the monastery); *Iambi* nos. 114–15, 1808CD (in honour of Leon and his wife who separated for the sake of the monastic life). Theodore's own parents separated to embrace monasticism: *Laudatio Platonis* 824B, *Laudatio Funebris* 889C ff.; *Vita B*, 240D.

[190] *PC* 131. 335.

[191] Ep. 396, to the *protospatharia* Albeneka. Basil the Great, in *RF* 12 (whom Theodore refers to in this letter), also refers to the breaking of the marriage bond for the sake of religion: 'We know of many cases, moreover, where the determination to lead a life of chastity prevailed with the aid of earnest prayer and unremitting penance; the Lord inducing those who had been quite obstinate, even, in many instances, by visiting them with bodily illness, to give consent to the right decision.' Cassian had the same attitude: *Collationes* 21, chs. 1–10, *PG* 49. 1169C–1184A.

[192] TC I. 60. 608. On entering the monastery to be saved (i.e. one's only road to salvation), TC I. 44. 560, TC I. 61, 610, TC I. 81. 653; TC III. 24. 48; *MC* 45. 127, *MC* 63. 176; PK 17. 114; *PC* 78. 202, etc.

[193] *MC* 90. 58; *PC* 53. 145; PK 36. 264, ep. 395. 23–5.

[194] *MC* 39. 110; *MC* 82. 23: πρὸς θειοτέραν ζωήν. Elsewhere Theodore denotes it as τὴν κατὰ Θεὸν ζωήν (PK 77. 536, PK 78. 537).

Monasticism, therefore, cannot be anything else but a way of living out one's baptism. Despite what Theodore says of the 'more divine life', he is the first to admit that there are no 'grades of perfection' as such in the Christian vocation.[195] With St Basil, for example, there is perfect identity in the terminology used to qualify monastic life and that used to qualify ordinary Christian life.[196] The same is true for Theodore. For this reason he would insist, contrary to contemporary custom, that there could be only one monastic schema, and not two (Small and Great), since there was but one baptism.[197] Holiness was one as there was but 'one Lord, one faith, one God, one Church'.[198]

As examples of Theodore's baptismal (or common Christian) language for monastic profession and the status of the monk the following can be given: To be a monk is truly to cross the desert away from the servitude of Egypt;[199] it is to move from darkness to light: 'He called us from out of the darkness into his wonderful light, the light of ascetical life.'[200] Monks are therefore those who 'walk in the newness of life';[201] they are 'sons of light' and 'sons of light and day', 'elected and sanctified vessels,' 'children/sons of God', 'disciples of Christ and little children of the Lord', 'sons and inheritors of the Kingdom of heaven', 'adopted in Christ our God', 'the holy people of God', a 'chosen people, holy race, royal priesthood', 'the flock of Christ', 'the Church of Christ'.[202]

---

[195] Cf. Neri, *Basilio di Cesarea*, 71. Dionysios' triad of the lay orders in the *Ecclesiastical Hierarchy* gives a misleading orientation of the true place of monasticism (and the same can be said of clerical orders).

[196] A table of some comparative terminology for St Basil is given in Neri, *Basilio di Cesarea*, 71–4. Basil, in fact, never uses the term 'monks', but 'brethren', or 'true Christians', or simply 'Christians': J. Fedwick, *The Church and the Charisma of Leadership in Basil of Caesarea* (Toronto, 1979), 165 n. 28.

[197] *Testamentum* 1820C; ep. 10. 47–9. Cf. ep. 499. 18–24 (as above), on the rejection of divisions of more perfect and inferior. The Barberini Euchologion, on the contrary, had separate rites for the small and great habits. On this division and its recent origins in relation to Theodore's time, see M. Wawryk, *Initiatio Monastica in Liturgia Byzantina*, OCA 180 (Rome, 1968), 78–103 and *passim*.

[198] Ep. 273. 31–2.   [199] Cf. PK 19. 132 (= *MC* 27. 75).

[200] *MC* 11. 32: ἐκάλεσεν ἡμᾶς ἀπὸ σκότους εἰς τὸ θαυμαστὸν αὐτοῦ φῶς τῆς ἀσκήσεως. Cf. 2 Pet. 2: 9.

[201] *PC* 40. 114.

[202] Cf. TC I. 67. 627, TC I. 84. 658; *MC* 34. 97: καὶ υἱοθετηθῶμεν Χριστῷ τῷ Θεῷ ἡμῶν; *MC* 52. 142; PK 15. 98 (= *MC* 54. 149), *MC* 58. 161, *MC* 62. 174, *MC* 70. 197, *MC* 90. 56; PK 46. 332, PK 57. 407, PK 19. 134 (= *MC* 27, 76): ὡς λαὸς τοῦ Θεοῦ ἅγιος ἐσώμεθα; *Catechesis Chronica* 1700A: ὁ τοῦ Κυρίου λαός; PK 86. 609: ὁ περιούσιος ὡς ἀληθῶς λαός, PK 109. 799: τῶν ὡς ἀληθῶς Χριστοῦ προβάτων, PK 113. 835 (= *MC* 11. 31): τὸ ποίμνιον τοῦ Χριστοῦ, PK 123. 721; ep. 397. 8–9: μία ἐκκλησία κοινοβιακή ἐσμεν.

'Second-Chance' Baptism

Theodore belonged to that ancient and well-established tradition of the East which considered the taking of the monastic habit to be akin to baptism, and to be indeed a sort of 'second' baptism. This was expressed in the rituals of his day for monastic profession.[203] It was a second chance to live out one's baptismal promises: 'How ineffable is (God's) philanthropy!' Theodore exclaims. 'From non-being He brought us into being; having fallen, He made us rise again. Thirdly, He gave us the grace of monastic perfection.'[204] In another sermon he proposes that thanksgiving should initiate prayer; thanksgiving, above all, for the three greatest goods God has given: existence, baptism, and the monastic profession.[205] All three are manifestations of God's life-creating activity; all three acts are acts of goodness and beauty. God 'beautified' us (ἐκάλλυνεν ἡμᾶς) in the first act of creation; He 'beautified' us in baptism, and thirdly, because we did not make proper use of the second, He 'beautified' us through the 'profession of virginity' (ἐν τῷ τῆς παρθενίας ἐπαγγέλματι). What had been lost since baptism is now regained.[206]

According to Gregory Nazianzene the tears of repentance or compunction were a 'fifth' type of baptism that purified the soul from the stain of sin.[207] Penitence and sincere conversion effected God's forgiveness, and the taking of the monastic habit was the commitment to a lifelong project to live in this spirit so as not to be

---

[203] See, on this, E. Malone, 'Martyrdom and Monastic Profession as a Second Baptism', *Vom Christlichen Mysterium*, ed. A. Mayer, J. Quasten, and B. Neunheuser (Düsseldorf, 1951), 115–34; D. F. Vandenbroucke, 'La Profession, second baptême', *La Vie spirituelle*, 76. (1947), 250–63; Wawryk, *Initiatio Monastica*, 3–38; A. Kavanagh, 'Notes on the Baptismal Ethos of Monasticism', *Studia Anselmiana*, 110 (1993), 235–44; P. Raffin, *Les Rituels orientaux de la profession monastique*, 177–181 and *passim*; Hausherr, *Penthos*, 135–51; J. B. Fuertes, 'Professio religiosa, complementum baptismi', *Commentarium pro religiosis et missionaribus*, 43 (1964), 292–319.

[204] *PC* 24. 72.   [205] *PC* 29. 84–5.

[206] *PC* 100. 254; PK 113. 836 (= *MC* 11, 32): ὃς ἦρε τὰ παραπτώματα ἡμῶν καὶ πάλιν ἐκ φιλανθρωπίας διὰ τῆς ἐπενδύσεως τοῦ ἁγίου σχήματος. Cf. PK 9. 59 (= *MC* 87. 45). . . . . πρῶτον μὲν ἐν τῷ δι' ὕδατος καὶ πνεύματος βαπτίσματι, ἔπειτα [δὲ] κατὰ μεγάλην φιλανθρωπίαν Θεοῦ, καὶ ἐν τῷ δευτέρῳ τῆς μετανοίας καὶ ἀποταγῆς βαπτίσματι.

[207] *Or.* 39, *In Sacra Lumina* (εἰς τὰ φῶτα) 17: *PG* 36. 356A. The other types of baptism listed by Gregory are that of Moses (in the cloud and sea), the baptism of John (baptism of repentance), the baptism of blood (of the martyrs), and the baptism of Jesus in the Spirit.

condemned for one's sins. On the vigil of the Feast of Epiphany
Theodore exhorts his listeners:

Let us carry ourselves in spirit to the (river) Jordan; let us see there the
Great Light, our Christ, baptized. Let us kiss in the waters his incomprehensible traces; let us not go back to the darkness of sin, but let us go and
walk with him, as true followers. But beforehand, let us receive baptism
with him, I mean the baptism of tears (τῷ τῶν δακρύων βαπτίσματι
λέγω), for in truth it purifies always luminously (καθαρτήριον καὶ
ἀείφωτον).[208]

It is the tears of repentance and penance, therefore, that purify
and cleanse in the way baptismal water purifies and cleanses.[209] In
a number of places Theodore states or implies that the forgiveness
of sins is actually effected through the reception of the monastic
habit. For example, he tells his brethren that there are two kinds of
moral fall: that committed after the reception of baptism and that
committed after receiving the schema, both being equal moments
of forgiveness of past sin. He recounts how a dying man requested
the schema, to which Theodore agreed, since 'the Lord wants all
to be saved'. This individual was saved because he confessed
before Theodore and to all the brethren when receiving the
habit.[210] Reception of the habit is equivalent to a spiritual birth
because a new bond with the Holy Spirit is formed, who cleanses
and purifies through the habit—the 'tunic of salvation and joy'.[211]
This thinking is clarified in the *Testament*: 'I further confess that the
monastic schema is lofty and sublime. It is angelic and cleanses
every sin by its perfect and complete manner of life (καθαρτικόν
τε πάσης ἁμαρτίας διὰ τελείας ἐπιβιώσεως).'[212] Taking the
habit is equivalent to forgiveness of sin because God looks with
favour on the monastic candidate who is about to embrace the life
of penance:

I have baptized you with this second baptism (ἐβάπτισα τὸ δεύτερον
βάπτισμα τοῦτο); I have clothed you with the tunic of gladness and

---

[208] PK 27. 190–1 (= MC 32. 89).
[209] Cf. TC I. 49 (on passing through the Jordan of tears to enter into the land of eternal life), TC III. 19. 39 (on the ever-flowing and living waters of repentance); PC 2. 13 and PC 56. 154 (on illumination through tears), PC 132. 334 (on purification through tears).
[210] TC I. 27. 522–3.
[211] TC I. 65. 620; MC 15. 42; PK 8. 53, PK 47. 340 (= MC 29. 81): κοινῶς μὲν οἱ πάντες ἐπὶ τοῦ ἁγίου βαπτίσματος, ἰδίως δὲ οἱ ἀπομονάζοντες διὰ τοῦ ἁγίου σχήματος); PK 57. 407, PK 70. 488, PK 111. 817; PC 79. 203.
[212] *Testamentum* 1816C.

chastity; I have absolved the sins that had not been absolved, in the hope that God above will absolve them through my poor absolution of here below, and I have bound unspeakable afflictions in the hope that God above will bind them through my poor binding of here below.[213]

To receive the habit is, like baptism, to receive 'the seal'.[214] The rite of profession, as given in the Barberini codex 336, is structured much like the baptismal ceremony.[215] Preparation on the part of the candidate had to be thorough so that he has an adequate knowledge and understanding of what he is doing, otherwise the whole affair of profession would be pernicious.[216] Once he is prepared the ceremony is performed by a priest in a sacred place, the habit being received in the sanctuary of the church.[217] His words in giving the habit are: 'Our brother N. is clothed in the tunic of gladness, in the name of the Father and of the Son and of the Holy Spirit.'[218] The ritual also considers the taking of the habit to be a second baptism for the remission of sins.[219]

To leave the monastic life was, for Theodore, the same as abandoning the Christian vocation and turning one's back on God: 'Removing the monastic habit is like removing baptism.'[220] For a professed monk to revert to being a layman (τελεῖν ἐν λαϊκοῖς) is like leaving paradise, leaving Christ's flock and Christ's church, subjecting oneself to the devil, turning away from the light and choosing darkness; it was to abandon honour and glory, to go from

---

[213] *MC* 12. 35.

[214] Ep. 549. 63, ep. 447. 14: (τὴν σφραγῖδα τῆς ἁγνείας). On the early use of this term to refer to the habit, cf. Wawryk, *Initiatio Monastica*, 13–14.

[215] For a description of the rite and commentary, see Raffin, *Les Rituels orientaux de la profession monastique*, 38–63.

[216] Ep. 467. 18–19, ep. 486. 51–3.

[217] Ep. 431. 14–15, ep. 536. 15–16, ep. 549. 115–16. The *hegoumenos* receives the candidate and interrogates him, the priest leads the prayers. It is probable that the vesting took place at the entrance to the sanctuary (at the Holy Doors).

[218] Goar, Εὐχολόγιον, 386. For the 'Great' habit, the words are, tunic 'of justice and gladness', ibid. 411. (There are, of course, other components to 'receiving the schema', e.g. receiving the belt, sandals, being tonsured, etc.).

[219] Ibid. 408 (in the Catechesis): Δεύτερον βάπτισμα λαμβάνεις σήμερον, ἀδελφέ, τῇ περιουσίᾳ τῶν τοῦ φιλανθρώπου Θεοῦ δωρεῶν, καὶ τῶν ἁμαρτιῶν σου καθαίρῃ, καὶ υἱὸς φωτὸς γίνῃ, καὶ αὐτὸς Χριστὸς ὁ Θεὸς ἡμῶν συγχαίρει μετὰ τῶν ἁγίων αὐτοῦ ἀγγελῶν ἐπὶ τῇ σῇ μετανοίᾳ . . . (The instructions and the prayers of this service (especially the rite of the Great habit) give a synopsis of the theology of monasticism, expressing in short form much of Theodore's thinking. It would be a useful exercise, and the subject for a possible future paper, to demonstrate the parallels).

[220] Ep. 486. 53: ἀλλὰ γὰρ καὶ ἀποσχηματίζειν μοναχὸν, ἴσον ἐστὶ τῷ ἀποβαπτίζειν.

being free to becoming enslaved, leaving the sacred for the polluted, and changing from one who is beloved to one who is
hated.[221] Rejecting the habit is to leave the conversation of heaven
for the sleep of the dead. 'For what else is it to be in sin, but to be
in death?'[222] The schema is also like the vow of marriage.
Theodore quotes Matthew 19: 6: 'What God has joined, let no
man separate', and then adds, 'If separation is prohibited in carnal
union, how much more so in spiritual union?'[223] The bond of the
monastic profession is a 'pact (σύμβασις) of the Holy Spirit',
vowed before God and men and witnessed by the angels.[224]

The same doctrine of the irrevocable nature of monastic profession is also to be found in the Barberini *Euchologion*:[225]

For you who have begun to advance along the road that leads to the
Kingdom of heaven, it is totally forbidden to turn back, for in this case
you will not be fit for the Kingdom.

Under no account turn back, for fear that you become a pillar of salt like
the wife of Lot, or like the dog that returns to its vomit, for fear, also, that
the word of the Lord be fulfilled: whoever puts his hand to the plough and
turns back is not suited for the Kingdom of heaven

6.6 CONCLUSIONS TO PART III

Holiness was a most serious business. Not only was it open to all,
but it was the duty of every Christian. The formula was straight-
forward: holiness (or its equivalent expressions—sanctification,
divinization, justification, or salvation) was coterminous with
being a 'complete', 'authentic', or *true* Christian. Theodore con-
ceptualized the process of sanctification in terms that were traditional to monasticism, especially Palestinian monasticism. Yet not
to be in monastic habit was no excuse for not being as earnest as a
good monk in making use of all the means the church, in its sanctifying rituals and customs, provides for its children to attain this
goal. Being thoroughly Orthodox was, of course, an essential pre-

---

[221] Ep. 431. 5, ep. 444. 7 ff.; *MC* 82. 24; PK 73. 504, PK 5. 28, PK 113. 835, etc.

[222] Ep. 444. 34–5.

[223] Ep. 530. 39–40. Cf. *MC* 70. 197 (purity to be guarded to preserve the 'indissolubility'
of profession).

[224] Ep. 530. 35–6; TC I. 15. 496, 497 ('you are bound in heaven as on earth, not just by
my ruling but by that of the Holy Spirit'); *MC* 82. 25; PK 9. 59 (= *MC* 87. 45), etc.

[225] Goar, Εὐχολόγιον, 384; 408.

requisite for the effective action of God on the soul. Receiving the help of those ministers of the church who had abandoned the right way was of no avail for one's sanctification and salvation. Indeed, according to Theodore, it jeopardized one's salvation.

The monk was a person who made a second promise to God, the first being that of his baptism. This promise was essentially the renewal of the baptismal promise. It would be appropriate at this concluding point to return to the question of the 'sacramental' nature of monastic consecration or profession. In later tradition this profession was indeed thought of as a sacrament or 'mystery'.

The letter to the monk Gregory, which formed the subject of analysis at the head of the third part of this study, did indeed refer to monastic profession as a μυστήριον.[226] Yet the analysis made in Ch. 4 demonstrated that this terminology had no special significance for Theodore. The 'baptismal' character of profession was not an invention of Theodore's and cannot of itself be advanced as an argument, as some have done, for the 'sacramentality' of monastic profession, in the sense of considering it one of a number (six or more) of church sacraments or *mysteria*.[227] A statement such as 'the theologian of today can hardly accept the teaching of Pseudo-Dionysius and Theodore Studites, who placed monastic profession on a par with the sacraments'[228] expresses a pseudo-problem created by a misreading of both Dionysios and Theodore. If my own understanding of Theodore is correct, the letter to Gregory was nothing more than a rhetorical means of arguing in defence of the monastic institution, and not a listing of sacraments. To him, the 'mystery' of monasticism was apostolic for an obvious reason: it was nothing more nor nothing less than living life according to how the founder of Christianity wanted it. Comparing the *koinobion* to life in apostolic times, Theodore asks, 'How else can we imitate the angels if not in such a life?'[229] The apostolic origins of monasticism, besides, had already been established among monastic authors through Cassian.[230] But what more convincing way to put this across, when engaged in polemic,

---

[226] Ep. 489. 12–13: Τὸ τῶν μοναχῶν σχῆμα παρθενίας ἐστὶν ἐπάγγελμα καὶ μυστήριόν ἐστι μοναχικῆς τελειώσεως . . ..

[227] Cf. Wawryk, *Initiatio Monastica*, 28–32.

[228] Malone, *The Monk and the Martyr*, 142.   [229] PK 75. 514.

[230] In the *Praefatio* to his *Institutions*. On this, see A. De Vogüe, 'Monachisme et église dans la pensée de Cassien', *Théologie de la vie monastique*, 213–40.

than to evoke the authority of the Pseudo-Areopagite who spoke (supposedly) as a witness of the apostolic church? Theodore, however, goes even further than Dionysios, and says that it was Christ himself ('the one who first legislated') who established the rites described in the *Ecclesiastical Hierarchy*.[231] Dionysios made no such explicit claim and this conclusion was Theodore's own inference or was perhaps a belief of the time. Theodore's interest was in showing that whoever attacked the credentials of monasticism was attacking Christ in person. Remove the monasteries and you destroy what Christianity is about. This is the sole message Theodore wanted to communicate. To the extent that later tradition was dependent on the authority of Dionysios and Theodore in postulating monastic profession as a sacrament or mystery, it was wrong.

---

[231] Ep. 489. 14–18.

General Conclusions

This study has attempted to give a new focus to the life and thought of Theodore the Stoudite. Byzantine historians have for long been interested in the facts and circumstances of Theodore's life, but no modern biography exists which brings together the insights gained from the more recent research into the eighth and ninth centuries, integrating these with the fruits of research of historical theologians. For history and theology cannot be separated when one's interest is the life and thought of a religious personality from ninth-century Byzantium. Part I of this work has attempted to give a rounded and comprehensive picture of Theodore's life and times. A review of the wider issues and major personalities of the period has been integrated into an account of the events in which Theodore was personally involved, together with an account of his scholastic formation, sources of thought, writings, and monastic reform.

It is his monastic reform that, although well studied by theologians (especially Julien Leroy OSB), has not been given its due weight by historians. Without an adequate understanding of the thinking behind this reform and of Theodore's religious and theological formation it is impossible to give a fair assessment of his involvement in the major religious issues of his day, namely the 'adulterous' marriage of Emperor Constantine VI, the 'Joseph affair' that followed on this, and the reintroduction of iconoclasm in 815. A reassessment of Theodore's interventions, seen from this perspective of Theodore as a monk and religious thinker, has been the subject of Part II of the book.

This second part, Principles of Order, analysed Theodore's understanding of obedience and authority and, in Ch. 3, of church and emperor. Theodore was a Byzantine, and Byzantines believed in the divinely ordained structures of society. That things should be done with order was a command of the Apostle (1 Cor. 14: 40), which meant a command from God. To keep order was to obey authority, whether this was the authority of God, the legitimate exercise of authority of the emperor, the authority of the church, or the authority of monastic rulers. The principles of order or authorities analysed in Ch. 2 were the commandments of God, monastic rulings, and church ordinances. God's commandments and church ordinances had equal moral binding force, along with the monastic rulings for the monk; they were the means by which holiness was ordered. Disobedience to any detail of this complex of authorities carried with it the potential for eternal damnation.

The commandments of God meant the whole Christian ethic of the New Testament. Anything that was associated with the Gospel or the style of living and thinking of the early Christian communities was understood as being normative for the Christian of any age. Along with this was the example of the Fathers who, as models of Christian living, were considered to be the most authoritative interpreters of the Gospel. Thus Theodore could consider the words of St Basil, to take one example, as having been spoken by the Holy Spirit; the other Fathers were likewise authentic mouthpieces of the Apostles. Theodore's monastic reform was a call to respect anew the witness of these Fathers. It was therefore a call to Byzantine society at large to return to authentic Christianity. Since the monk was nothing but a 'true' Christian, the Christian in the world, it followed, needed to look to the monks (and, by extension, to Theodore himself) to see how the Gospel was optimally to be lived.

The Fathers of the Councils, also, with their deliberations, credal statements, and synodal judgements and canons, offered to the Christian world the Gospel in interpreted, but authentic, form. Their work, if done within the accepted parameters for authoritative pronouncements (unlike the 754 or 815 councils), was the work of the Holy Spirit. It expressed the one and same living stream of tradition that gave continuity to the church's life from the apostolic age onwards.

These principles of order, the principles by which holiness was ordered, seem to have been an unchallenged part of the contemporary Christian world-view, and not just a phenomenon of the monks. The account of the martyrdom of lay Christians in Bulgaria over a rule of fasting (*PC* 63), a good example of the moral rigorism born of these principles, illustrates this point. The Second Council of Nicaea itself shared and propagated this mentality in its formulae and canons.

The Byzantine church of the late eighth and early ninth centuries was a church interested in preserving order and the status quo, rather than in fostering historical self-examination and critical thinking. This is the clear impression left by the iconophiles in their discussions at the Second Nicene Council, to take but one example. Those who are familiar with Theodore's icon theology would agree that this theology had a certain sophistication and refinement. Yet, he too lacked historical perspective, accepting, for example, along with like-minded contemporaries, miracle stories that purported to root icon veneration in apostolic times. In his case this ahistoricism extended to the origins of the monastic institution. Iconoclasts, such as John the Grammarian, may have fared a little better. They were willing to challenge accepted customs (and not just because of the emperor's will). But then, their case was weakened by imperially backed excesses. Yet even they claimed to be inheritors of authentic tradition, and their theology, like iconophile theology, was at the service of tradition (but differently understood). Absolute fidelity to authority or authorities was everybody's concern, for this gave authenticity to the regime of the church.

Theodore's struggles with the imperial authorities over Constantine's marriage and the Joseph affair were all to do with how economy was to be exercised in the church. It has been shown how the division of the opposing parties into 'economizers' as against those who held to *akribeia* or 'the rigorists' is a misleading, not to say false, representation of the terms of the conflict. Theodore accepted the principle of economy of the saints (contrary to what he had been accused of), as expounded by Patriarch Eulogios of Alexandria two centuries previously. The economizers, on their part, also accepted the principles of rigorism or *akribeia* traditional to the church. The conflict was not over the principle of economy but over the limits of its application. Theodore could not accept that the pernicious example of the priest Joseph could offset any good that might come in showing him favour. The Christian life was shaped by example: that of Christ, the apostles, the Fathers of the church, and all the saints. The Christian was to imitate them 'as far as possible'. If a prominent personage in the close-knit Byzantine society were permitted to set an example contrary to what was proper, there would be a corresponding detrimental effect on Christian morals.

It was no doubt an overreaction on Theodore's part to see heresy involved in this dispute—the moechian heresy. But it was an understandable reaction to the equally unmeasured condemnation by the 809 Synod of those who did not accept their synodal decision concerning Joseph. But for both condemners and condemned faith and discipline were so interconnected that disciplinary issues were also faith issues. The result was that both groups could interpret the actions, not just the words, of their opponents as heretical. But why should Theodore feel he could challenge the church of Constantinople? Was it arrogance, or was it politically motivated? A simpler motive is discernible: as it was the monk's professed business to live as a Christian, anything that publicly attacked the integrity of Christian living had to be resisted. Church leaders were required to exercise their ministry in the secular world, and so it was not surprising if on occasion they buckled under its pressure. Monasticism then received a mission to protect Orthodox faith and living.

The emperor had a special role within society. He was head of a Christian empire where it made little sense to separate out church and state. The empire was a Christian body with the emperor as supreme protector of all the interests of its citizens. Theodore accepted the role of the emperor in much the same way as delineated by Justinian in the preface to *Novella* VI. The relationship between emperor and priesthood was a relationship of concord where the former was expected to promote church doctrine and discipline, intervening in the affairs of the church to the degree that served this end. Theodore stood up against the emperor only when this harmony was breached, when the latter manifestly abused his position and promoted what was contrary to good faith and morals (these emperors, incidentally, always worked in conjunction with compliant bishops so as not to be seen to be deciding matters of doctrine). In opposing imperial might Theodore stood in the tradition of a John Chrysostom, a Maximos the Confessor, a John Damascene. But this is not to say, as some have concluded, basing themselves on certain statements taken in isolation, that Theodore was trying to depart from traditional theory concerning church and state or church and emperor. He did not argue for the complete autonomy of the church. After all, Theodore was a Byzantine and thought like a Byzantine. The emperor was what he was— having serious responsibilities towards the church—according to the terms of Christian political Hellenism. But the emperor was not above God's law, and he was subject to divinely established order. If Orthodoxy was threatened through the emperor's sin and through a departure from order, then this was not cause for redefining the emperor's role, but for the sin and disorder to be corrected and for Orthodoxy to be defended and upheld.

Monks were those who feared nothing other than God and the Last Judgement. Their mission in these circumstances was to oppose the emperor and be willing to suffer for the truth. Their example would counterbalance the bad examples of the errant and the submissive.

Part III of the study is entitled Principles of Holiness, and contains three chapters: Rites of Sanctification; Baptism, Eucharist, and Heresy; Sanctification of Lay Person and Monk. The external aspects of the ordering of holiness have been treated in Part II; Part III deals with the means internal to the church of leading its faithful to holiness. By holiness is meant salvation, for the task of the church is to save, to lead its people to their definitive home with God, namely with the saints. The church, as a holy people, lives in anticipation of its end and shares in the holiness of the elect. This it does principally through its rites of sanctification, the first of which are baptism and eucharist. Chapter 4 deals first with the rites of sanctification in general, taking as its starting point the epistle to the monk Gregory with the 'list' of mysteries or sacraments.

Gregory's letter became important in subsequent history because it seemed to present what Dionysios the Pseudo-Areopagite, and then Theodore, believed to be the sacraments (mysteries) of the church—baptism, eucharist, the myron, orders, monastic profession, and burial of the dead. But, as argued in Ch. 4, for neither of these authors was this a list of sacraments. In particular, the idea of monastic consecration being a sacrament/mystery (listed as such, for example, by Symeon of Thessalonike),[1] has no other foundation than a misunderstanding of Dionysios and Theodore; the source of the error is attributable to an early editor of Dionysios' *Ecclesiastical Hierarchy*.

To avoid overemphasis on the terms sacrament or mystery—whose meanings were analysed and found to be polyvalent and ultimately unhelpful—the subsections were listed as ecclesiastical

---

[1] *De Sacramentis* 39, PG 155, 180B. Cf. 177B.

rites of sanctification, corresponding more exactly to the language of the Euchologion of the time, found in the *Codex Barberini gr. 336*. The rites mentioned by Dionysios were commented upon to the extent that these rites are reflected in Theodore's writings, giving them a full context in which to be understood. Liturgical historians, it is hoped, will profit by some of the details noted which reflect ninth-century usage. Examples would be the relationship of marriage to the eucharist and Theodore's symbolism of virginity for the crowns, the nature of penance, and the fact that the priest's (or monk's) role in the process of forgiveness was that of a guarantor and not the means by which the forgiveness of God is effected. Non-clerical absolution of sins, described, for example, in the well-known letter on confession by Symeon the New Theologian,[2] finds its theological rationale in Theodore's writings.

Chapter 5 focused particularly on baptism and eucharist, the latter since early times being commonly designated as 'the mysteries'. A discussion on sacraments administered by heretics led to the conclusion that for Theodore iconoclast sacraments (baptism, eucharist, and orders) were null and non-existent. His position *vis-à-vis* the moechians is less clear, although he did think of their sacraments as being at least somehow defective.

Chapter 6, on the sanctification of lay person and monk, analysed the anthropological foundations for holiness followed by the baptismal framework for a comprehensive theology of holiness. Among the various insights of this section is that the Christian's objective in asceticism was the attainment of the state of *apatheia*, which by no means was opposed to *theoria*, its fruit and natural corollary. Control of unruly passions made it possible to experience the 'sight' of things divine and to re-establish the divine life lost through Adam's sin. Although Theodore's ascetical theology is thoroughly intellectualist in its terminology, following the well-trodden paths of earlier tradition, this is also balanced by a language of aestheticism. God and all of his creation has inherent beauty which is naturally lovable. Theodore's immediate sources for his ascetic theology include St Basil and the Cappadocians, St Dorotheos of Gaza, and the Palestinian school of spirituality.

Holiness has only one source: Christ and the action of the Holy

---

[2] This letter, once attributed to John Damascene, is found in K. Holl, *Enthusiasmus und Bussgewalt heim Griechischen Mönchtum: Eine Studie zu Symeon dem Neun Theologen* (Leipzig, 1898), 110–27.

Spirit. The life of Christ and of the Holy Spirit is conferred with baptism. As there is but 'one Lord, one faith, one baptism', holiness cannot be divided into perfect and imperfect, monastic and lay. Everyone is called to live baptismal life to the full, to live the Gospel to the full, to be a 'true' Christian. The difference between the lay person and the monk lies in the means by which this goal is attained. Virginity, above all, is what separates the two orders. In virginity the distractions of married life, and the worldliness associated with this, are avoided; the life of paradise is therefore more easily and more exactly reappropriated by the monk. Yet, as Theodore points out, there are also seculars who live in virginity who participate in the monastic ethos but without its renunciation or ἀποταγή. This is the second differentiating characteristic separating the monk from the lay world.

Yet lay married life without worldliness as the ideal for all non-monks was recognized and preached by Theodore, even though he insisted on its difficulties. Ultimately there was no difference between the monk and lay person other than the fact that the former avoids by his style of living the distractions and temptations that the latter is exposed to daily.

It is often said that Eastern spirituality looks upon the pious lay person as a monk living in the world (and certainly Orthodox liturgical practices do seem to encourage this perception). Lay Christian life, then, is measured in terms of the monastic ideal. But the real question for an Orthodox believer should be: what actually is a monk? The answer would be that a monk is nothing more than a fervent committed Christian; at least this is the monk's intention when making his profession. Any sharp theoretical distinction and division separating lay person from monk which may have developed historically, between the one aspiring to the perfect Christian life, and the one aspiring for less because of compromise with the world, should be rejected as unfortunate and unbiblical. This is a lesson that can be drawn from Theodore himself.

The development of monasticism could and should be defended as an authentic development of Christianity, as a movement that expresses discontent and dissatisfaction with the values of 'this present age'. But the strength and influence of this movement has often obscured the fact that it is also the Christian in the street who is called to share fully in the perfection of holiness as proposed in the Gospel.

Theodore's theology of holiness, which is a theology of living the reality of one's baptism, is most relevant to the needs of our own Christian age. His theology of second baptism is really a metaphor for a more profound understanding of the implications of being regenerated in the Spirit through the washing of the waters of baptism. Some would find here a metaphor for the modern sacrament of reconciliation. The monastic movement reminds all Christians of their duty to live according to the Gospel. Monasticism itself must be measured against the same rule.

Although it may seem a trite remark, Theodore's insights help one to see that the laity cannot be defined in terms of monasticism and be placed in the shadow of the latter. On the contrary, monks must be defined in terms of the laity. They are not more perfect lay people, but lay people who make a committment to live out their baptismal promises within a protected society with protective rules. Monks are lay people who live within monastery walls. There can only be one holy nation and royal priesthood of the baptized. There is but one λαὸς τοῦ Θεοῦ ἅγιος.

In ending this study some general remarks are called for to place and to interpret the historical importance of Theodore the Stoudite, Byzantine churchman and monastic reformer.

As a man Theodore was an energetic and strong leader with an obviously powerful personality. He was upper class and well educated. Although vowed by profession to abstain from involvement in the affairs of the world his connections enabled him to be effective in speaking out when this duty took priority over seclusion. After all, a monk was but a Christian, Byzantine society was Christian, and so a monk was as entitled as anyone to use his rights as a member of this society. The interaction of church and state, besides, meant that 'political activity' was not by nature restricted to non-churchmen. Theodore could perhaps be described as a politician as long as one keeps in mind that his society was quite different from modern societies where church and state are strictly separated. But one should also remember that, this being the case, Theodore was a reluctant politician. His love was his monastery, his preferred company his monks.

Theodore had obvious influence in the society of his own day. By the force of his personality and convictions he led many to take part in protest action. His leadership in the iconophile protest gained him a permanent place in the list of defenders of the Orthodox faith in the *Synodikon*. But how much influence did he have as a thinker? He was certainly not another John of Damascus, and his icon theology, although subtle and sophisticated, never became official Orthodox teaching. What originality there was in this theology seems to have been more an originality of the age. His monastic theology was even less 'original. He maintained strong views on certain issues, such as not accepting the division of the monastic schema into Great and Small. This division itself seems to have been a relatively recent development but Theodore did not command enough authority to stop it becoming entrenched in tradition. His call to return to the traditions of the Fathers was, in fact, little more than a call to live out the words of the rite of monastic profession already codified in liturgical texts. His own manner of expressing the realities of monastic and Christian living falls within well-established patterns. These patterns were the legacy of Palestinian religious thought and, more remotely, Basilian and Pachomian thought.

The interest in studying Theodore's thought, therefore, lies not in the expectation of discovering originality but in seeing this thought as a mirror of his age. To know how Theodore thought is to be able to assume how others of his day thought. To know what kind of books he read is to feel fairly certain about what books others read. A particular area not covered in this study but of some interest to modern ecumenists is Theodore's thinking on church unity. Not being an original thinker, his views on, for example, the Roman pontiff take on peculiar interest as an expression of ninth-century Byzantine understanding of who and what the pope is.

If it was not as a theorist, neither iconophile nor monastic, that Theodore had any lasting importance, then what was his contribution to subsequent generations? As a preacher he did leave his mark. His *Parva Catechesis* became an extremely popular monastic spiritual reader, and his predilection for Dorotheos of Gaza led to the latter receiving a prominence in the canon of Orthodox authorities that Dorotheos probably would not have otherwise achieved. Theodore himself was an authority for the Stoudite confederation; other monasteries in later ages, such as the Evergetis monastery, likewise looked to him as a guide. But Theodore's real influence was in what he had organized.

So effective were his organizational skills that the rule that was developed, the *Hypotyposis*, became the model for many other monasteries including some on Mount Athos and ancient Russia. In this way also Palestinian liturgical usages, adopted by the Stoudites, were propagated. The activities of the Stoudios monastery itself contributed much to Byzantine society. Scholars have indicated that the monastery, through its *scriptorium*, was a contributing factor to the revival of culture and humanism in the ninth century. Theodore himself places no special importance on this work nor does he indicate that such work was peculiar to Stoudite monasteries. What the Stoudites contributed in this regard was simply the result of having been extremely well organized. For the Stoudites themselves the *scriptorium* was one among many ministries, and not even its most important. The same can be said about its other activities. They were all a means to a more important task—that of holiness. Surprisingly, perhaps, not even icon painting gets a special mention or emphasis, leaving one to wonder to what degree icon veneration was considered an integral part of monastic spirituality.

Theodore contributed to the life of the church not primarily as an intellectual but as an organizer and leader. Tradition has also given Theodore a place amongst its great hymnographers. But his real legacy according to this writer is the legacy of a man of faith who passionately felt he had a special mission to accomplish: the strengthening and defence of the monastic institution. His involvement in other ecclesiastical issues in which venerable traditions of the church were thought to be at stake should be understood always keeping this in mind. Theodore unquestionably fulfilled his ecclesial mission with extraordinary zeal and dedication. Perhaps it is fitting, after all, to remember Theodore the Stoudite, in the words of Anastasius Bibliothecarius, as a *vir valde mirabilis*.

BIBLIOGRAPHY

PRIMARY TEXTS AND TRANSLATIONS OF THEODORE

Letters

Des heiligen Abtes Theodor von Studion Martyrbriefe aus der Ostkirche, ed. B. Hermann (Mainz, 1931).

Opera Varia, v. Sancti Theodori Studitae epistolae, ed. J. Sirmond (Paris, 1696), 221–753.

Theodori Studitae Epistulae, ed. G. Fatouros, Corpus Fontium Historiae Byzantinae, 31/1, 31/2, Series Berolinensis (Berlin and New York, 1992).

Catecheses

Dobrotolubie v russkom perevod, iv (Moscow, 1889; repr. 1901).

Sancti Theodori Studitae Sermones Magnae Catecheseos, ed. J. Cozza-Luzi, in A. Mai, NPB, 9/2 (Rome, 1888); 10/1 (Rome, 1905).

Sancti Theodori Studitae Sermones Parvae Catecheseos, ed. J. Cozza-Luzi, in A. Mai, NPB 9/1 (Rome, 1888).

Théodore Stoudite: Petites Catéchèses, trans. Anne-Marie Mohr. Introduction, notes, bibliography, thematic guide, glossary by Marie-Hélène Congourdeau, 'Les Pères dans la foi', Migne (Paris, 1993).

Τοῦ ὁσίου πατρὸς ἡμῶν καὶ ὁμολογητοῦ Θεοδώρου ἡγουμένου τῶν Στουδίου μικρὰ κατήχησις. Sancti patris nostri confessoris Theodori Studitis praepositi parva catechesis, ed. E. Auvray (Paris, 1891).

Τοῦ ὁσίου πατρὸς ἡμῶν καὶ ὁμολογητοῦ Θεοδώρου ἡγουμένου τῶν Στουδίου μικρὰ κατήχησις, ed. Nikodimos Skretta, *Ὀρθόδοξος Κυψέλη*, ii (Thessalonica, 1984).

Τοῦ ὁσίου Θεοδώρου τοῦ Στουδίτου Μεγάλη Κατήχησις. Βιβλίον δεύτερον. ed. Nikodimos Skretta, *Ὀρθόδοξος Κυψέλη*, 1 (Thessalonica, 1987).

Τοῦ ὁσίου Θεοδώρου τοῦ Στουδίτου Μεγάλη Κατήχησις. Βιβλίον δεύτερον, ἐκδοθὲν ὑπο τῆς Αὐτοκρατορικῆς Ἀρχαιογραφικῆς Ἐπιτροπῆς (St Petersburg, 1904) (known as the Papadopoulos-Kerameus edition).

Tvorenija prepodobnago otsa nashego i ispovidnyka Feodorja Studitja v russkom perevod, 2 vols. (St Petersburg, 1907).

Other works

Anastasius Bibliothecarius Sermo Theodori Studitae de Sancto Bartholomeo Apostolo, text ed. U. Westerbergh, Studia Latina Stockholmiensia, 9 (Stockholm, 1963), 41–8.

CONSTAS, N. P., *Saint Theodore the Studite. The Testament* (Monastery of the Holy Cross: Washington DC, 1991).

DE ROSA, M., *La Dormizione Vitale della Madonna. Panegirici di S. Teodoro Studita.* . . . *Trad. e commentario* [Atessa and Chieti, 1976], 11–20.

'Hymnae Theodori Studiti', *Analecta Sacra Spicilegio Solesmense Parata*, ed. J. B. Pitra (Paris, 1876), i. 336–80.

Laudatio Funebris in Matrem Suam (BHG 2422): A. Mai, NPB 6 (Rome, 1853), ii. 364–78 (repr. *PG* 99. 884–901).

Laudatio Sancti Platonis Hegumeni (BHG, 1553), *AA.SS Aprilis I* (Antwerp, 1675), xlvi–liv (repr. *PG* 99. 804–849).

'Le Panégyrique de S. Théophane le Confesseur par S. Théodore Studite (BHG 1792b). Édition critique du texte intégral', S. Efthymiadis, *AB* 111 (1993), 259–90.

NISSEN, T., 'Das Enkomion des Theodoros Studites auf den heiligen Arsenios', Byzantinisch-neugriechische Jahrbücher, 1 (1920).

ROTH, C. (trans.), *St Theodore the Studite on the Holy Icons* (New York, 1981).

Theodoros Studites, Jamben auf verschiedene Gegenstände: Einleitung, kritischer Text, Übersetzung und Kommentar besorgt von P. Speck, Supplementa Byzantina, 1 (Berlin, 1968).

VAN ESBROECK, M., 'Un Panegyrique de Théodore Studite pour la fête liturgique des sièges de Constantinople', *Studia Anselmiana*, 110 (1993), 525–36.

OTHER PRIMARY TEXTS AND TRANSLATIONS

Acta Romanorum Pontificum a S. Clemente I (an. c. 90) ad Coelestinum III (+1198). Pontificia commissio ad redigendum codicem iuris canonici orientalis. Fontes, Series 3/1 (Rome, 1943).

Acta Sanctorum (1st edn.), collegit I. Bollandus etc. (Antwerp, 1643; Brussels, 1925).

ARRANZ, M., *I Penitenziali Bizantini. Il Protokanonarion o Kanonarion Primitivo di Giovanni Monaco e Diacono e il Deuterokanonarion o 'Secondo Kanonarion' di Basilio Monaco*, Kanonika, 3 (Rome, 1993), 15–129.

AUZÉPY, M.-F., *La Vie d'Étienne le Jeune par Étienne le Diacre. Introduction, Édition et Traduction*. Birmingham Byzantine and Ottoman Mono-graphs, 3 (Ashgate/Variorum, 1997).

Basile de Césarée: Sur le Baptême, ed. J. Ducatillon, *SC* 357 (Paris, 1989).

Basilio di Cesarea, Il battesimo. Testo, trad., introd. e commento, U. Neri, Testi e ricerche di scienza religiosa (Brescia, 1976).

BASIL OF CAESAREA, *Saint Basile: Lettres*, ed. Y. Courtonne, 3 vols. (Paris, 1957, 1961, 1966).

BRIGHTMAN, F. E., *Liturgies Eastern and Western. Being the Texts Original or Translated of the Principal Liturgies of the Church* (Oxford, 1896).

Constantin VII Porphyrogénète: Le Livre des cérémonies, ed. A. Vogt (Paris, 1967), i.

CONYBEARE, F. C. (ed.), *Rituale Armenorum, being the Administration of the Sacraments and the Breviary Rites of the Armenian Church, together with the Greek Rites of Baptism and Epiphany Edited from the Oldest MSS* (Oxford, 1905).

Cyril of Scythopolis: The Lives of the Monks of Palestine, trans. R. M. Price (Kalamazoo, 1991). German original, Eduard Schwartz, *Kyrillos von Skythopolis*, Series Texte und Untersuchungen zur Geschichte der altchristlichen Literatur, 49/2 (Leipzig, 1939).

Corpus Dionysiacum, ed. B. Suchla (vol. i), G. Heil and A. M Ritter (vol. ii), Patristische Texte und Studien, 33, 36 (Berlin and New York, 1990–1).

DIONYSIUS, see *Pseudo-Dionysius*.

DMITRIEVSKIJ, A. A. (ed.), *Opisanie liturgičeskich rukopisej*, 3 vols. (Kiev, 1885–1917).

Dorothée de Gaza: Œuvres Spirituelles, ed. L. Regnault and J De Préville, *SC* 92 (Paris, 1963).

EFTHYMIADIS, S. *The Life of Patriarch Tarasios by Ignatios the Deacon (BHG 1698). Introduction, Text, Translation and Commentary*, Birmingham Byzantine and Ottoman Monographs, 4 (Ashgate/Variorum, 1998).

Georgius Cedrenus Ioannis Scylitzae opera, ed. I. Bekker, CSHB, 2 vols. (Bonn, 1838–9).

Georgius Monachus (Harmatolus), *Chronicon*, ed. C. de Boor, 2 vols. (Leipzig, 1904).

GOAR, J. (ed.), *Εὐχολόγιον sive Rituale Graecorum* . . . , 2nd edn. (Venice, 1730).

GREGORY OF NAZIANZUS, *PG* 35–8; critical edns. with Fr. trans. of the *Orations: Gregoire de Nazianze: Discours*, ed. J. Bernardi *et al.*, SC 9 vols. (vols. 247, 250, 270, 284, 309, 318, 358, 384, 405) (Paris, 1978–95).

HENNEPHOF, H. (ed.), *Textus Byzantinos ad Iconomachiam pertinentes etc.* (Leiden, 1969).

JOANNOU, P.-P., *Fonti*, 9, *Discipline Générale Antique*, Pontificia commissione per la redazione del codice di diritto canonico orientale, 2 vols. in 3 pts. and index (Grottaferrata/Rome, 1962–3): i. pt. 1, 'Les Canons des conciles oecuméniques'; i. pt. 2, 'Les Canons des Synodes Particuliers'; ii, 'Les Canons des Pères Grecs'; Index (1964).

KLIMAKOS, JOHN, *John Climacus, The Ladder of Divine Ascent*, The Classics of Western Spirituality (New York, 1982) (*PG* 88. 631–1164).

KOTTER, B., *Die Schriften des Johannes von Damaskos*, Patristiche Texte und Studien, 2 vols. (Berlin, 1969; 1975).

Martyrologium Romanum ad formam editionis typicae scholiis historicis instructum: *Propylaeum ad AA.SS. Decembris* (Brussels, 1940).

MOSCHOS, JOHN, *The Spiritual Meadow of John Moschos*, trans. J. Wortley, (Michigan, 1992) (*PG* 87. 3. 2855–3112).

Naucratii confessoris encyclica de obitu sancti Theodori Studitae (BHG 1756), ed. F. Combefis: *PG* 99. 1825–49.

Nicephori Archiepiscopi Constantinopolitani Opuscula Historica, ed. C. de Boor, (Leipzig, 1880); *Historia syntomos (Brevarium)*, 1–77.

Œuvres de saint Pakhôme et des ses disciples, ed. Th. Lefort, CSCO (1956), 159–60.

Pachomiana latina, ed. A. Boon (Louvain, 1932).

Patrologiae cursus completus: Series graeca, ed. J.-P. Migne, 161 vols. in 166 pts. (Paris, 1857–66).

Patrologiae cursus completus: Series latina, ed. J.-P. Migne, 221 vols. in 222 pts. (Paris, 1844–80).

PERCIVAL, H. R., *The Seven Ecumenical Councils*, The Nicene and Post-Nicene Fathers, series 2/14 (Edinburgh and Michigan, repr. 1988).

Photius Bibliothèque, ed. R. Henry, Collection Byzantine, 4, (Paris, 1965).

Pseudo-Dionysius: The Complete Works, ed., P. Rorem. The Classics of Western Spirituality (New York, 1987).

Regum libri Quattuor, ed. A. Lesmüller-Werner and H. Thurn (Berlin and New York, 1978).

Sacrorum Conciliorum Nova et Amplissima Collectio etc., ed. I. D. Mansi, 53 vols. in 58 pts. (Paris and Leipzig, 1901–27).

De schismate Studitarum (= *Narratio de sanctis Patriarchis Tarasio et Nicephoro*), *PG* 99. 1849–53.

Scriptor incertus de Leone Armenio, in I. Bekker (ed.), *Leonis Grammatici Chronographia*, CSHB (Bonn, 1842), 335–62.

Synaxarium Ecclesiae Constantinopolitanae: Propylaeum ad AA. SS. Novembris, ed. H. Delehaye (Brussels, 1902; repr. Louvain, 1954).

Synodicon Vetus, ed. J. A. Fabricius and Q. C. Harles, *Bibliotheca graeca* (Hamburg, 1809).

Le Synodikon de l'Orthodoxie, Édition et commentaire, J. Gouillard, *TM* 2 (1967), 1–316.

TANNER, N. (ed.), *Decrees of the Ecumenical Councils*, 2 vols. (London and Georgetown, 1990).

THEOPHANES *The Chronicle of Theophanes: An English Translation of Anni Mundi 6095–6305 (A.D. 602–813), with Introduction and Notes*, H. Turtledove (Philadelphia, 1982).

—— *The Chronicle of Theophanes Confessor*, trans. with introduction and commentary by C. Mango and R. Scott with the assistance of G. Greatrex, Byzantine and Near Eastern History AD 284–813 (Oxford, 1997).

Theophanis Chronographia, ed. C. de Boor, 2 vols. (Leipzig, 1883–5; repr. Hildesheim, 1963).

Theophanes Continuatus [*Chronographia*], ed. I. Bekker, CSHB (Bonn, 1838).
VAN DE VORST, Ch. (ed.), εἰς τὴν ἀνακομιδὴν καὶ κατάθεσιν τῶν λειψάνων τοῦ ὁσίου πατρὸς ἡμῶν καὶ ὁμολογῃ τοῦ Θεοδώρου: 'La Translation de S. Théodore Studite et de S. Joseph de Thessalonique', *AB* 32 (1913), 50–61.
Vita Georgii Amastridos (BHG 668), in V. Vasilievskij, *Trudy*, 3 (Petrograd, 1915), 1–71.
Vita Ioannicii, by Sabas (BHG 935), *AA.SS Novembris II*, 332–83.
Vita Ioannicii, by Petrus (BHG 936), *AA.SS Novembris II*, 384–435.
Vita Nicetae Mediciensis, by Theosteriktos (BHG 1341), *AA.SS Aprilis I*, pp. xviii–xxvii.
Vita Nicolai Studitae (BHG 1365), *PG* 105. 863–925.
Vita Nicephorii, by Ignatios Diakonos (BHG 1335), *Nicephori . . . Opuscula Historica*, 139–217.
Vita Tarasii, by Ignatios Diakonos (BHG 1698), ed. I. A. Heikel, Acta Societatis Scientiarum Fennicae, 17 (1891), 391–439.
Vita Theodori Studitae A (BHG 1755), ed. J. Sirmond, *Opera Varia*, v. 1–79 (repr. *PG* 99. 113–232).
Vita Theodori Studitae B (BHG 1754), A. Mai, NPB 9/2 (Rome, 1853), 293–363 (repr. *PG* 99. 233–328).
Vita Theodori Studitae C (BHG 1755d), ed. B. Latyšev, *VizVrem* 21 (1914), 258–304.
ZACHARIÄ VON LINGENTHAL, C. E., *Collectio Librorum Juris Graeco-Romani Ineditorum* (Leipzig, 1852).

REFERENCE WORKS AND SECONDARY LITERATURE

AHRWEILER, H., 'The Geography of the Iconoclast World', in *Iconoclasm*, ed. A. Bryer and J. Herrin (Birmingham, 1977), 21–7.
ALEXANDER, P. J., 'The Iconoclastic Council of St Sophia (815) and its Definition (*Horos*)', *DOP* 7 (1953).
—— *The Patriarch Nicephorus of Constantinople. Ecclesiastical Policy and Image Worship in the Byzantine Empire* (Oxford, 1958).
—— 'The Strength of Empire and Capital as seen through Byzantine Eyes', *Speculum*, 37 (1962), 339–57.
—— 'Religious Persecution and Resistance in the Byzantine Empire of the Eighth and Ninth centuries: Methods and Justifications', *Speculum*, 52/2 (1977), 238–64.
ALLATIUS, L., 'Diatriba de Theodoris', ed. A. Mai, NPB, 6 (Rome, 1853), 158–68.
AMAND, D., *L'Ascèse monastique de Saint Basile de Césarée: Essai historique* (Maredsous, 1948).
AMANN, E., 'Théodore le Studite', *DTC* (Pt 1, 1946), cli. 267–98.

ANASTOS, M. V., 'The Ethical Theory of Images as Formulated by the Iconoclasts of 754 and 815', *DOP* 78 (1954), 151–60.

—— 'The Argument for Iconoclasm as Presented by the Iconoclastic Council of 754', *Late Classical and Medieval Studies in Honor of Albert Mathias Frend, Jr.* (Princeton, 1955), 177–88.

ARRANZ, M., *Évolution des rites d'incorporation et de réadmission dans l'Église selon l'Euchologe byzantin* (Rome, 1978).

—— 'Christologie et ecclésiologie des prières pour les malades de l'Euchologe slav du Sinaï', in *L'Église dans la liturgie: Conférences Saint-Serge, XXVIᵉ Semaine d'études liturgiques* (Paris, 1979), 19–66.

—— *Istoricheskie zametki o chinoposledovanijakh Tainstv po rukopisjam Grecheskogo Evkhologija (3 Kurs.)* (St Peterburg, 1979).

—— 'Les Sacraments de l'ancien Euchologe constantinopolitain', (1) *OCP* 48 (1982), 284–335; (2) 49 (1983), 42–90, 284–302; (3) 50 (1984), 43–64, 372–97; (4) 51 (1985), 60–86; (5) 52 (1986), 145–78; (6) 53 (1987), 59–106; (7) 55 (1989), 33–62; (8) 57 (1991), 87–143, 309–29; (9) 58 (1992), 23–82, 423–59; (10) 59 (1993), 63–89, 357–86.

AUZÉPY, M.-F., 'La Place des moines à Nicée II (787)', *Byzantion*, 58 (1988), 5–21.

AZKOUL, M., 'Oikonomia and the Orthodox Church', *Patristic and Byzantine Review*, 6 (1987), 65–79.

BACHT, H., 'Pakhôme et ses disciples (IVᵉ siècle)', in *Théologie de la vie monastique*, Théologie Historique, 49 (Paris, 1961), 39–71.

BALDANZA, G., 'Il rito del matrimonio nell'Eucologio Barberini 336. Analisi della sua visione teologica', *EL* 93 (1979), 316–51.

—— 'Il rito matrimoniale dell'Eucologio Sinaitico Greco 958 ed il significato della coronazione nella *ΔΟΧΑ ΚΑΙ ΤΙΜΗ*. Proposte per una ricerca teologica', *EL* 95 (1981), 289–315.

BALFOUR, D., 'Extended Notions of Martyrdom in the Byzantine Ascetical Tradition', *Sobornost*, 5 (1983), 20–35.

BARKER, E., *Social and Political Thought in Byzantium* (Oxford, 1961).

BARNARD, L., 'The Theology of Images', in *Iconoclasm*, ed. A. Bryer and J. Herrin (Birmingham, 1977), 7–13.

BARRINGER, R., 'Ecclesiastical Penance in the Church of Constantinople: A Study of the Hagiographical Evidence to 983 A.D.', D.Phil. dissertation (Oxford, 1979).

—— 'The Pseudo-Amphilochian Life of St Basil: Ecclesiastical Penance and Byzantine Hagiography', *ΘΕΟΛΟΓΙΑ*, 51 (1980), 49–61.

—— 'Penance and Byzantine Hagiography: Le Répondant du péché', *Studia Patristica*, 17/2 (1979; pub. 1982), 552–7.

BAUDINET, M.-J., 'La Relation iconique à Byzance au IXᵉ siècle d'après Nicéphore le Patriarche: Un destin de l'aristotélisme', *Les Études philosophiques*, 1 (1978), 85–106.

BAYNES, N., 'The "Pratum Spirituale"', *OCP* 13 (1947), 404–14.

—— and Moss, H., ed. *Byzantium* (Oxford, 1948).

BECK, H. G., *Kirche und theologische Literatur im byzantinischen Reich* (Munich, 1959).

BEHR, J., *Asceticism and Anthropology in Irenaeus and Clement*, Oxford Early Christian Studies (Oxford, 2000).

BERNARDAKIS, P., 'Les Appels au pape dans l'église grecque jusqu'à Photius', *EO* 6 (1903), 249–57.

BORNERT, R., *Les Commentaires byzantins de la Divine Liturgie du VIIe au XVe siècle* (Paris, 1966).

BOUYER, L., *Mystery and Mysticism* (New York, 1956).

BRÉHIER, L., *La Civilisation byzantine* (Paris, 1950).

BROWN, P., 'A Dark-Age Crisis: Aspects of the Iconoclast Controversy', *English Historical Review*, 88 (1973), 1–34.

BRUBAKER, L. (ed.), *Byzantium in the Ninth Century: Dead or Alive?* Papers from the Thirtieth Spring Symposium of Byzantine Studies, Birmingham, March 1996 (Aldershot etc., 1998).

BURTON-CHRISTIE, D., *The Word in the Desert. Scripture and the Quest for Holiness in Early Christian Monasticism* (New York and Oxford, 1993).

BURY, J. B., *A History of the Eastern Roman Empire from the Fall of Irene to the Accession of Basil I (A.D. 802–867)* (London, 1912; repr. New York, 1965).

—— *A History of the Later Roman Empire from Arcadius to Irene (395 A.D. to 800 A.D.)* (London, 1889; repr. Amsterdam, 1966), ii.

CALLAHAN, J., 'Greek Philosophy and the Cappadocian Cosmology', *DOP* 12 (1958), 31–57.

CAMERON, A., *Continuity and Change in Sixth-Century Byzantium* (London, 1981).

—— 'The Language of Images: The Rise of Icons and Christian Representation', in D. Wood (ed.), *The Church and the Arts*. Studies in Church History, 28 (Oxford, 1992), 1–42.

CHADWICK, H., 'John Moschus and his friend Sophronius the Sophist', *JTS* NS 25 (1974), 41–74.

CHARANIS, P., 'The Monk as an Element in Byzantine Society', *DOP* 25 (1971), 63–84.

CHITTY, D. J., *The Desert a City: An Introduction to the Study of Egyptian and Palestinian Monasticism under the Christian Empire* (Crestwood, NY, 1995; 1st edn. Oxford, 1966).

COLONNA, M. E., *Gli storici bizantini dal IV al XV secolo: i. Storici Profani* (Naples, 1956).

CONGAR, Y., 'Neuf cents ans après. Notes sur le "Schisme oriental"' in *1054–1954: L'Église et les églises. Neuf siècles de douloureuse séparation entre l'Orient et l'Occident. Études et travaux sur l'Unité chrétienne offerts à Dom Lambert Beauduin*, 2 vols. (Brussels, 1954), i. 3–95.

—— *L'Ecclésiologie du haut Moyen Age. De Saint Grégoire le Grand à la désunion entre Byzance et Rome* (Paris, 1968).

258 *Bibliography*

CONGOURDEAU, M.-H., 'Théodore Stoudite', *DS* 15 (1990), 401–14.
CORMACK, R., *Writing In Gold. Byzantine Society and its Icons* (London, 1985).
COSTA-LOUILLET, G. da, 'Saints de Constantinople au VIIIᵉ, IXᵉ et Xᵉ siècles', *Byzantion*, 24 (1954–6), 179–263, 453–511; 25–7 (1957), 783–852.
CROUZEL, H., 'Origène: Précurseur du monachisme', in *Théologie de la vie monastique*, Théologie Historique, 49 (Paris, 1961), 15–38.
CUPANE, C., 'Appunti per uno studio dell'oikonomia ecclesiastica', *JÖB* 38 (1988), 53–73.
DAMIAN, T., 'The Icons: Theological and Spiritual Dimensions According to St Theodore of Studion', Ph.D. dissertation (Fordham University, 1993).
DANIÉLOU, J., *Sacramentum Futuri: Études sur les origines de la typologie biblique* (Paris, 1950).
—— *Bible et Liturgie* (Paris, 1951).
—— 'Saint Grégoire de Nysse dans l'histoire du monachisme', *Théologie de la vie monastique*, Théologie Historique, 49 (Paris, 1961), 131–41.
DARROUZÈS, J., *Documents inédits d'ecclésiologie byzantin* (Paris, 1966).
—— 'Le Patriarche Méthode contre les Iconoclastes et les Stoudites', *REB* 45 (1987), 15–57.
DAUVILLIER, J. and CLERCQ, C., DE *Le Marriage en droit canonique orientale* (Paris, 1936).
Delehaye, H., 'Stoudion—Stoudios', *AB* 52 (1934), 64–6.
DEVREESSE, R., 'Une lettre de S. Théodore Studite relative au synode moechien', *AB* 68 (1950), 44–57.
DIEHL, C., *Byzantine Portraits* (New York, 1927).
—— *Byzantine Empresses* (London, 1964) = *Figures Byzantines* (Paris, 1906).
DOBROKLONSKIJ, A. P., *Prepodobnij Feodor, ispovednik i igumen Studijskij. i. Ego epoha, dzizn i deyatelnost. ii. Ego tvoreniya* (Odessa, 1913–14).
DOBSCHÜTZ, E. VON, 'Methodios und die Studiten. Strömungen und Gegenströmungen in der Hagiographie des 9. Jahrhunderts', *BZ* 18 (1909), 41–105.
DODD, C. H., *Gospel and Law: The Relation of Faith and Ethics in Early Christianity* (Cambridge, 1950).
DRAGAS, G., Introduction to the facsimile of the 1860 Paris 1st edn. of *PG* 99, *S.P.N. Theodori Studitae Opera Omnia* (Centre for Patristic Publications, Athens, 1988), 7–14.
DUJČEV, I., 'San Teodoro Studita ed i Bulgari', *Bulletino dell'Istituto storico Italiano per il medio evo e Archivio Muratoriano*, 73 (1961), 71–83.
DUMEIGE, G., *Nicée II*, Histoire des conciles oecuméniques (Paris, 1978).
DVORNIK, F., *Les Légendes de Constantin et de méthode vues de Byzance* (Prague, 1933).
—— *Byzance et la primauté romaine* (Paris, 1964) (= *Byzantium and the Roman Primacy*, 2nd edn. (New York, 1979)).

—— *Early Christian and Byzantine Political Philosophy: Origins and Background*, Dumbarton Oaks Studies, 9, 2 vols. (Washington, 1966).

—— 'Constantinople and Rome', *The Cambridge Medieval History*, iv. I. ch. 10, 431–72.

EFTHYMIADIS, S., 'The Vita Tarasii and the hagiographical work of Ignatios the Deacon: A Contribution to the Study of Byzantine Hagiography', D.Phil. dissertation (Oxford, 1991).

EHRHARD, A., *Überlieferung und Bestand der hagiographischen und homiletischen Literatur der griechischen Kirche* (Leipzig, 1937), i.

ÉMEREAU, C., 'Hymnographi byzantini', *EO* 24 (1925), 177–9; 25 (1926), 178.

Encyclopedia of the Early Church, ed. A. di Berardino. Trans. from the Italian by A. Walford, 2 vols. (Cambridge, 1992).

ERICKSON, J. H., 'Oikonomia in Byzantine Canon Law', in K. Pennington and R. Somerville (eds.), *Law, Church and Society: Essays in Honor of Stephen Kuttner* (Philadelphia, 1977), 225–36.

—— 'Penitential Discipline in the Orthodox Canonical Tradition', *SVThQ* 21 (1977), 191–206.

—— 'Reception of Non-Orthodox into the Orthodox Church', *Diakonia*, 19 (1984–5), 68–86.

—— *The Challenge of Our Past* (Crestwood, NY, 1991).

ESQUERDA BIFET, J., 'Culto y devoción mariana en San Teodoro Estudita', *Burgense*, 13 (1972), 445–55.

FEATHERSTONE, J., and HOLLAND, M., 'A Note on Penances Prescribed for Negligent Scribes and Librarians in the Monastery of Studios', *Scriptorium*, 36 (1982), 258–60.

FEDWICK, J. F., *The Church and the Charisma of Leadership in Basil of Caesarea* (Toronto, 1979).

FRAIGNEAU-JULIEN, B., *Les Sens spirituels et la vision de Dieu selon Syméon Le Nouveau Théologien*, Théologie Historique, 67 (Paris, 1985).

FRAZEE, C., 'St Theodore of Studios and Ninth Century Monasticism in Constantinople', *Studia Monastica*, 23 (1981), 27–58.

FUENTES ALONSO, J. A., *El divorcio de Constantino VI y la doctrina matrimonial de San Teodoro Estudita* (Pamplona, 1984).

—— '"Oikonomia" en la iglesia bizantina ante el divorcio de Constantino VI', in *Hispania Christiana: Estudios en honor del J. Orlandis Rovira 24* (Pamplona, 1988), 239–55.

FUERTES, J. B., 'Professio religiosa, complementum baptismi', *Commentarium pro religiosis et missionaribus*, 43 (1964), 292–319.

GARDNER, A., *Theodore of Studium, his Life and Times* (London, 1905).

GARSOÏAN, N. G., 'Byzantine Heresy: A Reinterpretation', *DOP* 25 (1971), 85–114.

GEANAKOPLOS, D. J., *Byzantine East and Latin West* (Oxford, 1966).

GEMMITI, D., *Teodoro Studita e la questione Moicheiana* (Naples, 1993).

GERO, S., *Byzantine Iconoclasm During the Reign of Leo III, with Particular Attention to the Oriental Sources*, CSCO 346 suppl. 41 (Louvain, 1973).

GERO, S., 'Notes on Byzantine Iconoclasm in the Eighth Century', *Byzantion*, 44 (1974), 23–42.

—— 'The Eucharistic Doctrine of the Byzantine Iconoclasts and its Sources', *BZ* 68 (1975), 4–22.

—— 'The Resurgence of Byzantine Iconoclasm in the Ninth Century According to a Syriac Source', *Speculum*, 51 (1976), 1–5.

—— *Byzantine Iconoclasm During the Reign of Constantine V, with Particular Attention to the Oriental Sources*, CSCO 348 suppl. 52 (Louvain, 1977).

—— 'Byzantine Iconoclasm and Monachomachy', *JEH* 28 (1977), 241–8.

GESTEIRA GARZA, M., 'La Eucaristía, imagen de Cristo? Ante el 12º centenario del Concilio 2º de Nicea', *Rivista espanola de teología* (1987), 281–339.

GILL, J., 'St Theodore the Studite against the Papacy?', *BF* 1 (1966), 115–23.

—— 'An Unpublished Letter of St Theodore the Studite', *OCP* 34 (1968), 62–9.

GOUILLARD, J., 'L'Église d'Orient et la Primauté Romaine au temps de l'Iconoclasme', *Istina*, 21 (1976), 25–54.

—— 'La Femme de qualité dans les lettres de Théodore Studite', *JÖB* 32/2 (1982), 445–52.

GOULD, G., 'Ecclesiastical Hierarchy in the Thought of Pseudo-Dionysius', in *Studies in Church History*, 26 (Oxford, 1989), 29–42.

GRABAR, A., *L'Empereur dans l'art byzantin* (Paris, 1936).

—— *L'Iconoclasme byzantin: Le Dossier archéologique*, 2nd edn. (Paris, 1984).

GREENFIELD, R., *Traditions of Belief in Late Byzantine Demonology* (Amsterdam, 1988).

GREENSLADE, S. L., *Schism in the Early Church* (London, 1953).

GRIBOMONT, J., 'Obéissance et Évangile selon saint Basil le Grand', in *Supplément de la Vie Spirituelle*, 5 (1952), 192–215.

—— 'Les Règles morales de saint Basile et le Nouveau Testament', *Studia Patristica*, 2 (= TU 64) (Berlin, 1957), 416–26.

—— 'Le Renoncement au monde dans l'idéal ascétique de saint Basile', *Irénikon*, 31 (1958), 282–307, 460–75.

—— 'Commandements du Seigneur et libération évangélique: Saint Basile', *Studia Anselmiana*, 70 (1977), 81–105.

GROSSU, N., *Prepodobnij Teodor Studit: Ego vremya i tvoreniya* (Kiev, 1907).

GRUMEL, V., 'Saint Théophane le Chronographe et ses rapports avec saint Théodore Studite', *VizVrem* 9 (1902), 31–102.

—— 'L'iconologie de saint Théodore Studite', *EO* 20 (1921), 257–68.

—— *Les Regestes des actes du patriarcat de Constantinople*. i. Les Actes des patriarches, pt. II; 'Les Regestes de 715 à 1043', Le Patriarcat byzantin, 1 (Paris 1936).

—— 'Jean Grammaticos et saint Théodore Studite', *EO* 36 (1937), 181–9.

—— 'Les Relations politico-religieuses entre Byzance et Rome sous le règne de Léon V l'Arménian', *REB* 18 (1960), 19–44.

HALDON, J. F., *Byzantium in the Seventh Century: The Transformation of a Culture* (Cambridge, 1990).

HALKIN, F., *Bibliotheca Hagiographica Graeca*, 3rd edn. (Brussels, 1957).

HARVEY, A. E., 'The Use of Mystery Language in the Bible', *JTS* NS 31 (1980), 320–36.

HATLIE, P., 'Abbot Theodore and the Stoudites: A Case Study in Monastic Social Groupings and Religious Conflict in Constantinople (787–826)', Ph.D. dissertation (Fordham University, 1993).

—— 'Theodore of Stoudios, Pope Leo III and the Joseph Affair (808–812): New Light on an Obscure Negotiation', *OCP* 61 (1995), 407–23.

—— 'The Politics of Salvation: Theodore of Stoudios on Martyrdom (*Martyrion*) and Speaking Out (*Parrhesia*)', *DOP* 50 (1996), 263–87.

—— 'Women of Discipline during the Second Iconoclastic Age', *BZ* 89 (1996), 37–44.

HAUSHERR, I., *Saint Théodore Studite: L'Homme et l'ascète (d'après ses catéchèses)*, Orientalia Christiana, 6/1 (Rome, 1926).

—— 'Les Grands Courants de la spiritualité orientale', *OCP* 1 (1935), 114–38.

—— *Penthos: La Doctrine de la componction dans l'orient chrétien*, OCA 132 (Rome, 1944) (= *Penthos. The Doctrine of Compunction in the Christian East*, trans. A. Hufstader, Cistercian Studies, 53 (Kalamazoo, 1982)).

—— *Direction spirituelle en orient autrefois*, OCA 144 (Rome, 1955) (= *Spiritual Direction in the Early Christian East*, trans. A. P. Gythiel, Cistercian Studies, 116 (Kalamazoo, 1990)).

—— 'L'Hésychasme', *OCP* 22 (1956), 5–40, 247–85.

—— 'La Théologie du monachisme chez saint Jean Climaque', in *Théologie de la vie monastique*, Théologie Historique, 49 (Paris, 1961), 385–410.

HEAD, C., *Justinian II of Byzantium* (Madison, 1972).

HENRY, P., 'Theodore of Studios, Byzantine Churchman', Ph.D. dissertation (Yale University, 1968).

—— 'The Moechian Controversy and the Constantinopolitan Synod of January A.D. 809', *JTS* NS 20 (1969), 495–522.

—— 'Initial Eastern Assessments of the Seventh Oecumenical Council', *JTS* NS 25 (1974), 75–92.

—— 'What Was the Iconoclastic Controversy About?', *Church History*, 45 (1976), 16–31.

—— 'Images of the Church in the Second Nicene Council and in the *Libri Carolini*', in K. Pennington and R. Somerville (eds.), *Law, Church and Society*, 237–52.

HENRY, P., 'The Formulators of Icon Doctrine', in P. Henry (ed.), *Schools of Thought in the Christian Tradition* (Philadelphia, 1984), 75–89.

HERGENROTHER, J., *Photius, Patriarch von Konstantinopel: Sein Leben, seine Schriften und das griechische Schisma nach handschriftlichen undgedruckten Quellen* (Regensburg, 1867; repr. Darmstadt, 1966), i.

HERMAN, E., ʽΕὐχὴ ἐπὶ διγάμων᾽, *OCP* 1 (1935), 467–89.

—— *Textus selecti ex operibus commentatorum byzantinorum iuris ecclesiastici*, ed. I. Croce, Fonti, S. Congregazione per la chiesa orientale, Codificazione canonica orientale, 2/5 (Vatican City, 1939), 7–35, esp. 10–11.

—— 'Il più antico penitenziale greco', *OCP* 19 (1953), 71–127.

HERMANN, B., *Theoktista aus Byzanz, die Mutter zweier Heiligen* (Freiberg, 1919).

—— 'Eucharistische Sitten im Leben des hl. Theodor Studites', *Liturgie und Kunst*, 4 (1923), 76–80.

—— 'Der hl. Abt Theodor von Studion (+11 Nov. 826): Erneuerer des basilianischen Mönchtum, im Lichte seiner Schriften', *Benediktinische Monatschrift*, 7 (1925), 418–35.

—— 'Bekennertum des hl. Abtes Theodor von Studion und seiner Mönche', *Benediktinische Monatschrift*, 8 (1926), 31–45, 111–24.

—— 'Der hl. Abt Theodor, der asketische Meister von Studium und die Studient Mönche', *Zeitschrift für Askese und Mystik*, 4 (1929), 289–312; ibid. 5 (1930), 121–47.

HERRIN, J., 'The Context of Iconoclast Reform', in *Iconoclasm*, ed. A. Bryer and J. Herrin (Birmingham, 1977), 15–20.

—— *The Formation of Christendom* (London, 1989).

HOTZ, R., *Sakramente—im Wechselspiel zwischen Ost und West* (Cologne, 1979).

L'HUILLIER, P., 'L'Économie dans la tradition de l'Église Orthodoxe', *Kanon*, 6, Yearbook of the Society for the Law of the Oriental Churches (Vienna, 1983), 19–38.

—— *The Church of the Ancient Councils: The Disciplinary Work of the First Four Ecumenical Councils* (Crestwood, NY, 1996).

HUSSEY, J. M. (ed.), *The Cambridge Medieval History* (Cambridge, 1966), iv.

—— *The Byzantine World*, 3rd edn. (London, 1967).

—— 'Byzantine Monasticism', in *Camb. Med. Hist.* iv, II. 161–84.

—— *The Orthodox Church in the Byzantine Empire* (Oxford, 1984).

Iconoclasm, Papers given at the Ninth Spring Symposium of Byzantine Studies, University of Birmingham, March 1975, ed. A. Bryer and J. Herrin (Birmingham, 1977).

ISČENKO, D. S., 'La Publication des Catéchèses de Théodore Studite à Byzance et les Slaves', *VizVrem* 40 (1979), 157–71.

JANIN, R., *La Géographie ecclésiastique de l'empire byzantin*, i. *Le Siège de Constantinople et le patriarcat oecuménique*, iii. *Les églises et les monastères* (Paris, 1969).

—— *Les Églises et monastères des grands centres byzantins: Bithynie, Hellespont, Latros, Galesios, Trebizonde, Athènes, Thessalonique* (Paris, 1975).

JUGIE, M., 'La Doctrine mariale de saint Théodore Studite', *EO* 25 (1926), 421–7.

—— *Theologia Dogmatica Christianorum Orientalium.* 5 vols. (Paris, 1930), iii.

KARAGIANNOPOULOS, I. E., and WEISS, G., *Quellenkunde zur Geschichte von Byzanz (324–1453)* (Wiesbaden, 1982), ii.

KARLIN-HAYTER, P., 'A Byzantine Politician Monk: Saint Theodore Stoudite', *JÖB* 44 (1994), 217–32.

KAVANAGH, A., 'Notes on the Baptismal Ethos of Monasticism', *Studia Anselmiana*, 110 (1993), 235–44.

KAZHDAN, A., 'Hermitic, Cenobitic and Secular Ideals in Byzantine Hagiography of the Ninth Century', *Greek Orthodox Theological Review*, 30 (1985), 473–87.

KUCHAREK, C., *The Sacramental Mysteries: A Byzantine Approach* (Allendale, NJ, 1976).

LADNER, G., 'Origin and Significance of the Byzantine Iconoclastic Controversy', *Medieval Studies*, 2 (1940), 127–49.

—— and SYMONDS, H. E., *The Church Universal and the See of Rome. A study of the relations between the Episcopate and the Papacy up to the Schism between East and West* (London, 1939).

LAIOU, A. E., and SIMON, D. (eds.), *Law and Society in Byzantium, Ninth–Twelfth Centuries* (Washington DC, 1994).

LAMPE, G. W. H., *The Seal of the Spirit: A Study in the Doctrine of Baptism and Confirmation in the New Testament and the Fathers* (London, 1951).

—— *A Patristic Greek Lexicon* (Oxford, 1961).

LANNE, E., 'Le Mystère de l'Église dans la perspective de la théologie Orthodoxe', *Irénikon*, 35 (1962), 171–212.

LASCARIS, A. F., 'The "Monastic" Ecclesiology of the Byzantine Church', *Communio*, Commentarii Internationales de Ecclesia et Theologia, 3 (Seville, 1970), 145–74.

LATYŠEV, B., 'Vita S. Theodori Studitae in codice Mosquensi musei Rumianzoviani n° 520', *VizVrem* 21 (1914), 258–304.

LEMERLE, P., *Le Premier Humanisme byzantin: Notes et remarques sur enseignement et culture à Byzance des origines au Xe siècle* (Paris, 1971).

LEROUX, J.-M., 'Monachisme et communauté chrétienne d'après saint Jean Chrysostome', in *Théologie de la vie monastique*, Théologie Historique, 49 (Paris, 1961), 143–90.

LEROY, J., 'Les capitula ascetica de Saint Théodore Studite', *Revue d'Ascétique et de Mystique*, 27/106 (1951), 175–6.

—— 'La Vie quotidienne du moine studite', *Irénikon*, 27 (1954), 21–50.

—— 'Le Cursus canonique chez Saint Théodore Studite', *EL* 68 (1954), 5–19.

LEROY, J., 'Un nouveau témoin de la Grande Catéchèse de St Théodore Studite', *REB* 15 (1957), 73–88.

—— 'La Réforme studite', in *Il monachesimo orientale. Atti del convegno di studi orientali che sul predetto tema si tenne a Roma, sotto la direzione del pontificio istituto orientale, nei giorni 9, 10, 11 e 12 Aprile 1958*, OCA 153 (Rome, 1958), 181–214.

—— 'Les Petites Catéchèses de S. Théodore Studite', *Le Muséon*, 71 (1958), 329–58.

—— 'Un témoin ancien des petites catéchèses de Théodore Studite', *Scriptorium*, 15 (1961), 36–60.

—— 'S. Théodore Studite', in *Théologie de la vie monastique*, Théologie Historique, 49 (Paris, 1961), 423–36.

—— *Studitisches Mönchtum, Spiritualität und Lebensform*, Geist und Leben der Ostkirche, 4 (Graz, 1969).

—— 'L'Influence de saint Basile sur la réforme studite d'après les Catéchèses', *Irénikon*, 52 (1979), 491–506.

—— 'Études sur les "Grands Catéchèses" de S. Théodore Studite, Studi e Testi' (pro manuscripto).

LOMBARD, A., *Constantin V, empereur des Romains (740–775)* (Paris, 1902).

LOT-BORODINE, M., 'Le Mystère des larmes', *Vie spirituelle*, 48 (1936), 65–110.

LOUTH, A., *The Origins of the Christian Mystical Tradition: From Plato to Denys* (Oxford, 1981).

—— 'Pagan Theurgy and Christian Sacramentalism in Denys the Areopagite', *JTS* NS 37 (1986), 432–8.

—— *Denys the Areopagite* (London, 1989).

MALONE, E., 'Martyrdom and Monastic Profession as a Second Baptism', in A. Mayer, J. Quasten, and B. Neunheuser (eds.), *Vom Christlichen Mysterium* (Düsseldorf, 1951), 115–34.

—— 'The Monk and the Martyr', *Studia Anselmiana*, 38 (1956), 201–28.

MANGO, C., 'The Availability of Books in the Byzantine Empire, A.D. 750–850', in *Byzantine Books and Bookmen*, a Dumbarton Oaks Colloquium (Washington DC, 1975), 29–45.

—— 'Historical Introduction', in A. Bryer and J. Herrin (eds.), *Iconoclasm* (Birmingham, 1977), 5–6.

—— 'The Liquidation of Iconoclasm and the Patriarch Photios', in Bryer and Herrin (eds.), *Iconoclasm*, 133–4.

—— 'Who Wrote the Chronicle of Theophanes?', *Zbornik radova Visantološkog Instituta*, 18 (1978), 9–17.

—— 'The Date of the Studius Basilica at Istanbul', *BMGS* 4 (1978), 115–22.

—— *Byzantium: The Empire of the New Rome* (London, 1980).

—— *The Art of the Byzantine Empire 312–1453: Sources and Documents* (Englewood Cliffs, NJ, 1972; repr. Toronto, 1986).

MARIN, E., *De Studio coenobio Constantinopolitano* (Paris, 1893).

—— *Les Moines de Constantinople depuis la fondation de la ville jusqu'à la mort de Photius (330–898)* (Paris, 1897).

—— *Saint Théodore (759–826)* (Paris, 1906). Italian edn., *San Teodoro* (Rome, 1908).

MARSH, H.G., 'The Use of μυστήριον in the Writings of Clement of Alexandria with Special Reference to his Sacramental Doctrine', *JTS* 37 (1936), 64–80.

MARTIMORT, A. G. (ed.), *L'Église en prière: Introduction à la liturgie. III, Les Sacrements* (Bruges, 1984). Trans. M. J. O'Connell (new edn.), *The Church at Prayer*, iii. *The Sacraments* (Minnesota, 1988).

MARTIN, E. J., *A History of the Iconoclastic Controversy* (London, 1930; repr. New York, 1978).

MATEOS, J., *Le Typicon de la Grande Église*, *OCA* 166 (Rome, 1963), ii.

DE MEESTER, P., *De monachico statu iuxta disciplinam byzantinam: Statuta selectis fontibus et commentariis instructa* (Sacra congregazione per la chiesa orientale. Codificazione canonica orientale, fonti, 2/10) (Vatican City, 1942).

MEYENDORFF, J., 'L'Image du Christ d'après Théodore Studite', *Synthronon*, 3 (Paris, 1967).

—— *Byzantine Theology: Historical Trends and Doctrinal Themes*, 2nd edn. (New York, 1979).

MINISCI, T., 'Riflessi studitani nel monachesimo orientale', in *Il monachesimo orientale*, *OCA* 153 (1958), 215–33.

MOGENET, H., 'L'Obéissance religieuse, vertu évangelique et humaine', *Revue d'Ascétique et de Mystique*, 27 (1951), 75–95.

MORRIS, R., *Monks and Laymen in Byzantium 843–1118* (Cambridge, 1995).

MOFFATT, A., 'Schooling in the Iconoclast Centuries', in *Iconoclasm*, ed. A. Brier and J. Herrin (Birmingham, 1977), 85–92.

MULLETT, M., and KIRBY, A. (eds.), *The Theotokos Evergetis and Eleventh-Century Monasticism* (Belfast, 1994).

NERI, U., see under *Basilio di Cesarea. Il battesimo.*

NIAVIS, P. E., *The Reign of the Byzantine Emperor Nicephorus I (AD 802–811)* (Athens, 1987).

O'CONNELL, P., 'The Letters and Catecheses of St Theodore Studites', *OCP* 38 (1972), 256–9.

—— *The Ecclesiology of St Nicephorus I (758–828), Patriarch of Constantinople: Pentarchy and Primacy*, *OCA* 194 (Rome, 1972).

ORPHANOS, M. A., *Creation and Salvation according to St Basil of Caesarea* (Athens, 1975).

OSTROGORSKY, G., *Studien zur Geschichte des byzantinischen Bilderstreites* (Breslau, 1929).

—— 'Les Débuts de la querelle des images', *Mélanges Charles Diehl* (Paris, 1930), i. 235–55.

—— *History of the Byzantine State*, 2nd edn. (Oxford, 1968).

Oxford Dictionary of Byzantium, ed. A. P. Kazhdan, A.-M. Talbot, A Cutler, T. E. Gregory, N. P. Ševčenko, 3 vols. (Oxford and New York, 1991).

PAPACHRYSSANTHOU, D., 'La Vie monastique dans les campagnes Byzantines du VIIIᵉ au XIᵉ siècle: Ermitages, groupes, communautés', *Byzantion*, 43 (1973), 159–80.

PAPADOPULOS, C., "Ὁ Ἅγιος Θεόδωρος Στουδίτης ἐν τῷ ἀγῶνι αὐτοῦ ὑπὲρ τῶν ἱερῶν εἰκόνων', Ἐπετηρὶς Βυζαντινῶν Σπουδῶν, 15 (1939), 3–87.

PARGOIRE, J., 'Une loi monastique de S. Platon', *BZ* 8 (1899), 98–106.

—— 'Les Débuts du monachisme à Constantinople', *Revue des questions historiques*, 65 (1899), 101–13.

—— 'A quelle date l'higoumène saint Platon est-il mort?', *EO* 4 (1900–1), 164–70.

—— 'Saint Théophane le Chronographe et ses rapports avec Saint Théodore Studite', *VizVrem* 9 (1902), 31–102.

—— 'La Bonita de S. Théodore Studite', *EO* 6 (1903), 207–12.

—— *L'Église Byzantine de 527 à 847*, 3rd edn. (Paris, 1905, 1923).

—— 'Saint Thaddée l'homologète', *EO* 9 (1906), 37–41.

—— 'Saint Joseph de Thessalonique', *EO* 9 (1906), 278–82, 351–6.

PARKER, T. M., *Christianity and the State in the Light of History*, Bampton Lectures (London, 1955).

PARRY, K., 'Theodore Studites and the Patriarch Nicephoros on Image-making as a Christian Imperative', *Byzantion*, 59 (1989), 164–83.

—— *Depicting the Word: Byzantine Iconophile Thought of the Eighth and Ninth Centuries*, The Medieval Mediterranean Peoples, Economies and Cultures, 400–1453 (Leiden etc., 1996), xii.

PATLAGEAN, E., 'Les Studites, l'empereur et Rome: Figure Byzantine d'un monachisme réformateur', in *Bisanzio, Roma e l'Italia nell'alto Medioevo*, Settimane di studio nel centro Italiano di studi sull'alto medioevo, 34, 3–9 April 1986 (Spoleto, 1988), 429–60.

PENNINGTON, K., and SOMERVILLE, R. (eds.), *Law, Church and Society: Essays in Honor of Stephen Kuttner* (Philadelphia, 1977).

PRATSCH, T., *Theodoros Studites (759–826)—zwischen Dogma und Pragma: Der Abt des Studiosklosters in Konstantinopel im Spannungsfeld von Patriarch, Kaiser und eigenem Anspruch*, Berliner Byzantinistische Studien, 4 (Frankfurt am Main etc., 1998).

PRESTIGE, G. L., *God in Patristic Thought*, 2nd edn. (London, 1952).

PUJOL, C., 'La eucharistia y la paz en el monaquismo bizantino segùn Teodoro Estudita (759–826)', *Actos del XXV Congreso Intern. Eucharístico*, 2 (Barcelona, 1952).

—— 'Baptismus infantium in ecclesiis orientalibus', *Periodica*, 72 (1983), 203–37, 563–91.

RAFFIN, P., *Les Rituels orientaux de la profession monastique*, Spiritualité Orientale, 4 (Maine-et-Loire, 1992).

RAHNER, K., 'Le Début d'une doctrine des cinq sens spirituels chez Origène', *Revue d'Ascétique et de Mystique*, 13 (1932), 113–45.

RAÏ, P., 'L'Économie dans le droit canonique byzantin des origines jusqu'au XIe siècle: Recherches historiques et canoniques', *Istina*, 18 (1973), 273–7.

REGNAULT, L., 'Théologie de la vie monastique selon Barsanuphe et Dorothée (VIe siècle)', in *Théologie de la vie monastique*, Théologie Historique, 49 (Paris, 1961), 315–22.

RICHTER, J., 'Des heiligen Theodor, Abtes von Studium, Lehre vom Primat des römischen Bischofs', *Der Katholik Zeitschrift für katholische Wissenschaft unter Kirchliches Leben*, 54 (1874), ii. 385–414.

ROQUES, R., *L'Univers dionysien: Structure hiérarchique du monde selon le Pseudo-Denys* (Paris, 1954).

—— 'Le Sens du baptême selon le Pseudo-Denys', *Irénikon*, 31 (1958), 427–49.

—— 'Éléments pour une théologie de l'état monastique selon Denys l'Aréopagite', in *Théologie de la vie monastique*, Théologiie Historique, 49 (Paris, 1961), 283–314.

ROREM, P., *Biblical and Liturgical Symbols Within the Pseudo-Dionysian Synthesis*, Studies and Texts, 71, Pontifical Institute of Medieval Studies (Toronto, 1984).

—— *Pseudo-Dionysius: A Commentary on the Texts and an Introduction to their Influence* (Oxford, 1993).

ROUSSEAU, O., 'Le Rôle important du monachisme dans l'église d'Orient', in *Il monachesimo orientale*, OCA 153 (1958), 34–56.

ROUSSEAU, P., *Basil of Caesarea* (Berkeley and Oxford, 1994).

RUGGIERI, V., *Byzantine Religious Architecture (582–867): Its History and Structural Elements*, OCA 237 (Rome, 1991).

RUNCIMAN, S., *Byzantine Theocracy* (Cambridge, 1977).

SACHSEN, PRINZ MAX VON, *Der heilige Theodor, Archimandrit von Studion* (Munich, 1929).

SAHAS, D. J., *Icon and Logos: Sources in Eighth-Century Iconoclasm* (Toronto, 1986).

SALAVILLE, S., 'De "quinivertice ecclesiastico corpore" apud S. Theodorum Studitam', *Acta Academiae Velehradensis*, 7 (Prague, 1911), 177–80 (= *Studia Orientalia*, Liturgico-Theologica (Rome, 1940)).

—— 'La Primauté de Saint Pierre et du pape d'après Saint Théodore Studite (759–826)', *EO* 17 (1914), 23–42.

—— 'Messe et Communion d'après les Typika monastiques byzantins du Xe au XIVe siècle', *OCP* 13 (1947), 282–98.

SALTET, L., *Les Réordinations: Étude sur le sacrament de l'ordre* (Paris, 1907).

SANSTERRE, J.-M., 'Les Informations parvenues en Occident sur l'avènement de l'empereur Léon V et le siège de Constantinople par les Bulgares en 813', *BZ* 66 (1996), 373–80.

Scazzoso, P., 'La terminologia misterica nel corpus Pseudo-Areopagiticum: Provenienza indiretta e diretta dei termini misterici nel corpus', *Aevum*, 37 (1963), 406–29.

—— *Introduzione alla Ecclesiologia di San Basilio* (Milan, 1975).

Schiwietz, S., *De S. Theodoro Studita Reformatore Monachorum Basilianorum* (Bratislava, 1896).

Schmemann, A., 'Byzantium, Iconoclasm and the Monks', *St Vladimir's Seminary Quarterly*, 3 (1959), 18–34.

Schneider, G. A., *Der Hl. Theodor von studion. Sein Leben und Wirken: Ein Beitrag zur byzantinischen Mönchsgeschichte* (Münster, 1900).

Schönborn, C. von, ' "La lettre 38 de saint Basile" et le problème christologique de l'iconoclasme', *Revue des Sciences Philosophiques et Théologiques*, 60 (1976), 446–50.

Sevčenko, I., 'Hagiography of the Iconoclast Period', in *Iconoclasm*, ed. A. Bryer and J. Herrin (Brimingham, 1977), 113–31.

Sheils, W. J. (ed.), *Monks, Hermits and the Ascetic Tradition*, Studies in Church History, 22 (Oxford, 1985).

Sideris, T., 'The Theological Position of the Iconophiles during the Iconoclastic Controversy', *SVThQ* 17 (1973), 210–26.

Speck, P., *Kaiser Konstantin VI: Die Legitimation einer fremden und der Versuch einer eigenen Herrschaft. Quellenkritische Darstellung von 25 Jahren byzantinischer Geschichte nach dem ersten Ikonoklasmus* (Munich, 1978).

Špidlik, T., *La Spiritualité de l'orient chrétien: Manuel systématique*, OCA 206 (Rome, 1985).

—— 'Il monachesimo bizantino sul crocevia fra lo studitismo e l'esicasmo', *Vetera Christianorum*, 23 (1986), 117–29.

—— 'Superiore-padre: l'Ideale di san Teodoro Studita', *Studia Missionalia*, 36 (1987), 109–26.

Stein, D., *Der Beginn des byzantinischen Bilderstreites und seine Entwicklung* (Munich, 1980).

Streza, N., 'Aspect dogmatique du culte des icônes chez saint Théodore le Studite', *Studii Teologice*, 29 (Bucharest, 1977), 298–306.

Taft, R., *The Liturgy of the Hours in East and West* (Collegeville, 1986).

—— 'Penance in Contemporary Scholarship', *Studia Liturgica*, 18 (1988), 2–21.

—— *The Diptychs*, iv. *A History of the Liturgy of St John Chrysostom*, OCA 238 (Rome, 1991).

Tailliez, F., 'Βασιλικὴ ὁδός', *OCP* 13 (1947), 299–354.

Théologie de la Vie Monastique, Études sur la tradition patristique, Théologie Historique, 49 (Paris, 1961).

Thomas, C., *Theodor von Studion und sein Zeitalter: Ein Beitrag sur byzantinischen Kirchengeschichte* (Osnabrück, 1892).

Thompson, F. J., 'Economy', *JTS* ns 16 (1965), 368–420.

TREADGOLD, W., 'The Unpublished Saint's Life of the Empress Irene', *BF* 7 (1982), 237–51.

—— *The Byzantine Revival 780–842* (Stanford, 1988).

TOUGARD, A., 'La Persécution iconoclaste d'après la correspondance de St Théodore Studite', *Revue des Questions Historiques*, 26 (1891), 80–118.

TSIGARAS, G., 'Philosophisches Instrumentarium der Christologie von Theodoros Studites über die Darstellung des menschgeworden Logos', *Annuarium Historiae Conciliorum*, 20 (1988, pub. 1989), 268–77.

TURNER, D., 'The Origins and Accession of Leo V (813–820)', *JÖB* 40 (1990), 171–203.

VALENTINE, F., *Religious Obedience* (London, 1951).

VANDENBROUCKE, D. F., 'La Profession, second baptême', *La Vie spirituelle*, 315, 76/2 (Feb. 1947), 250–63.

VAN DE VORST, C., 'Un panégyrique de S. Théophane le Chronographe par S. Théodore Studite', *AB* 31 (1912), 11–23.

—— 'S. Thaddée Studite', *AB* 31 (1912), 157–60.

—— 'Les Relations de S. Théodore Studite avec Rome', *AB* 32 (1913), 439–47.

—— 'La Translation de S. Théodore Studite et de S. Joseph de Thessalonique', *AB* 32 (1913), 27–62.

—— 'La Petite Catéchèse de S. Théodore Studite', *AB* 32 (1914), 31–51.

—— 'A propos d'un discours attribué à S. Jean Damascène', *BZ* 23 (1914), 128–32.

VIDOV, B., *St Theodore the Studite*, Studite Spiritual Library (Toronto, 1985).

DE VOGÜÉ, A., 'Le Monastère, Église du Christ', *Studia Anselmiana*, 42 (1957), 25–46.

—— 'Monachisme et église dans la pensée de Cassien', in *Théologie de la vie monastique*, Théologie Historique, 49 (Paris, 1961), 213–40.

WAGNER, G., 'Bussdisziplin in der Tradition des Ostens', in *Liturgie et remission des péchés* (Rome, 1975), 251–64.

WALTER, C., *L'iconographie des conciles dans la tradition byzantine* (Paris, 1970).

—— *Art and Ritual of the Byzantine Church* (London, 1982).

WARE, K., 'The Spiritual Father in Orthodox Spirituality', *Cross Currents*, 24 (1974), 296–313.

—— 'What is a Martyr?', *Sobornost*, 5 (1983), 7–18 (repr. *The Seed of the Church: The Universal Vocation of Martyrdom* (Witney, 1995)).

—— Introduction, in *John Climacus: The Ladder of Divine Ascent*, 1–70.

—— 'Prayer and the Sacraments in the *Synagoge*', in M. Mullett and A. Kirby (eds.), *The Theotokos Evergetis and Eleventh-Century Monasticism* (Belfast, 1994), 341–4.

WAWRYK, M., *Initiatio Monastica in Liturgia Byzantina: Officiorum schematis monastici magni et parvi necnon rasopharatus exordia et evolutio*, OCA 180 (Rome, 1968).

WELLESZ, E., *A History of Byzantine Music and Hymnography*, 2nd edn. (Oxford, 1961).

WERNER, E., 'Die Krise im Verhältnis von Staat und Kirche in Byzanz: Theodor von Studion', *Berliner byzantinische Arbeiten*, 5 (1957), 113–33.

WESTERBERGH, U., *Anastasius Bibliothecarius Sermo Theodori Studitae de Sancto Bartholomeo Apostolo: A Study*, Studia Latina Stockholmiensia, 9 (Stockholm, 1963).

WILSON, N. G., *Scholars of Byzantium* (London, 1983).

WORTLEY, J., 'Iconoclasm and Leipsanoclasm: Leo III, Constantine V and the Relics', *BF* 8 (1982), 253–79.

ZERVOS, G., 'La spiritualità eucharistica del sacerdote nella tradizione bizantina', *Nicolaus*, 7 (1979), 145–52.

INDEX

commandments 98–100, 102, 103, 106, 207,
    212, 224, 232
communion *see* eucharist
communion with heretics 121–3, 175,
    201–3
compunction, see *penthos*
confession of faults, see *exagoreusis*
Constantine V 10, 12, 13, 14, 25
Constantine VI 19, 26, 39, 40–2, 106, 130,
    134, 135, 136, 137
contemplation, see *theoria*
Cozza-Luzi, J. 66, 69
creation 207–9, 222, 230
Cyprian of Carthage 4, 73, 196
Cyril of Alexandria 117, 118
Cyril of Jerusalem 156 n. 19
Cyril of Scythopolis 86 n. 27

Damascene, *see* John Damascene
Desert Fathers 86 n. 27, 87 n. 30, 95
    see also Fathers of the Church
deuteros 31
devil 191, 192, 209, 212, 213, 214, 218,
    221 n. 121, 229, 237
Dionysios the Pseudo-Areopagite 24,
    133 n. 34, 154–5, 159–63, 165,
    167 n. 110, 185 n. 15, 211 n. 37,
    216, 226 n. 151, 234 n. 195, 239, 240
Dobroklonskij, A. P. 6
Dorotheos of Gaza 24, 36, 86 nn. 27 and
    28, 95, 96, 200, 214 n. 64, 217–18,
    228 n. 159
Dositheos 36, 87 n. 30

ecclesiology 199–200, 203–5
economy of the saints, see *oikonomia*
emperor:
    role within society 127–30
    relationship to the church 131–4, 138–48
    relationship to the law 134–7
Enklistos, Theodore's spiritual guide
    181 n. 223, 221 n. 121
epigrams 24, 27, 32 n.185, 77
epitimia, see penance
Epiphanios 24, 166, 203 n. 138
Erickson *see* John Erickson
ethical theory of images 87 n. 32
eucharist 197–9 , 203, 204
    heretical eucharist 200–5
Euchologion 164, 165, 166, 169, 170, 171,
    172, 174 n. 158, 178 n. 193, 179,
    180 n. 204, 181 n. 216, 183, 184, 185,
    237, 238

Eulogios of Alexandria 116–18, 124
Euphrosyne (daughter of Constantine VI)
    63, 108 n. 162
Eusebius 127
Euthymios (brother of Theodore) 17
Euthymios (Palestinian monk) 37, 87 n. 30
Evagrius 214, 218
Eve 212 n. 43
Exagoreusis (manifestation of thoughts) 35,
    92 n.59, 174, 180, 181

Fathers of the Church:
    basis of Catecheses 35
    imitation of 23, 35, 87, 93, 126
    source of education 23
Fatouros, G. 74
forgiveness of sins, *see* absolution

Gerontikon (collection of stories and say-
    ings) 33, 37, 86 n. 27
gnosis 218, 219
Gregory Asbestas, Archbishop of Syracuse
    21
Gregory II, Pope 129
Gregory Nazianzene (Gregory of
    Nazianzus) 22, 23, 30, 128, 170 n. 138,
    185, 215 n. 70, 221 n. 122
Gregory of Nyssa 24, 119 n. 222, 128,
    207 n. 2, 221 n. 123, 222 n. 130

hagiography 8, 86, 187
Hatlie, Peter 5
Hausherr, I. xii, 25, 66, 96
hellenism, christian political 127–30
Henry, Patrick xiv, 6 n. 17, 107, 109, 111,
    112, 123, 134, 135 n.45, 139
heresy, heretics 36 n. 216, 50–1, 61,
    120 n. 225, 121, 122, 143, 178 n. 190,
    190–7, 200–4
hesychasts, *hesychia* 29, 30 n.173, 220, 221
    n. 121
Hieria, Synod of (754) 13–14, 38, 55,
    56
Hilarion 37, 87 n. 30
holiness:
    common calling 224–8
    monastic calling 229–38
humanity of Christ 215–16
Hussey, J. M. 147
hymnography 20 n. 106, 32
Hypotyposis (Stoudite rule) 28 n. 166, 29,
    34 n. 203, 65 n. 382, 77, 90, 103,
    181 n. 221

Index

273

icons:
    as baptismal sponsor 183–4
    restoration of icon worship 26, 38,
        theology 25, 33, 59–60, 208
iconoclasm 11–15, 25–6
    persecution and martyrdom 57–8, 61–2,
        87 n. 34, 93–4, 144
    return of 53–60, 144–5, 147
imitation of saints, *see* Fathers of the Church
interior senses, *see* spiritual senses
Ioannikios 29, 30 n. 173
Irene, Empress 26, 38–9, 42–3, 46, 132, 133
Irene, Patrician 93, 173 n. 151

John Cassian 36, 239
John Chrysostom 23, 101 n.118, 122, 125
    n. 259, 128, 171 n. 143, 193 n. 61, 201
John Climacus, *see* John Klimakos
John Damascene (John of Damascus) 21,
        144 n. 96, 148 n. 111, 172 n. 150,
        209 n. 15, 246 n.2
John Erickson 115 n. 195, 166 n.104, 193
John the Evangelist (Stoudite church) 27
John the Grammarian 20 n. 111, 55
John Klimakos 24, 36, 86 nn. 27 and 29, 95,
        214 n. 60
John Meyendorff 155 n. 10
John Moschos 24, 86 n. 27, 179 n. 201,
        185 n. 16, 187–8, 189
John the Prophet 96
Joseph, archbishop and brother of Theodore
        8, 17, 42, 48, 49, 50, 52, 64, 108, 135
Joseph affair (second phase of moechian
        controversy) 49–53, 108–10, 120–2,
        124–6, 141
Joseph the Hymnographer 17 n. 86
Joseph of Kathara, steward of St.Sophia 40,
        42, 58 n. 346
    see also Joseph affair
Justinian, Emperor 131 n.22, 136
Justinian II, Emperor 129

Kalogeros (stoudite monk) 50
Kathara monastery 40, 42
Karlin-Hayter, P. 5
Klimakos, *see* John Klimakos
koinobion 29, 84
    see also coenobitic life
koinonia 121, 122
    see also communion with heretics

Ladder of Divine Ascent, *see* John Klimakos
Laity, theology of 224–7, 232–4, 237, 238

lapsi 177, 204
lavra 29
Lent 105, 197 n. 84
Leo III, Emperor 11, 129, 138 n. 69
Leo III, Pope 46, 53, 190 n. 46
Leo IV, Emperor 18, 25–6
Leo V, Emperor 54–55, 59–60, 89, 93,
        144–5
Leroy, J. xii, 20 n.110, 29, 34 n. 203, 66, 68,
        69
letters (of Theodore) 4, 7, 73–74
liturgy 33, 197
    see also eucharist
logismoi 92, 93 n. 63, 214, 218

Manicheans 177, 192, 197
manifestation of thoughts, see *exagoreusis*
Maria of Amnia 39, 40
Mark the Hermit 36
marriage, theology of 169–71, 226, 228,
        229, 231, 232, 233, 238
    corruption of virginity 230
    marital continence 16
    married monks 233
    result of sin 213
    second marriage 170
martyrdom, *see under* monks
Mary of Egypt 179
Matthew Blastares 189 n. 41
Maximos the Confessor 130 n. 20
menaion 21
metanoia (repentance) 176, 178, 179
    see also penance
Methodios of Olympos 91
Meyendorff, *see* John Meyendorff
Michael, the Biographer 4, 7, 65, 66
Michael I Rhangabe, Emperor 52–4
Michael II the Amorian, Emperor 60–1,
        87 n. 34, 89, 108 n. 162, 145
minuscule script 4
moechian controversy:
    first phase 38–43, 106–8
    second phase 49–53, 75, 108–10; *see also*
        Joseph affair
monastery, stoudite 43–5, 52, 53
    catechetical instructions 34–5
    child members 31
    confederation 27, 45
    craftsmen 32
    liturgical practices 33–4
    offices and ministries 31–2
    school 31
    study and learning 32–3